Queens Around the World, 1520–1620

Dror Ze'evi

Queens Around the World, 1520–1620

A Century of Female Power

Dror Ze'evi
Ben-Gurion University of the Negev
Beersheba, Israel

ISBN 978-3-031-58633-0   ISBN 978-3-031-58634-7 (eBook)
https://doi.org/10.1007/978-3-031-58634-7

© The Editor(s) (if applicable) and The Author(s), under exclusive license to Springer Nature Switzerland AG 2024

This work is subject to copyright. All rights are solely and exclusively licensed by the Publisher, whether the whole or part of the material is concerned, specifically the rights of translation, reprinting, reuse of illustrations, recitation, broadcasting, reproduction on microfilms or in any other physical way, and transmission or information storage and retrieval, electronic adaptation, computer software, or by similar or dissimilar methodology now known or hereafter developed.

The use of general descriptive names, registered names, trademarks, service marks, etc. in this publication does not imply, even in the absence of a specific statement, that such names are exempt from the relevant protective laws and regulations and therefore free for general use.

The publisher, the authors and the editors are safe to assume that the advice and information in this book are believed to be true and accurate at the date of publication. Neither the publisher nor the authors or the editors give a warranty, expressed or implied, with respect to the material contained herein or for any errors or omissions that may have been made. The publisher remains neutral with regard to jurisdictional claims in published maps and institutional affiliations.

Cover illustration: IanDagnall Computing / Alamy Stock Photo GRANGER - Historical Picture Archive / Alamy Stock Photo

This Palgrave Macmillan imprint is published by the registered company Springer Nature Switzerland AG.
The registered company address is: Gewerbestrasse 11, 6330 Cham, Switzerland

If disposing of this product, please recycle the paper.

To Dana, Lior, Bareket, Alice, Robin-Saar, Luna Gaia and Aya
You make our world a better place.
And to the memory of my mother Galila

NOTE ON THE SPELLING OF NAMES PLACES AND EVENTS

Dozens of political entities are mentioned in this book, each involving numerous languages, often coupled with multiple systems of transliteration. To further complicate the matter, before their orthography became standardized in the seventeenth century, they could be encountered in a variety of spellings in each of the vernacular languages concerned. English, the world's most widely spoken language that today has, largely, a single (with some minor differences with, for example, American English) overarching system of grammar, was still rife with local dialects and spelling variations, and even within the written language of the governing elite, English spelling was quite chaotic. The same is true of most of the languages dealt with in this book.

To add to the confusion, kings and queens were addressed differently in different places and stages of their lives. Many of the book's protagonists were born in one country but lived in another and often adopted their new country's culture. This situation forces us, in the twenty-first century, to face, for example, the question of whether we should use Katherine, Catherine, Catarina, Catalina, or some other variation of the name. What about Isabelle, Isabella, or Elizabeth? Louise of Savoy or Louise de Savoie? Should we refer to the Ottoman sultana (whose original name, before she was abducted and enslaved in the royal harem, may have been Anastasia) as Hurrem or Roxelana? Should we call the Safavid shah's sister by her childhood name, Mahin Banu, or Shahzada Sultanum, the title-name she was given at court in later life? Should we write "Süleyman" as a Turk would, Sulaymān, as the name is usually transcribed from Arabic, or Suleiman, as is common in most European languages?

Several academic transliteration systems exist, but they are mostly used by experts of a specific region, and trying to decipher them might hamper the flow of reading. A common system for the transliteration of names of people, places, and events throughout the book must therefore be arbitrary. To simplify the system and avoid cumbersome transliterations, names in this book appear most often as they are commonly spelled in English. This does not necessarily reflect the correct spelling in the original language, and it is certainly not always consistent, but its use is intended to make it easier for the reader to follow up on people, places, and events by searching for them online. In certain special cases, the so-called professional transliteration of a name will appear in a footnote. Exact transliterations will be given in the text only for rare and unfamiliar names.

Acknowledgements

I would like to thank those who read the many drafts of this book and commented on them. Unfortunately, my mother, Galila, did not live to see the book's publication. She was always very supportive of the project. Before she passed away, she had read all the drafts and always had original and thought-provoking feedback to share. Dana, my partner, could always be counted on to be unflinchingly honest, both when she pointed out that more work was needed and when she (finally!) approved of what I had written. Roly Hadas read each chapter carefully and made good suggestions throughout. Long discussions over lunch and coffee with Nimrod Hurvitz, Ehud Toledano, Tami Sarfatti, and Dror Wahrman pointed me in the right directions.

Leslie Peirce's encouragement at the outset meant a lot to me, as did her pioneering work on royal harem women. Kathryn Babayan offered important insights into the Safavid world and Afsaneh Najmabadi's books were an important inspiration. Talks with Menashe Anzi directed me to new scholarship on trade between the Ottomans and the Mughals. Naghmeh Sohrabi's suggestions were sharp and thoughtful, and talks with Ilanit Swissa caused me to see Gracia Mendes in a different light.

I'm very grateful to the anonymous readers of the manuscript, who had excellent comments and suggestions, and to the editors at Springer Nature, to Will Wiseman, who led me through the first phases to Sam Stocker, Emily Russell, Carly Silver, and Linda Berlin.

I would like to thank the photographers, from Iran to Germany, who graciously allowed me to use their photographs, and to those museums and galleries that gave me permission to use their art.

I conducted most of my research at Ben Gurion University of the Negev, and The European University Institute in Florence hosted me through the last phase of this project. I'm grateful to both for their hospitality and assistance.

Finally, thanks also go to my siblings, children, and grandchildren, whose support and love sustained me over the years.

If I've forgotten some of you who helped me along the way, please accept my apologies and gratitude. Responsibility for all errors, mistakes, and blunders rests with me alone.

Contents

1 **Introduction** — 1
   The Comet — 1
   How Was the Sixteenth Century Different? — 4
   Forerunners — 11

2 **Sultanas of the Ottoman Empire** — 13
   The Harem Game — 14
   Hurrem/Roxelana — 17
   Nurbanu — 32
   Safiye — 40
   Kösem Sultan: Zenith and Decline — 47

3 **Mughal Queens of Hindustan** — 57
   The Mongol Legacy of Female Rule — 58
   Aisan Daulat Begum — 59
   Khanzada Begum — 63
   Hamida Banu Begum: Gulbadan Tells the Story — 69
   Harkha Bai/Mariam uz-Zamani — 80
   Mihr un-Nisa/Nur Jahan — 84
   Aftermath: Mumtaz Mahal and Jahanara — 92

4 **The Safavid Queens of Iran** — 95
   The Birth of the Safavids — 95
   Tajlu Khanum and the Rise of Safavid Queendom — 99
   Mahin Banu/Shahzada Sultanum — 103
   Parikhan Khanum — 110
   Mahd-i Ulya — 118
   Zaynab Begum — 122

5	**Queens of the Jews**	131
	Queen Isabella of Castile and the Expulsion of the Jews	132
	Gracia Mendes	135
	Benvenida Abrabanel	161
	The Kiras: Esther Handali and Esperanza Malchi	165
	Jewish Ladies as a Bridge to European Queendom	170
6	**Queens of France**	173
	Anne of France	176
	Louise of Savoy	177
	Catherine de Medici	185
	Marie de Medici	205
7	**Queens of the British Isles and Ireland**	213
	Katherine of Aragon and the Rise of Queendom in England	214
	Anne Boleyn	220
	Mary I	222
	Elizabeth I	230
	Elizabeth and Mary, Queen of Scots	242
	Elizabeth and Grace O'Malley (Ireland)	246
8	**The Three Phases of Sixteenth-Century Female Rule**	249
	The Power of Character	252
	Neither East nor West	252
	The Three Phases of Queendom	256
	Constructing Sovereignty	258
	Weaving a Net	260
9	**Conclusion: How and Why Did It End?**	263
	Bibliography	267
	Index	283

List of Figures

Fig. 1.1	The 1577-8 comet as it appears on an English tract published six years after its appearance. The writing in Hebrew says: *Jehovah*: I shall come to judge. STC 1416, Houghton Library, Harvard University	3
Fig. 2.1	La Sultana Rossa, Titian's workshop c. 1550. John and Mable Ringling Museum of Art, Sarasota, Florida	19
Fig. 2.2	Cameo of Bona Sforza, circa 1540, Metropolitan Museum of Art, New York	22
Fig. 2.3	Haseki Hurrem Sultan Külliyesi. Photo: Dosseman, 2008	24
Fig. 2.4	Mihrimah's mosque and the city walls (photo: 123rf)	33
Fig. 2.5	Miniature painting of Nurbanu's funeral, by Seyyid Lokman, *Shahanshanameh*. Top: Sultan Murad III walks in front of his mother's casket exiting the third court of Topkapı. Topkapı Museum	41
Fig. 2.6	The New Valide Mosque (*yeni cami*), one of the largest mosques in Istanbul. Construction was begun by Safiye in 1597. Photo: Sinoplu Diyojen	46
Fig. 2.7	Kösem Sultan with her son Murad (portrait attributed to Hans Ludwig Graf von Kuefstein after an original, c. 1650–1699). Unknown artist, circle of Franz Herrmann and Hans Gemminger, Austrian School, second quarter of the seventeenth century	49
Fig. 2.8	Kösem's Büyük Valide Han. Photo by Jacob Historian	52
Fig. 3.1	Timur's empire at his death. Map by Stuntelaar	60
Fig. 3.2	Babur seeks his grandmother's advice, surrounded by other women. Read Mughal Album, from the Baburnama. The Morgan Library and Museum	61
Fig. 3.3	Babur's conquests	66
Fig. 3.4	Gulbadan Begum smoking a waterpipe, Delhi, Mughal India, c. 1800	71
Fig. 3.5	Hamida Banu Begum as a young woman (Probably an imaginary likeness, no attribution)	72
Fig. 3.6	Baby Akbar reunites with his mother Hamida from Akbarnama, c. 1596–1600, National Museum of Asian Art	75
Fig. 3.7	The royal harem in Fatehpur Sikri. Photo: Tanu Chaudhary	77

Fig. 3.8	Rani Durgavati, 1988 Indian stamp	79
Fig. 3.9	Harkha Bai after the birth of Jahangir, miniature, royal album, c. 1600. The grandmother, Hamida Begum, is sitting on a chair by the bedside. Attributed to Bishandas, Boston Museum of Fine Arts	81
Fig. 3.10	Nur Jahan in a manly pose, loading a musket. Painting by Abul-Hasan Nadiruz Zaman. Seventeenth century	87
Fig. 3.11	Itimad ud-Daula's tomb. Photo: Wikijib	90
Fig. 3.12	Jahanara Begum attributed to Lalchand c. 1631–3. British Library	93
Fig. 4.1	The Kingdom of Trebizond on the shores of the Black Sea	96
Fig. 4.2	A portrait, said to be of Theodora. From a fresco in Verona by Pisanello, c. 1436–1438	97
Fig. 4.3	Stylized portrait of Ismail I by the Italian painter Cristofano dell'Altissimo (c. 1552–1568), Uffizi Gallery	98
Fig. 4.4	Shrine of Ali Reza, Mashhad. Photo by Mostafameraji, 2017	105
Fig. 4.5	Detail of a later-era wall painting describing the reception given by a sword bearing Shah Tahmasp (right) to the Mughal Emperor Humayun, seen here in a pose of supplication. Muhammad Mahdi Karim, dated to 1646–7, Chehel Sutun Palace, Isfahan. Photo: Muhammad Mahdi Karim	106
Fig. 4.6	Safavid princess, probably Parikhan, sixteenth century Persian miniature by Muhammadi	113
Fig. 4.7	Palace in Qazvin, one of 274 vintage photographs, late nineteenth-early twentieth century. Brooklyn Museum, Purchase gift of Leona Soudavar in memory of Ahmad Soudavar, 1997.3.44	117
Fig. 4.8	The Safavid Empire and its enemies, sixteenth century. Map by F. Dany (Fabienkhan)	121
Fig. 4.9	The young Shah Abbas I, engraving by Dominicus Custos, Atrium heroicum, Augsburg 1600–1602. Public domain	126
Fig. 5.1	Ferdinand and Isabella on the throne. The youth on their right is almost certainly their son, Don Juan Prince of Asturias. Author unknown	133
Fig. 5.2	Gracia Nasi the Younger by Pastorino di Giovan Michele de' Pastorini. Source: The Jewish Museum, New York	144
Fig. 5.3	Map of the Duchy of Ferrara in the sixteenth century, copper engraving by Joan and Cornelius Blaeu, c. 1640. Koninklijke bibliotheek, The Hague	151
Fig. 5.4	Dona Gracia on an Israeli stamp issued in 1992	159
Fig. 5.5	Shlomo Molcho's signature. Source: Jewish Encyclopedia (1901–1906)	163
Fig. 6.1	Virtuous ladies building their city. Meister, Illustration from *The Book of the City of Ladies*, 1410. Bibliothèque nationale de France	175
Fig. 6.2	Map of the Habsburg Empire during Charles V's reign. Source: *Cambridge Modern History Atlas*, 1912	179

Fig. 6.3	An allegorical painting depicting Louise of Savoy as a winged woman holding the rudder of the ship of state and talking to the Ottoman Sultan Suleiman, lying at her feet. Source: Etienne Leblanc, Frontispiece of Geste de Blanche de Castille, c. 1520–1522. Bibliothèque nationale de France	182
Fig. 6.4	The opening page of a tract by Jean Thibault, the royal astrologer, with the three signatories of the Peace of the Ladies: Louise of Savoy, Margaret of Austria, and Margaret of Navarre	185
Fig. 6.5	Young Catherine de Medici, sixteenth-century painting. French School, Galleria Palatina di Palazzo Pitti, Inv. 1890 n. 2448	189
Fig. 6.6	Peter Paul Rubens, Marie de Medici's portrait presented to Henry IV by the gods of love (detail). At Henry's back, the helmeted "France" urges the smitten king to propose. Part of the 24-painting series known as the "Marie de Medici Cycle" commissioned by the queen in 1622 (now in the Louvre) (see René Langlois, "Comparing the French Queen Regent and the Ottoman Validé Sultan" in Woodacre et al. *A Companion to Global Queenship*, 273)	208
Fig. 6.7	Assassination of Henry IV	209
Fig. 7.1	Young Katherine of Aragon as the Magdalene. Painting by Michael Sittow (late fifteenth or early sixteenth century), oil on oak panel. Detroit Institute of Arts, Founders Society Purchase, General Membership Fund, 40.50	216
Fig. 7.2	Young Henry VIII. Attributed to Meynnart Wewyck, about 1509. Denver Art Museum: Gift of the Berger Collection Educational Trust, 2021.29. Photography courtesy Denver Art Museum	217
Fig. 7.3	House of Tudor family tree, by Muriel Gottrop (enwiki)	222
Fig. 7.4	Cover of the pamphlet "A View of certain wonderful effects," by Thomas Twyne, 1578	238
Fig. 7.5	Mary, Queen of Scots, by François Clouet (1558–1560) Royal Collection Trust	245
Fig. 7.6	Meeting between Elizabeth (right) and Grace O'Malley. Illustration from Anthologia Hibernica, 1793	248

CHAPTER 1

Introduction

THE COMET

In late October 1577, the night sky suddenly became more luminous. Soon a huge comet appeared on the horizon. It outshone the moon, its tail covered a sixth of the sky dome, and it was naturally interpreted as a sign from heaven, but a sign of what?[1]

In Qazvin, capital of the Safavid Empire, the comet appeared in the midst of a series of upheavals that threatened to break the dynasty's hold on power. Shah Tahmasp had died the previous year and his daughter, Princess *Parikhan Khanum*, who governed the empire during his final months, had one crown prince killed and another crowned in his stead. But a year later, just as the comet was blazing in the winter sky, the new shah was also assassinated, and the princess once again took the reins of government in her own hands.[2] Her subjects connected the appearance of the great star to these events, and many believed it to be a warning against women meddling in the affairs of state.

Far away in the west, in Elizabethan England, Thomas Twyne, an amateur astronomer and astrologer, wrote an entire tract about the significance of the amazing comet. To counter the views of many who claimed it was proof that government by women was anathema, he offered a positive assessment. According to his astrological map, the event portended peace, and although it did not necessarily bode well for other ruling women around the world, it had arrived in order to endorse the advancement of women in England. Among other things, it indicated the coming union of *Queen Elizabeth*[3] with the Church:

---

[1] This comet is known to us today as non-periodic C/1577 v1.

[2] There is no definite proof that Parikhan Khanum assassinated Shah Ismail, but circumstantial evidence points to her as the culprit.

[3] Throughout this introduction, names of ruling women are italicized at the first mention, to introduce the reader to the extent of female government in Europe and Asia during the period.

© The Author(s), under exclusive license to Springer Nature Switzerland AG 2024
D. Ze'evi, *Queens Around the World, 1520–1620*,
https://doi.org/10.1007/978-3-031-58634-7_1

it doth not only portende the inseparable coniunction & marriage, as it were, of our most true and naturall souveraigne Queene Elizabeth, with the holy Church and Gospel of Jesus Christ, indissolubly united: but also of sutch oridnancies, leagues, & confederacies, as she hath taken, or meaneth to take ... And moreover, I am of this opinion, contrary to the trayterous iudgement of some hollow harts, that the lengthening of her maiesties long life and prosperous reigne over her realmes, is hereby most effectually sygnifyed; which the lord grant to our endlesse comfort.[4]

Twyne's astrological prognostications were echoed by another lover of science, Henry Howard, Earl of Northampton, whose writings were imbued with the spirit of early scientific empiricism. Contemptuous of people's superstitious ignorance about women as rulers, Howard praised Elizabeth's dismissive reaction when advised to draw the curtain, avert her gaze, and not look directly at the comet:

[S]he caused the window to be set open, and cast out this word, 'Iacta est alia' the dice are thrown, affirming that her steadfast hope and confidence was too firmly planted in the providence of God, to be blasted or affrighted with those beams, which either had a ground in nature whereupon to rise, or at least no warrant out of scripture, to portend the mishaps of Princes. Behold a woman and a Queen, which seem to be the kinds and callings upon which the Comets (if Astrologers speak truth) are wont to prey: and yet not only she relenteth not to common fear, but insulteth rather upon common folly.[5]

Said to be shaped "like a Turban sash over Ursa Minor," the comet caused a stir when recorded by the court's great astronomer, Takiyuddin, in Istanbul's state-of-the-art observatory.[6] His patron, Sultan Murad III, had only recently acceded to the throne, and, as a war was just declared between the Ottomans and the Safavids, the astronomer believed the appearance of the comet signified a glorious victory. A year later, when the campaign faltered and plague ravaged the capital city, it was reinterpreted by religious authorities as a warning about the impious conduct of the empire's elite. The main cause, it was whispered, was the unprecedented influence of the queen mother, *Nurbanu Sultan*, and the sultan's favorite concubine, *Safiye Sultan*, on affairs of state. The sultan (or perhaps his mother) decided to placate the clerics by virtually killing the messenger. The observatory, perhaps the most advanced in the world at the time, was demolished, and Takiyuddin was sent away (Fig. 1.1).[7]

As it rose over Agra, capital of the Mughals, the comet was observed by Abu'l-Fazl, Grand Vizier to Emperor Akbar of India, who mentions it in his chronicle. The emperor saw the comet as a bad omen and, to counter its

---

[4] Twyne, *A View of Certain Wonderful Effects*, Section VI. Hellman, "the Comet of 1577," 288–9.
[5] Howard, Henry. *Preservative against the Poison of supposed Prophecies*," iv.
[6] Taqi al-Dīn in Arabic.
[7] Özgen, *Grand Vizier Koca Sinan Paşa*, 32. Ben Zaken, "The Revolving Planets," 141. Taqi ad-Din Muhammad ibn Ma'ruf established his observatory near Istanbul only three years earlier, in 1574.

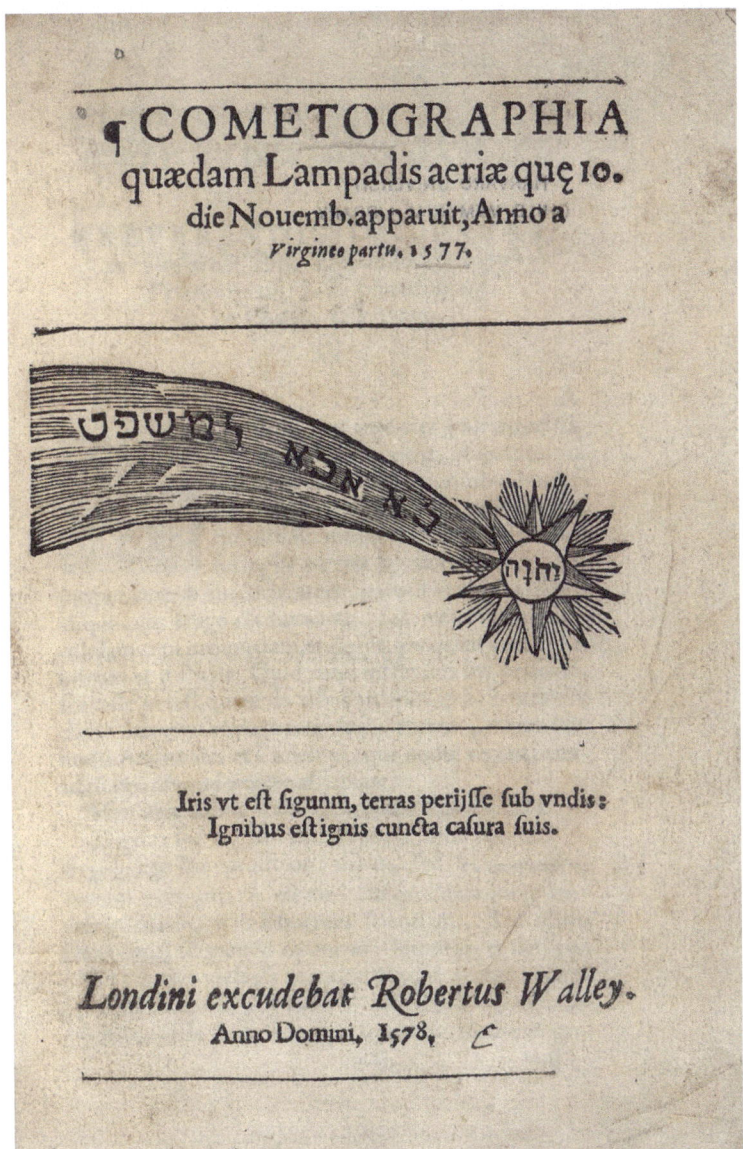

Fig. 1.1 The 1577-8 comet as it appears on an English tract published six years after its appearance. The writing in Hebrew says: *Jehovah*: I shall come to judge. STC 1416, Houghton Library, Harvard University

negative impact, distributed alms to the populace. The comet may have been one of Akbar's reasons for forsaking Islam and embracing his newly created religion and personal cult, "the divine religion" (*din-i ilahi*), a couple of years later. What the emperor did not know was that the appearance of the comet coincided with the birth of *Nur Jahan*, his future daughter-in-law, destined to be the greatest queen in the history of the Indian subcontinent.[8]

At the same time, in Safed, city of Upper Galilee, the famous mystic scholar Haim Vital saw the comet and wrote about it in his *Book of Visions*: "On the first day of Kislev 5338 (November 1577) after sunset, one could see a big star in the sky on the west side ... with a very long tail rising upwards and tilting a bit to the east. It stayed there for three hours and then set behind the mountain in Safed. This continued for over fifty nights." Witnessing the great upheavals all around him, including the rise to power of his patroness, Dona Gracia, Vital saw this comet as an omen heralding Armageddon, to be followed by the redemption of the Jews. "On the fifteenth of Kislev," he writes, "I moved to Jerusalem," probably to await the Day of Judgment.[9]

It might seem strange that a comet, bright though it may be, would raise the specific issue of female rule, but comets were tightly intertwined in the human imagination with heavenly signs for monarchs and princes. The fact that this comet's appearance was so often interpreted as proof of God's approval or disapproval of women's rule is a measure of how heavily the question weighed on people's minds. Indeed, the ubiquity of women's rule in the mid-sixteenth century made this issue one of the most heated topics of debate in the period.

How Was the Sixteenth Century Different?

The reasons for the astonishing rise of women across the globe to supreme positions of power in the sixteenth century can be clustered into two large categories. The first is *structural and timebound* and has to do with upheavals brought on by the Age of Exploration, religious disruption, and scientific advances. The second is *circumstance-based* and has more to do with serendipitous coincidences, the power of character, and the determination of specific women at critical junctures.

In terms of human understanding of the world and the universe, the dawn of the sixteenth century was a turning point unlike any other. In a trip funded by the Spanish crown, seeking a new route to India, the Genoese explorer Christopher Columbus "discovered" a new continent previously unknown to Europeans. Several years later, Vasco da Gama of Portugal rounded the Cape of Good Hope at the southern tip of Africa and found a new sea route to India and China. Another Portuguese fleet, led by Ferdinand Magellan, circumnavigated the globe. The Ottomans sent a fleet of their own to the Red Sea and the Indian Ocean, opening new sea routes to India, China, and Africa. Hard on

---

[8] Kapoor, "Abu'l Fazl," 249–260. Lal, *Empress*, 14–15.
[9] Faierstein, *The Book of Visions* (Sefer Ha-Hezyonot), 88.

their heels, Dutch, French, and English ship captains made new inroads into all these continents.

Sustained by new shipbuilding, sailing, and navigation technologies and by huge financial investments, these new routes connected the globe as never before, changing long-held notions of movement in space and time, as well as conceptions of imperial policy, international trade, and travel. A few decades later, the voyage from western Europe to India, which took many months by land, could be made by sea in less than a month, and one ship, crewed by several dozen sailors, could load as much merchandise as a caravan of a thousand pack animals. The exchange of letters between rulers, which previously took years, could now be accomplished in a tenth of that time. As a result of all these transformations, banking, trade, and the capitalist worldview also evolved.

But aside from their impact on global commerce, knowledge, the quickening pace of human transactions, and the political balance of power, these new discoveries shook the foundations of seemingly incontrovertible truths that were preached for millennia by religious authorities. Every day new facts were revealed about the universe and its treasures: the heliocentric solar system, the earth as an orb revolving around its own axis; the motions of stars, planets, and moons; vast new oceans and island civilizations; legendary kingdoms, new and previously unknown political systems, animals, plants, foods, and spices and along with them new diseases, pandemics, and forms of human cruelty that wiped out millions. Every day offered a new piece of the vast cosmic puzzle of being, bringing into question the teachings of age-old religions. The sixteenth century was thus the swan song of a disappearing medieval system of belief. This was the music that accompanied the rise of women to power across Eurasia.[10]

The Rise of Gunpowder Empires

At the same time, in a separate shift, a new type of polity came into being. It would be the most important contributor to the rise of women to positions of power in the sixteenth century.

In the medieval period, "the state" was a relatively modest set of institutions. Kings rode to war at the head of smallish semiautonomous feudal armies, often bringing along with them the entire machinery of the state—scribes, legal experts, administrators, tax collectors, judges, and keepers of the royal seal. But the fifteenth century saw the emergence of new centralized states that based their power on big musket-wielding armies and expensive artillery. These gunpowder empires were much more expensive to run and maintain and,

---

[10] Freitag and Von Oppen, *Translocality*, 7–11. These were not always new ideas. It may also be, as Carlo Ginzburg pointed out in *The Cheese and the Worms*, that by breaking "the crust of religious unity," the reformation indirectly caused older beliefs to resurface. Also discussed by Miller is the idea that Menocchio's adoration of "the empress" was greater than of the Madonna in the mid-sixteenth century (ibid., 34–35).

hence, required a more elaborate bureaucracy. The state apparatus became too cumbersome for kings to simply take along with them wherever they went. The previously portable nucleus of the state was thus compelled to stay in one place, and the royal palace in the capital city became the permanent center of political and administrative life. This shift was accompanied by an ideological reordering. The central government was now imagined as a keep, a strong tower, from which the entire realm was to be viewed and ordered. As one historian of France added, the ideological change "went far beyond making law and judging; the [monarchs] actively interfered in more and more aspects of daily life. They made the state a part of everyone's daily existence."[11]

From this point on, when kings led their armies to war, they had to leave behind trusted confidants to manage their council of state, central treasury, and scribal services. In most cases, the king's female next of kin—mother, sister, wife, and daughter—were the ones the king relied on not to usurp power while he was away. Closer to the locus of power, and with the sovereign away in war, palace women could now wield more influence in matters of state.[12]

But while global travel, gunpowder, the Renaissance, and the first stirrings of Enlightenment were at work changing gender paradigms, a ferocious struggle was still tearing religious dogmas apart. Forced conversions, mass deportations, torture of suspected heretics, the burning of apostates at the stake, and even widespread massacres of unbelievers were not a rare sight in Europe. To the east, the heterodox sects on the marches between the Ottomans and the Safavids gradually had to opt for one of the two rival camps, Sunni or Shia. Untold numbers were massacred for their suspected misalliance.[13] Myriads of Jews and Muslims were forced to convert or be expelled from Spain in the wake of the conquest of Granada in 1492 and, later, from Portugal and other Catholic kingdoms. Many opted for exile under harsh conditions. But, as often happens in times of trouble, those with the presence of mind, wit, and courage to lead came to the fore. For some Catholic, Protestant, Jewish, and Muslim women, such hardship presented a singular opportunity to prove their mettle in leadership roles.[14]

Taken together, these structural developments opened a new space for noble women and, at the same time, conditioned society to view their authority as more legitimate. Women who were quick to perceive these openings and bold enough to make use of them would be given the opportunity to lead.

---

[11] Collins, *The State in Early Modern France*, 3. See also pp. 6–10. 17: "In 1520, France had 11 *generaux* and 11 treasurers; by 1620, it had 200 treasurers of France, and by 1640, about 500." See also pp. 21–22.

[12] Friedrich, "Government and Information," 541. Collins, Ibid.

[13] See, for instance, Abdurrahman Atçıl, "The Safavid threat and juristic authority in the Ottoman Empire during the 16th century." *International Journal of Middle East Studies* 49.2 (2017): 295.

[14] Yvonne Yazbeck Haddad and Ellison Banks Findly, eds., *Women, Religion and Social Change* (Albany: SUNY Press, 1985).

A New Opening for Women

The rise of women was such a widespread phenomenon at midcentury that at some point people began to suspect that it was another piece of the unfolding new world of marvels. Most, in East and West alike, still believed that women are by nature inferior, that they are emotional, capricious, and deficient in logic, and therefore should be subservient to men, whose minds are ruled by reason and logic. But could these people be wrong? Many authors now suggested the possibility that women were, if not superior, then equal to men. When the great comet appeared in the night sky in October 1577, in the full bloom of the phenomenon, it certainly seemed as though the order of the world had changed permanently. Could it be that men's rule was at an end and that henceforth the world would be ruled by women?

But in order for the levee of patriarchal rule to burst, and for such a widespread phenomenon as female rule to emerge, a series of other changes had to take place. One of these was the slow disintegration of belief in the divine right of kings. In medieval times the rule of male kings was believed to represent the will of God. Kings themselves were convinced that their crowning was divinely ordained and that, as a result, even their gaze and touch held healing powers. But during the Age of Exploration, great ruptures appeared in the fabric of religion, and previously unshakeable dogmas unraveled. Although some of these medieval convictions lingered for centuries and entrenched themselves, the biblical idea of kings being ordained "by the grace of God" was called into question by both the aristocracy and the masses. If men could hold divinely ordained supernatural powers, perhaps, then, women could, too.[15]

Another medieval notion, that of women as a less-developed creature, was also shaken by shifts in medical knowledge. The Greco-Roman medical tradition suggesting that females' articulation in the womb was somehow stunted before they reached the final stage of development, and that therefore they were inferior to men, was no longer accepted at face value. Furthermore, kings may have continued to claim a divine right to the throne, and the aspiration for an eternal royal male line was still prevalent—as it is today in some monarchies—but the dynasty now received its legitimacy from the nation, rather than from God, and the public often understood that the real force behind the crown was a woman.[16]

Such reverberations were already felt in 1405, long before the great discoveries, when Christine de Pizan wrote her famous *Book of the City of Ladies*.[17] Although her story about the imaginary creation of a city by and for women depicted their societal roles in the traditional way—a font of compassion, homemaking, and obedience to their male kin—her book gave women a sense

---

[15] Anderson, *Imagined Communities*, 18–22. Collins, *The State in Early Modern France*, 11.

[16] Matthias Range, "Dei Gratia and the Divine Right of Kings" in Woodacre et al., *The Routledge History of Monarchy*, 130–145. It was James I&VI who reintroduced the idea in the early seventeenth century, perhaps as a way of reasserting male privilege.

[17] Christine de Pizan and Earl Jeffrey Richards, *The book of the city of ladies*. (Pan Books, 1983).

of purpose and self-worth. It was soon translated from French into several other languages, including Spanish and Dutch. De Pizan's main contribution to the idea of female power was showing elite women throughout Europe that they shared more than just a predicament—they also shared the power to challenge it.

De Pizan's ideas, read by many upper-class women, were later taken up and developed by a group of proto-feminist Enlightenment scholars. Among them were Queen Anne of France in her book of lessons for her daughters; the Italian Balthazar Castiglione in his book of court etiquette; the Englishman Thomas More, who devised an advanced educational curriculum for the female members of his household; and the Spaniard Juan Luis Vives, who wrote an important book on women's education for Princess Mary of England at the request of her mother, Katherine of Aragon.[18]

A similar effect was produced in Jewish culture by women such as Dona Gracia Mendes and Dona Benvenida Abrabanel, who encouraged research, literature, and pioneering theology, offering grants of money for projects such as the translation of the Bible into local vernaculars. Parallel shifts occurred in Safavid Iran, where Fakhrī of Herat wrote *The Jewels of Wonder*, extolling great women of his time and highlighting their talents. His book had a noticeable impact on royal Safavid and Mughal women of the age.[19] Such ideas circulated alongside budding notions of social and economic equality between genders, races, and classes of people.[20] The newly invented printing press spread these progressive ideas about the intellectual abilities of women and the need to educate them far and wide in the sixteenth century.

Sixteenth-Century Queens and Women's Liberation
From the early 1800s historians worked under the implicit assumption that history is in essence the relentless march of human progress.[21] Democracy, abolition of slavery, racial equality, human rights, and, indeed, women's slow march to liberation developed from the Renaissance on and are bound to reach their culmination in the future. This is true in essence. Most humans are better off today in terms of security, opportunity, relative wealth, life expectancy, and health than they were even fifty or a hundred years ago. But events in the mid-twentieth and early twenty-first centuries belie this image of constant progression toward the end of times. When the winds of war blow again around the world, when women's rights to abortion or choice of attire are challenged, when hard-won liberties taken for granted are threatened, we must question this view of historical time as a linear journey toward redemption.

---

[18] See Chap. 6. See also Hilary Mantel, *Wolf Hall*, p. 370.
[19] See Chap. 3.
[20] Alfani and Frigeni, "Inequality (Un)perceived."
[21] This is sometimes referred to as "the Whig interpretation of history," based on the historical approach of English progressive historians such as Macaulay and Acton.

Historians tell us that the movement for women's liberation got under way in the late eighteenth century with authors such as Mary Wollstonecraft in England and Olympe de Gouges in France. Some claim that even *that* was a false start, and real change only began a century later.[22] Yet over two hundred years before these pioneers, women governed much of the Eurasian landmass. When the 1577 comet streaked through the skies, they acted as sovereigns in the majority of empires between the Atlantic Ocean and the Bay of Bengal. This period of female rule endured for over a century. Although the dates of its beginning and end vary from state to state, its early manifestations could be traced to the 1520s and its swan song to a century later.

Should we then revise our periodization? Did this century-long period of female rule leave a trace in people's collective memory? Did it have an impact on the movement of women's liberation? And if it did, where can we find its traces? If it simply rose and then ebbed like a wave on the shore, should we assume that the Early Enlightenment did not contribute much to the liberation of women but, on the contrary, remarginalized them for almost two centuries before the first harbingers of liberation?

A caveat is in order here. The protagonists of this book—sultanas, queens, princesses, and other female nobles—were all rich, powerful, and far more privileged even than most males. Theirs was not the predicament of the majority of women in the early modern period, and their stories are not typical of women's history. And yet it is not merely the remarkable fact that, as we shall see, women were at the forefront of political power. Their period of rule was accompanied by lively debates and literary pieces claiming women's equality with men in terms of intellect and sagacity and upholding their right to govern. How, then, does this story fit within the narrative of women's march to liberation? This book will try to lay the ground for an answer to some of these questions. It is my hope that revisiting this era and showcasing the female power that stood at the cradle of modernity will enable us to take a fresh look at the historical narrative and redefine it.

What follow are a few examples of women whose stories will be told in the following chapters.

From the inception of the Mughal empire in the first years of the sixteenth century women figured prominently in its ruling elite. *Aisan Daulat Begum*, grandmother of its founder, Babur, set the stage for subsequent generations and bequeathed her leading role to Babur's sister, *Khanzada Begum*. In the next generation, when Babur's son, Humayun, was on the verge of losing his entire empire, his wife, *Hamida Begum*, played a crucial role in forging alliances with the Safavids of Iran and restoring Mughal dominion over Hindustan. A few decades later, queendom reached its apex when Emperor Jahangir's formidable wife, *Nur Jahan*, became sovereign in everything but the formal title. The era of women's rule in India practically ended with the death of her niece *Mumtaz Mahal*, wife of Shah Jahan, in 1631.

---

[22] Schwartz, "Infidel Feminism," 2–4.

In the Ottoman Empire, *Hurrem Sultan* (known in the West as Roxelana), wife of Sultan Suleiman, played a critical role in government and politics from the 1520s to the 1550s. She was succeeded by a long line of great sultanas, including *Nurbanu* and *Safiye*, who ruled the empire with few interruptions from the mid-sixteenth century onward. The most powerful of all Ottoman queens, *Kösem Sultan*, was murdered in 1651, putting an end to that illustrious line.

In Safavid Iran, *Shahzada Sultanum* governed the emerging dynastic realm in tandem with her brother Tahmasp from the 1530s and was a powerhouse in the state during his rule.[23] Her niece, *Parikhan Khanum*, was officially head of state for a while and exerted a major influence on the realm, as did her rival and sister-in-law *Mahd-i Ulya Begum*, who had Parikhan executed and ruled the empire for several years in the name of her incompetent husband. Her place as leading woman of the realm was later taken up by *Zaynab Khanum*, who served as guide and elder stateswoman to the following shahs until her death in 1640.

In England, *Katherine of Aragon*, Henry VIII's first wife and daughter of Spain's warrior queen Isabella, paved the way for women's rule. Her daughter *Mary I* was the first woman to be formally crowned queen in England, and Mary's half-sister *Elizabeth*, daughter of the executed Anne Boleyn, took over for almost half a century until her death in 1603. Their cousin, *Mary* of the Stuart household, queen consort of France in her teens, was crowned queen of Scotland and ruled until being ousted, taken prisoner, and finally executed by Elizabeth in 1587. Another woman, Gráinne Ní Mháille, better known by her English name *Grace O'Malley*, governed western Ireland at the same time.

In France it was *Louise of Savoy*, mother of King Francis I, who first took the reins of government into her hands when her son was taken prisoner during a campaign in Italy. Her grandson's wife, *Catherine de Medici*, became queen by a fluke of fate and later regent for her minor son. In the 1560s, she finally became *de facto* sovereign of France and held power for more than a decade. In subsequent years another scion of the Tuscan ruling family, her distant relative *Marie de Medici*, governed France intermittently as regent in the early decades of the seventeenth century. Her exile in the early 1630s put an end to France's era of female rule.

Other women were prominent in Europe and the Mediterranean basin throughout the sixteenth century. The Habsburg Empire's *Margaret of Austria* and her niece, *Mary of Hungary*, governed the Netherlands and Flanders in succession as autonomous queens. *Bona Sforza*, an Italian from Lombardy who married King Sigismund of Poland, gained strength and influence as her husband's power waned. Her daughter *Isabella* was regent in Hungary and Transylvania, allying herself with the Ottomans. In western North Africa, a Muslim refugee from Spain, *Al-Sayyida al-Hurra*, governed northern Morocco as an independent ruler and pirate queen.

---

[23] Mahin Banu was known as Shahzada Sultanum throughout her adult life.

Finally, though not officially part of any formal state, *Dona Gracia Mendes*, a Crypto-Jewish (Marrano) businesswoman, led the rich and powerful Sephardic diaspora in the mid-sixteenth century.[24] Throughout her fascinating career, she behaved like royalty, establishing great banking houses, hobnobbing with kings and queens, and making loans to monarchs all over Europe and the Middle East. Her friend *Dona Benvenida Abrabanel* was patroness of the Jewish communities on the Italian peninsula, and two other women—*Esther Handali* and *Esperanza Malchi*—were personal assistants to Ottoman sultanas. They were also leaders of the empire's Jewish communities until the end of the century.

Forerunners

The empowerment of women in general, and specifically in the context of the sixteenth century, is often believed to be a uniquely Western phenomenon. Yet for its earliest precursors we should look eastward. During the Middle Ages and the early modern period, women acted as sovereigns most conspicuously in Asia, and only later in Europe. As we shall see in Chap. 3, the Mughals, who founded their empire in Hindustan in the early sixteenth century, imagined their state as a resurrection of the Mongol world empire and were imbued with its traditions. To some extent, so did the Safavids in Iran, whose mythical lineages and invented traditions stretched back to Genghis Khan and his Mongolian homeland, and the Safavids' court decorum was also influenced to a large extent by Mongol precedents (through their Timurid and Aq-Qoyunlu successor states). With some reservations—after all, the Turks and Mongols were rivals in Central Asia even before their westward migration—so did the early Ottomans in Asia Minor.

In the vast empire founded by Genghis Khan in the thirteenth century, and in the Mongol-led states established in its wake, the governing elites perceived themselves as confederations of tribes, and rulership was decided by a council of elders. Once a khan was elected, sovereignty was bestowed not just on the male ruler but on the family as a whole. Thus, on many occasions, a woman was recognized as a great khan, as a proxy for an absent husband, or as the actual head of the state after his death. The last great Mongol queen before the sixteenth century was *Mandukhai*, queen of the northern Yuan, who proved herself a wise and powerful ruler for several decades. Based on Mandukhai's example, from the early days of the Indian Mughal and Safavid dynasties women played a crucial role in building, governing, and defending the realm.

Although European examples of sovereign queens before the sixteenth century are rarer, with a fair amount of time separating them, one important

---

[24] Marrano was the pejorative term used to describe Jews who outwardly converted to Christianity but kept the Jewish faith in the privacy of their homes. Muslims who outwardly converted were called Moriscos. Nowadays "Marranos" is used interchangeably with "crypto-Jews."

example should be mentioned here. Just as Queen Mandukhai was a forerunner for Muslim women in power, so Queen Isabella of Castile played that role for powerful European women. A formidable monarch who fought her incompetent brother for the throne against the background of a country in turmoil, Isabella began the unification of Spain through marriage to Ferdinand of Aragon. With her husband's help she vanquished the Muslim kingdom of Granada and completed the *reconquista* of the Iberian Peninsula, brought law and order to a society in anarchy, and sponsored Columbus's adventurous trip around the world to India. Through her daughter Katherine she had a direct impact on the rise of queens in England; through her daughter Joanna "the Mad" and her grandson, Emperor Charles V, on female power in the Habsburg Empire; through her great-granddaughter *Marie de Medici* on France; and through *Isabella* and *Maria*, her other daughters, on Portugal. Indirectly she served as an inspiration for countless other queens and princesses around Europe.[25] Like Mandukhai in the East, Isabella offered an early model for the unprecedented phenomenon of queendom throughout the sixteenth and early seventeenth centuries.

To put the Eurocentric paradigm of women's liberation in perspective and challenge its hold on our historical imagination, the first three chapters of this book will be devoted to ruling women in Muslim empires, beginning with the Ottomans, and then moving on to the Mughals and the Safavids. One of the reasons for opening the book with a discussion of the Ottomans is that, situated between Europe and Asia, they acted as a key civilizational conduit between East and West and a crucial hub of the emerging female grid. Another reason is the fact that women in the Ottoman Empire held onto power almost uninterruptedly for longer than any other dynastic state in the period.

The second part of the book will be devoted to European examples of queendom, with an opening chapter focusing on the role of Jewish and Marrano women as mediators between East and West. There was no Jewish kingdom in early modern Europe, and the women discussed in this chapter did not hold formal power at any time. Yet, dispersed in all corners of the Mediterranean and reaching new colonies, these women were in many respects the neurons that connected the queendom network. The next chapter will trace female rule in France, whose women had to struggle against a formal legal prohibition on women as sovereigns. The final chapter in this section will trace the rise and fall of queendom in the British Isles, where, in the late sixteenth century, women ruled over England, Scotland, and western Ireland concurrently.

In the last chapter we will try to answer three questions from a wider perspective: How and why did women rise to power in the sixteenth century? How did they build their power base and their authority? And how did they construct their internal and external networks.

---

[25] Isabella is also blamed for the expulsion of the Jews from Spain (although modern historians ascribe this action mostly to her husband Ferdinand). Her role in that episode will be discussed further in Chap. 5.

CHAPTER 2

Sultanas of the Ottoman Empire

> *It is a common occurrence that [Sultan Murad III] shies away from any action necessitated by the day ahead, resting ... principally on the counsel of his mother, believing that he could never obtain more affectionate and faithful advice than hers, stemming from the reverence that he nurtures for her and his esteem for her rare qualities and many virtues. Another [woman] who has authority over His Majesty is the Sultana, his wife, who is also engaged skillfully in the affairs of state and makes her opinions heard, because she is loved infinitely by the Signor. As a result, this empire more and more has come to be governed by the two Sultanas, who use the magnificent pashas as the executors of their wishes and who summon them at their will as their counselors.*
> Venetian ambassador Paolo Contarini, Relazioni *(1583)*

There are three reasons to begin with an account of the Ottoman Empire. First, of the three great powers of the early modern Muslim world—Ottomans, Mughals, and Safavids—the Ottomans were the oldest and survived longest.[1] The Ottoman state, named after its eponymous founder, Osman Ghazi, emerged at the turn of the thirteenth century, spread over three continents from Budapest to Mecca and from Algiers to Baghdad, and lasted as a world empire long after the other two dynasties had disappeared. The second reason is that the period known in Turkish historiography as "the sultanate of women" was the longest and most impressive example of continuous government by women, lasting from the 1520s to the 1650s. And finally, straddling the Bosphorus Strait, the empire was the main cultural conduit between Europe and Asia. More than any other governing elite, Ottoman queens maintained

---

[1] *Relazioni* ([1583]) III:3, 234–235. Quoted and translated in Kayaalp, *Empress Nurbanu and Ottoman Politics*, 32–33.

© The Author(s), under exclusive license to Springer Nature Switzerland AG 2024
D. Ze'evi, *Queens Around the World, 1520–1620*,
https://doi.org/10.1007/978-3-031-58634-7_2

close relations with their counterparts on both sides. The story of Ottoman female rule could therefore serve as the best exposition of this book's theme.

Yet the Ottomans were also very different from their neighbors to the east and west. While, as we shall see in the next two chapters, late Mongol culture was the principal model for women's authority in the royal households of Asia, the Ottomans were ambivalent about this heritage. In the sixteenth century the Mongols were a distant memory and their respect for women in government had little bearing on Ottoman household practices. Moreover, the Ottomans considered Genghis Khan and the first generations of Mongol rulers idolators, sinners, and destroyers of early Islamic civilization.[2] Be that as it may, in the 1400s, the Sultans decided to eschew the practice of political marriage, prevalent in Europe and Asia alike, and instead filled their harems with slave women who were groomed to bear the future sultans. This shift was intended to curtail the danger of infighting, meddling by foreign princesses, and rival loyalties. The sultans assumed that slaves would not present such a danger. But a series of bondswomen challenged these assumptions throughout the sixteenth century. Their impressive personalities led them to positions of power, just as they did to highborn Safavid and Mughal princesses.

This chapter traces the lives of four women who began their careers as harem slaves and ended up governing the empire: Hurrem, wife of Sultan Suleiman "the Magnificent" and mother of Selim II; Nurbanu, wife of Selim II and mother of Murad III; Safiye, wife of Murad III and mother of Mehmet III; and Kösem, wife of Ahmed I and mother of Murad IV and Ibrahim I. Taken together, their careers spanned almost 130 years.

THE HAREM GAME

In its first decades, during the early 1300s, the Ottoman emirate took over a small territory in western Anatolia. Its leaders usually married the daughters of neighboring emirs. This was common practice among their predecessors and contemporaries. As their power and dominions grew, Ottoman princes took to marrying Byzantine and Serbian princesses and the daughters of neighboring Muslim monarchs, cementing political alliances. But after the conquest of Constantinople in 1453, they began to see their empire as a rightful heir to Alexander the Great and to the Roman-Byzantine, and Abbasid world empires. No other dynasty on earth could match their military and economic power, and political alliances by marriage with neighboring monarchs of petty kingdoms seemed unbecoming for such a great empire. From that time on, only

---

[2] In the sixteenth century, attitudes toward the Mongols began to change, perhaps in an attempt to introduce their close allies, the Tatar Khans of Crimea, of Mongol descent, into their lineage as a lesser branch of the dynasty. Ottoman chroniclers now described the Mongols as distant cousins of the Turks, and even as part of the same lineage. But the ambivalence toward the early Genghisid rulers remained. On Ottoman historiography of the Mongols see Ogasawara, "Enter the Mongols." It is interesting to note that in the Republic of Turkey, Genghis Khan has been adopted as one of the forefathers of the Turks.

harem slave women, known in the West as "odalisques" (from *odalık*, "girl of the chamber," meaning slave intended for sexual purposes in Turkish), would bear the sultans' children. Most of them were abducted in raids on enemy territory. A few were sold to palace envoys in slave markets around the empire. Once brought into the harem, these women were cut off from their families and friends, told to forget their past lives, schooled and resocialized as Ottoman ladies, and finally integrated into the sultan's household.[3]

The harem they were brought into was a strict hierarchical institution that comprised five distinct groups. One was the royal family: the sultan's mother and sisters, his child-bearing concubines, and his minor sons and daughters. The second included other concubines serving as acting or potential sexual companions for the sultan and his sons. The third was a group of young or even prepubescent female slaves in training, who could either become royal concubines or be married off to the empire's grandees. The fourth included women who served as administrators (*kalfas*) and domestic servants. Finally, there was a contingent of eunuchs—castrated male slaves of African descent—who were posted there to guard the harem's gate against intrusion, keep discipline inside, and maintain constant contact with the outside world.[4] Until the sixteenth century the harem was separate from Topkapı, the sultan's palace in Istanbul, and located in an older palace. At the end of the century, the current sultan's family along with its slaves and servants resided in the Topkapı, while the deceased sultan's female family members, as well as those in training, resided in the old palace.

The operating principles of the harem were reminiscent of those guiding the male Ottoman governing elite, known as *kul* (short for *kapı kulları*, meaning "slaves of the gate"). Most of the *kul* during this period were boys gathered from the empire's Christian villages or captured in war, formally enslaved, converted to Islam, and educated in the palace under very strict discipline. Talented *kul* would end up as governors, viziers, and army commanders in the "outer" service (*birun*) or as attendants and personal servants to the sultan in the "inner" service (*enderun*). Emulating this system, the harem developed a rigorous training scheme. The best slaves soon rose to influential positions inside the palace or were married off to members of the empire's elite. A woman who was often invited to share the sultan's bed was entitled to a moderate daily stipend from the treasury and to better lodgings. If she bore him a child, she was moved to an even higher rung on the ladder, especially if that child was a boy and a possible heir to the throne. She could then earn the title of "sultan's favorite" (*haseki sultan*) or "chief consort" (*baş kadın*). The highest perch in

---

[3] The most detailed descriptions of the institution and its workings are Leslie Peirce's *The Imperial Harem* and *The Empress*. The next few paragraphs are based mostly on Peirce's accounts. On social death as a basic condition of slavery see Orlando Patterson, *Slavery and Social Death* (Harvard University Press, 2018).

[4] While those eunuchs who oversaw the harem were labeled "black" (meaning brought over from sub-Saharan Africa), a contingent of "white" eunuchs, mostly from the Caucasus and the Balkans, oversaw the male part of the palace and mainly the sultan's young palace slaves in training.

the harem was reserved for the sultan's mother, the *valide*, or, if she were no longer alive, for the chief consort. In the late sixteenth century, as we shall see, *valides* ruled side by side with the sultans and at times even surpassed them in power. They played a major role in internal and external politics, casting a net of relations that encompassed the empire's governing elite as well as foreign dignitaries.[5]

With the stakes running so high, struggles between concubines for the sultan's favor, between mothers to eliminate their sons' rivals in line for the throne, and between the *valide* and the sultan's chief consort for influence and power were often brutal and in some cases involved physical violence. Like their male counterparts who rose through the ranks to become army commanders and civil governors, only those women who could bear the heat of the struggle, anticipate their rivals' moves, protect the lives of their offspring from multiple threats, and see them through to the throne remained standing for the last act: reigning supreme over the palace and the empire.[6]

From her apartment in the harem, the sultan's mother or his favorite consort would oversee the selection of the sultan's sexual partners and arrange the marriages of other harem women, including the sultan's sisters and daughters, to members of the governing elite. She could wield considerable political power over the sultan but, at the same time, was a prisoner in her own house. Ottoman etiquette demanded that women stay inside the harem at all times, except for travel to other palaces or ceremonial purposes, in which case they usually traveled in a closed carriage and wore a veil. Even women who performed administrative tasks at the harem were usually locked inside. This made communication between the ruling women and the world outside difficult. The only ones who could come and go as they pleased, besides the sultan himself, were the eunuchs, who were not perceived as a threat to the sultan's sexual prerogative. This freedom of movement gave the chief black eunuch a unique position in the empire as the ruling woman's main point of contact to other members of the elite.

Succession to the sultanic crown during this period was determined through a race to the throne between the sons of the deceased sultan. Once a prince reached his early teens, he would be sent by the sultan along with his mother to govern one of several districts in Anatolia. The real burden of governing would often fall to the mother, who, if politically savvy, would also build potential power coalitions for her son.[7] When news of the sultan's death reached them, each of his sons would rush from his province to the imperial capital (or to wherever the sultan and his retinue were at the time), calling on his supporters in the army and officialdom to help him secure the throne. Those who had

---

[5] Starting in the early sixteenth century, the sultan's mother, his chief consort, and his sons were also given the title "sultan," but while the sovereign's title came before his name (Sultan Suleiman), for the women and princes the title followed the name (Hurrem Sultan, Mustafa Sultan). See also Leslie Peirce, "Beyond Harem Walls," in Walthall (ed.) *Servants of the Dynasty*, 83–84.

[6] Peirce, *Empress*, 77.

[7] Leslie Peirce, "Beyond Harem Walls," in Walthall (ed.) *Servants of the Dynasty*, 86.

access to intelligence from within, had better assistance, and built stronger military and political alliances would arrive first and entrench themselves as sultans. Once they did, they usually executed their brothers to prevent further challenges to their rule.

When Sultan Selim I died in 1520, the situation was different. All his sons, except the 26-year-old Prince Suleiman, died at a young age. Suleiman, who at the time was governor of Manisa, near the Aegean coast, ascended the sultanic throne without any competition. Soon after his coronation he brought his beloved mother, Hafsa, to the Topkapı palace, asked her to head the royal harem, and bestowed on her the title "sultan," to be added after her name.

Hurrem/Roxelana

As governor of Manisa, Prince Suleiman already had a harem with several concubines. One of them, Mahidevran, a slave of Circassian or Albanian origin, bore his first son, Mustafa. When Suleiman became sultan, he appointed Mahidevran chief consort, but she soon lost this position to another woman.

In the early sixteenth century, Tatars from the Crimean peninsula regularly raided Ukrainian and Ruthenian settlements. They raped and abducted thousands of young men and women and then carted them off to Crimea to be sold for profit. According to some estimates, over a million youths were enslaved in this manner. The cream of the crop, attractive women who somehow escaped sexual assault by the marauders, were sent to the household of the Ottoman sultan, a close ally of the ruling Tatar dynasty.[8] One of them was a young girl of fifteen. The raiders apparently knew enough to keep her virginity intact, but no one cared to register her name.

According to old local traditions, the girl was born Anastasia Lisowska, daughter of a priest from the town of Rohatyn near Lviv. She may have been taken in a raid around 1517, but there is no written record and no way to verify these claims.[9] Like many other enslaved girls, she was traumatized and rebelled against her captors' attempts to tame her, but soon after her arrival at the royal harem she understood that resistance was pointless, resigned herself to the situation, and decided to make the most of it. She was given the name *Hurrem*, meaning "cheerful," either mocking her sullen expression or reflecting her change of mood. Roxelana (or Roxolana, Rosselane, La Rossa), the name she was known by in the West in later years, was suggested by visitors who heard stories about her. It referred both to her Ruthenian origins and to her reddish hair.

Pietro Bragadin, a Venetian ambassador who described her to the Republic's senate, said she was "young but not beautiful, although graceful and petite."[10]

---

[8] Peirce, *Empress*, 14–16. Yermolenko, "Roxolana," 234–238. Ruthenia was an old name for the territory that comprised parts of Ukraine, Poland, and parts of western Russia and Lithuania.
[9] Jačov, "La Tragica Fine," 47.
[10] Peirce, *Empress*, 32–33. Yermolenko, "Roxolana," 234.

Soon after her arrival, the sultan fell in love with the sharp-witted youth, to the dismay of Mahidevran, who regarded herself as the undisputed head of the harem. At one time Mahidevran quarreled with Hurrem and scratched her face. The issue was brought to Suleiman and, according to another Venetian envoy, Bernardo Navagero, when the sultan asked Mahidevran what happened, she replied *"that she had done less to [Hurrem] than she deserved, and that she believed that all the women should yield to her and recognize her as mistress since she had been in the service of his majesty first."*[11] A short time later, even though Mahidevran was well liked and her son, Prince Mustafa, was adored by the public, Hurrem replaced her and became Suleiman's only sexual partner.[12]

Years later, the great painter Titian, who never saw her in person, painted her likeness. He may have had sketches sent from Istanbul or based his painting on detailed descriptions. His masterpiece disappeared, but extant copies based on his original depict a majestic figure with ivory-white skin, a long neck, straight nose and full lips, wavy auburn hair, and shiny brown eyes. On her head she is wearing an ornate crown over a long sleeve of gauze-like material—reminiscent of the famous headdress of Ottoman Janissary soldiers—with a simple pearl necklace and earrings to match. Her satin gown, worn over a white cotton dress, is embroidered with gold filigree, echoing the crown on her head (Fig. 2.1).[13]

Suleiman was clearly smitten. He penned verses for her under the pseudonym *Muhibbi* (the lover). During a campaign in Persia, he composed a poem of love and yearning:

> *My solitude, my everything, my beloved*
> *My gleaming moon*
> *My companion, my intimate,*
> *My all, lord of beauties, my sultan.*
> *My love's essence and span, my sip from*
> *The river of paradise, my Eden*
> *My springtime, my bright joy, my secret,*
> *My idol, my laughing rose.*

Hurrem reciprocated with love letters of her own: "*If you ask after your wretched poor slave, day and night I burn in the fire of grief over separation from you.*" And: "*My sultan, there is no limit to the burning anguish of separation. Now spare this miserable one and do not withhold your noble letters. Let my soul gain at least some comfort.*" The love they shared never abated. Even three

---

[11] Quoted in Isom-Verhaaren, "Süleyman and Mihrimah," 68. In England around the same time, Katherine of Aragon scratched Anne Boleyn's face, for exactly the same reason. See Chap. 6.
[12] Isom-Verhaaren, "Süleyman and Mihrimah," 68–69.
[13] Madar, "Renaissance Representations," 14–19. Yermolenko, *Roxolana in European Literature*, 23–24.

Fig. 2.1 La Sultana Rossa, Titian's workshop c. 1550. John and Mable Ringling Museum of Art, Sarasota, Florida

decades later, as Hurrem lay on her deathbed, the French ambassador to the Porte informed his minister that Suleiman "*promised her and swore by the soul of his father Selim that he would never approach another woman.*"[14]

Soon after becoming the sultan's favorite (*Haseki Sultan*) she received the title of chief consort (*baş kadın*) and was given her own spacious apartment in the harem. When her first son, Mehmed, was born, her salary and status were raised further.[15] By that time she was recognized even by those outside the empire as a power to be reckoned with. In 1526, summing up his term in Istanbul with a speech to Venice's government, Ambassador Bragadin predicted that her star would soon rise.[16]

Since then, violating palace conventions that permitted each concubine to have only one child, Hurrem bore the Sultan a daughter, Mihrimah, and four more sons in succession.[17] To the courtiers' dismay, breaking another

[14] Peirce, *Empress*, 73, 142–143, 301.
[15] Ibid., 4–5, 55.
[16] Ibid., 69.
[17] Her name, of Persian origin (Mehr o māh), means "the sun and the moon."

time-honored practice, she was not sent off with any of her sons to govern a province. She remained in the old harem and later moved to the new one in the Topkapı palace, taking care of her children and mainly of her youngest, the beloved Cihangir, who suffered from severe scoliosis and other medical problems.[18]

Now that her salary was raised to an unprecedented 2,000 aspers a day from the treasury, on top of the frequent presents of land and property from Suleiman, Hurrem could spend more money on acquiring power and its trappings, including items of luxury. Her relationship with her young and energetic *kira* (assistant and jeweler) Esther Handali, who served as her main conduit to the outside world, became intimate.[19] Esther was more attuned to her style and tastes than the older *kira*, Fatma Hatun, who served Suleiman's mother. She used her connections in Istanbul's artisan community and in the Italian embassies in Galata to procure ornaments of rare beauty.[20] One gets a sense of the expenses involved from a letter sent by a Florentine merchant in Istanbul to Duke Cosimo de Medici, assuring him that the jewels entrusted to him would be sold as soon as the sultana was back in Istanbul. In his reply, Duke Cosimo asks the merchant to demand at least 8,000 scudi, an enormous sum, for the sale.[21] Since there was no way for the merchant himself to enter the harem, the *kira* must have made the decision and bought the jewels for Hurrem.[22]

First Glimmers of an International Female Network

Harem women were taught languages, music, dancing, embroidery, and religion, but not politics, and few inside the imperial harem knew enough about the world outside to instruct them. For guidance on negotiating the maze of state affairs, the young favorite, whose understanding of international relations was inadequate at best, depended on the chief black eunuch, who was her main link to the palace, and on her *kira*, who spoke European languages and was in touch with foreign ambassadors in Istanbul. In their meetings, Esther updated her on the royal gossip of the times and talked about events taking place in Europe in order for Hurrem to be able to hold her own when talking to Suleiman.

---

[18] Yermolenko, "Roxolana," 235–236.

[19] On the Jewish *kiras* of the harem, see Chap. 5. Abraham Galante suggests an etymology for the title *kira* which was previously unknown in the Ottoman Empire. Since the name Esther sounds to the Turkish ear like the verb *ister*, which means "to want," he suggests it may have been translated back to Spanish as "querer," hence *kira*. Another possible source is the Greek *Kyrazza* meaning "pretty woman." Galante, *Esther Kyra*, 3.

[20] In the mid-sixteenth century, one Venetian ducat (about 3.45 grams of pure gold) was worth about 84 aspers.

[21] The scudo was a general name for large silver coins weighing approximately 23 grams. Eight thousand scudi were therefore worth about 184 kilos (slightly more than 400 pounds) of silver.

[22] *Medici Archive*, Vol. 653, Fol. 52 (March 4, 1545).

One tidbit of gossip that must have fascinated Hurrem was the story of Poland's queen, Bona Sforza, with whom she was to have a long and fruitful relationship. Bona was a noble woman from the ruling family of Lombardy in northern Italy who was sent to Poland about the same time as Hurrem herself was abducted from her village. She married Poland's widowed king, Sigismund, and soon distinguished herself at his court as a perceptive statesperson. Besides an appreciation of Renaissance style, she brought to the palace in Krakow a keen mind, strong political intuitions, and a dislike for the House of Habsburg and its creeping domination of central Europe. Hurrem must have felt a sense of shared destiny with the Italian Queen of Poland, who had traded places with her.

Five years after Suleiman's accession to the throne, the two queens finally had the opportunity to communicate. In February 1525, King Francis I of France was taken prisoner in Italy and sent to Spain as hostage of Habsburg Emperor Charles V. In her efforts to release him, his mother, Louise of Savoy, sent two delegations, one to Sultan Suleiman, asking for his intercession, and another to Poland with the same request.[23] Having received Louise's envoys in Poland, Bona Sforza decided to write to Hurrem, her counterpart in the sultan's court, and update her about the situation. Hurrem, who probably saw Bona's overture as an incentive to establish a connection with royal women in Poland and France, brought the matter up with Suleiman.

Thus, when the French delegation received an audience with the sultan and presented Louise of Savoy's request, Suleiman promised his support. If any *active* steps were taken by the Ottomans at that point, no written record of it has survived in the archive, but the Sultan's public endorsement of the French king must have had an impact on Emperor Charles V's decision. Soon a treaty was signed between Charles and Francis, some land was ceded, and the king of France was set free. As a gesture of gratitude, when the Ottomans set out on a campaign against the Habsburgs in Hungary later that same year, King Francis announced that the treaty with Charles had been signed under duress and was therefore illegal and opened a second front in Lombardy. The military buildup forced the Habsburg emperor to split up his armies. Queen Bona and King Sigismund of Poland also assisted the Ottoman endeavor by instructing their Hungarian protégé, John Zapolya, to refrain from attacking the Ottoman army. With French and Polish assistance, and with Hungarian neutrality, the Sultan's army crushed the emperor's forces at the battle of Mohács (August 29, 1526) and occupied all of Hungary (Fig. 2.2).[24]

After the victory, Suleiman returned to Istanbul without reorganizing Hungary's government, and the Hungarian aristocracy was in crisis, split between supporters of the Habsburg claimant, Ferdinand I, and those of John

---

[23] The first delegation sent by Louise of Savoy to Istanbul was attacked and robbed on the way. Louise immediately sent another, headed by the experienced diplomat Frangipani, who went in disguise and reached Istanbul later than planned. For more details, see Chap. 6.

[24] Jačov, "La Tragica Fine," 49.

Fig. 2.2 Cameo of Bona Sforza, circa 1540, Metropolitan Museum of Art, New York

Zapolya who opposed him. Bona informed Hurrem of the crisis and recommended Zapolya as a trusted vassal. As a result, when Zapolya's emissary was received by Suleiman and his grand vizier, Ibrahim, they promised him their backing. Three years later, during Suleiman's first attempt to capture Vienna in 1529, he passed through Buda and restored order to its government, recognizing Zapolya as its king.[25] Through such actions Hurrem Sultan and Bona Sforza forged a tacit alliance between Poland and the Ottoman Empire, which was then cemented in an "Eternal Peace Treaty" signed in 1533. Piotr Opalinski, Poland's ambassador to Suleiman's court, confirmed that it was Hurrem's insistence that convinced the sultan to forbid raids of Polish lands by the Crimean khan.[26] A few years later, another link was added to the alliance when Bona's daughter, Isabella, married John Zapolya. Hurrem and Bona remained friends and political allies throughout their lives.

Building a Power Base

He didn't dare do it while his mother Hafsa was alive, but in 1534, right after her death, Suleiman decided to marry his slave Hurrem, once again scandalously breaking with tradition. Love was surely a strong incentive for

[25] Ibid., 49.
[26] Yermolenko, "Roxolana," 239.

manumitting her and making her an official wife, but another motivation was also at play. Suleiman and his Grand Vizier Ibrahim were headed out to Iraq for a long campaign against the Safavids. Suleiman needed someone to take control of the state in his absence, and his beloved Hurrem was the only one he fully trusted. The idea may have been inspired by the letter he received a decade earlier from the strong-willed Louise of Savoy, who asked for his help when she served as regent for her son Francis. Suleiman and Hurrem's wedding was held in secret to avoid angering conservative circles, but the well-connected Venetians soon reported the fact.[27] Since then, during Suleiman's frequent military campaigns, Hurrem held court—from behind a curtain—honing her political instincts and expanding her circle of acquaintances both inside the realm and in foreign lands.[28]

She soon figured out that in order to be respected and obeyed, she needed to build a stronger foundation of political and social power. She used all the weapons in her arsenal, including playing palace factions against each other and using the harem's main assets—marriageable princesses and palace-trained odalisques—to cement alliances with senior officers and bureaucrats. But the main obstacle on her path to power, she realized, was the grand vizier, Ibrahim Pasha.

Captured as a boy in a piracy raid, Ibrahim was taken into Suleiman's service when they were both teenagers. He became the sultan's closest companion, soon making himself indispensable by running foreign relations and controlling access to the sultan. No love was lost between the best friend and the beloved wife. He suspected her (rightly, it turned out) of trying to replace him, and she suspected him of favoring Mustafa, Mahidevran's son, as heir to the throne, rather than one of her own sons. Assisted by allies inside the palace, including the head royal physician and the *kira*, Hurrem relentlessly strove to undermine Suleiman's faith in his advisor and to portray him as untrustworthy. Finally, in March 1536, she succeeded. Suleiman relented and had the vizier executed. Hurrem soon took his place as Suleiman's right-hand person and sought public recognition of her status.[29]

In his famous book *The Prince*, her contemporary Niccolo Machiavelli suggested that there were two ways for a ruler to get his subjects to obey: fear and love. A combination of the two would be best, he asserted, but if the prince is unable to inspire both fear and love, fear is preferable.[30] Hurrem was certainly feared by members of the elite who knew of the hold she had over the sultan, but the public at large was a different matter. As a foreign-born veiled woman, a former slave bound to the harem most of the time, with no autonomous source of power, Hurrem could hardly instill fear in the hearts of her subjects. She chose to court their love instead and demonstrated it by founding crucial welfare institutions.

---

[27] Peirce, *Empress*, 119. Pedani, "Safiye's Household," 17–18.
[28] Peirce, *Empress*, 100–101, 117.
[29] Heyd, "Moses Hamon," 164. Peirce, *Empress*, 150–154. Ibrahim was strangled in his sleep.
[30] Niccolo Machiavelli, *The Prince*, Chap. XVII.

In 1538, she began building her own urban complex of institutions (*külliye*) combining a mosque, law academies, soup kitchens for the poor, and hospitals. The complex she had in mind defied tradition. Previously building such grand institutions had been the privilege of the sultan. Suleiman's mother, Hafsa, had built a modest one in Manisa, far away from the capital, and even that was regarded as a bold move for a *valide* of slave origins. Hurrem had decided to build hers smack in the middle of the capital city. At that point Suleiman had still not begun to build his own mosque, and upstaging him might have been construed as disrespectful, so she made two important decisions at the outset. One was to build her *külliye* on a hillside, not on top of a hill. There it would be less imposing but still visible. The spot she chose for the structure, right by the women's slave market (*Avret Pazarı*), may have symbolized for her the long way she had come from her humble origins. The other decision was to employ a relatively unknown architect named Sinan, who at the time was still a military engineer but was to become the empire's most famous architect. Hurrem immediately recognized his talent and gave him his first civilian project in the capital: a set of structures that would convey power and beneficence without treading on powerful men's toes (Fig. 2.3).[31]

Fig. 2.3 Haseki Hurrem Sultan Külliyesi. Photo: Dosseman, 2008

---

[31] The Avret Pazarı was close to today's Nuruosmaniye Mosque in central Istanbul. See also René Langlois, "Comparing the French Queen Regent and the Ottoman Validé Sultan" in Woodacre et al. *A Companion to Global Queenship*, 273–274.

The finished structure was exactly what she aimed for: built in the new austere imperial style, restrained but broadcasting power.[32] Careful not to outshine the sultanic privilege, it was not as extravagant as the house that her rival Ibrahim Pasha built across the road from the sultan's palace, but it echoed the quiet elegance of the Topkapı. The complex proudly bore her name for all the world to see: *Haseki Hurrem Sultan Külliyesi*. In later years she built similar complexes in Edirne and Ankara and in the 1550s established sultanic soup kitchens in Mecca and Jerusalem (locally known as *khasikiyya*). One of her crowning architectural achievements was a majestic public bathhouse facing the Hagia Sophia mosque. Such legitimizing structures, on an even grander scale, were later used by her female successors to make their power and beneficence known.[33]

Foreign Relations

In July 1540, as the *külliye* broke ground, the king of Hungary John Zapolya suddenly died, only sixteen months after his marriage to Bona's daughter, Isabella, and just a week after their son was born. The widowed Isabella was pressured by the Habsburgs to accept their control in Hungary and Transylvania. To block Habsburg rule, the Hungarian lords elected Isabella's baby, John Sigismund, as heir to the throne and appointed Isabella herself as regent until his maturity. Two years later Suleiman arrived in Buda and, in view of the imminent Habsburg danger, decided to take full control of the country and formally annex it as an Ottoman province, divesting Isabella and her son of their kingdom. Remembering the friendship between Hurrem and her mother, Isabella wrote to her and enclosed gifts for her daughter Mihrimah. Upon receiving the letter, Hurrem conferred with Mihrimah's husband, Grand Vizier Rustem Pasha, and the two discussed the matter with Suleiman. Under Hurrem's pressure the sultan agreed to allow Isabella to keep Transylvania as regent on behalf of her son. To allay Isabella's fears of a Habsburg occupation, Hurrem sent a letter to let her know that she was now under Hurrem's personal protection. It is clear from the letter that she saw her assistance to Isabella as part of a deep feminine bond that transcended religion and ethnicity: "*Dearest daughter,*" she wrote, "*we are both born from one mother, Eve, and we are both created from the same matter, and we both serve the same man*" (that is, Suleiman).[34] As a further confidence-building measure, she later supported Bona's position on the marriage of her son (Isabella's brother) Sigismund Augustus, heir to the throne of Poland.

---

[32] On the emergence of an imperial style in Suleiman's time, see Gülru Necipoğlu, "A kanun for the state, a canon for the arts: the classical synthesis in Ottoman art and architecture during the Age of Süleyman." *Soliman le Magnifique et son temps* (1990): 195–216.

[33] Peirce, ibid. Yermolenko, "Roxolana", 237–238. Singer, *Constructing Ottoman Beneficence*, esp. pp. 88–104. Godfrey Goodwin, *Ottoman Turkey*, 38.

[34] Peirce, *Empress*, 223–225. Jačov, "La Tragica Fine," 50.

Once they established cordial relations with the ruling women in Poland and Transylvania, Hurrem and her *kira*, Esther, turned their attention to Moldavia, the last bit of Eastern Europe left out of the Ottoman sphere of influence, and secured it for the Ottomans as well. In 1541 they decided to support Petru Rareş, who had been *voivode* of Moldavia but was removed from the throne several years previously.[35] Until that time Rareş shifted his support between the Ottomans, the Habsburgs, and Zapolya. Under Hurrem's pressure he finally accepted the position of vassal to the Ottomans and remained loyal until he was killed in battle a few years later.[36]

When the king of Poland, Sigismund, died in 1548 and his son Sigismund Augustus was crowned, both Hurrem and Mihrimah wrote to congratulate him and sent their condolences over the death of his father. Sigismund replied, thanking them for their letters and expressing his wish for continued good relations with the Ottoman Empire. In an intimate gesture of familial relationship, Hurrem sent the new king gifts of clothes and towels that she herself had embroidered and informed him that the Sultan expressed joy upon receiving his letter: "*The old king and I were like two brothers,*" Suleiman said, "*and if it pleases God the Merciful, this king and I will be like father and son.*" Suleiman himself demonstrated how deep these feelings ran when, in a letter to Sigismund Augustus written in 1551, he referred to Hurrem as "*your sister and my wife.*"[37]

Now that the western front was securely under the Ottoman sphere of influence, Hurrem turned her attention to the eastern borders. From the beginning of the century, the rising Safavid state in northern Iran was at war with the Ottomans. Its rulers, hailing from a militant Shiite Sufi order, incited a like-minded segment of Anatolia's population to rise against their Ottoman Sunni masters.[38] The first great battle between Suleiman's father, Sultan Selim, and the founder of the Safavid dynasty, Shah Ismail, was fought on the plain of Chaldiran, to the east of Lake Van. Faced with the firepower of Ottoman artillery and the disciplined musket-wielding Janissary troops, the shah's army was overpowered, and the Ottomans swept its encampment, capturing his harem and sending the women to Istanbul. Suleiman's troops even ransacked the Safavid capital, Tabriz.[39] But in the dead of winter, with mutiny simmering in

---

[35] Voivode (voivoda) was a common title for military governors, leaders, and warlords in the Balkans, later used by the Ottomans in these regions.

[36] Roth, *House of Nasi*, 33.

[37] Peirce, *Imperial Harem*, 221, 251–252. Peirce, *Empress*, 251–2. Yermolenko, "Roxolana," 231–2, 240–242. Jačov, "La Tragica Fine," 42.

[38] It is interesting to note that until the sixteenth century, most of Iran's population was Sunni and the population of Anatolia was mostly heterodox Shiite. Once the Safavid dynasty chose Shiism as their banner, the Ottomans shifted more and more toward Sunni orthodoxy. See also Chap. 3.

[39] For the Safavid perspective on this battle, see Chap. 4.

the ranks, the sultan decided to retreat to the army's barracks back home, forsaking his territorial gains. Two decades later, in 1534, he and Ibrahim set out once again, this time against Ismail's son, Shah Tahmasp. They retook Tabriz and Baghdad, but soon they had to withdraw again, and the Safavids clambered back into Iraq and eastern Anatolia. The fighting between the two dynasties seemed to flare up again in a never-ending cycle of violence. Hurrem was determined to help solve this problem as well.

From her first years in the harem, she was intrigued by the Safavids. They may have been the enemy, but they were still unmatched as a source of elegant craftsmanship and style. Ceramic tiles, carpets, and miniature drawings made by artisans brought over from Tabriz and employed by the royal artisanal workshops were emulated by Ottoman artists. Their bracelets and necklaces were finer than those produced by the court's jewelers, and even their language, Farsi, was admired as the most poetic. Hurrem spent long hours in the harem listening to stories told by the women carried off from Shah Ismail's harem shortly before she herself was captured in Ukraine.[40]

In 1547, an event took place that shook the foundations of Ottoman–Safavid relations. Shah Tahmasp's rebellious younger brother, the handsome Prince Alqas Mirza, found refuge in the Ottoman court and offered to lead an army against his brother were he to be given Ottoman backing and financial means.[41] To show his commitment and his readiness to fight shoulder to shoulder with his Ottoman peers, he even converted to Sunnism.[42] His retinue brought dazzling pieces of jewelry and illuminated manuscripts as gifts that served as models for palace artisans long after he was gone. Excited by the possibility of using this Safavid prince to undermine his enemy, Suleiman lavished upon Alqas slaves, gold, sable furs, swords, and horses. Hurrem, who took charge of the women in Alqas Mirza's retinue, was just as active. She and her harem servants sent the prince shirts, quilt covers, and pillows that she had embroidered in her own hand with silver thread.[43]

The end was tragic. Alqas accompanied Suleiman's armies to the eastern border but failed to recruit an Iranian force and defeat his brother. He surrendered to Tahmasp in 1549, was incarcerated, and six months later mysteriously died when he fell off the ramparts of his prison.[44] In a strange epilogue

---

[40] Peirce, *Imperial Harem*, 37. Jackson and Lockhart, *Cambridge History of Iran*, vol. 6, 224.

[41] Mirza, short for "emirzadeh," much like the ungendered "shahzadeh," is a common title for princes of the realm.

[42] C. Fleischer, "Alqās Mirza." *Encyclopædia Iranica*, I/9, pp. 907–909 (https://iranicaonline.org/articles/alqas-alqasb-alqas-mirza-safawi). Peirce, *Imperial Harem*, 220. Beck and Nashat, 154–157. Clot, *Suleiman the Magnificent*, 153–154.

[43] Peirce, *Empress*, 254–256. Clot, *Suleiman the Magnificent*, 154.

[44] "Alqas Mirza," *Encyclopedia Iranica*. Clot, *Suleiman the Magnificent*, 154. For an account of the Alqas affair, see Chap. 3.

to the story, many years later, Hurrem's own son, Prince Bayezid, who fled with his family to the Safavid Empire, found refuge with Shah Tahmasp. The Shah probably saw this as a way of getting back at Sultan Suleiman for sheltering his brother Alqas and threatening his rule. But two years later, in return for a hefty payment and promises of a renewed peace agreement, he handed Bayezid and his four sons back to the Ottoman delegation. They were executed on the spot.[45]

But long before Alqas's tragic end, during their stay in the palace, the Safavid ladies in his retinue told Hurrem wondrous stories about Shah Tahmasp's sister, Shazada Sultanum. In intimate conversations they claimed that she shared the throne with her brother and joined his campaigns and hunting expeditions, riding horses like a practiced warrior.[46] As long as the war with Iran went on, there could be no contact between the two royal women, but as soon as the 1549 campaign was over and a ceasefire declared, Hurrem and her daughter Mihrimah contacted Shahzada Sultanum, and the three worked diligently together to bring the two empires to the negotiating table and achieve peace. In 1555, due in large part to their efforts, a peace treaty was signed by Suleiman and Tahmasp in the city of Amasya.

In the wake of the Amasya treaty, the three women exchanged several letters. In one of them, Hurrem wrote about the need to appoint ambassadors to safeguard the peace and prevent further conflict.[47] Two years later, when work on Suleiman's great mosque complex in Istanbul was under way, it was Shahzada Sultanum's turn to send Hurrem and Mihrimah a congratulatory note, letting them know that she was preparing illuminated Qurans and carpets for the mosque. As in many other letters exchanged between royal women in this period, Shahzada Sultanum emphasized the importance of peace between the two empires and commended Hurrem Sultan and her son-in-law, grand vizier Rustem Pasha, for their role in bringing it about. Hurrem thanked her and assured her that the Ottoman Empire was committed to the peace agreement.[48]

---

[45] Clot, *Suleiman the Magnificent*, 166–167.

[46] Beck and Nashat, *Women in Iran*, 151–152. Uluç, "Execution of Safavid Begum." More on Shahzada Sultanum see Chap. 3.

[47] Birjandifar, *Women and Politics in Safavid Iran*, 43.

[48] Peirce, *Empress*, 295–296. Peirce, *Harem*, 221. Birjandifar, *Royal Women*, 33, 43–44. Beck and Guity, *Women in Iran*, 154.

2 SULTANAS OF THE OTTOMAN EMPIRE   29

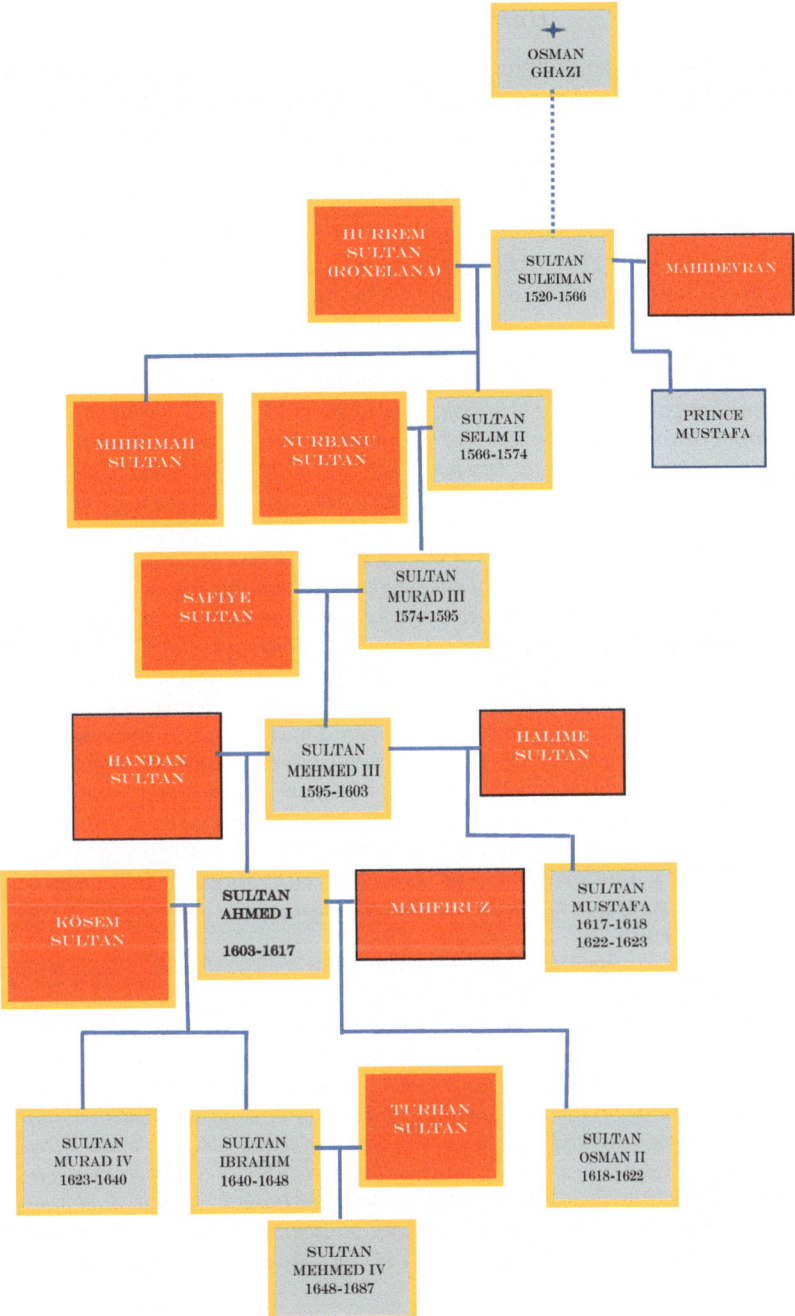

Lineage 1: Hurrem Sultan to Kösem Sultan

Hurrem and Dona Gracia

Dona Gracia, a Jewish shipping magnate who came to Venice from Antwerp in 1546, must have found the stories about Hurrem captivating. She felt that the sultana was a kindred spirit—an intelligent and powerful woman holding her own in a world of men—and was determined to meet and join forces with her. A few years later, when she found refuge in Istanbul in 1553, Gracia had an appointment with the sultana.[49] We have no record of this meeting and the discussion that took place. The following is an imaginary description based on what we do know about the connections between the two.

> With a train of servants carrying fine dresses and gem-studded jewels crafted in Florence for the sultana, Gracia entered the royal harem. Summoning one of her own servants to put them aside, Hurrem thanked her and reclined on silken pillows, inviting Gracia to sit by her side. A low padded stool was brought over for the lady, who was unaccustomed to the Ottoman style. A long chat ensued that Esther kira, fluent in both Spanish and Turkish, translated, sometimes conveying more than just the literal meaning of the words.
>
> Gracia opened by thanking the sultana for her assistance in opening the gates of the empire wide for Jews in general and specifically for her own family. Hurrem nodded and politely asked about the trip through the Balkans, and Gracia recounted her impressions of the Ottoman provinces she traveled through after leaving Italy. They then discussed politics, and Gracia did her best to explain the intricate rivalries and alliances between Venice, Milan, Florence, Ferrara, Naples, and the papal state, as well as the nuances of Christian faith that seemed to be tearing Europe apart. She told the story of her own flight from Lisbon and Antwerp, recounted anecdotes about her acquaintance with Mary of Hungary, the Habsburg governor of the Netherlands, described the beauty of Venice's canals and palaces, and expressed her frustration with the persecution of Jews and New Christians in Europe. Hurrem nodded in sympathy and praised the tolerance of Islam. They briefly discussed business matters, the importation of spices from India, and other commercial opportunities for the Ottoman Empire.
>
> The tragic execution of Crown Prince Mustafa, a few months earlier, hung heavy in the air but was not mentioned. Hurrem's eyes shone as she talked about her eldest remaining son, Prince Selim, whom she hoped would one day be sultan. Gracia then mentioned her nephew, Don João Miques (Joseph Nasi), who was a frequent visitor to most of Europe's royal courts, and expressed her hope that he would arrive in Istanbul soon. Both agreed that someone like Don João could be a perfect companion and counselor for the aspiring Prince Selim. Gracia vowed to help as best she could, offered the services of her agents and intelligence gathering network in Europe, suggested her mediation between Hurrem and various ladies in the Italian city-states, and promised to invest in Hurem's central European ventures. Hurrem hinted she would update the sultan and would keep in touch with her. She told Esther to make sure this relationship continued.

---

[49] For Dona Gracia's story, see Chap. 5.

Shortly afterwards, Gracia contacted Hurrem once again, asking for her intercession. Pope Paul IV, known for his hatred of Marranos (Jews who converted to Christianity but were suspected of still practicing Judaism in the privacy of their homes), had arrested a group of them in the city of Ancona, accused them of performing Jewish rituals, and executed some of them, including Dona Gracia's own commercial agents. She was furious and wanted to take revenge by punishing the pope and those doing his bidding. She planned a boycott of the port of Ancona, the main point of entry to Europe for commerce from the Ottoman Empire and the Eastern Mediterranean. As a shipping magnate she could divert her own ships and those of her partners to other ports, but in order to achieve a complete shut-down of commerce in the port, she needed the sultan's backing. Hurrem agreed to help and talked to Suleiman, who supported the move, dispatched an envoy to Ancona to protect those listed as Ottoman subjects, and even sent a personal letter to the pope. But the boycott failed, mainly because of dissent inside the Jewish trader community.

By that time Hurrem's health was already failing. She still corresponded with other royal women but was confined to her chambers in the harem. In early 1558, she contracted malaria, which worsened her condition, and died in mid-April. The widowed Suleiman was inconsolable for a long time and, as he promised, never took another wife or consort. He died eight years later.[50]

Hurrem's unprecedented power and influence paved the way for her daughter Mihrimah, her daughter-in-law Nurbanu, and a chain of later *valides* who ruled the empire until the mid-seventeenth century. She also left an indelible mark on Western European culture. Gabriel Bounin's play, *La Soltane*, staged for Queen Catherine de Medici, depicted Hurrem/Roxelana, thinly disguised as "Rose," as a devious queen conspiring to have her rival's son, Prince Mustafa, killed, so that her own son would inherit the throne. Suleiman had indeed killed Prince Mustafa on the campaign trail to Iran. He may have been incited by Hurrem to do so, but, to be fair, he also knew—and knew that Hurrem understood—that the accession of Mustafa to the throne would mean death for all her male offspring. It came down to a choice between his sons. The Venetian Navagero describes a conversation—probably apocryphal—that took place between Suleiman and his beloved youngest son, Cihangir. In the conversation, Cihangir said he believed that if Mustafa were sultan, he would let him live because of his deformity. But Suleiman shook his head. "*Son*," he said, "*Mustafa will become sultan and will take the lives of all of you*."[51] Be that as it may, in Bounin's play, and in many other stories and plays staged around Europe, Hurrem was always depicted as an ambitious and ruthless queen pulling her husband's strings behind the scenes.

Although such plays and books were meant to present the cruelty and wiles of the Ottoman sultana, they also presented Hurrem as a strong-willed and

---

[50] Yermolenko, "Roxolana," 235.
[51] Quoted in Isom-Verhaaren, "Süleyman and Mihrimah," 73.

determined queen and may have influenced Catherine de Medici to assume full control in France on her own merit.

Hurrem's story was also widespread in England. In his misogynistic *First Blast of the Trumpet against the Regiment of Women*, published in 1558, the Protestant reverend John Knox drew a parallel between Hurrem and the Catholic Mary I, Queen of England, describing in disgust the Ottoman "monstiferouse empire of women" and its imitation by the English monarchy. Others, such as Bishop John Aylmer, took offense at such comparisons, suggesting that Elizabeth (who replaced Mary as queen in 1558) was different from the Turks because they were heathens and she was a devout Christian.[52] However, misogynistic and anti-Islamic claims notwithstanding, there is no doubt that the debate about women in government, in both England and France, was heavily influenced by Hurrem's rise to power and the place she carved out for herself and her female successors in the greatest empire of the time.

Nurbanu

When Nurbanu, the next great queen of the Ottoman Empire, arrived on the scene, the position of first lady was already taken. As Hurrem lay dying, her daughter Mihrimah took over as head of the imperial household. Educated in languages and law, trained by her mother and the *kira* in affairs of state, and accustomed to corresponding with foreign royals, she easily slipped into her role as Suleiman's main female counsellor and peace emissary.[53] Initially, she wielded power mainly through her much older and experienced husband, Grand Vizier Rustem Pasha, but once he died in 1561, she came into her own as the court's most influential politician.[54] Although her stipend was lower than her mother's, during Rustem Pasha's life the couple amassed legendary fortunes, and she was eager to initiate her own construction projects. Building on the precedents established by her mother, she chose her sites carefully. Her first mosque project was finished in 1548. It stood proud on the water's edge across the Bosphorus Strait, visible from her favorite vantage point in the Topkapı palace. Being the first such imperial mosque built by a princess in Istanbul, it proclaimed her status as a privileged daughter of the sultan.[55] Soon after the death of her husband, Mihrimah started constructing a second mosque complex bearing her name, atop the highest hill in Istanbul, right by Edirne Gate, the city's main entryway. Elegant, resplendent, and feminine in decoration, the

---

[52] Andrea, "Women and Islam," 15. Many of these descriptions of the event rely on descriptions written by Busbecq, Habsburg ambassador to Istanbul, that circulated widely in Europe. See Ogier de Busbecq, *Turkish Letters*, 43, 52–55.

[53] Isom-Verhaaren, "Süleyman and Mihrimah," 70. Unlike Hurrem, who studied Ottoman Turkish late and had scribes write most of her letters, Mihrimah wrote letters to her father in her own hand.

[54] Peirce, *Imperial Harem*, 65.

[55] Isom-Verhaaren, "Süleyman and Mihrimah," 77–81.

Fig. 2.4 Mihrimah's mosque and the city walls (photo: 123rf)

single-minaret mosque was designed by Sinan and built on a raised platform, towering above the high city walls.[56] It was the first edifice a traveler on the road from Europe would see when approaching the city. A law school, an ablution fountain, a public bath, and a row of shops for the upkeep of the mosque were also part of the complex (Fig. 2.4).[57]

Mihrimah may have hoped that the soaring dome and minaret would be ready in time to welcome her father upon his return from yet another campaign against the Habsburgs in Hungary, but it was not to be. In 1566, the seventy-two-year-old Suleiman insisted on leading his army in an attempt to breach the walls of the formidable Szigetvar fortress in Hungary. Tens of thousands of Ottoman soldiers were killed in this futile siege, and right before his army finally broke through the walls, the ailing sultan breathed his last. His death was kept secret while the grand vizier, Sokollu Mehmed Pasha, ordered a retreat and summoned Suleiman's son, Selim, from his governorship in the town of Kütahya, to take his father's place.

Selim and Nurbanu's Accession

Selim immediately ordered his harem and courtiers to pack up and prepare to go to Istanbul and galloped to the Balkans with his retinue to take charge of

---

[56] Minaret (*minare* in Turkish) is the mosque tower from which the call for prayer is sounded.
[57] Ibid., 82–83.

the kingdom. His close friend Don Joseph Nasi, Dona Gracia's nephew, joined him. When the party reached Belgrade and Selim ascertained that he was indeed to be the next sultan, he bestowed on Don Joseph the Duchy of Naxos in the Aegean Sea.[58]

Twenty-five years earlier, in 1541, young Selim was sent to govern the district of Manisa, where he assembled an elegant group of courtiers, poets, and musicians. His mother, Hurrem, did not accompany him to his posting, but the pleasure-seeking sixteen-year-old boy already had a harem of his own. His favorite new concubine, who was given the name Nurbanu (also spelled Nur Banu, meaning "lady of light"), bore her first daughter in 1544. She was nineteen years old at the time. Two years later she had a son, Murad, and was formally recognized as the prince's chief consort.

There is no clear record of Nurbanu's early years. It was believed that she was taken prisoner on or around the Venetian-held island of Corfu. Selim suspected, perhaps based on her childhood memories, that she came from an aristocratic family and sent a special envoy to Venice to inquire about her origins. A short while later the Venetians replied that she was indeed of noble stock, that her original name was Cecilia Venier-Baffo, and that she was an illegitimate child (meaning born out of wedlock) of two young aristocrats. Their claim was accepted at face value both by the Ottomans and by later historians, but in recent years several documents have surfaced that put that identification in doubt. The new documents suggest that she was actually Greek, from the island of Paros, and that her original name was Kalé Kartanou.[59] The Venetians may have confused Nurbanu with another girl abducted in the same raid, or they may have embellished the story on purpose, hoping to curry favor with a future sultana. In any case, Nurbanu immediately understood the advantages of identifying as a noble daughter of the *Serenissima Republica*, presented herself as a lady of aristocratic provenance, and tended to conduct a pro-Venice policy. Closely following her career, the Venetians reported that she was beautiful and exceptionally intelligent and that Selim was deeply in love with her. Although there is no official record of a wedding between the two, the Venetian ambassador reported in 1571 that Selim married her, following his father's precedent of marrying his mother.[60]

When the new sultan and his favorite consort arrived at Topkapı palace to begin their reign, two things became immediately clear. One was that the empire was in deep financial crisis. Enormous sums were spent on the construction of imperial buildings, tax collection was neglected, and the remaining funds were siphoned off to Suleiman's final unsuccessful campaign. The treasury vaults were empty and the tired returning soldiers, whose expectations for spoils of war or at least a special coronation bonus were dashed, were once again on the brink of mutiny.

---

[58] Roth, *House of Nasi*, 40–41, 75.
[59] Arbel, "Nur Banu."
[60] Peirce, *Imperial Harem*, 92–93. Pedani, "Safiye's Household," 17.

From Nurbanu's point of view, another problem soon arose. Mihrimah, who was about the same age as she, was *de facto* sovereign in Suleiman's final months and was expected to continue as her brother's co-sultan. Although Mihrimah first supported her other brother, Bayezid, and even sent him money to help secure his accession, she immediately recognized her mistake, shifted her allegiance, and supported Selim.[61] She then helped rebuild the defunct navy, equipped the army with new weapons and uniforms, and magnanimously loaned Selim 50,000 gold coins from her private funds for his accession expenses. Under these circumstances Nurbanu was relegated to second place in the female pecking order. Both women, however, understood that it would be in their best interest to work as a team. Until Selim's death and the ascent of Nurbanu's son, Murad, to the throne, they collaborated, with Nurbanu gradually moving to the fore as Mihrimah receded to the background until her premature death in 1578.

From Haseki to Valide

Like her predecessors, Nurbanu built up and carefully nurtured her own power on the traditional pillars of female influence that her predecessor, Hurrem, had erected—marrying off harem women to state officials, social beneficence for the masses, and a foreign policy aimed at stability. Unlike Hurrem, by the time she arrived at the imperial palace, she was no longer a novice. She already had experience as Selim's favorite when he was governor of Manisa and knew the basics of running a household and holding her own within the dynasty.

Soon after her arrival, she summoned Hurrem's aging lady-in-waiting, Esther *kira*, and asked for her support in continuing the work done by Hurrem and Mihrimah with foreign ambassadors and envoys.[62] Like theirs, her central European policy was predicated on intimate relations with the Polish Commonwealth.[63] Poland sought an alliance both against the Habsburgs and against the new rising power, Russia, which began its westward push under Tsar Ivan IV, "The Terrible."[64] As her opening move Nurbanu encouraged Joseph Nasi to offer King Sigismund Augustus a loan of 150,000 ducats for which he was given guarantees in the form of a monopoly on the export of Beeswax from Poland. But when Augustus died with no male heir a few years later, Nurbanu needed to recalibrate her eastern European policy. She sought the advice of her counselors, including that of her physician, Solomon Ashkenazi, who began his career in Poland's royal court and was well versed in

---

[61] Isom-Verhaaren, "Süleyman and Mihrimah," 77, 84.
[62] Pedani-Fabris, "Veneziani a Constantinopoli," 68. Nina Ergin, "Ottoman Royal Women's Spaces," 96.
[63] Dumas, "Une diplomatie par les femmes," 20–21.
[64] Robert Frost, "The Roads Not Taken: Liberty, Sovereignty and the Idea of the Republic in Poland-Lithuania and the British Isles, 1550–1660." *Transactions of the Royal Historical Society* 32 (2022): 93–112.

its politics. At their behest she opted for Catherine de Medici's suggestion to crown her son king of Poland.⁶⁵ Ashkenazi, Esther *kira*, and other well-connected courtiers used their connections in Poland to assist the efforts of Monluc, the French envoy to Krakow, who tried to convince the Polish peers to vote for Henry de Valois.

Promised an alliance with France and the friendship of the Ottomans, the notables finally consented, and in 1573 invited Henry to wear the Polish crown. Initially, this series of events also strengthened diplomatic relations between the Ottomans and the French, but soon things went sour. In his first year, the French king proved himself a bungling monarch and, by foolishly allowing a group of hawkish Polish nobles to threaten Ottoman interests in the Balkans, almost initiated a war between the two countries. Fortunately for all sides, less than a year after Henry's accession, his brother King Charles died, and he was recalled to Paris to be crowned Henry III of France.⁶⁶

Soon after this episode Sultan Selim died, and Nurbanu took swift and decisive action to have her son, Murad, crowned. Ottoman chroniclers recount that upon her husband's death, she resorted to the tactics used by Grand Vizier Sokollu Mehmed when Suleiman died. She packed Selim's body in ice and hid his death from all but the grand vizier and the admiral of the navy, until she could make sure that Murad had arrived safely by boat from his governorship in Manisa, giving him an edge over his half-brothers.⁶⁷ Once he was crowned Murad III and had his brothers strangled, she became the uncontested head of the harem—and then the empire.

Although the title *sultan* was already added by Suleiman to his mother Hafsa's formal designation of *valide* (mother), only during Nurbanu's tenure did it become the queen mother's formal title, making her co-head of the house of Osman and officially investing her with executive power. To make that power visible to the empire's subjects and to the world at large, she initiated a tradition that in later years became a formal ritual: an orchestrated day-long ceremonial procession of the *valide sultan* from the old palace in the center of Istanbul to the Topkapı palace at the tip of the peninsula. During this mile-long procession, which the empire's grandees and army commanders were required to attend on horseback in full regalia, Nurbanu doled out fistfuls of coins to the troops as she solemnly made her way to the Topkapı gate. Her son waited at the entrance to the palace's second court and made his obeisance when she arrived, bowing and kissing her hands. Upon arrival, she devised another tradition, dispatching a formal notice to the grand vizier to inform him that she was now on the premises. All was designed to relay a clear message:

---

⁶⁵ Ashkenazi was known in Istanbul as *Almanoğlu*, meaning "German," which is a translation of the Hebrew "Ashkenazi."

⁶⁶ Roth, *House of Nasi*, 196. Isom-Verharen, "Allies with the Infidel," 47. Catherine de Medici to Cosimo de Medici, 31 May 1574, *Medici Archives*, Vol. 4727, Fol. 227. Gurkan, *Espionage*, 449–450. Peirce, *Imperial Harem*, 226–227. For the details of this episode, see Chap. 5.

⁶⁷ Keating, "Feminine Roles in the Ottoman Empire," 8. Peirce, *Imperial Harem*, 261. See also Chap. 5.

henceforth, the royal mother is the sultan's equal and should be treated as such.[68]

Murad III was less interested than his predecessors in cabinet meetings and the daily running of the empire.[69] Instead, a short tunnel was dug from inside the harem to an opening in the wall above the government's meeting hall. A metal lattice was placed over the opening, so that the sultan could sit at the small chamber above the hall and listen in. He could either intervene in the discussions or stay silent and hidden from view for as long as he wished. The tunnel may have been installed at Nurbanu's specific request and in any case enabled her to sit there instead of her son when she so wished. We do not know whether she made her voice heard in the cabinet chamber, but she almost certainly eavesdropped on the meetings and could advise her son on various state matters. Protocols from later years indicate that at least one of her successors, Kösem Sultan, vocally participated in the cabinet's meetings from her perch and even berated politicians in the chamber for their conduct.[70]

Like Hurrem and Mihrimah, Nurbanu understood that her subjects' support depended on public manifestations of power and beneficence, and she built her own great complex of welfare structures, later known as the Old Valide Mosque (*atik valide camii*) on a hill in Üsküdar, overlooking Mihrimah's complex. The site was chosen carefully. As the old walled city became overcrowded, building on the Asian (eastern) side of the Bosphorus became more fashionable. The new neighborhoods were in dire need of public facilities. A booming trade brought goods by caravans from eastern Anatolia, Iran, and the Arab provinces, and merchants required services such as lodging, food, medical treatment, and prayer before they crossed the straits to the main markets on the European side.

But Nurbanu's choice of building site was also a declaration of status and power. While on the less prestigious side of the strait it was placed prominently on top of a hill. During her husband's first few years on the throne, the project was designed as a medium-sized mosque with a single minaret, but once she became *valide* and concentrated imperial power in her hands, it was greatly expanded. One of the first additions was another minaret, previously considered a prerogative of the sultan. It made clear that hers was now an imperial center to rival those of the male rulers of the dynasty. The site surrounding the mosque comprised a hospital, a big caravansary, religious schools, a Sufi convent, and a bathhouse. In fact, it was the only great sultanic complex built in Istanbul during the half century between the construction of Suleiman's in the 1550s and the so-called Blue Mosque built by her grandson, Ahmet I, in the early seventeenth century. Selim, her husband, built his own great mosque in Edirne, the second imperial capital, and her son Murad built it in his beloved

---

[68] Peirce, *Imperial Harem*, 188.
[69] Kayaalp, *Empress Nurbanu and Ottoman Politics*, 31–33.
[70] Ergin, "Ottoman Royal Women's Spaces," 96–97.

Manisa, where he was born and raised. Work on Nurbanu's *Külliye* ended only after her death.[71]

Foreign Relations

In a departure from her regular pro-Venice policy, Nurbanu supported the Ottoman conquest of Venetian Cyprus in 1570, perhaps on the advice of her *kiras*, who cooperated with the plan hatched by Joseph Nasi, the Duke of Naxos. But after the pyrrhic Ottoman victory in Cyprus and the subsequent defeat of the navy at the battle of Lepanto, she regretted her mistake and did her best to resume peace negotiations with the Serenissima. In a move coordinated with Grand Vizier Sokollu Mehmed Pasha, she sent Solomon Ashkenazi as an envoy to Venice with clear instructions to prepare a new treaty of alliance. Soon after that, Nurbanu became Venice's leading voice in the sultan's government.[72] In 1583 Ambassador Contarini wrote: "*[She] appears to have great affection for this Most Serene Republic and wants to be recognized as such and to do what she can.*" In the same year, the Venetian Senate awarded her two thousand gold ducats as a token of appreciation for her support.[73] Through the years she corresponded directly with the Venetian doges, and at one point prevented an Ottoman attack on the Venetian island of Crete, arguing that such an invasion would be detrimental to Ottoman interests. Her letters indicate that she and Esther *kira* were in almost daily contact with the Venetian authorities. The letters she sent were direct and brief, suggesting an informal contact. They thanked her correspondents for gifts, informed them of political problems, demanded their cooperation in freeing Muslim captives and giving permits to traders, and suggested avenues of action, sometimes even in trifling matters. In 1582, for instance, she wrote to the doge on behalf of her personal physician, Emmanuel Brodo, to request his intervention in a debt owed him by a merchant residing in Venice.[74]

She also corresponded with Catherine de Medici, France's queen mother. Through the years, once it found some accommodation with the Habsburgs, the French monarchy neglected its alliance with the Ottomans. By writing to Catherine, Nurbanu aimed to jump-start relations and return to the old treaty. One immediate problem to be solved—perhaps an excuse for the initiation of correspondence—was the imprisonment of two Ottoman ladies who had been abducted in a piracy raid and, according to the reports that reached her, were

---

[71] Necipoğlu, *The Age of Sinan*, 280–285. Duzbakar, "The Hospital of Nurbanu Sultan," 14. Peirce, *Imperial Harem*, 188–189. Goodwin, *Ottoman Turkey*, 140–143.

[72] Roth, *House of Nasi*, 153–155, 196. Gurkan, *Espionage*, 364–365. See also *Medici Archives*, Vol. 3082, Fol. 647, March 4, 1579, "A report by the Medici envoy of gold brocade vests sent by Nurbanu to the Venetian ambassador and the Doge."

[73] Peirce, *Imperial Harem*, 222–223. Gold ducats or sequins (zecchini) were regular gold coins minted in Venice and elsewhere.

[74] Pedani, "Safiye's Household," 29. Peirce, *Imperial Harem*, 226. Lushchenko, "Correspondence of Ottoman Women," 13.

engaged as servants in the French court. Mihrimah, Nurbanu, and Ismihan, Nurbanu's daughter, each wrote a letter to Queen Catherine, interceding on behalf of the ladies' families. This exchange opened a line of communication with Catherine who, keen to offer a counterweight to the growing power of Catholics in France and Spain, was interested in renewing the relationship. Quickly realizing that Nurbanu should be treated as an equal, Catherine opened her letter with the words *"from the Queen Mother of the King to the Queen Mother of the Grand Seigneur"* and suggested a renewal of the commercial agreements called "capitulations" that allowed French merchants to trade in the Ottoman Empire on special terms. Nurbanu, in turn, invited Catherine to Istanbul in the hope of strengthening relations between the two countries.[75]

It is also certain that Nurbanu corresponded with Safavid royal women. When Selim II ascended the sultanic throne, diplomatic contacts with the Safavids were handled by Nurbanu's co-queen Mihrimah, who, along with her mother, had corresponded with Shahzada Sultanum and had established cordial relations with her. When Nurbanu arrived on the scene, however, Shahzada Sultanum was already dead, and Shah Tahmasp's beloved daughter, Parikhan Khanum, took the lead in the Safavid court. Parikhan became her father's closest advisor when still a teenager, exchanged letters with the Ottoman court, and was in charge of diplomatic relations with Istanbul on his behalf.[76] Since accommodation with the Ottomans was viewed as a crucial part of Safavid foreign policy by her aunt and father, she corresponded with Nurbanu. After the death of her father, Shah Tahmasp, in 1576, Parikhan took control of the Safavid Empire and ruled it on her own, continuing the policy of peace with the Ottomans. Her career ended when she was strangled to death under orders from Mahd-i Ulya, the next shah's wife, who wanted her out of the way. After Parikhan's death, Mahd-i Ulya sent Nurbanu gifts in her husband's name to let her know that the government in Iran had changed hands but that the peace was still intact.[77]

Nurbanu may have also had some contacts with Mughal Indian ruling women, although we have no clear indication of a correspondence. In the 1570s, as the Mughal empire flourished under Emperor Akbar, his Aunt Gulbadan, who was also one of his closest advisors, decided to go on a pilgrimage to Mecca, taking several of the court's ladies and many servants along with her. After completing the *hajj*, they decided to stay in Mecca, giving alms to the poor and making a name for themselves and their empire as magnanimous benefactors. Their long sojourn in the holy cities worried Ottoman officials, who believed this might be an attempt to gain a Mughal foothold in the heart

---

[75] Peirce, *Imperial Harem*, 226–227. Lushchenko, "Correspondence of Ottoman Women," 15. "Grand Seigneur" was a common title for the sultan in Europe.

[76] Birjandifar, *Pari Khan Khanum*, 51.

[77] *Medici Archive*, Vol. 4026, Fol. 548/R (July 14, 1576). A report from a Medici envoy in Istanbul that "the sultanas" have also sent presents to Shah Tahmasp, which, the report says, is unusual. Arcak, "Ottoman Safavid Cultural Exchange," 131. Beck and Nashat, *Women in Iran*, 157–158. Soudavar, *The Early Safavids*, 18–19. On Mahd-i Ulya, see also Chap. 4.

of the Islamic world. We do not know if there was any direct contact between Nurbanu and these women, but the issue was surely brought to her attention. Finally, the Mughal women were respectfully told to pack up and leave. They went back to Agra in 1580 through the port of Aden.[78]

In 1583, her fifty-eighth year, Nurbanu succumbed to illness. Right before her death, she counselled her son Murad on three matters: "*ensuring that swifter and more impartial justice be rendered to his subjects, restraining his natural avidity for gold and money, and above all, keeping watch on the conduct of his son.*"[79] Once again, in contravention of palace etiquette, the broken-hearted son accompanied his mother's coffin *on foot*, in a solemn funeral procession to the Conqueror's Mosque on the other side of town, where prayers for her soul were recited. The faraway location was chosen on purpose since Murad wished the entire city to weep for his mother. After the prayers, her coffin was escorted back to Sarayburnu, the palace neighborhood, and she was buried beside her husband Selim II in his Hagia Sophia mausoleum. For forty days Quran verses were constantly read over the grave as the empire's notables paid their respect (Fig. 2.5).[80]

When Hafsa was referred to as "*valide sultan*," the title simply meant "the sultan's mother," and her main function was still that of a beloved family relation, not a state official. Her daughter-in-law, Hurrem, died before her son ascended the throne and never held the title of *valide*. It was thus left to Nurbanu to infuse the role with the political and cultural content that would define it for many decades. She succeeded in elevating the role of the sultan's mother to the unprecedented position of the empire's leading statesperson, but the struggle between *haseki* and *valide* was by no means over. Hurrem and Nurbanu accumulated their political power as sultans' consorts, not as mothers, and when Nurbanu's son was finally crowned sultan and she assumed the title of royal mother, there was already a new favorite wife in the harem, and it was only natural that *she* would wish to emulate the example of her predecessors and become the dominant power in the palace.

Safiye

In 1563, a thirteen-year-old slave girl, probably of Albanian origin, arrived at the old palace. She was soon given the name Safiye (meaning "pure" or "innocent") and presented to the seventeen-year-old Prince Murad, who fell in love with her physical beauty and her wits. At the time, Murad was in transition between two governorships, and Safiye joined his harem on the way to Saruhan, near Izmir. Two years later she had her first son, the future Mehmed III. When

---

[78] Farooqi, "Six Ottoman Documents," 45–47. Lal, "Rethinking Mughal India," 60. Zaman, "Instructive Memory," 695. Shanim, "Status of Women in the Mughal Empire," 54. Lal, *Empress*, 38–42. For the full story see Chap. 3.
[79] Peirce, *Imperial Harem*, 238.
[80] Ibid., 189.

Fig. 2.5 Miniature painting of Nurbanu's funeral, by Seyyid Lokman, *Shahanshanameh*. Top: Sultan Murad III walks in front of his mother's casket exiting the third court of Topkapı. Topkapı Museum

Murad's father, Selim, was enthroned in 1566, Murad was sent on yet another posting, this time to govern the district of Manisa, and by the time Selim died, Murad was already an experienced governor. Safiye, his only sexual partner until that time and well into his reign, already had three children and, like him, was adept at the business of government. Several years later she was described by a Jewish courtier as "prudent, wise, clever and most patient."[81] Mustafa Ali, an Ottoman author of the period, claims that, following the example of his

---

[81] Pedani, "Safiye's Household," 11. Skilliter, "Three Letters," 144–145.

father and grandfather, Murad married her. The claim makes sense, but if true, it was done only after his mother passed away, and he must have kept the secret better than his forefathers did. The Venetian ambassador Morosini, who left Istanbul in 1585, claimed he had no knowledge of such a wedding, but it may have taken place after his departure.

When Safiye met Nurbanu, she immediately realized the sway that the *valide* held over her son and over state affairs, but when Murad was crowned, she was determined to hold her own. She soon partnered with Sinan Pasha, an up-and-coming provincial governor who disapproved of Nurbanu's political intervention and even earned her wrath by claiming that in the Ottoman state women's formal authority resided with the *haseki*, not the *valide*.[82] Eager to maintain her position vis-à-vis her ambitious daughter-in-law, Nurbanu joined forces with the cunning Grand Vizier Sokollu. To keep Safiye at bay, she also enlisted the harem's chief administrator, Canfeda Hatun, and convinced Murad that his chief consort was using witchcraft and concocting potions to make him impotent and prevent him from having sex with other concubines. Murad was so shaken by these allegations that he arrested and interrogated Safiye's servants, including one of her *kiras*, and although he found no evidence to support the allegation of witchcraft, some were exiled to the island of Rhodes for a while.[83] On Nurbanu's instructions, her daughter Ismihan offered Murad two young slave women whom he apparently found irresistible. From that moment on, Murad's sexual appetite was insatiable. He ended up fathering twenty sons and twenty-seven daughters. Safiye, however, kept her cool. If she was offended by Selim's philandering or by Nurbanu's intrigues, she hid her disappointment well, bided her time, and positioned herself instead as the sultan's best friend and wisest counsel. Eventually, when Nurbanu died in 1583, Safiye became head of the harem and reorganized it, dismissing Canfeda Hatun and replacing her with her own loyal servants.[84]

Safiye's Foreign Policy

As long as the old *valide* controlled the harem, despite the simmering power struggle between them, Safiye cooperated with her on matters of foreign policy, including Nurbanu's favorite issue, the Venetian file. She was so committed to maintaining good relations with Venice, in fact, that many diplomats and travelers assumed that she too was of Venetian origin. In 1585, the Venetian ambassador commended her for her financial support throughout the years, even after Nurbanu's demise.

By then, Safiye was clearly the head of the family and the leading statesperson. One of the first international crises she had to deal with was the war between Spain and England. As the Spanish Armada was making its way to

---

[82] Peirce, *Imperial Harem*, 91.
[83] Pedani, "Safiye's Household," 13.
[84] Peirce, *Imperial Harem*, 94. Pedani, "Safiye's Household," 24.

England in 1588, the Venetians were suspected of sending ships to assist Spain, the Ottomans' nemesis, and of planning an attack against the Ottomans as well. Fearing Ottoman retaliation, the Venetian ambassador asked for her intercession: "*Great favor has your highness done me by informing me through your slave the Chirazza [kira], of the calumnious report to the Grand Signor. It is false that the Republic has sent galleys to the King of Spain to assist in an attack on England ... The Venetian Ambassador begs your Highness to point all this out to the Grand Signor.*" Another smitten ambassador reported in 1595: "*She is a woman of her word, trustworthy, and I can say that in her alone have I found truth in Constantinople.*" Venice's envoys made it a habit to bring her gifts and supply her and her "chirazza" with whatever they wished for.[85]

Safiye surrounded herself with competent women. She shared with the *valide* the services of Esther Handali, and as the veteran *kira* got older, Safiye showed a daughter's concern for her well-being, mixed in with a plea for continued political advice and assistance. In 1588, when Esther fell ill, Safiye sent her a note. "*How are you?... Why didn't you send your dish here today? Please, send it at the time of dinner every day ... Why do the Venetians build castles near the border? Please tell them to destroy the castles or they know what will happen.*"[86] Yet, realizing that Esther was getting old, she also engaged a second *kira*, Esperanza Malchi, who had excellent relations with the European ambassadors, and especially with the Venetians. In the following years Esperanza's influence in court grew as Esther's waned.[87]

Another woman in Safiye's service was Beatrice Michiel, a Venetian convert to Islam who joined Safiye's retinue in 1591. Many years earlier, two of Beatrice's brothers were abducted in an Ottoman raid and castrated to serve as eunuchs in the palace. Only one survived the ordeal and, after being given the name Gazanfer Ağa, rose through the ranks of the inner service and became chief white eunuch (*kapı ağası*) and, later, chief chamberlain (*Hasodabaşı*), both key positions in the palace. Safiye soon spotted his talent and joined forces with him to govern the empire. When Gazanfer's sister, Beatrice, who lived in Venice, learned of her brother's senior position in the sultan's court, she came over to Istanbul and converted to Islam, adopting the name Fatma Hatun. Her brother introduced her to the *valide*'s service. Like Esther and Esperanza, Fatma/Beatrice was sent by Safiye on errands to the European embassies. At the same time she worked as a Venetian agent, perhaps in order to protect her children, who remained in Venice. Esperanza suspected Fatma of spying and saw her ties to the embassies as a threat to her own position. The two often bickered over political and personal issues.[88]

---

[85] Peirce, *Imperial Harem*, 223. The ambassador request for her intercession with the sultan ("the Grand Signor") may have been just a polite way of asking Safiye herself to trust Venice, without casting public doubt on the sultan's actual power.
[86] Pedani, "Safiye's Household," 19.
[87] Ibid, 13–16.
[88] Ibid., 14–15, 25–28.

Safiye was also assisted by the local Jewish and Marrano network, with people such as David Passi, Solomon Ashkenazi, Moses Benveniste, and Alvaro Mendes working alongside her. Known to the Ottomans as *Frenk* Davut ("David the European"), Passi was a rich merchant born in Portugal who moved to Ragusa, thence to Venice, and later to Istanbul. His brother held a similar position in Poland's royal court, and other relatives resided in Ferrara and Salonica, with connections all over Europe. He soon became a favorite of the *valide* and, like his famous predecessor, Joseph Nasi, was awarded a dukedom, this time of the island of Mytilene (Lesbos). His main concern was forming an alliance between the Ottomans and the rising power, England, against Spain. The Venetian ambassador claimed that Passi had a network of spies "in all the Christian courts."

David Passi was party to all strategic discussions in court. His associate, the elusive Alvaro Mendes, was another Portuguese merchant who made a fortune in India and moved to the Ottoman Empire after traveling around Europe. Once settled in Istanbul, he returned to Judaism, called himself Solomon Abenaish (Ibn Yaish), and was soon favored by the court and later also appointed Duke of Mytilene. Abenaish had his own European and Indian network that included his cousin, the ill-fated Rodrigo Lopez, who settled in England and served as Queen Elizabeth's physician.[89]

Safiye's most famous diplomatic feat was her correspondence with Queen Elizabeth. Mary, Elizabeth's older half-sister, who was crowned queen in 1553, married King Philip II of Spain, and as long as England was viewed as part of Habsburg-dominated Spain, contacts between the Ottoman Empire and England were constrained. But once Mary died and Elizabeth acceded to the throne in 1558, the tide shifted. Although Elizabeth's sympathies clearly lay with the Protestants, for political reasons she maintained a semblance of peace with Spain and the Habsburgs, but by the late 1570s it had become clear that she had no intention of taking orders from Rome. Relations with France had greatly improved, and Spain became England's main enemy. Under these conditions, England needed a strong ally who would deter Spain from planning another invasion. Elizabeth approached the Ottomans and sent her ambassador William Harborne with gifts. The ambassador's assistant, Edward Barton, who stayed behind after Harborne's return, quickly established a close friendship with the *kira*, Esperanza Malchi, and through her with Safiye Sultan.[90]

As may be gleaned from Safiye's correspondence with the Venetian ambassador, she had also set her sights on cooperation with Elizabeth's kingdom. From her vantage point England seemed very much like Venice: an island nation with a strong navy and a vibrant mercantile culture, keen on preserving its political independence from Rome. It was Safiye, more than anyone else in court, who understood the importance of this alliance, likely because of her

---

[89] Roth, *House of Nasi*, 204–207. Gurkan, "Espionage," 326, 385–387. Ozgen, "Disgrace of Murad III's Favorite."

[90] For more details, see Chap. 6.

appreciation for its queen, and the encouragement of Esperanza Malchi, who followed European politics and witnessed the rise of England.[91] In March 1593, after several emissaries had come and gone, the queen of England sent Safiye a letter and several presents, including a portrait of herself set in rubies and diamonds, a sort of personal introduction. After that, Elizabeth and Safiye exchanged a few presents and letters, in which they assured each other of their good intentions and indicated their support for an alliance between their countries.

The original of the first letter sent by Safiye in December 1593 was destroyed, and we only have it in copy and translation. It was clearly a formal state letter, a product of the sultanic scribal service written in flowery rhymed prose on heavy paper, decorated in gold leaf and lapis lazuli. The opening fourteen lines include the usual greetings, self-aggrandizement, and exchange of compliments between heads of state, the most interesting of which in this context is Safiye's reference to Elizabeth as "the pillar of Christian womanhood".[92] Much of the rest includes assurances by the *valide* of the empire's friendship and good intentions toward England and Elizabeth.

In the other two extant letters, written six years later, Safiye assures Elizabeth of her friendship and support, promises to work for a bilateral economic treaty, thanks her for sending a carriage as a gift, and informs her that she is sending back gifts of her own. As Skilliter, who studied the letters, points out, these two documents are much cruder in appearance and in style. The handwriting is "awkward and unskilled" and the spelling often incorrect.[93] Unlike the first, state-produced letter, these were clearly dictated by Safiye to the nonnative Esperanza, who wrote them in her less-than-perfect Ottoman Turkish and later had them translated into Italian. Although Safiye could have used the scribal service, it was important for the sultana to compose the messages herself, perhaps to make it clear to Elizabeth that she—Safiye—was writing in person and that no one was dictating it to her. The letters once again assure Elizabeth of Safiye's good intentions and promise, "*We do not cease to admonish our son, His Majesty the Padishah, and to tell him: 'Do act according to the treaty [with England]!.'*"[94] Esperanza *kira* cheekily tacked on her own letter, in which she expressed admiration for Elizabeth and asked her for skin-care products, including special distilled water and aromatic oils for the face and hands "*on account of Your Majesty's being a woman I can without any embarrassment employ you with this notice.*" It also seems that she had secreted one of Safiye's valuable gifts, a gem-studded tiara, which she may have sent later as her own gift.[95]

---

[91] Skilliter, "Three Letters". Ergin, "Ottoman Royal Women's Spaces," 94. Holmberg, "Jews of All Trades," 39. Adler, "Auto de fé and Jews," 701.
[92] Skilliter, "Three Letters," 131 (*'umdat firqat al-khawātīn al-'īsāwiyāt*).
[93] Ibid., 134.
[94] Ibid., 139. Original (badly misspelled) Turkish in 136.
[95] Ibid., 143.

Fig. 2.6 The New Valide Mosque (*yeni cami*), one of the largest mosques in Istanbul. Construction was begun by Safiye in 1597. Photo: Sinoplu Diyojen

In 1603, Safiye's son, Mehmed III, died, and his thirteen-year-old son Ahmed ascended the throne. Now there was a new *valide* in the palace—Mehmed's consort, Handan Sultan. Safiye and her entire retinue were summarily packed off and sent to the old palace. For a while, the old *valide* tried to pull the strings of government from afar, but soon Handan made sure that her supporters and favorites were chased away from court (Fig. 2.6).

Handan herself did not last long as *valide*. She fell ill shortly after Ahmed's accession and died two years later, in 1605. But although Safiye survived until 1619, and saw even her great-grandsons, Mustafa and Osman II, ascend the throne, she never regained the status she had had as *valide*.

By the end of the sixteenth century the pattern of women's government was clearly inscribed as a sacred dynastic tradition. A woman in the royal harem would reach her apogee as *valide*, at which time she would become co-sultan with her son, often preceding him as the initiator of government policy. But although in most cases she wielded just as much power as the sultan, or even more, the arc of her career would be hitched to his fortunes, his enthronement, and his death. Arriving in the palace as a lowly slave, usually uneducated in the ways of the empire and speaking a foreign language, she would be brought up in strict discipline by the harem's attendants. A first opportunity might present itself if she were selected for sexual service by a young sultan or by a royal prince. If lucky, she would then be chosen to share his bed on a regular basis.

Once she bore him a son she could rise to the position of chief consort. If luck struck again, when the reigning sultan died, the prince would beat his brothers to the throne and bring his beloved to the palace. Then, if his chief consort proved herself smart, patient, and politically savvy at this stage, she would stay the course under the watchful eye of her mother-in-law. Upon the death of her husband, the reigning sultan, and the ascent of her own son, *she* would become the most powerful woman in the empire, banishing the former *valide* to the old palace, to spend her days in the company of other former consorts.

Valides' power was supreme, but they were always threatened by their sons' consorts, who were eager to reach the same summit. The next powerful *valide*, Kösem Sultan, challenged this pattern and managed to hold on to power for almost half a century.

Kösem Sultan: Zenith and Decline

When a new slave arrived in the harem in 1604 and was given the name Kösem, it was clear that there was a chance—slim though it might be—that she would become the sultan's favorite and go on to become queen mother. Knowing that, it would have made sense for Ottoman officialdom to inquire about the origins and upbringing of slave girls brought to the harem, at least for posterity's sake. But the Ottomans still regarded the arrival of a slave at the royal harem as a rebirth. Whatever preceded it—her ethnic origins, family relations, class, circumstances of enslavement, even her former name—was of no consequence. Court functionaries did not even bother to find out where she was born or try to locate her family when the slave *did* become queen. Kösem's origins, like those of most other *valides*, are therefore shrouded in mystery. Later Ottoman and Turkish historians claimed that she was originally from the island of Tinos in the Aegean Sea, but even her ethnicity is doubtful. What we do know is that she was abducted from her home at the age of fourteen, that she was bought by, or given to, the Ottoman governor of Bosnia, and that, impressed by her beauty, he sent her right away to the palace in Istanbul.

When she arrived, the reigning sultan was Ahmed I, Mehmed's son, crowned a couple of years earlier. The seventeen-year-old Ahmed already had at least one mistress, who bore him a first son, Osman. But a year later, by 1605, Kösem was already his new favorite, and the couple would ultimately bear eight children, two of whom would become sultans.[96]

The premature death of Ahmed's mother, Handan, opened the way for the new favorite, still a young girl of sixteen or seventeen, with hardly any knowledge of Turkish or Ottoman etiquette, to govern the harem and become

---

[96] Tezcan, "The Debut of Kösem's Career," 348. Görgün-Baran, "A Woman Leader," 76. Kösem has several meanings, the most common of which is "bellwether," the ram that leads the herd. Another possible meaning comes from "köse," hairless. Tezcan, "The Debut of Kösem's Career," 348.

first lady of the empire.[97] Yet from early on, she demonstrated wisdom, strong character, and far-sightedness. When Ahmed ascended the throne, the sultanate was in a predicament. The new sultan was not sexually active—he wasn't even circumcised yet—and there was no guarantee that he would have children of his own. To secure the perpetuation of the dynasty, it was decided that, in contravention of the age-old custom that the new sultan must kill all claimants to the throne except his own progeny, his baby brother, the two-year-old Mustafa, will be kept alive. But a few years later, once Ahmed had several sons, everyone at court expected him to execute his brother in the time-honored manner. The fact that he did not owes much to Kösem's far-sightedness and powers of persuasion. Kösem knew that Ahmed's eldest, Osman, was most likely to become sultan after him and that his enthronement would automatically entail the assassination of her own sons. She therefore did all she could to keep the sultan's brother, Mustafa, alive and create a precedent. In fact, her success in convincing Ahmed not to kill his brother signaled a change in the Ottoman principle of succession, from fratricide to seniority. Henceforth, at least in principle, upon the sultan's death, the crown would go to the oldest living male in the dynasty.[98]

Although she was careful to stay in the shadows during those first years, it soon became clear that Kösem ruled Ahmed's heart and stood behind many of his decisions. In 1612, the Venetian ambassador Simon Contarini remarked that she was a woman of *"beauty and shrewdness, and furthermore, of many talents. She sings excellently, whence she continues to be extremely loved by the king."* And another Venetian, Cristoforo Vanier, wrote a few years later, *"She can do what she wishes with the king and possesses his heart absolutely, nor is anything denied her."* Vanier also suggested that the Venetians compensate her for her support of their policies, as they did her predecessors (Fig. 2.7).[99]

When Ahmed I died of typhus in 1617, still a young man, it was indeed his brother Mustafa who was taken out of the harem and crowned, rather than his son Osman. Mustafa's mother, Halime, was appointed *valide*, and Kösem reluctantly retired. A year later, however, Mustafa was diagnosed as mentally unstable, deposed, and sent back to the old palace with his mother. As former sultan, he was placed under guard in a locked suite of rooms in the harem, later known as "the cage" (*kafes*). After that, all Ottoman princes kept alive during the reign of a sultan languished in this sumptuous cage. When a sultan died, the eldest of the remaining princes was taken out and crowned in his stead.

---

[97] Some sources claim that Ahmed poisoned his own mother, perhaps to stop her meddling in his affairs. One proof adduced is that four days prior to her death, the sultan replaced the chief black eunuch with his own appointee. See Tezcan, "The Debut of Kösem's Career," 351.

[98] Peirce, *The Imperial Harem*, 106. Imber, *The Ottoman Empire*, 110. It took time for the principle of seniority to take hold. Later sultans in the seventeenth century, including Kösem's sons, also executed their brothers at the smallest hint of rebellion or factionalism.

[99] Peirce, *Imperial Harem*, 105, 223–224.

Fig. 2.7 Kösem Sultan with her son Murad (portrait attributed to Hans Ludwig Graf von Kuefstein after an original, c. 1650–1699). Unknown artist, circle of Franz Herrmann and Hans Gemminger, Austrian School, second quarter of the seventeenth century

Ahmed's eldest son, the precocious fourteen-year-old Osman, now replaced Mustafa on the throne. But since his mother had died a few years earlier, there was no queen mother to share the throne and guide him through palace conspiracies and world politics. Osman soon decided that in order to restore the power of the empire radical change was needed. He signed a peace treaty with the Safavids and rashly declared war against Poland, which he lost. Then he secretly planned to move his capital from Istanbul, which he saw as a den of corruption, to another city in the empire. Three years after his accession, during an unusually harsh winter that caused many deaths and a huge hike in the price of basic foodstuffs, he decided to set out on another campaign against the Poles. This time the Janissary commanders, fearing another defeat, refused to obey his orders. Frustrated, Osman hatched another plan: to get rid of the unreliable Janissaries and replace them with another force more willing to do his bidding, but his plan was exposed prematurely and he soon faced an uprising. In a Janissary raid on the palace, he was abducted, imprisoned, and later strangled to death.

Mustafa, the previously deposed sultan whose mental instability was only exacerbated by his isolation in the cage and fear of assassination by his nephew, was summoned back to the throne, but refused to come out of his room unless shown proof that Osman was indeed dead. When he finally consented to be crowned, it became clear to all that his condition had deteriorated. Finally, the government had no other options. Having been promised that his life would be spared, Mustafa's mother agreed to have him deposed once again. They were both sent back to the old palace, and Kösem was invited back to Topkapı with her eleven-year-old son, now crowned Sultan Murad IV.[100] In time, Murad would turn out to be a formidable sultan, but since he was still a minor, the imperial council asked Kösem to govern the empire as regent.

For almost ten years Kösem ruled supreme, heading meetings from her perch above the royal council under the great dome of the Council Hall (*kubbe altı*) and, when her son reached majority, continued to govern along with him. But the couple encountered serious challenges along the way. After many years of internal fighting and neglect, exacerbated under Mustafa and Osman's bumbling rule, with the state in disarray and a child sultan on the throne, the empire's enemies pounced. The Safavids retook Baghdad, the Habsburgs and the Poles raided the Balkan regions, and rebellions led by disgruntled officers erupted in Anatolia. To make things worse, a plague decimated the population of Istanbul. As long as her son was a minor, Kösem Sultan was unable to bring the factions in the elite to heel. Only when he was old enough to appear as the man in charge did mother and son manage to rein in the unruly elite and reestablish law and order inside the realm.

To do so, they resorted to draconian measures, beginning with the closing down of taverns and coffee houses, which they saw as dens of sedition, and strictly banning the use of stimulants such as tobacco, coffee, and alcohol. Then they broke down resistance among the soldiery and the *ulema*, sometimes resorting to torture and even assassinations.[101] At one point, believing that a group of clerics intended to publish a learned opinion (*fetva*) denouncing the sultan's harsh measures as inhumane and illegal, Kösem explained to her son that governing an empire required unflinching determination. As the British consul Paul Rycaut wrote, "*with like expedition, [Murad] dispatched a boat to bring over the mufti and his son to Prusa [Bursa], who were no sooner arrived than they were strangled, being not permitted to speak for themselves, or to alledge any plea or excuse for their lives. This act of cruelty beyond the example of former ages, and never practised by the most tyrannical of his predecessours, struck a terrour on the whole Empire.*"[102]

---

[100] The saga of Mustafa I and Osman II's reigns are described in detail in Gabi Piterberg's book *An Ottoman Tragedy*. See also Görgün-Baran, "A Woman Leader," 77–80. Rycaut, *History of the Turkish Empire*, Book 1: *The Reign of Sultan Morat*, 2–3.

[101] Turkish *ulema*, from the Arabic *ulamā*, is the common name for religious clerics in Islam.

[102] Rycaut, *History of the Turkish Empire*, 43.

Only after he ensured that their actions had the desired impact on the home front did Murad set out against his external enemies. In a war that he finally won in 1638, he retook Baghdad and other lands that the Safavids had conquered previously and forced the shah to endorse once again the Peace of Amasya, drawn up by Hurrem Sultan and Shahzada Sultanum in 1555. Although we have no written proof, Kösem may have been instrumental in this resumption of the peace treaty, along with her Safavid counterpart, Zaynab Begum, great-aunt of the Safavid shah. While staying with his armies in Baghdad, Sultan Murad also met with a delegation sent by Shah Jahan of the Mughal Empire to confirm the friendly relations between the two empires.[103]

By that time the formal status of *valide* was so entrenched that, unlike her predecessors, Kösem had no need to advertise her sovereignty by building imperial mosques or charitable foundations. Yet it was also incumbent on the *valide* to contribute to society, and Kösem did her part, concentrating on public welfare. Her huge inn and commercial center, later named after her "Inn of the Elder-*Valide*" (*Büyük Valide Han*), near the entrance to Istanbul's covered bazaar, was Istanbul's biggest commercial hub until the twentieth century, a city unto itself with the mosque at its center dwarfed by the buildings around it. She gave alms to the poor, had local prisoners released by paying off their debts, and assisted poor girls with trousseaus for their marriage. By now she also had an elite network of her own, based on daughters and harem slaves married to powerful pashas in key positions in the empire (Fig. 2.8).[104]

Kösem and Murad did not always see eye to eye. One of their main disagreements concerned their respective attitudes to Spain. While the bellicose and impatient Murad wanted to take on Spain as well by attacking its colonies in North Africa, Kösem advised patience and thought that the right approach at this stage would be to offer peace. She recruited two of her allies to assist her in this argument, the governor of Egypt Bayram Pasha and the navy's admiral, Recep (Rejeb) Pasha, both married to her daughters. With their assistance she managed to avert war with Spain throughout Murad's reign. Another bone of contention was Murad's intention to attack Poland again, to regain the lands his predecessors had lost, which Kösem succeeded in stalling.[105]

In 1640, still a young man, Murad died from cirrhosis of the liver, probably caused by excessive drinking. By that time, he had ten sons and five daughters, but all his sons died young, and none made it to the throne. Rycaut claims that at one point, even though he only had daughters by his favorite concubine, Ayşe, he resolved to marry her, but Kösem, sticking to what has become sacred tradition by that time, blocked the move, claiming that it is "*a thing not usual*

---

[103] See also Rycaut, *History of the Turkish Empire*, 23ff.
[104] Peirce, *The Imperial Harem*, 143–144.
[105] Ibid, 226. See also *A Vaunting, Daring, and a menacing letter, sent from Sultan Morat the great Turke, from his Court at Constantinople, by his embassadeur Gobam, to Vladisllaus King of Poland &c.* (London, 1638).

Fig. 2.8 Kösem's Büyük Valide Han. Photo by Jacob Historian

for any woman to be honoured with that title before she had supplied the inheritance by birth of a male child."[106]

Although under Kösem the empire changed the system of succession from fratricide to seniority, Murad was paranoid, always afraid that one of his brothers would champion a disgruntled group of pashas and overthrow him. During his reign he executed four of his brothers but left the youngest alive, perhaps because he believed that the simple-minded Ibrahim would pose no danger. At one point, Rycaut writes, Kösem had insisted that the sultan ride around the city of Istanbul on horseback along with his brother, to accustom the public to the change in succession rules and to the possibility of coexistence between brothers.[107] But apart from such rare episodes, Ibrahim was locked up in the harem cage and lived in constant fear that his brother would execute him as he did his brothers. In 1640, on his deathbed, Murad actually ordered his servants to execute Ibrahim and may have even suggested that the crown should pass on to the Tatar Giray Khans in Crimea. But Kösem managed to thwart his plan and keep Ibrahim alive.[108]

Like Mustafa, his mentally inadequate uncle some eighteen years earlier, Ibrahim refused to believe that his brother was really dead and suspected that

---

[106] Rycaut, *History of the Turkish Empire*, 36.

[107] Ibid., 23.

[108] Rycaut, *History of the Turkish Empire*, Book 2, *The Reign of Sultan Ibrahim*. Peirce, *The Imperial Harem*, 102. Görgün-Baran, "A Woman Leader," 80.

he was simply taunting him before his execution. When the viziers came to escort him to the palace, he refused to come out of his room. Cajoled by the pashas, he said that he had no interest in ruling the empire and that his only wish was to stay in the cage. Kösem herself had to go there and convince him to come out.[109] He finally opened his door, looked at the body of Murad, and only then reluctantly agreed to be crowned.

As in Mustafa's case, it was clear from the first day that Ibrahim was not fit to govern. Ottoman chronicles are replete with stories about his childish pranks, his fetish for sable furs, his debauchery, and his insatiable lust for corpulent women, music, and wine. Some of these stories may have been exaggerated gossip, but it is clear that he devoted very little time to state affairs, and the onus of governing once again fell on Kösem's shoulders. It is also probable that after three decades at the helm, Kösem was certain that she could rule the empire better than anyone else. She exploited Ibrahim's weaknesses and provided him with a constant supply of the women he coveted in order to distance him even further from state affairs and allow her to assume power.

At this stage, many at court were weary of her domineering conduct and of Ibrahim's mental disorder. She clashed with the grand vizier and had him executed in 1644, and continued to run things until the ministers and courtiers approached her in 1648 and told her that they could no longer agree to being governed, even nominally, by such an unstable and capricious sultan. They asked her permission to depose Ibrahim and crown Mehmed, his son and her grandson, instead. While Kösem mulled the issue, Ibrahim, who had learned of the plot to oust him and whose greatest fear was to be unseated and assassinated like all his brothers, had his recently appointed grand vizier executed and exiled Kösem to the village of Florya, south of Istanbul. But a short while later the situation became so dire that she was secretly brought back. The Venetians invaded and blocked the entrance to the Dardanelles, halting all ship movement between the Aegean and the Black Sea, and attacked Ottoman lands in the Balkans. There were food shortages in the capital, and the unpaid Janissaries were once again on the brink of revolt.

Back at the Topkapı, Kösem headed an emergency meeting in the royal divan. After a long discussion, the ministers asked for her consent to depose Ibrahim. "*Her mother's heart was shattered*," recounts court historian Naima. She must have known that a deposed sultan would surely be executed. But at one point a senior cleric addressed her, alluding to her role as mother not just to a son but to the entire nation. "*My sultan*," he said, "*we are all at your mercy and the believers trust in your pity and compassion. As the mother of all believers (umm al-mu'minin*, a title usually reserved for prophet Muhammad's righteous wives*) you must pity those who believe in the oneness of God, and this is an urgent matter for the world.*" The ministers and clergy convinced her that her role in the dynasty extended beyond safeguarding her own sons' rule.

[109] Rycaut, *History of the Turkish Empire*, Book 2, *The Reign of Sultan Ibrahim*.

Replying to the ministers, she chided them for not providing the necessary guidance to her two sons when they needed it, but she reluctantly agreed to have Ibrahim deposed.[110]

She then went into the harem and brought out her seven-year-old grandson, who was duly crowned Mehmed IV under his grandmother's watchful eye. Ibrahim was unseated and ten days later, as foreseen, executed by order of the şeyhülislam, the chief mufti, who claimed that it was forbidden by sacred law to have two sultans at the same time. The grief-stricken Kösem claimed she would retire to the old palace, but perhaps she already knew that the ministers would insist that she stay, since Mehmed's mother, the young Turhan, was too inexperienced to govern the state during her son's minority.[111] At first Turhan acquiesced and consented to have Kösem guide her through the motions of wielding sovereign power, trusting that the old lady would retire in due course and let her take her rightful place beside her son. But a year later, when Kösem invested herself with the title "elder mother" (büyük valide), allotted herself an even larger daily stipend, and made clear that she was here to stay, tensions mounted.[112]

Kösem continued to head divan meetings and dictated her orders to her daughter-in-law, to her grandson, and to the ministers of state. Some of the ministers and clerics who were now infuriated by her behavior approached Turhan. At one point, after a failed assassination attempt on Kösem's life, several heads were chopped off, the grand vizier was replaced, and others were exiled. Finally, in 1651, with fear and intrigue swirling around the palace, Turhan was informed that her mother-in-law planned to have *her* assassinated. Whether or not these rumors were true, it is almost certain that Kösem planned to get rid of her grandson, Sultan Mehmed, perhaps have him assassinated, and replace him with Suleiman, another grandson whose mother, she believed, would be more compliant.

Ahead of the game, Turhan and her loyalists decided it was time to play their hand. A *fetva* ordering Kösem's execution was penned by the chief mufti and signed by her grandson, the young sultan himself, and on the night of September 2, 1651, the conspirators broke into her room. She immediately understood what this meant, ran and hid, but was discovered, dragged out into the courtyard, and strangled with a curtain rope. At one point, lying on the ground and believed dead, she rose and tried to escape but was caught once again. This time the executioners made sure she was no longer breathing.

When her coffin was carried in a funeral procession through the streets, many in the city, unaware of the drama at court, mourned her passing, but the empire's elite was relieved. Mehmed stayed on the throne, and all Kösem's treasures and assets were confiscated. Turhan, now officially proclaimed regent,

---

[110] Naima, *Tarih Naima*, Cild 4, 323. See also Colin Imber, *The Ottoman Empire*, 113.

[111] Peirce, *The Imperial Harem*, 251–252. Imber, *The Ottoman Empire*, 114–115. Görgün-Baran, "A Woman Leader," 81.

[112] Leslie Peirce, "Beyond Harem Walls," in Walthall (ed.) *Servants of the Dynasty*, 90–91.

attended divan meetings and tried to take Kösem's place as acting sultan, but, lacking experience in state affairs, she stumbled time and again. Five years later, after a series of debacles, as the capital was threatened once again by the Venetian navy, with empty coffers and a dearth of good options, Turhan turned to her experienced minister, Köprülü Mehmed Pasha, and asked him to be her grand vizier. The pasha agreed on condition that there would be no more meddling by the *valide* in the conduct of the state. The *valide* consented.

Her decision to step down and entrust the grand vizier with the task of overseeing the government put an end to the long line of great queens in the Ottoman Empire. Turhan herself died in 1683, a few years before her son, but from 1656 onward, mothers and consorts rarely intervened in affairs of state, and power shifted to the grand vizier's office. The name of the next *valide*, Aşub Sultan, mother of Mehmed's brother Suleiman II, is almost unknown, as are the names of most of the *hasekis* and *valides* who followed her. They remained in the shadows and are hardly ever mentioned.

* * *

For over a century consorts and *valides* defined their role in the state and established a set of rules of conduct. One guiding principle was the importance of diplomacy as a complement to war and as a formal end to hostilities. If the main political instrument in the sultans' toolbox was war, that of their wives and mothers was political alliances. It was more than a mere division of labor between men and women. During the sultanate of women, sultans spent more time in the palace and less on the battlefield, and political agreements and treaties were more common.

Another principle bequeathed from one sultana to the next was reinforcing the western frontier against Habsburg encroachment, mainly by allying with Venice, their long-time business partner and rival, with Poland, their neighbor to the north, and with France and later England, which could, if required, join forces with the Ottomans to curb Habsburg aggression. A third leading tenet of their rule was stabilizing the eastern front by maintaining cordial relations with the Safavids and the Mughals. Each of these queens inherited these principles of foreign policy as the mainstay of her government and developed the means to advance them. In addition, each of the *valides* sought to bolster her position and advertise her power by constructing great complexes in the capital. While the early ones, Hurrem and Mihrimah, built relatively modest edifices, their successors in the early 1600s clearly rivalled the complexes built by the sultans themselves.

In retrospect, beyond the specific historical narratives, we can trace the rise and fall of queendom in the Ottoman Empire. The period is bookended by two very exceptional women—Hurrem in the 1520s and Kösem until the mid-seventeenth century. Against all odds, the young Ruthenian slave succeeded in breaking the mold of the Ottoman concubinage system by making Suleiman marry and recognize her as his only consort and his political mainstay. By her actions she laid the foundations on which her successors built their authority. A hundred years later Kösem, who already inherited the official path to power created by Hurrem and perfected by Nurbanu and Safiye, took it to a new level. While for her predecessors it was clear that their careers were hitched to those of their sons, and when the sultan died his mother would retire and relinquish the role of *valide* to the next sultan's mother, Kösem continued as virtual leader of the empire through the reigns of two sons and one grandson. At some point her despotic behavior endangered the survival of the dynasty, at least in the eyes of the state's governing elite, and her assassination marked the fall of the *valide* institution. It was her bride, Turhan, who gave it the *coup de grace* by deciding to give up her status. The role of executive ruler of the empire was passed on to the grand vizier, where it remained for at least the next half century. After 1656, *valides* never recovered their status and power.

CHAPTER 3

Mughal Queens of Hindustan

By the order of Shah Jahangir
The gold got a hundred honors added to it
By getting impressed on it the name of Nur Jahan Padshah Begum
Inscriptions on silver and gold coins bearing the name of Nur Jahan.

The Mughal Empire, which in its heyday reigned over most of today's India, Pakistan, and Afghanistan, sprouted at the beginning of the sixteenth century from a small emirate governed by a local ruler named Zahir al-Din Babur.[1] While all three great Muslim empires of the period—the Ottomans, Safavids, and Mughals—claimed *some* connection to Genghis Khan, both in their lineage and in their foundation myths, the Mughals were closest to, and proudest of, their Mongol ancestry.[2] The name by which they are now known, Mughal or *Mogul*, a derivative of "Mongol," was applied to the family mainly by outsiders. They referred to themselves as *Gurkani*, meaning "sons-in-law" (of the Great Khan), a name that in and of itself puts women in the center.

From the outset, women played a major role in Mughal political, social, economic, and cultural life, and from the mid-sixteenth century until the late 1620s they actually governed the empire alongside their male counterparts, often taking the lead. Understanding the Mongol attitude to women in leadership roles is therefore crucial for understanding the founding myths of the Mughal Empire, and to some extent of the Safavids and Ottomans as well.

---

[1] Quoted from Ruby Lal, *Empress*, 143.
[2] See references to Mongol heritage even a century and a half later, in Jahangir's day: Jahangir, *The Tuzuk-i Jahangiri*, Vol. 1, 23, 68, 76.

The Mongol Legacy of Female Rule

In the early thirteenth century, the Mongol tribal chief Temüjin, later known as Genghis Khan, founded the biggest land empire that the world has ever known, stretching from China and Korea in the east to Kyiv and the Black Sea in the west. It soon broke up into smaller kingdoms, but the series of Mongol dynasties spread over most of Asia remained the most memorable civilizational event of the early modern world. Mongol royal women, usually bearing the title *khatun*, the female equivalent of "khan," were central figures in the creation myths of the Mongols and in Genghis' own lineage. Since marriages were the main instrument for forging political alliances between tribes, the women given in marriage were ambassadors of their original clans and powerful tribal leaders in their own right. Both Genghis' mother and his wife played a major role in securing his political supremacy. When Temüjin's father died and the members of his clan decided to leave and seek another patron, it was his mother, Hö'elün, who rode out carrying the tribal flag and brought half of them back to their encampment. Genghis' wife, Börte, helped him take on the great shaman who challenged him in an effort to maintain his superior status. She then assisted him in conquering and managing the fledgling empire.[3]

In later years other women were called on to lead the Mongols. Töregene was elected by the tribes to rule the federation as regent for her son from 1241 to 1246. She even broke with tradition by appointing a woman, a former slave named Fatima, to be her highest counsellor. And again, when the Mongol Empire was already divided among Gengis' heirs, another woman, Orghina Khatun, ruled over the Chagatai kingdom, which included parts of today's northern China, Uzbekistan, and Afghanistan. She was in power for ten years, from 1251 to 1260, and is known to have kept the peace in the region and to have held control of the region against threats from China and rival Mongol khanates.[4]

Finally, shortly before the rise of the Mughals, a queen named Mandukhai ruled a Mongol kingdom to the north of China.[5] At the age of sixteen, Mandukhai, daughter of a noble family, married Manduul Khan, who ruled the vast area of Northern Yuan. When her husband died in 1479, the thirty-year-old queen brought out of hiding a child who was said to be the last direct descendent of Genghis Khan. She pronounced him *Dayan Khan* (Great Khan) and during his adolescence served as regent and *de facto* empress. When her protégé reached the age of nineteen, she married him and kept control of the realm even during his adulthood. Mandukhai defended her kingdom against the Chinese Ming dynasty, and her armies even made incursions into Chinese

---

[3] De Nicola, *Women in Mongolian Iran*, 41–43, 47–49.
[4] Ibid, 76–80.
[5] See Chap. 4.

territory. To block her army's advance the Chinese expanded the Great Wall during this period. Riding at the head of her forces, wearing armor and carrying a sword, she vanquished her Mongol rivals, the Oirats, who threatened her control. She survived several attempts on her life and died in 1510, just as Babur, the founder of the Mughal Empire, began to expand his own kingdom.

Stories about the great Mongol warring Queen Mandukhai and myths and lore about Hö'elün, Börte, Töregene, and Orghina were told around campfires in the budding Mughal dynasty, serving as an archetype for royal women in subsequent generations.

Aisan Daulat Begum

Babur, the founder of the Mughal Empire, was the great-great-grandson of Timur (Tamerlane), the conqueror of a vast kingdom stretching from Samarkand to Constantinople. Timur himself claimed descent from the Mongol royal lineage, and this imagined ancestry drove him, in the early fifteenth century, to reunite the tattered Mongol realm, long since divided into smaller kingdoms, under his rule.[6] In a sweeping campaign, he defeated the Mamluks on the banks of the Euphrates River, took Asia Minor from the Ottomans, and occupied northern India. But by the time Timur's grandsons were born, his empire had already shrunk to a quarter of its original size. The Ottomans, the Mamluks, and the sultans of Hindustan had all regained their lost territories, and the remaining land was divided between Timur's descendants in a mosaic of small independent kingdoms (Fig. 3.1).[7]

Babur's father, Umar Shaikh Mirza, one of Timur's many great-grandsons, reigned over the Fergana Valley, a sliver of the once-great kingdom in the northern foothills of the Himalayas. His brothers and cousins ruled over other slices of Timurid heirloom.[8] Umar Shaikh's claim to a Mongol royal pedigree was just as shaky as Timur's, but his first wife and chief consort, Qutlugh Nigar Khanum, had a much stronger relationship to that pedigree. She was a direct descendant of Genghis through both her father, Yunus Khan, and her mother, Aisan Daulat Begum. She married Umar Shaikh in 1475. Their eldest daughter, Khanzada Begum, was born three years later, and their son, Babur, was born in 1483.

Twelve years later Umar Shaikh died in battle, and the child Babur was crowned ruler of Fergana Valley. He soon learned that with his Timurid relatives ready to pounce at the first sign of weakness, holding on to power was a contest of wits at which he had very little experience. His grandmother Aisan

---

[6] Timur, hit by an arrow in the leg in his youth, was often referred to as Timur Lenk (Timur the Lame) or Tamerlane.
[7] De Nicola, *Women in Mongol Iran*, 65.
[8] As in Safavid Iran, the title "mirza" referred to princes and rulers of relatively small regions.

Fig. 3.1 Timur's empire at his death. Map by Stuntelaar

Daulat Begum, a contemporary of Queen Mandukhai, soon emerged as the real power behind Babur's throne. Well-educated, courageous, and witty, as a young woman Aisan Daulat mixed freely with the men of her clan, competed with them, and participated in their wars and hunting expeditions.[9] Her life was the stuff of legend. During the reign of her husband Yunus in the eastern Chagatai kingdom, she fought alongside him and was captured twice and given to his enemies' army commanders. In both cases she managed to free herself from captivity and escape. During one of those incidents, she and her servants killed her captor and found their way back to her husband's camp.[10]

When Yunus died and his kingdom was divided among his heirs, Aisan Daulat came to reside with her son-in-law Umar Shaikh Mirza and her daughter Qutlugh Nigar. But Babur's father, on whom she pinned her hopes of taking back her old kingdom, was a disappointment. In his memoirs, Babur himself describes his father as a generous and courageous man but also as a figure of ridicule. He was a dandy, a gambler, a habitual consumer of wine and opium, and very obese. In one paragraph, Babur writes: "*He used to wear his tunic so very tight that to fasten the strings he had to draw his belly in, and if he let himself out after tying them, they often tore away.*"[11]

In contrast, Babur admired his maternal grandmother, and it is clear that she was the true leader of the family, at least in his early years.[12] By the time her son-in-law Umar Shaikh died and Babur ascended the throne, the battle-hardened Aisan Daulat was better poised to understand Central Asian politics

[9] Beveridge, *Babur-Nama*, 20–21. Godden, *Gulbadan*, 17.
[10] Mukhoty, *Daughters of the Sun*, 4. Lal, "Rethinking Mughal India," 53.
[11] Beveridge, *Babur-Nama*, 14. Thackston, *The Baburnama*, 9.
[12] Mukhoty, *Daughters of the Sun*, 3. Beveridge, *Babur-Nama*, 43–44.

than anyone else at court. In his memoirs, Babur admits that his grandmother was the main influence on his life at this stage: "*Few among women will have been my grandmother's equals for judgment and counsel. She was very intelligent and a good planner. Most affairs were done by her counsel.*"[13] Through her stories, the proud old matriarch made clear to her grandson that he was destined to be the embodiment of that past Timurid and Mongol glory, the true scion of Genghis Khan (Fig. 3.2).[14]

Fig. 3.2 Babur seeks his grandmother's advice, surrounded by other women. Read Mughal Album, from the Baburnama. The Morgan Library and Museum

[13] Lal, *Domesticity and Power*, 84. Beveridge, *Babur-Nama*, 43. Thackston, *Baburnama*, 49.
[14] https://wp-en.wikideck.com/Aisan_Daulat_Begum.

Although many had their eyes on the Fergana Valley, her political wisdom and decisive actions enabled Babur's coronation and secured his first years in power. Using her elaborate networks around Central Asia and her deep understanding of strategy, Aisan Daulat Begum took swift action to save her realm and her grandson's crown from the schemes of ambitious relatives and to govern the state until he was able to gain enough experience to rule on his own. Soon she turned the tables on her enemies and sent her grandson on campaigns of conquest. Guided by her steady hand, Babur gradually extended his realm, first taking Timur's capital, Samarkand, and then putting Kabul in his sights. Even when Babur was old enough to rule on his own, he depended on his grandmother to defend his flank. In 1501, as recounted in what follows, when the eighteen-year-old Babur was forced to leave Samarkand during an enemy siege, Aisan Daulat remained in charge of the group of women and children in the castle. She commanded the garrison and only joined him "*with the hungry and lean family members*" when the siege was lifted."[15]

Aisan Daulat paved the way for the Mughal sultanate of women, which would reach its zenith with Nur Jahan a century later. The model of royal womanhood she left behind was very different from the one chosen by the Ottomans and more akin to that of the French or the Safavids (as we will see in subsequent chapters). Unlike the Ottoman slavery and concubinage system, Mughal consorts and imperial mothers were all free women, mostly from noble or well-to-do families. This had an impact not only on the lineage, its political connections, and the tensions inside the court, but also on the visibility of women in public. Mughal women resisted constant attempts to lock them up in harems and to curb their participation in public life.

---

[15] Lal, *Domesticity and Power*, 110. Beveridge, *Babur-Nama*, 151. See also Sunita Sharma, "Women Protagonists in the Formative Years of Babur," 359.

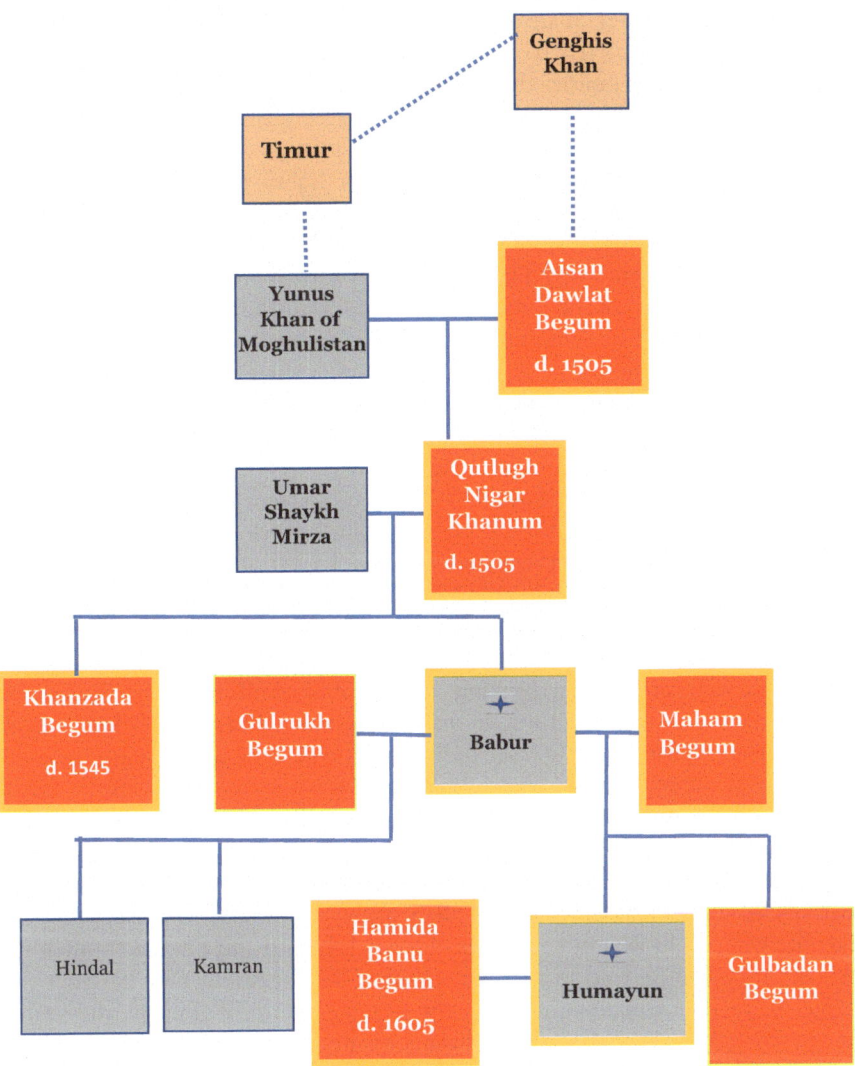

Lineage from Aisan Daulat Begum to Hamida Begum. Only names relevant to the narrative are mentioned

KHANZADA BEGUM

Both Aisan Daulat Begum and her daughter, Babur's mother Kutlugh Nigar, died in 1505. The role of chief woman and close adviser passed on to Babur's beloved older sister, Khanzada Begum, who turned out to be just as quick-witted and daring as her grandmother. As in the case of the Safavid Shah

Tahmasp and his sister Shahzada Sultanum, she and Babur had an intimate connection and completely trusted each other.[16]

Khanzada learned politics the hard way, just as her grandmother did. A few years after her brother's accession, the Uzbek leader Shaybani Khan, a distant relative, lay siege to Babur's newly conquered fortress of Samarkand. At some point, fed up with sitting idly and waiting for Babur to surrender, Shaybani offered him and his men a chance to walk away if Babur would let him marry his twenty-two-year-old sister (thereby laying the groundwork for a future claim to Babur's dominions). Finding no other way to break the siege and sensing the imminent fall of the fortress, Babur and Khanzada reluctantly agreed to the deal. She stayed in Samarkand, and Babur set out on foot with two hundred of his men. The incident must have been a shameful memory for both brother and sister, and in his memoirs Babur glosses over it, as does his daughter, Gulbadan, in the *Humayun-nama*, the biography she wrote about her brother.

Khanzada remained in Shaybani's captivity for ten long years. Sometime after their marriage, as a further insult to Babur, Shaybani accused Khanzada of disloyalty, divorced her, and sent her off to the harem of one of his retainers, a man of lower rank.[17] But then, in 1510, Shaybani himself was defeated in battle and killed by Shah Ismail, the founder of the Safavid dynasty in Iran. The shah's hatred and contempt for Shaybani was such that after the battle, he asked his jewelers to make a drinking cup out of his skull. But Ismail was also a shrewd statesman. By that time, he must have figured out that Babur was an up-and-coming leader and so concluded that it would be best to have him and his sister as allies on his eastern flank. As a gesture to Babur, Ismail took Khanzada away from his enemy's camp, brought her to his own encampment, and showered her with gifts.

Since at that time Safavid royal wives accompanied their husbands to the battlefield, we may assume that in Shah Ismail's quarters, Khanzada met his favorite wife, Tajlu Khanum, mother of Shah Tahmasp and Shazada Sultanum, whose story will be told in the next chapter. This meeting may have set the stage for further female contacts in the next generation.[18] Finally, the shah's men escorted her back to the Mughal camp, along with an offer of friendship and alliance. At Babur's court, Khanzada received a hero's welcome and helped seal a treaty between the Mughals and the Safavids, which would save the Mughal Empire in later years.

Soon after the emotional meeting with her brother Babur, Khanzada became his partner in government, as well as the budding empire's repository of Mongol lore and a treasure trove of royal connections throughout Asia. She later married one of her relatives, but the marriage seems to have been one of

---

[16] See Chap. 4.

[17] Mukhoty, *Daughters of the Sun*, 5–6. Gulbadan, *Humayun-Nama*, 85. Sunita Sharma, "Women Protagonists in the Formative Years of Babur," 360.

[18] See Chap. 4.

convenience. Being married afforded her the freedom to come and go as she pleased and to act with independence in court. Yet one important outcome that did materialize out of Khanzada's marriage was her adoption of the husband's younger sister, Sultanum, destined to play a role in future politics.

While Khanzada was still held by Shaybani in captivity, Babur married several women, including Maham Begum, the daughter of a famous Sufi leader and mother of his eldest son, future Emperor Humayun. In later years, after the conquest of Delhi and Agra, when Babur crowned himself *Padshah* (emperor), Maham was the first consort to be given the title "Padshah Begum" (Lady Emperor) and to formalize the status of favorite consorts as co-monarchs.[19] But in this case the formal title failed to convey the court's hierarchy. Ever since her return from Shaybani's captivity, Khanzada was Babur's compass and anchor and the chief negotiator of the realm. In later years, after Babur died, she became the great arbiter of the family, the settler of disputes between his sons, Emperor Humayun, and his brothers in times of strife and unrest.

Khanzada looms large in her brother's biography, the *Humayun-nama*, written by her niece Gulbadan. Humayun, she writes, always deferred to "my dear lady" (*aka janam*). When Khanzada first arrived at the head of a large royal convoy after her nephew Humayun completed the reconquest of northern Hindustan, Humayun rode a long way from Agra to meet and escort her in.[20] When the ladies' ceremonial tents were pitched during an outing or a celebration—each of the royal women had her own decorated tent—his sister's was always "*at the top of the row*," with Babur's wives' and daughters' tents behind hers and Humayun's own consorts' even farther away.[21] In this, too, the Mughals were very different from the Ottomans, in whose palaces the current sultan's mother reigned supreme and the previous sultan's consorts were usually packed away to another palace (Fig. 3.3).

One of the reasons for Khanzada's continued sway over the emperor and the rest of the family was Babur's bold decision to change the rules of succession. By tradition, Timurid rulers divided their realms among their sons. This is what Babur's ancestors did, and it resulted in the fragmentation of each kingdom into ever smaller statelets. But aiming to establish a world empire, the ambitious Babur changed the system of succession before he died in 1530. In accordance with his instructions, only one son would replace him, and the rest would have to satisfy themselves with subservient positions.

---

[19] Mukhoty, *Daughters of the Sun*, 11.
[20] Ibid., 23.
[21] Ibid, 32–33.

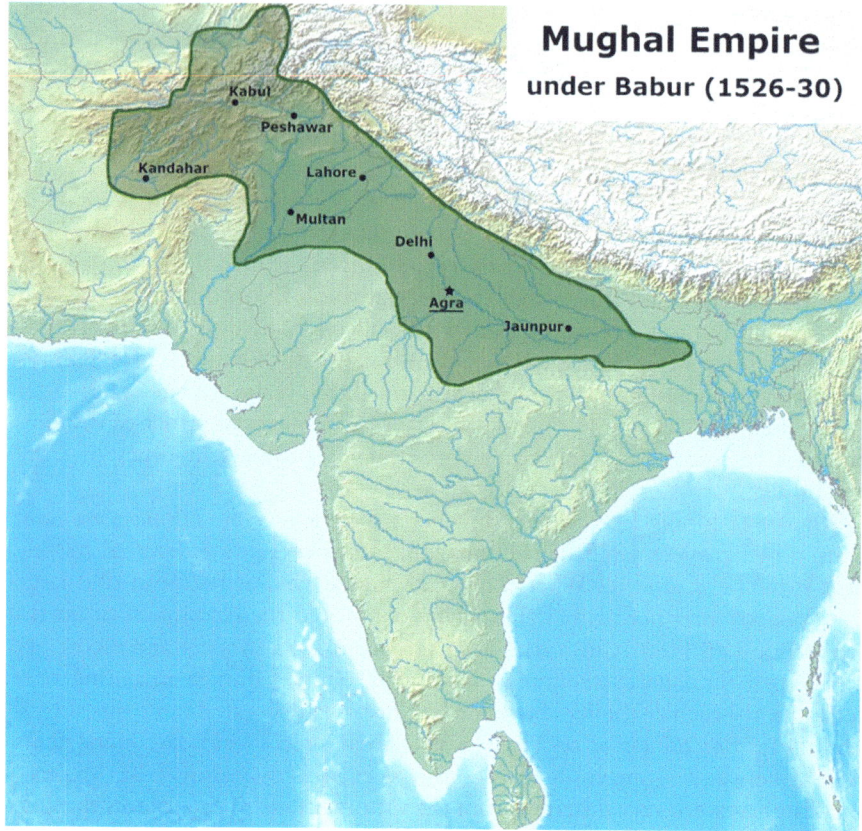

Fig. 3.3 Babur's conquests

He finally decided to leave his empire to his eldest son, Humayun. Expecting to receive a chunk of the empire for themselves as was customary, the other sons—Kamran, Hindal, and Askari—felt cheated out of their birthright. Humayun counted on Khanzada, by now the great matriarch of the family, to endorse his father's decision and give it her seal of legitimacy. His brothers, on the other hand, expected her to support *their* claim for a division of the realm. Playing her cards wisely, Khanzada succeeded both in upholding Humayun's rule, recognizing him as the rightful heir to the throne, and in being regarded by his brothers as an authoritative arbitrator, the only person trustworthy enough to negotiate on their behalf and represent their interests.[22]

---

[22] On Babur's deviation from the old Timurid tradition, see Sunita Sharma, "Women Protagonists in the Formative Years of Babur," 364.

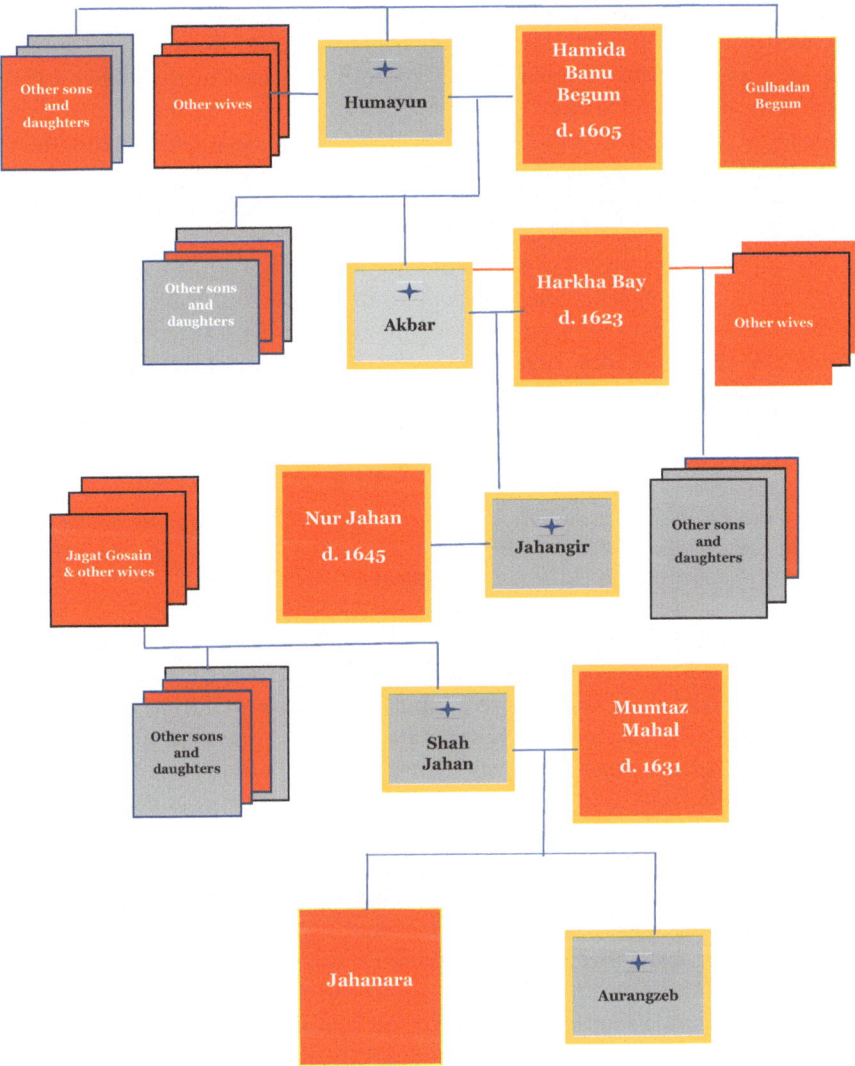

Lineage from Hamida Banu Begum to Jahanara. Only names relevant to the narrative are mentioned

The Mystic Feast

In 1533, three years after Humayun's coronation, it was again his aunt Khanzada who arranged the legendary "mystic feast," perhaps so named for the octagonal spiritual hall in which it took place on the bank of the Yamuna River. In addition to publicly acknowledging Humayun's ascension, the event reaffirmed the dynasty's connection to its Mongol roots. In the *Humayun-nama*, Khanzada's niece Gulbadan mentions dozens of women who participated in the feast. In addition to those of Humayun's household, many attended from the households of Mughal grandees and from other Timurid and Mongol kingdoms. Some had been recently displaced by the Uzbek tribal federation and found shelter in the Mughal kingdom. The list of attendees reads like a gathering of princesses from all of Central Asia, emphasizing once again the importance of women in the Timurid world.[23]

One of Khanzada's goals in arranging the mystic feast was to make clear that by the 1530s her brother's bequest was indeed a world empire, full of strong princes and illustrious royal women. Another was to show Humayun's brothers that there was enough here for everyone in the family to partake. Yet another purpose was to formalize her own standing at court. As Catherine de Medici would do three decades later during the coronation of her second son, Khanzada Begum used the event's seating arrangements to make her own status official and her superior position in the empire known. Understanding the full impact of the move, Gulbadan writes:

> *The jeweled throne which my lady had given for the feast was placed in the forecourt of the house, and a gold embroidered divan was laid in front of it, (on which) his majesty and dearest lady* [Khanzada] *sat together.*[24]

Humayun, who clearly acquiesced in his aunt's role as co-emperor, agreed to her demand to forgo the formal bejeweled throne and sit with her on the divan, and played along when he requested her permission during this celebration to fill up the palace pool with water and invite the guests to splash around in it: *"His Majesty was pleased to say 'Dearest Lady! If you approved, they might put water in the tank.' She replied: 'Very good,' and went herself and sat at the top of the steps."*[25]

Khanzada's adopted daughter, Sultanum Begum (not to be confused with Iran's Shahzada Sultanum), later married Humayun's brother Hindal.[26] Their wedding was once again planned and executed by Aunt Khanzada, who choreographed the feast, investing *"everything she had collected"* in it.[27] The marriage was an added incentive for the bridegroom, Hindal, to maintain his loyalty to Khanzada's authority. Later in the century, when Humayun was at war with his other brothers, Kamran and Askari, Khanzada again emerged as the family's lodestone. When Hindal considered declaring independence, it was she who refused to authorize it and suggested instead that he recognize Humayun's sovereignty in the Friday sermon (*khutba*). Hindal followed her advice.

---

[23] Balabanlilar, "The Begims of the Mystic Feast," 123–124.
[24] Gulbadan, *Humayun-nama*, 118. Mukhoty, *Daughters of the Sun*, 30–31. For Catherine de Medici's coronation act, see Chap. 5.
[25] Gulbadan, *Humayun-nama*, 124. Mukhoty, *Daughters of the Sun*, 28–30.
[26] On Shahzada Sultanum, see Chap. 4.
[27] Gulbadan, *Humayun-nama*, 126–128.

In 1545 Humayun and his wife Hamida returned from exile in Iran with an army of Safavid soldiers to reclaim his kingdom, as will be told in the next chapter. As they approached his fort at Kandahar Kamran sent Hamida's son, the future emperor Akbar, whom he had held hostage, to Khanzada, trusting her to parlay on his behalf with Humayun.[28] Later on, understanding that the battle was lost, Kamran beseeched his old and ailing aunt to go and make peace between him and Humayun. She died in 1545, at the age of 67, while on the road to perform this peacemaking task.[29]

Without Khanzada's commanding presence, Humayun, Kamran, Askari, and Hindal would have torn the young Mughal Empire into small pieces, and Humayun would never have been able to restore it. In the dynasty's history, she should be remembered as the woman who succeeded in placing the Mughal Empire squarely in the Mongol and Timurid tradition, in holding the empire together against powerful centrifugal forces, and in preventing its breakup into small khanates until her nephew, Humayun, secured it once again under his rule.

Hamida Banu Begum: Gulbadan Tells the Story

When Babur's daughter Gulbadan ("rose body") was born in 1522, the Mughal kingdom stretched from today's Uzbekistan and Afghanistan to the foothills of the Himalayas. Gulbadan's older full brother, Humayun, was fifteen years old. Three years later her father defeated Ibrahim Lodi, the ruler of Delhi, in the Battle of Panipat, conquered northern Hindustan, and crowned himself first padshah of the Mughal dynasty. Four years later he suddenly died in Agra, perhaps a belated response to poisoning by his enemies.

Humayun was crowned at eighteen, and from his first day on the throne he encountered bitter opposition from both his enemies in the Indian subcontinent and his envious brothers. At the time of his ascension, his brothers still governed provinces of the empire, which they wanted to hold on to and make their own. The most ambitious, Kamran, was in charge of the region of Kandahar, and the younger Hindal ruled parts of northwest Hindustan. Two other powerful threats were Sher Shah Suri, a former commander in the Mughal army who rebelled against the young new emperor, carving out a kingdom for himself in Bengal and central India, and Sultan Bahadur of Gujarat, an ally of the Portuguese on the shores of the Indian Ocean. These combined forces gradually drove Humayun, a courageous fighter but an inadequate strategist, out of his empire and into exile.

Gulbadan, who was merely eight years old when her father died, was raised and educated by her mother and by aunt Khanzada. As a Mughal princess she received the best education and is still remembered as the only royal woman in the sixteenth century to have written her own detailed memoir of her brother's

[28] Lal, "Rethinking Mughal India," 57.
[29] Gulbadan, *Humayun-nama*, 175, 251. Mukhoty, *Daughters of the Sun*, 58–59.

era, the *Humayun-nama*. Apart from being an indication of her high level of education and her succinct no-nonsense style, her book reveals a different facet of the dynasty. As Ruby Lal points out, it tells us something about the place of women in the early Mughal dynasty that would have otherwise been glossed over by subsequent male authors. It also differs from many other chronicles by being very candid and honest. Unlike the regular sycophantic accounts written by Mughal court historians, it speaks frankly of weaknesses, mistakes, and failures. Her literary portraits of her father and her brothers are very revealing, and her descriptions of kindred women in the royal harem are distinctive and unparalleled.

For most of her childhood Gulbadan moved about with her father, her siblings, and the Mughal peripatetic royal camp, joining the emperor's entourage on military campaigns and hunting expeditions. In her teens, she settled in the city of Kabul, which soon became the center of a rapidly shrinking Mughal state and a hotbed of rebellion and conspiracies. At the root of many of these conspiracies stood Kamran, who tried to oust his brother and take his place. The other siblings waited on the sidelines, ready to support whoever won the contest. But the main threat at this point came from the rebellious former general Sher Shah Suri, who defeated Humayun in a battle not far from his capital in 1540 and took control of Agra and Delhi (Fig. 3.4).

When he was chased out of his palace in 1540, Humayun was already thirty-two years old and married several times over. He first laid eyes on Hamida Banu Begum, who would become his beloved wife and the mother of his heir, while finding refuge with his brother Hindal in Rajasthan. The pretty fourteen-year-old was the daughter of Hindal's Persian teacher and distantly related to the Mughal family. As Gulbadan recounts Humayun's courtship, we can picture Hamida, now in her late sixties, telling her best friend Gulbadan the details of the story, and both of them laughing at Humayun's bungling attempts to woo her.

Although Gulbadan doesn't say so outright, at the time Hamida may have been attracted to Humayun's brother Hindal, and he was not oblivious to her charms:

> *[Humayun] asked: "Who is this?" They said: "The daughter of Mīr Bābā Dost." … In those days Hamida Bānū Begam was often in mīrzā [Hindal]'s residence. Another day when his Majesty [Humayun] came to see Her Highness my mother, he remarked: "Mīr Bābā Dost is related to us. It is fitting that you should give me his daughter in marriage." Mirza Hindāl kept on making objections, and said: "I look on this girl as a sister and child of my own. Your Majesty is a king. Heaven forbid there should not be a proper alimony, and that so a cause of annoyance should arise."*[30]

---

[30] Beveridge, *Humayun-Nama*, 14; also 239–240. Gulbadan's mother was also Hindal's mother, and Hamida's father was in principle in Hindal's employ. It probably therefore made sense for Humayun to ask her to tie the knot between him and Hamida.

Fig. 3.4 Gulbadan Begum smoking a waterpipe, Delhi, Mughal India, c. 1800

Perhaps in an attempt to forestall his brother's attempts, Hindal implied that in the present situation, with Humayun practically running for his life, he would not be able to offer Hamida the kind of dowry that a king should bring to a marriage. In such a case, it would be improper to ask for the woman's hand. But the smitten Humayun refused to let go. A few days later *"he came to my mother and said: 'Send someone to call Hamīdā Bānū Begam here.' When she sent someone, the begam did not come, but said: 'If it is to pay my respects, I was [already] exalted by paying my respects the other day. Why should I come again?'"*[31] When he sent someone for her a third time, she came up with another lame excuse: *"To see kings once is lawful; a second time it is forbidden. I shall not*

[31] Ibid., 150.

come."³² When Gulbadan's mother, Dil Dar, tried to convince her to go along, saying *"After all you will marry someone. Better than a king, who is there?"* Hamida cheekily replied, *"Oh yes, I shall marry someone; but he shall be a man whose collar my hand can touch, and not one whose skirt it does not reach."*³³ Yet after forty days, and perhaps some soul searching with her beloved Hindal, Hamida gave up and was betrothed to Humayun. By that time the terms of the relationship between them were set for years to come. Even though he was almost twenty years her senior, he a king and she a commoner, she was the one who finally deigned to marry him, and he was the one who begged (Fig. 3.5).

Fig. 3.5 Hamida Banu Begum as a young woman (Probably an imaginary likeness, no attribution)

---

³²Ibid.
³³See also Mukhoty, *Daughters of the Sun*, 42–43.

The wedding took place in September 1541, but soon after the celebrations the couple had to keep running. Hamida left her home and joined Humayun's campaign against his enemies (at this stage Gulbadan stayed in Kabul). Soon afterward she became pregnant, and during a rare respite, in October 1542, in the desert fort of Market near Lahore, gave birth to her son Akbar. But Humayun's troubles were far from over. He lost battle after battle. His officers deserted him, and his brother Kamran defied him, taking the city of Kabul and making it his capital. Seeing how weak Humayun was, and perhaps bearing a secret grudge, Hindal also came close to launching a rebellion and planned to take Kandahar and make it his capital. At this point Kamran asked his Aunt Khanzada for permission to have the Friday pledge of allegiance read in his name. The old woman refused to authorize it and demanded obedience to the lawful heir, Humayun. Yet Kamran disobeyed, ignored her advice, and proclaimed himself emperor in his brother's place.

In the Safavid Empire

In the dead of winter, with no sanctuary inside their kingdom, Hamida and Humayun entrusted the baby Akbar to his third brother, Askari, in Kandahar, along with his wet nurse, Lady Maham Anaga, knowing full well that Askari was in cahoots with Kamran and ready to stab them in the back. Through snow and arid desert, protected only by a small group of retainers, they crossed the Afghan mountains and reached the Safavid border. Despite being unaccustomed to life in the field and having given birth just a few months earlier, young Hamida proved a match for the toughest soldiers and never complained about the hardship on the road.

To their surprise, when the small, harried contingent finally arrived, tired and destitute, in the legendary city of Herat, they were cheered by crowds of people lining the streets and the local governors who hosted them. It was soon revealed that Shah Tahmasp and his sister Shahzada Sultanum sent orders to treat them as honored guests. This may have had to do with the relationship forged some thirty years earlier between Babur and Tahmasp's father, Shah Ismail, who freed Khanzada from her Uzbek captivity and sent her back to her brother, and that forged between Shahzada's mother, Tajlu Khanum, and Khanzada herself at the same time. Since then, despite the religious differences—the Mughals were Sunni and the Safavids Shia—relations between the dynasties were cordial. Tahmasp and Shahzada had surely heard the news about Humayun's woes back home, but they decided to recognize him as the true emperor of Hindustan and to receive him in accordance with his status.

After touring the country for almost six months, accompanied by royal troops, the Mughal couple were finally invited to the royal Safavid presence, and a great feast was prepared in their honor. Shahzada Sultanum immediately found common ground with the plucky Hamida. She was as adept as her brother in riding horses and often joined the royal hunt, and Hamida proved her mettle by crossing the mountain range on horseback with Humayun through the winter snows. Besides, Persian was both ladies' mother tongue, and they could converse directly without an interpreter.

Humayun enjoyed his stay in Iran and would have stayed longer, reveling in the pleasures of its magnificent palaces. His host, the shah, would probably have been happy to add this former emperor to his own retinue. But by that time Hamida was no longer the reserved and shy young girl that Humayun married. Hardened by the journey, assuming her role as Mughal empress, and longing to see the son she left behind, she insisted on returning to confront their enemies and reconquer the empire that was theirs by right. During long conversations with Shahzada Sultanum a plan was hammered out.[34]

The next stage was to convince the shah to put part of his army under Humayun's command. But Tahmasp was reluctant. He was not impressed by Humayun's resolve and was heard to grumble about his ineptitude, demonstrated by the loss of his kingdom. Besides, he asked, why should I put my best cavalry under the command of a Sunni heretic? If he wants my help, let him embrace the tenets of the Shia first. Humayun was then persuaded to declare his allegiance to Shia Islam, and to prove it, he donned the symbolic *taj haydari*, a turban wrapped around a red felt cap, and professed his love for Ali and his descendants, the imams of the Shia community. The shah finally relented. One factor that swayed Tahmasp in favor of the decision may have been his sister's strong endorsement of Hamida Banu and her appreciation for the young woman's charisma and character.[35]

When Kamran's spies at the Safavid court reported that an alliance between Tahmasp and Humayun was taking shape, he sent a messenger to the shah, offering him the entire province of Kandahar in return for turning Humayun over to him. But the shah refused and decided to bet on the older brother. He equipped Humayun with an army of 12,000 trained cavalry, and the Mughal couple headed back to Kabul. Then, in short order, their forces defeated those of Humayun's brothers. The first to fall was Askari's castle in Kandahar, where Humayun's forces freed the other brother, Hindal, from custody. Next in line was Kamran's army in Kabul. At that point, after Humayun's show of force, many of Kamran's officers decided to switch camps. Kamran himself escaped with some of his men and tried, unsuccessfully, to rebuild his base. In November 1545, three years after they were separated, Hamida and her son, Akbar, were reunited, a momentous event immortalized in painting and verse. She stayed with little Akbar in Kabul, while Humayun went on to recover his lands in Hindustan. Shah Tahmasp's consent to assist Humayun renewed the friendship treaty between the Safavids and the Mughals (Fig. 3.6).

Soon after his return to Kabul, his archenemy Sher Shah Suri's short-lived kingdom disintegrated, and Humayun went on to recover his former territories in Hindustan. By 1555, more than a decade after he left, he was once again in control of Delhi and Agra, and the recovery of his father's empire was

---

[34] For an imaginary reconstruction of the first meeting between Hamida Begum and Shahzada Sultanum, see Chap. 3.

[35] Mukhoty, *Daughters of the Sun*, 53–55.

Fig. 3.6 Baby Akbar reunites with his mother Hamida from Akbarnama, c. 1596–1600, National Museum of Asian Art

complete. But he had precious little time to relish his victory. A year later, while descending the staircase of his library in Delhi carrying an armful of books, he stumbled and fell, hitting his head on a stone edge. He died three days later, and his young son Akbar acceded to the throne.

Ousting Bairam Khan

Akbar's reign would span almost half a century, exactly in parallel with Queen Elizabeth's in faraway England.[36] Soon after his coronation, when the situation of the empire was still dire, Akbar asked his mother Hamida and his Aunt Gulbadan, who remained in Kabul, to join him in Agra. They bid farewell to

---

[36] Abu'l-Fazl, *Akbarnama*, Vol. 1, 262–263. Jahangir, *The Tuzuk-i Jahangiri*, Vol. 1, 193–196.

the home they were used to and made the long journey from Kabul to Agra through the arid plains of Rajasthan. Since Akbar was in the midst of a campaign, he sent his foster mother, Maham Anaga, to meet them in Lahore and accompany them to his encampment. When the convoy was a day's march away, he left his headquarters, rode to prostrate himself before his mother, and accompanied them to their quarters, exactly as his father, Humayun, had done when his aunt, the great Khanzada, arrived.[37] "*The army greatly rejoiced at the arrival of their highnesses,*" writes the chronicler Abu'l-Fazl "... *And recognizing their arrival as a means of victory they increased their efforts.*"[38]

Proximity to the padishah was important, and in Fatehpur Sikri, Akbar's sleek new palace compound, royal women were given sumptuous lodgings. Gulbadan and Hamida now held more sway over state affairs, but they also felt confined. By that time, new state traditions were being established, and the powerful regent, Bairam Khan, who held the reins of government until Akbar reached maturity, designed the emperor's future harem like those of the Ottoman and Safavid courts: a separate part of the palace to which access is restricted and from which women could leave only with the emperor's permission. One explanation, as Ruby Lal suggests, is that "*the inviolability of the royal harem, penetrable only by the emperor ... was meant to be further proof of his near-divinity.*"[39] Although the formally married Gulbadan was not bound by the rules of harem seclusion, the freedom of movement she had enjoyed in previous eras—joining the hunt and mingling in society—was no longer possible (Fig. 3.7).[40]

But this was still a transition period, and changes were not set in stone. Although Hamida was given a suite of rooms in the harem and a contingent of servants, she was determined to move freely around the royal precinct and beyond, openly defying Bairam's regulations.[41]

Soon after their arrival in the capital, Hamida and Gulbadan conferred with Maham Anaga. Akbar's wet nurse and foster mother during Hamida's exile in Iran remained close to him after his accession. She proved herself a wise and knowledgeable counsel, and the emperor made her his chief steward. Akbar's historian, Abu'l Fazl, who held her in high regard, remarked:

> *Though Bahadur Khan had the name of Vakil, yet in reality the business was transacted by Maham Anaga. O ye worshippers of form, what do you behold? For this noble work [of governing], wisdom and courage are necessary, and in truth Maham Anaga possessed these two qualities in perfection.*
>
> "*Many a woman,*" *he added wistfully,* "*treads manfully wisdom's path.*"[42]

---

[37] Godden, *Gulbadan*, 113–114. Abu'l-Fazl, *Akbarnama*, 44, 86.
[38] Abu'l-Fazl, *Akbarnama*, 86–87. See also Ruby Lal, "Mughal Palace Women," in Walthall (ed.) *Servants of the Dynasty*, 99–100.
[39] Lal, *Empress*, 41.
[40] Ibid, 40–41.
[41] Schimmel, *Empire of the Great Mughals*, 121, 146. See also Ruby Lal, "Mughal Palace Women," in Walthall (ed.) *Servants of the Dynasty*, 96–97, 105–106.
[42] Abu'l-Fazl, *Akbarnama*, Vol. 2, 150–151.

Fig. 3.7 The royal harem in Fatehpur Sikri. Photo: Tanu Chaudhary

Concerned about Bairam Khan's high-handed behavior, and worried about Akbar's hesitant hold on power, the three women—Hamida, Gulbadan, and Maham Anaga—determined to get rid of the domineering regent. A Shia Muslim who joined the imperial service at the age of sixteen, Bairam Khan became the former emperor's closest male companion and Akbar's adoptive father. He was courageous, a good strategist, and a gifted poet with great ambitions, who accompanied Humayun throughout his years of exile in Iran. During the reconquest of Hindustan he commanded Humayun's forces, ending up as his chief of staff. When Humayun died, young Akbar immediately appointed "Uncle Bairam" regent and retained him as commander of the imperial army. With a young and inexperienced emperor on the throne, Bairam Khan took on more and more executive powers, often making decisions about war and peace without consulting his young liege. His success on the battlefield against the empire's enemies made him even more powerful and arrogant. He now behaved as if *he* were the real emperor, ordering the monarch about and constantly annoying him by dismissing, imprisoning, and even executing some of his favorite courtiers as punishment for trifling transgressions.

Persuaded by Maham Anaga that Bairam Khan aimed to gradually hijack the empire and use the emperor as a puppet ruler, they advised Akbar to dismiss Bairam. At their suggestion, the emperor gave him two options—either stay in the palace with no official position or save face and announce his intent to set out to perform the Hajj, an elegant way to have him retire without hurting his pride. Bairam decided to opt for the pilgrimage. But then, goaded by Maham Anaga and her son Adham Khan, whom he suspected of orchestrating this move in order to take his place, he changed his mind on the way and decided to rebel against Akbar.[43]

After a long and arduous campaign, Bairam Khan finally surrendered to the imperial army, and in a forgiving mood Akbar consented to his request to continue on his way to Mecca. Bairam Khan set out once again but was assassinated by a posse of his enemies in Gujarat, on his way to the harbor, in a belated act of vengeance for a long-forgotten slight.[44]

For a short while, Maham Anaga herself replaced Bairam as Akbar's closest advisor and co-ruler, but at one point her ruthless son, Adham Khan, whom Akbar considered a foster brother, overplayed his hand. In his rush to take over Bairam's role, he killed an elderly state minister, one of Akbar's most beloved courtiers. The furious Akbar had Adham thrown off a balcony—twice—killing him and ending his family's hold on power. Maham Anaga remained in the harem but lost much of her influence in court, while Hamida and Gulbadan emerged as the emperor's main guides and counsels, even issuing edicts (*farmans*) in his name. For a long while they kept the emperor's seal (*uzuk*) in the harem and affixed it on official documents. Later on, when Akbar went to war against his brother who invaded Punjab, he appointed Hamida regent in his place and head of the palace at Fatehpur Sikri.[45]

The War Against Rani Durgavati

Although it has no direct bearing on the Mughal female lineage, one more episode should be mentioned here, because it sheds light on another brave contemporary queen of Hindustan, a woman whose actions and bravery may have had an influence on Akbar's wives and, later, even on Nur Jahan, the greatest queen of the empire (Fig. 3.8).

While Akbar was away putting down a rebellion in Uzbekistan, Hamida was engaged in a campaign against Rani Durgavati, who ruled the kingdom of Gondwana (also called Garha), southeast of Delhi. The rani, appointed regent for her minor son, was famous for her hunting and riding skills, and her reign had brought peace and riches to her kingdom for fourteen years. Here is Abu'l-Fazl's admiring description:

> When [her husband, the former ruler] died, he left a son named Bir Narayan, only five years of age ... [T]he rani assumed the government showing no lack of courage and ability, and managing her foreign relations with judgment and prudence. She carried on some great wars against Baz Bahadur and his officers and was everywhere

---
[43] Abu'l-Fazl, *Akbarnama*, Vol. 2, 159.
[44] Mukhoty, *Daughters of the Sun*, 74–75. Schimmel, *Empire of the Great Mughals*, 146–147.
[45] Schimmel, *Empire of the Great Mughals*, 156. Schrieve, "Gulbadan and Nur Jahan," 10, 34. Mukhoty, *Daughters of the Sun*, 74–77.

Fig. 3.8 Rani Durgavati, 1988 Indian stamp

victorious. She had as many as twenty thousand excellent horse soldiers and a thousand fine elephants. The treasures of the Rajas of that country came into her possession. She was a good shot, both with the bow and musket, and frequently went out hunting, when she used to bring down the animals with her own gun ... But she had one great fault. She listened to the voice of flatterers, and being puffed up with ideas of her power, she did not pay her allegiance to the emperor.[46]

Gondwana was of interest to the Mughals both for its riches and for the abundance of elephants in its jungles, but although Abu'l-Fazl does not say so outright, his writing makes clear that Akbar, and perhaps Hamida herself, did not push for this war. It seems to have been a pet project of Asaf Khan, Akbar's general at the time, who coveted it for himself and who, after the war, fell out with Akbar over possession of its riches. Though trained and disciplined, Rani Durgavati's old-style army was no match for the Mughal cannon and musket forces, and eventually, wounded by two arrows, the rani killed herself rather than fall into Mughal hands.

---

[46] Abu'l-Fazl, *Akbar-Nama* (abridged printed version), 35.

Harkha Bai/Mariam uz-Zamani

In 1562, Akbar married Harkha Bai, a Rajput princess known for her beauty and grace. She was the daughter of Raja Bharmal, the ruler of Amber, and her betrothal to Akbar was a cold political arrangement, part of the Raja's contract of vassalage with the Mughals. But in time, she and Akbar found love and intimacy. Akbar allowed her to keep her Hindu faith—as he did with his other non-Muslim wives—and was influenced by her views on Hinduism when he decided to create his own eclectic religion.

After a decade of failed attempts to produce an heir to the throne, the desperate Akbar, whose wives already had a number of abortions and stillbirths, made a symbolic twenty-mile pilgrimage on foot from Agra to the village of Sikri and implored Shaikh Salim Chishti, the local Sufi holy man, to give him a special blessing. The Shaikh promised a male heir, and when Harkha Bai gave birth to a son in 1569, Akbar named him Salim in his honor.[47] As a further gesture of thanks for the miracle, Akbar decided to move his capital to Salim Chishti's village, renaming it Fatehpur (city of victory) Sikri and building a huge royal complex there.

Even though she was now the emperor's favorite, as a Hindu, and in the shadow of the older women in the palace—Hamida, Gulbadan, and Maham Anaga—it was not easy for Harkha Bai to find her place in the harem. But she gradually became a powerbroker in her own right and an important counselor to the emperor. Soon after Prince Salim's birth Akbar conferred on her the title by which she was known ever since, *Mariam-uz-Zamani* (the Mary of our times), perhaps implying that he himself was the Holy Spirit and Prince Salim would be the Jesus of our (that is, their) times. Akbar was so thrilled over finally having an heir that he bestowed on his wife unimaginable riches.[48] Gulbadan was also elated, and the proud grandmother, Hamida, presented Akbar with a huge ruby that he kept attached to his turban henceforth.[49] Like Mary, mother of Christ, Mariam walked around with a virtual halo around her head (Fig. 3.9).

After the establishment of Akbar's new capital in Fatehpur Sikri, Mariam uz-Zamani and her son were assigned their own sumptuous villa in the royal precinct. Soon she became one of only four members of the court to hold the lofty rank of 12,000 *Suwar* (holder of a force of 12,000 horsemen), which came with a sizable sinecure, as well as precious gems from every nobleman during celebrations and holidays, and special gifts from those seeking her intercession. Gradually she amassed a huge fortune. She was the first to *officially* be given the right to issue royal edicts and used part of her income to build public buildings, gardens, and mosques.[50]

---

[47] Or, as Abu'l-Fazl refers to him, the "world-illuminating pearl of the mansion of dominion and fortune, the night gleaming jewel of the casket of greatness and glory, Prince Sultan Salim."

[48] Abu'l-Fazl, *Akbarnama*, Vol. 2, 502–503.

[49] Jahangir, *The Tuzuk-i Jahangiri*, Vol. 1, 409.

[50] Findly, "Capture of Maryam-uz-Zamani's Ship," 232–233. Around 1571, Akbar introduced the elaborate *mansabdari* system, a hierarchical grading of state officials. Those holding the highest

Fig. 3.9 Harkha Bai after the birth of Jahangir, miniature, royal album, c. 1600. The grandmother, Hamida Begum, is sitting on a chair by the bedside. Attributed to Bishandas, Boston Museum of Fine Arts

Mariam uz-Zamani's Business Ventures

Looking for other ways to invest her great wealth, she soon became an international entrepreneur, building her own ships, competing with the Portuguese and the English in commerce, developing trade routes across the Indian Ocean, and transporting pilgrims to Mecca. She gradually edged the Portuguese out of their monopoly on trade in the northwestern part of India. In 1613, in an attempt to regain full control of seaborne trade in these regions, a Portuguese

---

offices were ranked according to the number of horsemen—*suwar* or *sawar*—they were obliged to maintain based on their salaries. See also Subrahmanyam, *Three Ways to Be Alien*, 133–135.

contingent of soldiers boarded the *Rahimi*, Mariam uz-Zamani's largest ship trading with the Gulf and the Red Sea. Even though it carried a Portuguese safe passage card, the ship was confiscated along with its crew. The empress was livid. She saw this blatant act of piracy as an affront to the empire, and as deliberate religious persecution. She convinced her son Salim, now Emperor Jahangir, to block Portuguese trade, shut down churches, and seize the town of Daman, which was under Portuguese control. These acts are rightly perceived as the beginning of the end of Portugal's supremacy and the shift to English dominance in the Indian Ocean.

But when she felt English traders were undermining her business ventures, they were not spared her wrath, either. In 1603, Queen Elizabeth's last year on the throne, an English merchant named John Mildenhall arrived in Akbar's court. It is not known whether he was actually sent by Elizabeth or was traveling on his own initiative. In any case, he presented Akbar with a set of impressive gifts, including twenty-nine first-rate horses and fine jewelry. During this visit he also offered some gifts from the queen of England to the queen of India, Mariam uz-Zamani, and to her son, established an informal embassy, and received permission to trade.[51] But then, in a thoughtless *faux pas*, one of the English traders working in India, a certain William Finch, offered farmers a higher price than she had for a load of indigo, taking it off her hands in a clear affront to the Mughal court. The result was the expulsion from India of the English envoy, William Hawkins.[52]

The Question of Succession

In the end, Salim, the long-awaited son, proved a disappointment to his father. Worried that Akbar, by that time almost half a century on the throne, would outlive him or would bypass him and appoint Khusrau, Salim's own son, to succeed him as emperor, he took up arms against his father and established his own court in Allahabad, several days' ride east of Agra.

His foolish next move was to kill Abu'l-Fazl, one of Akbar's dearest friends. Commissioned by the emperor to deal with Salim's rebellion, the statesman, famous for writing the *Akbar-nama*, was assassinated by Salim's Rajput accomplices on the way to Agra.[53] Akbar was so devastated that he resolved to destroy his son and crush the rebellion by any means. But Hamida and Gulbadan, along with Mariam uz-Zamani and Salim's wet nurse, Salima, convinced the emperor to invite his son, now cowering before the empire's mighty power, and to forgive him. As the eighty-year-old Gulbadan lay on her deathbed, Salima brought Salim back to court. On his way, the rebel prince paid a visit to his grandmother Hamida and to his mother, no doubt to prostrate himself

---

[51] Carlson, "Power, Presents, and Persuasion."
[52] Findly, "Capture of Maryam-uz-Zamani's Ship," 227, 232–233.
[53] And see Jahangir's own admission of ordering his killing, Jahangir, *The Tuzuk-i Jahangiri*, Vol. 1, 25. *Rajputs* are the Hindu warrior and ruling class.

before them and ask for guidance. They gave him clear instructions on the proper behavior during his meeting with Akbar, but although the father and son seemingly reconciled, tensions between them continued to smolder until Akbar's death.[54]

After these tragic events and the death of Gulbadan, her dearest friend, Hamida retired to her quarters in the palace. In 1604, a messenger returning from the court of Shah Abbas in Iran brought a letter reaffirming the good relations between the Mughals and Safavids and another letter addressed to Hamida Begum from a woman in the shah's palace. The letter's author may have been Zaynab Begum, the current shah's aunt and Iran's leading elder statesperson, whose aunt was Hamida's old friend Shahzadeh Sultanum. Zaynab, who was born after Hamida's departure from Iran, must have heard stories about Shahzadeh Sultanum's friendship with Hamida, and she sent her greetings.

Hamida passed away later that same year, slightly before the demise of her son Akbar. After her death she received the honorific Mariam Makani (Occupying the Place of the Virgin Mary), perhaps a last attempt by Akbar to defy death by claiming to be the Jesus of his era.[55]

Like his father and grandfather, Akbar's son, now Emperor Jahangir, made obeisance to his mother when she arrived at Lahore to meet him. His description of the meeting, written in his own hand, gives us a sense of the relationship between mothers and sons in the empire and of the way it related in their minds to ancient Mongol traditions:

> *I ordered my son [Khurram, the future Shah Jahan] to attend upon Hazrat [honorable] Maryam-zamani and the other ladies, and to escort them to me. When they reached the neighborhood of Lahore ... I embarked in a boat and went to a village named Dahr to meet my mother, and I had the good fortune to be received by her. After the performances of obeisance and prostration and greeting which is due from the young to the old according to the custom of Chingiz, the rules of Timur and common usage ... I obtained leave to return.*[56]

More than a century after the death of Aisan Daulat Begum, the empire's founding matriarch, Mongol etiquette was still a powerful model for courtly behavior in the state. Although he reigned over the richest empire in Asia, Jahangir still prostrated himself before his mother and requested her permission to leave.

Mariam uz-Zamani survived Akbar by eighteen years and kept developing her huge assets, sumptuous palaces, and elevated formal status. Her commercial activities continued unabated, but politically she was soon pushed aside by another woman, who would become the greatest Mughal queen of all.

---

[54] Mukhoty, *Daughters of the Sun*, 115–120. Lal, *Empress*, 77–82.
[55] Schimmel, *Empire of the Great Mughals*, 143. Choksy, "An Emissary from Akbar to Abbas I," 19–29. See also Edwards, "Relations of Shah Abbas the Great," 247–248.
[56] Jahangir, *The Tuzuk-i Jahangiri*, Vol. 1, 76.

Mihr un-Nisa/Nur Jahan

Between 1576 and 1579 Safavid Iran was wracked by a series of tragedies in quick succession. It began with the death of Shah Tahmasp and then, in less than two years, the killing of Haydar, the heir apparent who had declared himself shah; the murder of the next shah, Ismail II; the execution of Parikhan Khanum, the princess who held the reins of government; the accession of Tahmasp's remaining son, the purblind Mohammad Khodabanda; and the gradual takeover by Khodabanda's wife, Mahd-i Ulya.[57] These events shook the empire, and all those suspected of supporting the ousted monarchs were in danger of being persecuted by those who ousted them.

Ghiyas and Asmat, a couple belonging to the Khorasani upper class in Iran, were troubled by these events and perhaps feared for their safety. As the great comet of 1577 lit up the sky, they decided to leave Herat and join a caravan that traveled east in search of a better future. Akbar's illustrious empire across the mountains must have held the same attraction for aspiring young Asians that America did for adventurous Europeans at the same time—a rapidly growing land of riches and infinite possibilities. When a baby girl was born near Kandahar as the caravan snaked through the mountains, Ghiyas and Asmat named her Mihr un-Nisa (sun of womankind), swaddled her on the road, and carried on. After a long journey, they arrived in Lahore and a few months later moved on to Agra. Ghiyas was given an audience with Emperor Akbar, who at the time needed all the professional help he could get to run the rapidly expanding empire. He was appointed accountant and tax supervisor, low grade at first, but the talented Persian swiftly rose through the ranks.

Their comfortable house in Fatehpur Sikri soon became a meeting place for Persian-speaking state officials, intellectuals, and poets. Ghiyas' young daughter, Mihr, was given the best education available and soon revealed herself to be a prodigy. She could recite volumes of Persian poetry by heart and later began to compose her own poems under the penname *Makhfi* (the hidden one). Taught history and literature by Iranian exiles, she probably heard stories about the legendary Princess Parikhan Khanum and her Aunt Shahzada Sultanum who practically ruled the Safavid Empire in previous decades. She may even have read *Jawāhir al-ʿAjāib*, the famous book written by Fakhri of Herat—perhaps an acquaintance of her father's—which included biographies of successful Iranian women. Growing up in and around Akbar's court, she was also acquainted with the female heritage of the Mughal dynasty and perhaps heard stories from Hamida, Gulbadan, and Harkha Bai.[58]

Legend has it that as a young girl, Mihr un-Nisa had met the young Prince Salim, and the two fell in love, but there is no real evidence to support such a claim. Be that as it may, at seventeen she was married off to Ali Quli Beg, a

---

[57] For these events see Chap. 4. The following section on Nur Jahan relies heavily on Ruby Lal's book, *Empress*.
[58] See Chap. 4.

promising young officer of Persian descent, formerly an attendant of Shah Ismail II who, like Ghiyas, fled to India after his master was assassinated and found employment in the Mughal army. The young couple moved to Bengal in the east, where Ali Quli served as an imperial officer. Their baby girl, Ladli, was born in 1601.

Jahangir's Accession and Marriage

In 1605, Akbar died and Salim was crowned Padshah Jahangir. Soon after his accession his own son, Khusrau, the future Emperor Shah Jahan rebelled against him. Mihr's husband Ali Quli joined Khusrau's rebellion, but after the father and son made peace, Ali Quli was pardoned and summoned back to the army. A couple of years later, he was suspected of joining another rebellion, this time initiated by Jahangir's brother. The suspicions may have been unfounded, but when the emperor's envoys came to arrest him, he refused to go quietly and was killed in battle. His widow, Mihr, and her daughter, Ladli, were taken to Agra and sent to the royal harem.

At the time the harem was overseen by Jahangir's mother, Mariam uz-Zamani, and her co-wives, who guided Mihr through the first steps in the intricate politics of the palace. At first Mihr was almost invisible in the multitude of harem women. Her only advantage was that her father, Ghiyas, was already a senior executive. It is not clear whether there was an immediate attraction between her and Jahangir in that initial phase, but in 1611 he asked for her hand in marriage. She consented, of course, and, following the custom of the Mughal dynasty, by now another respected tradition, her name was changed to Nur Mahal (light of the palace). Soon afterward, Ghiyas was promoted to the position of chief finance minister and put in charge of land grants. On the occasion, he held a magnificent celebration for the emperor and for his new wife, giving them numerous expensive gifts. To reciprocate, Jahangir changed Mihr's name once more, this time to Nur Jahan (light of the world). This was the name she was known by ever since.[59] Ghiyas was also given a new name—I'timad ud-dawla (pillar of the dynasty).

Initially, marrying Nur Jahan may have been a political move intended to strengthen ties between Jahangir and his rich and gifted finance minister, but it soon developed into love and an unprecedented power alliance. When Jahangir, who kept a diary, started writing about his wife in 1614, he described her as *"a sensitive companion, superb caregiver, accomplished adviser, hunter, diplomat, and aesthete."*[60] He soon realized that his wife was much more than that. She was the smartest person around, and he depended more and more on her advice.

---

[59] Jahangir, *The Tuzuk-i Jahangiri*, Vol. 1, 319.
[60] Lal, *Empress*, 103.

Empress

Jahangir preferred the ascetic life of a soldier and the contemplative musings of a philosopher to the onus of government and the luxury of the palace. At every opportunity he traveled to his military second capital near Ajmer in Rajasthan. Nur Jahan, now his favorite, joined him on many of these trips. It soon became clear to everyone that *she* was the real power behind the throne. If anyone still had doubts about her influence, they got their answer in 1617 when, in the heat of a hunting expedition, separated from her posse, she found herself alone atop a restless elephant, surrounded by four tigers. The angry predators, scared out of their lairs by bush-beating servants, gathered around her, growling and threatening to attack. Nur acted like a trained soldier. Seated in her *howdah* atop the elephant, she loaded her cumbersome musket and fired six shots in quick succession, killing all four. "*Until now*," wrote her proud husband, "*such shooting was never seen.*"[61] Among the warlike Mughal elite, where soldiery and marksmanship were so highly appreciated, she became a legend overnight.[62]

In another instance, once again on an elephant, this time in the company of Jahangir, a tiger that threatened a nearby village came dangerously close during an attempt to track it down and hunt it: "*As I had vowed that I would not injure any living thing with my own hand, I told Nur Jahan to shoot at him,*" wrote Jahangir. "*An elephant is not at ease when it smells a tiger, and is continually in movement, and to hit with a gun from a litter is a very difficult matter, so much that Mirza Rustam, who, after me, is unequalled in shooting, has several times missed three of four shots from an elephant. Yet Nur Jahan so hit the tiger with one shot that he was immediately killed*" (Fig. 3.10).[63]

Jahangir's son Khurram quickly understood the new pecking order and on visits to the palace showed Nur Jahan the required respect even before visiting his own mother. When he returned victorious from a campaign in the south and was elevated to crown prince and given the name Shah Jahan, he offered her presents worth 200,000 rupees, which was more than he gave all the other royal women combined, including his own mother. She, in turn, presented him, his consorts, and his children with lavish presents of her own: caftans, bejeweled swords, fine horses, and trained elephants.[64]

Like ruling women elsewhere, Nur Jahan understood that if her orders were to be carried out, she needed to demonstrate her power to the elite, build a popular base, and invest in social welfare. She constructed inns and khans, mosques, and public gardens, and lavished alms on the poor. One of her pet projects was arranging weddings for orphan girls, an excellent way to make her generosity widely known. Another was the restoration and building of gardens,

---

[61] Jahangir, *The Tuzuk-i Jahangiri*, Vol. 1, 375.

[62] Lal, *Empress*, 129–130.

[63] Jahangir, *The Tuzuk-i Jahangiri*, Vol. 2, 105.

[64] Ibid., Vol. 1, 397–404. According to my calculations, 1 rupee = ~12 grams of silver. Hence 200,000 = 2.4 metric tons of silver.

Fig. 3.10 Nur Jahan in a manly pose, loading a musket. Painting by Abul-Hasan Nadiruz Zaman. Seventeenth century

such as the famous Shalimar Bagh in the vicinity of Srinagar, or the royal garden in Agra itself, named after Babur.

Her power and influence grew even more when her brother's daughter, Arjumand, later known as Mumtaz Mahal, married Crown Prince Khurram in 1612. To celebrate the event, Nur Jahan's brother, Asaf, was elevated to chief steward in charge of the royal household, and the governorship of Lahore was added to her father's already enormous ministerial portfolio. One last thread connecting the two families was the marriage of Ladli, Nur Jahan's daughter, to Shahryar, the emperor's youngest son.[65] Jahangir's Mughal dynasty and Nur Jahan's Persian clan were now fused together almost as one family. And with her father, I'timad ud-dawla, and her brother Asaf practically running the state, Nur's power over her husband, and hence the empire, seemed boundless. The

[65] Jahangir, *The Tuzuk-i Jahangiri*, Vol. 2, 187–188.

English ambassador Thomas Roe ridiculed Jahangir for becoming Nur Jahan's plaything: "*yet one governs him, and wynds him up at her pleasure.*"[66]

She now began issuing imperial edicts of her own. In the Mughal court there was a hierarchy of edicts. Those issued by her female predecessors, Hamida Begum and Mariam uz-Zamani, were defined as *hukms* or *nishans*, documents of a lesser degree, usually used to regulate specific issues. Nur Jahan's edicts were of a higher level, akin to *farmans*, royal decrees inscribed as bylaws of the land. The decrees she issued concerned taxation, internal affairs, and even military issues. Though written in a formal style akin to that of *hukms*, their content and embellishment were closer to those of *farmans*, and they were signed in her own name: "*Nur Jahan Padshah Begum.*" At the same time, the royal couple ordered the mint to cast gold coins that bore Jahangir's name on one side and Nur Jahan's on the other. Other coins were in her name alone, a never-before-seen phenomenon in the Muslim world. Coins were not just a medium of exchange. In the absence of mass media, they were the surest way to spread the news of her power far and wide.

Many years before Nur Jahan arrived on the scene, Akbar had made a habit of appearing on the palace's public viewing balcony (*Jharokha*) every morning at sunrise. Borrowing the Hindu custom of *darshan*, worship of deities and holy monarchs, he used it as a way to connect to non-Muslims and even made it part of his new personality cult. Although it was viewed as idolatry by devout Muslims, Jahangir continued the tradition. Soon Nur Jahan herself began appearing on the *Jharokha* at sunrise, making it clear to the adoring multitudes that she was at least Jahangir's equal, if not his senior. As the chronicler Bhakkari wrote, at that point she was a sovereign in everything but having the Friday sermon and oath of allegiance read in her name.[67] "*Her authority,*" wrote another contemporary historian, "*reached such a pass that the king was such only in name.*"[68]

Emperor Jahangir was aware of her gradual seizure of kingly prerogatives, but he did not seem to mind. His passions lay elsewhere, in the realms of aesthetics, art, and contemplation, as well as in his growing addiction to alcohol and opium. At one point, realizing that her own power drew legitimacy from the formal authority of the sovereign and seeing that his health was slowly deteriorating, Nur insisted that he cut down on drink and drug consumption. Jahangir agreed and maintained a strict diet for a time, which improved his health. After one yearly weighing ceremony—the padshah was weighed on the scale every year against gold and precious stones, which were then given as alms and presents—Jahangir wrote that Nur Jahan, presumably delighted about his increased weight, made a special gesture to his caretakers:

[66] Lal, *Empress*, 139.
[67] Ibid., 152. Iftikhar, "Analytical Study," 14.
[68] Iqbal in *Nama-i Jahangiri*. See Iftikhar, "Political Domain of Mughal Women," 22.

[S]he had paid greater attention than ever to adorn the assembly and arrange the feast. All the servants of approved service and the domestics who knew my temperament, who in that time of weakness had constantly been present and been ready to sacrifice their lives, and had fluttered round my head like moths, were now honoured with suitable kindnesses, such as dresses of honour, bejewelled sword-belts, bejewelled daggers, horses, elephants, and trays full of money, each according to their positions.[69]

In the 1620s, recognized by all as the real sovereign, she ventured into the field of foreign relations. One of her main accomplishments at that time was repairing relations with Imam Quli, ruler of Turan, a kingdom to the north of the Himalayas. Years earlier, offended by Jahangir, who had made fun of his pederastic inclinations, Imam Quli had broken off relations. In 1622, his mother sent Nur Jahan a letter, perhaps signaling her intention to resolve the crisis. Understanding that an alliance with the kingdom of Turan could be crucial for the safety of the empire as the Safavids (who at that point in time were rivals) were preparing a campaign in the east, Nur sent back precious gifts and a letter actively pursuing reconciliation, which were received and reciprocated. This was followed by a series of negotiations with leaders of Indian principalities to the south, which also led to a period of peaceful coexistence.[70]

A year later, Nur Jahan's father, Itimad ud-Daula, died, bequeathing most of his legendary fortune to his daughter. Jahangir followed suit by passing on to her all her father's commissions, state positions, and sources of income and wrote in his diary: "*On the first of the divine month of Isfandārmuz*[71] *I gave the establishment and everything belonging to the government and Amirship of I'timādu'd-daula to Nūr Jahān Begam and ordered that her drums and orchestra should be sounded after those of the king.*"[72] While making her even more powerful, these decisions exacerbated tensions between Nur Jahan and her brother, Asaf, who felt cheated out of his rightful inheritance. These tensions would rise to the surface years later.

The huge inheritance and new government positions were added to Nur's already substantial income from her own business ventures and taxes on imports. Francisco Pelsaert, a contemporary traveler, gives us an idea about one of these money-making ventures:

In Sikandra [facing Agra on the other side of the Yamuna River], the officers of Nur Jahan Begam, who built their sarai there, collect duties on all these goods before they can be shipped across the river; and also on innumerable kinds of grain, butter, and other provisions, which are produced in the Eastern provinces, and imported thence.[73]

[69] Jahangir, *The Tuzuk-i Jahangiri*, Vol. 2, 214.

[70] Lal, *Empress*, 171. Mutribi Samarqandi's conversations with Emperor Jahangir (trans. Richard Foltz) https://depts.washington.edu/silkroad/texts/mutribi.html. H.V. Bowen, *The Worlds of the East India Company* (2003), 81.

[71] The zodiac month of Aquarius (January 20 to February 17).

[72] Jahangir, *The Tuzuk-i Jahangiri*, Vol. 2, 228.

[73] Findly, "The Capture of Maryam uz-Zamani's Ship," 230.

Fig. 3.11 Itimad ud-Daula's tomb. Photo: Wikijib

In addition, she received a yearly salary of two hundred thousand rupees from the state treasury and took over the office of land grants to nobles, which also increased her wealth. All these sources made Nur as rich as the emperor himself, and perhaps even richer (Fig. 3.11).

In memory of her father—and later also her mother—she constructed a tomb in Agra, built on the axis of a Persianate four-garden (*Chaharbagh*) plan, with a magnificent pavilion around the burial site, built of marble and inlaid with semi-precious stones in the style known in the West as *pietra durra*. This tomb and its style of decoration are said to have been the main inspiration for the Taj Mahal, constructed some two decades later by Jahangir's son, Shah Jahan.

But peace did not last long in the Mughal Empire. Soon war broke out between father and son. Crown Prince Shah Jahan always suspected that his father would prefer to bestow the crown on one of his siblings, and now with Ladli, Nur Jahan's daughter, betrothed to his youngest brother, Shahryar, he began to suspect that she was pulling strings behind the scenes to make her son-in-law the next emperor. The relationship was further complicated by the fact that Mumtaz Mahal, Nur Jahan's niece and Asaf's daughter, was married to Shah Jahan, and Asaf himself was torn between his loyalty to his sister and his duty to his son-in-law, the rebellious prince. The war raged on until 1625, when the prince's forces, encircled by the imperial army, capitulated, and he pleaded with his father to pardon him. The emperor consented but, perhaps heeding Nur Jahan's advice, demanded that Shah Jahan send his young sons,

Aurangzeb and Dara Shukoh, as hostages to guarantee his good behavior. Shah Jahan complied, but his hatred toward his mother-in-law, whom he saw as the architect of his failure, never abated.

Mahabat Khan's Coup, Shah Jahan's Accession, and Nur's Fall from Grace

Just when it seemed that there were no more threats to their rule and the empress and her beloved Jahangir could rest on their laurels, another crisis rocked the empire. Accusations of corruption leveled at Mahabat Khan, Jahangir's military chief of staff, led to his son's imprisonment and his daughter's interrogation, dealing a blow to his status and pride. In a brazen act of retaliation, he abducted the ailing Jahangir from his tent in an encampment up north, crossed a local river, and burned the main bridge connecting the two banks. A hastily organized attempt by Nur Jahan to rescue her husband failed, and, with no good options left, she agreed to join him under Mahabat Khan's control, and be taken to Lahore. Mahabat's plan was to use them as puppet rulers in order to prevent rebellion while he gathered strength to take over the empire, and then do away with them and crown himself.

But as the convoy with the two royal hostages meandered through the countryside, Nur quietly sent emissaries and letters to her supporters across the country and gathered an armed force, which finally confronted the convoy on the way to Lahore. Mahabat's army was defeated and the couple was liberated, unscathed but seriously affected by the affair. As the crisis unfolded, the prodigal son Shah Jahan also renewed his rebellion, and this time his army was reinforced by his father-in-law's soldiers. Asaf Khan understood that this was the crucial moment. Many of Jahangir's and Nur Jahan's loyalists deserted and joined the rebellion, and the time seemed ripe for change.

Throughout this harrowing affair, Jahangir's dementia increased and his health deteriorated. By the time he died, in October 1627, Nur Jahan had no army left to defend herself and the palace. Three months later, while still on the road, Shah Jahan was recognized as emperor in the Friday sermon, and in a series of quick tactical moves his forces took the capital. Soon his brother Shahryar was apprehended and executed, as were other members of the family who might pose a threat to Shah Jahan's throne. With no male champion under whose banner she could put up a fight, Nur Jahan relented. She was soon sent away to Lahore, where the once all-powerful queen spent the rest of her life in charity work, clad in black.[74]

Clearly at the order of their master, court historians diligently erased Nur Jahan's deeds from the history books. But when she died in 1645, even the famous chronicler of Shah Jahan's reign, the author of the *Shah Jahan Nama*, could not ignore her critical importance for Mughal history. Mentioning her death in that year, the author acknowledged:

---

[74] Iftikhar, "Analytical Study," 23.

> *From the sixth year of late Emperor [Jahangir]'s reign, when she was united to him in the bond of matrimony, she gradually acquired such unbounded influence over his Majesty's mind that she seized the reins of government and arrogated to herself the supreme civil and financial administration of the realm, ruling with absolute authority till the conclusion of his reign.*[75]

Just as in the case of her contemporaries Elizabeth I in England and Kösem Sultan in the Ottoman Empire, this unprecedented stage of sovereignty which Nur Jahan attained also marked the decline of female power in the Mughal Empire. Her daughter-in-law, Mumtaz Mahal (immortalized in the Taj Mahal built in her honor), still held on to some symbols of sovereignty, and her granddaughter, Jahanara (Jahan Ara), was powerful in her own right, but none of them reached the glory and power attained by Nur Jahan. Henceforth, women would gradually move to the sidelines.

Aftermath: Mumtaz Mahal and Jahanara

Nur Jahan's niece, Arjumand Banu Begum, was the daughter of her brother Asaf, who at that point became Shah Jahan's right-hand man. She was born in 1593 and raised in and around the palace. Like her aunt, she was highly educated and conversant in Persian and Arabic. She is said to have been a woman of extraordinary character, honest, straightforward, and compassionate. At nineteen she married the future Shah Jahan as his second wife.[76] After the wedding he changed her name to Mumtaz Mahal (the exalted one of the palace). Soon he fell so deeply in love with her that, although he had many other women in his harem, the relationship between them became monogamous. During her life she bore Shah Jahan *fourteen* children, of whom seven survived, including Dara Shukoh and future Emperor Aurangzeb, who earlier on were sent as hostages to Jahangir's palace.[77]

In his adoration for his beloved wife, the emperor decreed a million rupees a year as her allowance (a rupee weighed 14 grams of silver), as well as many tax-yielding properties, which she used for alms and charity and to support poets and artists she adored. Like her predecessors, she kept the royal seal in her chambers inside the harem and affixed it to imperial documents. The seal bore the following words: "*By the grace of God, Mumtaz Mahal became the companion in the world of Shahjahan in the shadow of God.*"[78] Like her husband's grandmother, Mariam uz-Zamani, she was interested in trade and commercial expansion, built a fleet of merchant ships, and resented the continued Portuguese presence in India. But she died of post-partum hemorrhage in 1631, in her thirty-eighth year, before she had a chance to carry out all her plans. The heartbroken Shah Jahan could not be consoled even by the magnificent project of the Taj Mahal, built to honor her memory.

---

[75] Lal, *Empress*, 220.
[76] Jahangir, *The Tuzuk-i Jahangiri*, Vol. 1, 224–225.
[77] Iftikhar, "Analytical Study," 23.
[78] Ibid., 23.

Fig. 3.12 Jahanara Begum attributed to Lalchand c. 1631–3. British Library

Mumtaz Mahal's eldest daughter Jahanara Begum, her father's favorite, gradually took her place as leading lady of the palace, carrying the by now formal title of Padshah Begum. Building on the preceding generations' achievements, her power was such that she kept a palace and retinue of her own. She also received from her father half of her mother's substantial inheritance, while her other siblings had to split the other half among them. She continued her mother's unfinished work, employing a fleet of merchant ships and trading with the English and Dutch in the Indian ocean (Fig. 3.12).

Like her great aunt Gulbadan, Jahanara was a devout Muslim and sent a shipload of grain to the holy city of Mecca every year; and like her great-great-aunt Khanzada, more than a century earlier, she assumed the mantle of arbitrator in the royal family. She initially supported her brother Dara Shukoh as heir to the throne, but when Shah Jahan's other son, Aurangzeb, rebelled, took over, and locked the grief-stricken Shah Jahan in Agra fort, Jahanara refused to play along and remained with her father in his suite of rooms, tending to him for the rest of his life. After his death she reconciled with Aurangzeb and became his main advisor, retaining much of her former power. But she was also the last great Mughal empress.

From that time on, Mughal royal women mostly operated in the shadows, and most of them were unknown to the public.

CHAPTER 4

The Safavid Queens of Iran

When her justice crushed oppression under foot, wolves bowed to shepherds' feet.
Now that her governance has humbled cruelty, guard dogs
inflict thieves with multiple wounds.
When she asks those informed directions to the house of her enemy,
sudden death always comes calling.
Unknowing, like fate, each arrow from disaster's bow directed
itself, certain and sure, to her foes.
The Poet Muhtasham's Panegyric to Parikhan Khanum.[1]

Another great Muslim dynasty—the Safavids—emerged along with the Mughals in the early sixteenth century. The political and cultural roots of both could be traced to the Turko-Mongol kingdoms of the Middle Ages, which assigned leadership roles to women. But both were also typical of a new breed of mega-state—the gunpowder empire. In that sense they were as much a product of the great discoveries, the new international order and technical advances of the era, as they were descendants of the previous one.[2] This chapter follows the rise and fall of queendom in the Safavid Empire.

THE BIRTH OF THE SAFAVIDS

In April 1453, the Ottoman sultan Mehmed II, known as "The Conqueror," lay siege to the great city of Constantinople. Using never-before-seen fire power, he breached its formidable walls and ended the thousand-year reign of the Byzantine Empire. Only one branch of Byzantium's royal elite managed to survive: the kingdom of Trebizond, on the southeastern shores of the Black Sea. Threatened by the relentless march of the Ottomans who now turned

[1] Translated and quoted from Khafipour, *Empires of the Near East and India*, 411.
[2] Szuppe, "Status, Knowledge, and Politics," 141.

© The Author(s), under exclusive license to Springer Nature
Switzerland AG 2024
D. Ze'evi, *Queens Around the World, 1520–1620*,
https://doi.org/10.1007/978-3-031-58634-7_4

their attention eastward, Trebizond's rulers scrambled to build political alliances with their neighbors. They approached the powerful Turkic tribal Confederation of the Aq-Qoyunlu, ruled by the charismatic Uzun Hasan ("Hasan the tall"), who claimed descent from Timur/Tamerlane and through him—nebulously—from Genghis Khan.[3] The Aq-Qoyunlu, an assemblage of warlike tribes, controlled large swaths of Iran, Mesopotamia, and eastern Anatolia, but it too was concerned with the rising power of the Ottomans and their new terrifying gunpowder army (Fig. 4.1).

After long negotiations, the king of Trebizond, John IV, reached an agreement with Uzun Hasan. To seal the bargain, he agreed to give him his daughter Theodora's hand in marriage. It was a common opinion, as one traveler wrote, that *"there was at that time no woman of greater beauty."*[4] Even more importantly, Theodora descended from ancient Christian royalty on her

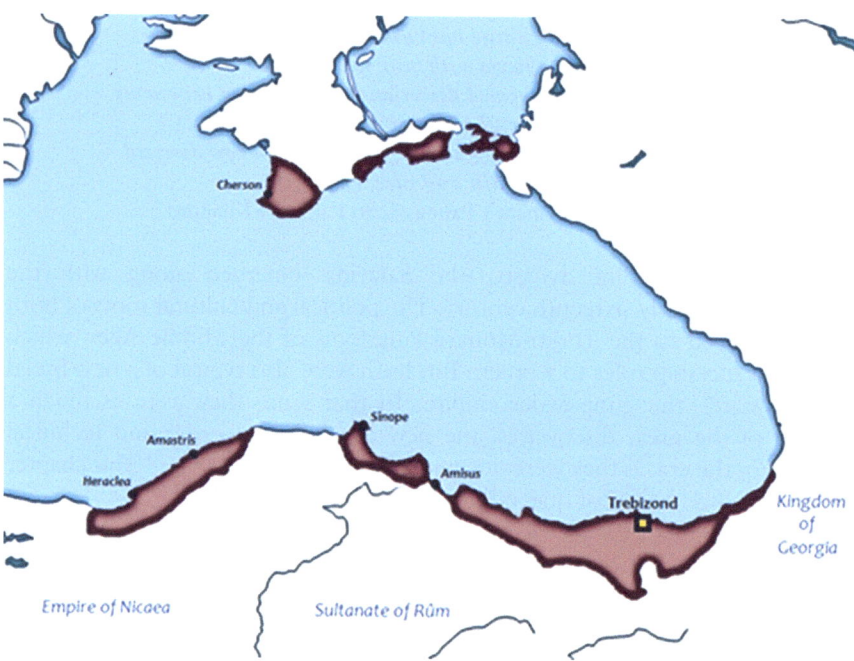

Fig. 4.1 The Kingdom of Trebizond on the shores of the Black Sea

[3] Aq-Qoyunlu means "Those of the White Sheep", their rivals in the Caucasus for a long time were another confederation of tribes named the Qara-Qoyunlu ("Those of the Black Sheep"). But in the late 1400s the Aq-Qoyunlu had defeated their rivals and were already an established state with a Mongol-style court culture, minting their own coins and creating their own architecture. It is not clear whether Uzun Hasan's claims of descent from Tamerlane are justified. We only know that Tamerlane appointed his grandfather governor of eastern Anatolia. See Babinger, *Mehmed the Conqueror*, 190.

[4] Miller, *Trebizond*, 88f.

maternal side as well. Her mother was Bagrationi, daughter of King Alexander I of Georgia. Theodora's marriage to Uzun Hasan thus created a strong alliance between the three eastern states around the Black Sea—Trebizond, Georgia, and the Aq-Qoyunlu federation—forging a connection between Christians and Muslims against the rising Ottomans.

As part of the marriage contract, Theodora and her father stipulated that the young princess be allowed to keep her Christian faith. Uzun Hasan consented. He invited her to bring along a group of priests and built churches for her in the cities of Diyarbakir and Tabriz. The marriage turned out to be a success. Theodora, who after her marriage was known as Despina Khatun (literally "Lady Lady" in Greek and Turkish, respectively), proved herself a capable stateswoman and soon devoted her time to improving the Aq-Qoyunlu's foreign relations and strengthening their alliances. Her envoys traveled by sea to Europe, met with the Venetians and the Moldavians, bought firearms, and formed alliances against the looming Ottoman threat (Fig. 4.2).

But Despina's bold diplomacy failed to rescue her father's kingdom, and the last outpost of the Byzantine empire ceased to exist. In 1461, Trebizond was run over by the Ottomans. Yet the Aq-Qoyunlu state survived for several more decades and even managed to defeat the Ottoman army in a major battle near the town of Erzincan. According to one historian, Despina Khatun herself was

Fig. 4.2 A portrait, said to be of Theodora. From a fresco in Verona by Pisanello, c. 1436–1438

present on the battlefield and egged her husband on to finish the job, chase the retreating sultan, and destroy his forces.[5]

Despina Khatun and Uzun Hasan had a daughter, Martha (also called Halima), whom they had offered in marriage to Shaykh Haydar, leader of the powerful Safavi brotherhood, a religious order named after its founder, Sāfi al-Din, Haydar's great-grandfather.[6] The brotherhood's devotees who wore red felt caps and were known as *Qizilbash* ("red heads"), combined heterodox Shi'a-leaning religious ideas with military power. Martha, who after her marriage to Haydar was given the name 'Alamshah Begum, gave birth to Ismail, the founder of the Safavid dynasty that would come to rule Iran and parts of modern Iraq, Afghanistan, and the Caucasus, from the early sixteenth until the mid-eighteenth century (Fig. 4.3).

Fig. 4.3 Stylized portrait of Ismail I by the Italian painter Cristofano dell'Altissimo (c. 1552–1568), Uffizi Gallery

---

[5] Babinger, *Mehmed the Conqueror*, 314.
[6] *Don Juan of Persia*, 107. Dale, *The Muslim Empires*, 64–68. The Safavid order (Safaviyya) was a Sufi heterodox brotherhood that combined Shia beliefs, mystical teachings, and military power. In terms of faith and ritual it was a continuation of an earlier Sufi brotherhood established by Zahed Gilani in Iran during the early thirteenth century.

Aquiline-nosed and red haired, reminiscent more of his grandmother's Greek-Roman lineage than of his father's Turkic one, Ismail believed that he was destined to rule the world. His ancestry pulled together the heritage of the greatest kingdoms of east and west: the Byzantine Empire, the ancient kingdom of Georgia, the Mongolian khanates, the Turkic Aq-Qoyunlus, and the Sufi Saint Safi al-Din (of Kurdish origin). To quote Don Juan of Persia, a secretary to the Safavid ambassador to Spain who crossed the lines and converted to Christianity: "*[T]he half of his house and blood comes, in direct descent, from that most noble Christian House of the Greek Emperors of Constantinople.*"[7] Later on, Ismail claimed to be a reincarnation of Moses, Jesus, Muhammad, and other legendary saints of yore.[8] Offering an early European assessment, the contemporary Italian diarist Marin Sanudo wrote that a new prophet had appeared in the East, a descendant of Muhammad who claimed to be "*either God himself or his anointed messenger.*"[9] In Europe, hopes of an eastern ally against the Ottoman steamroller were rekindled.[10]

TAJLU KHANUM AND THE RISE OF SAFAVID QUEENDOM[11]

Ismail based his power on Turkmen tribal leaders and on the Qizilbash emirs of the Safavid order who swore allegiance to him, but these same emirs would soon become a burden on the new empire and a threat to Safavid rule. Throughout the sixteenth century the main struggle inside the kingdom was between Shah Ismail's heirs, who pushed for a centralized state, and the Qizilbash leaders, who assisted the Safavids in the early days but then fought to preserve their power and resisted efforts at centralization.[12]

As the power of the Aq-Qoyunlu khans waned and the confederation was riven by civil war, Ismail led his militant disciples to take over its lands. Rapidly expanding his domains, he conquered the great city of Tabriz in 1501, had himself crowned shah of Iran, and set his sights on his next target, the Ottoman Empire. After several violent skirmishes, the Ottomans realized that Ismail and his Qizilbash army were not just another nuisance on the eastern border. They presented a serious challenge and would have to be dealt with.

Originally, the Ottomans were lax in terms of religion, eclectically mixing Shi'a and Sunna. But by the beginning of the sixteenth century, perhaps in reaction to the Safavids, who fought under the banner of militant Shi'a, they gradually became champions of Sunnism, and the Safavid-Ottoman conflict

---

[7] *Don Juan of Persia*, 107. See also Subrahmanyam, *Three Ways to Be Alien*, 80–81, 133.
[8] Babayan, *Aqāid al-Nisa'*, 36–37, 359.
[9] Meserve, "The Sophy," 581.
[10] Ibid, 581–584.
[11] The titles "khanum" "Khatun" and "Begum/Begam" (feminine forms of "khan" and "beg/bey") were all honorifics for women and were to a large extent interchangeable. The same lady could sometimes be referred to as Khatun and at other times as Begum.
[12] Szuppe, "Status, Knowledge, and Politics," 142.

took on an ideological hue. In 1514, Sultan Selim I, known as "the Grim," made his way to the eastern front, massacring thousands of Anatolian Qizilbash on the way, and finally facing Shah Ismail's forces on hills overlooking the plain of Chaldiran, close to Lake Van. Ismail gathered his infantry and cavalry on the opposite hills and, following custom, took his entire state bureaucracy, including his harem, with him to the battlefield.[13] The Safavids fought valiantly, but their swords, arrows, and few muskets were no match for the Ottoman artillery and the coordinated Janissary infantry. The battle was lost and the victorious Sultan Selim raided his enemy's camp, capturing Ismail's entire harem—wives, concubines, and servants. Then, as the Safavids retreated, he chased them to their capital city, Tabriz, sacked it, and sent the loot, including the harem women and the city's superb artisans, to Constantinople.

Shah Ismail, whose messianic belief in constant victory was deeply shaken, never fully recovered from the rout of his army and the loss of his womenfolk. The only piece of good news in the following days was the surprising reappearance of his beloved wife Tajlu Khanum, who was pregnant at the time. Tajlu was a princess from the Mawsillu, one of the great tribes comprising the Aq-Qoyunlu confederation. When they overran the harem, the Ottoman soldiers wounded her, but she hid and slipped away. A few days later a Safavid army officer found her wandering in the fields. Not long after her return, she gave birth to Ismail's first son, the future Shah Tahmasp. In the following years she bore Ismail another son, Bahram, and a daughter, given the name Mahin Banu, who was to govern the Safavid Empire along with her brother.[14] As Shah Ismail gradually retreated from political life, Tajlu got more involved in state affairs and set the stage for future Safavid princesses and wives to play an active governing role.[15]

At the age of two, Tajlu's son, Tahmasp, was separated from the rest of his family and sent with his wet nurse and several officials to Herat in the province of Khorasan, as nominal governor.[16] But in 1524, when he was ten years old, his father died, and he ascended the throne under the guardianship of his mother and several Qizilbash leaders. It took him six years to finally assert his authority and shake off his supervisors one by one. During that period, with power struggles between courtiers and tribal leaders spinning around him, the young shah could trust no one in the palace, not even his brothers who, as he knew well, eagerly awaited his downfall and set their sights on his throne. The only people he could rely on were his mother, Tajlu, and his younger sister, Mahin Banu, who impressed him with her perception and sharp wits even as a little girl.

---

[13] Selim I, known in Turkish as Yavuz Selim ("the stern" or "the grim"), was Sultan Suleiman's father.

[14] Roger M. Savory, Ahmet T. Karamustafa, "ESMĀ'ĪL I ṢAFAWĪ," *Encyclopaedia Iranica*, VIII/6, pp. 628–636. Szuppe, "La participation des femmes," Seconde Partie, 64.

[15] Szuppe, "Status, Knowledge, and Politics," 145.

[16] Welch, "Two Shahs," 10.

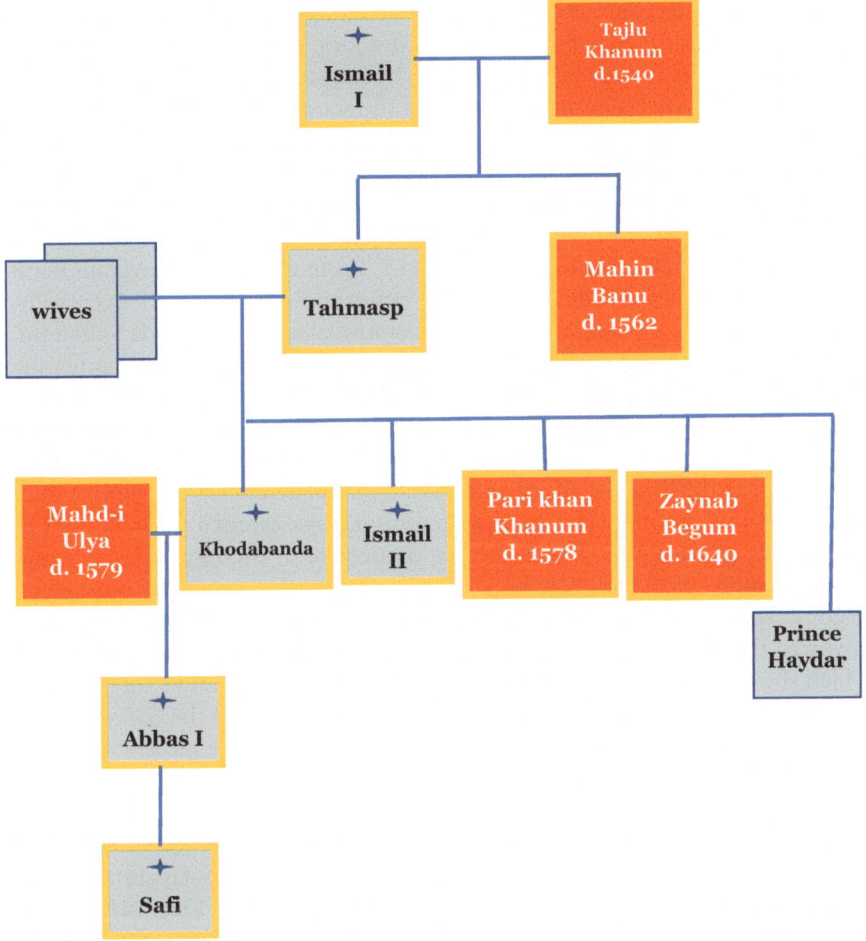

Lineage from Tajlu Khanum to Zaynab Begum. Only names relevant to the narrative are mentioned

In the early years of Tahmasp's autonomous rule, Tajlu still served as a close advisor. She became even more powerful and, as Maria Szuppe writes, "*dominated the political scene.*"[17] In 1534, she helped her son protect the kingdom against an Ottoman invasion by corresponding with the Safavid governor of Baghdad and guiding him through negotiations with the Ottoman commander. She thus cut short the escalating war that the young shah seemed destined to lose. Meanwhile, she amassed land and other property and

---

[17] Szuppe, "La participation des femmes," Seconde Partie, 72. See also Szuppe, "Status, Knowledge, and Politics," 156.

established several religious endowments, including a famous one dedicated to the sainted Fatima al-Ma'suma in the city of Qom.[18]

However, several years later, frustrated by her son's growing independence and by what she saw as mismanagement of the state, Tajlu colluded with other powerful men of the state to oust him and crown her other son, Bahram. The Venetian traveler and businessman Michele Membré, who was visiting Iran at the time, heard that she intended to poison Tahmasp and that the shah discovered the plot and accused his mother of treason. In 1540, he banished her to Shiraz and confiscated her numerous assets.[19] From that point on Mahin Banu replaced her mother as Tahmasp's closest companion, advisor, and, eventually, co-ruler.[20] Henceforth she was known by her formal name, Shahzada Sultanum.

Although Tajlu was banished, during her thirty years in the Safavid court she was the main inspiration for a woman-dominated model of government. The system most readily available to the Safavids was the Turko-Mongol one manifested in the Ilkhanid state, a dynasty harking back to Genghis Khan that ruled Iran from the thirteenth century and was later emulated in Aq-Qoyunlu courts as well. In this recent Turko-Mongol tradition, royal women were entitled to part of the spoils of war, had a right to participate in the *quriltay*, the grand tribal assembly, mixed freely in society and could, under certain circumstances, become sovereigns. In the early fifteenth century, for example, a Castilian envoy to the Timurid court was entertained at a feast hosted by a princess, in which she and her ladies sat with other men and women, eating and drinking wine with them.[21] This tradition endured until the time of the Safavids. The most recent Aq-Qoyunlu queen of pre-Safavid times, whose memory was still alive, was Saljuq-Shah Begum, mother of Ismail's paternal uncle. She played a major part in state politics.[22]

But while empowering women to take an active part in government was a distinct option, there were also other models that the young Safavid state could have opted for, including the more entrenched slave-based Ottoman one, in which women's involvement in politics was curtailed until the early sixteenth century. Tajlu Khanum's active role was an essential precedent in opting for the Mongol-based model that encouraged active participation of women.

The idea of female participation in government received support from a wider cultural movement in Iran. In the mid-sixteenth century a famous author known as Fakhrī of Herat wrote a book called *The Jewels of Wonder* (*Javāhir al-Ajāyib*), which included biographies of twenty great women in pre-Safavid days. The protagonists were upper-class women, and the ostensible reason for offering their life stories was that they wrote poetry, but the book also described their extensive education and their active participation in cultural and social

---

[18] See Szuppe, "Status, Knowledge, and Politics," 152. Fatima al-Ma'suma ("the innocent" or "the infallible") was the daughter of Musa al-Kadhim, the seventh Shia imam.
[19] Membré, *Mission to the Lord Sophy of Persia (1539–1542)*, 31. Zarinebaf-Shahr, "Economic Activities," 248–249.
[20] Szuppe, "Status, Knowledge, and Politics," 149, 156.
[21] Ibid, 141. See also Szuppe, "La participation des femmes," 105.
[22] Szuppe, "Status, Knowledge and Politics," 142.

life. Just like Christine de Pizan's *City of Ladies* in western Europe (described in Chap. 6), Fakhrī of Herat's book provided an intellectual rationalization for women's role in government during the sixteenth century.[23] Taken together with the crucial roles performed by Tajlu Khanum and other Qizilbash ladies of the early days, these literary contributions make clear why, by the mid-sixteenth century, as Kathryn Babayan suggests, there was no longer any need to apologize for the active role that women played in the realm.[24]

During the first century of Safavid rule, royal women were often visible in the public arena. In an article comparing the royal palaces of the Ottomans, the Safavids, and the Mughals, Gülrü Necipoğlu points out that the structure of the Safavid palace was more akin to French ones than to those of the Ottomans. Whereas the Ottoman sultanic family manifested its power by keeping its distance from public view, usually ensconced within three increasingly private courtyards in the Topkapı palace, the Safavid shah, like the French king, "*manifested his royal power through constant visibility, spectacle, and display.*"[25] Among other reasons, this had to do with the shah being head of a Sufi order and expected to lead his adherents. Even as late as the early seventeenth century sources describe Shah Abbas "the Great" strolling through the city, tasting street food, and chatting with random people. Abbas's palace in Isfahan was built as a set of open courts, pavilions, and gardens, reflecting Timurid and Mongol practices. Some of the courtyards were reserved for private assemblies, and some were more accessible to the public. The palace grounds merged almost seamlessly with major squares and boulevards in the city. In its more secluded gardens, men and women would assemble together. As in Louis XIV's Versailles, the grounds on the connecting boulevard were inhabited by princes, amirs, and other notables of the state who erected their own houses close to their sovereign's palace.[26]

Mahin Banu/Shahzada Sultanum

Mahin Banu, Tajlu and Ismail's daughter, received the best education that the age could offer, and was taught religion, law, languages, arts, and sciences. One of her teachers was the famous painter and calligrapher Dost Muhammad, and soon the talented girl produced fine works of penmanship and art, some of which have survived to the present day. She also memorized and could recite entire Quran verses verbatim, a skill usually mastered by religious scholars. Later on, she used her knowledge of the Quran and the Hadith to make clear to members of the clergy that she could argue with them as an equal even about issues concerning law and religion.[27]

---

[23] On Christine de Pizan see Chap. 6.
[24] Szuppe, "The Jewels of Wonder," 326–327. Babayan, *Aqāid al-Nisa'*, 351.
[25] Necipoğlu, "Framing the Gaze," 306.
[26] Necipoğlu, "Framing the Gaze," 306–312.
[27] Szuppe, "The Jewels of Wonder," 329–330. Szuppe, "Status, Knowledge, and Politics," 150. Birjandifar, "Royal Women and Politics," 34. Nazari, "Influence of Safavid Women," 7. Babayan, *Aqāid al-Nisa'*, 367.

Like Hurrem Sultan in the Ottoman Empire and Anne of France in the French court, Mahin's tenure as co-shah set the legal basis for queendom in the Safavid Empire and formally established the position.[28] With her education and quick intelligence, watching her mother's example in the early years, she needed little preparation for her role as the kingdom's mainstay.[29] Tahmasp soon became so dependent on his sister that she was asked to accompany him everywhere. Using his prerogative as shah, he refused to let her marry and instead forced her to stay single by "betrothing" her to the twelfth Imam, Muhammad al-Mahdi, who is in occultation according to Shia tradition, and will return to save the world at the end of days. There was even malicious gossip that Tahmasp and his sister Mahin—now given the royal name Shahzada Sultanum—had an incestuous relationship.[30] According to one unverifiable story, when she was eighteen, Tahmasp had a young man burned at the stake for openly courting her.[31]

The shah needed her to advise him and approve each of his decisions. "*Since she was a learned, wise woman,*" wrote a contemporary Iranian chronicler, "*all the financial and administrative affairs of the state were carried out according to her advice and the shah would not do anything without consulting her and without her knowledge.*"[32] He lavished money, land, and properties on her, much of which she devoted to charitable endowments. She particularly favored the shrine of Ali Reza, the scholarly eighth Imam of Shia Islam, in the town of Mashhad. She constantly funded the renovation of the shrine, which by that time became the holiest site of visitation in Iran, and added to it until it became the largest and most elaborately decorated mosque in the world. She made sure that her protégé, Prince Sultan Ibrahim, would be appointed governor of the province. The princess was also an avid collector of artwork, mainly porcelains, which she later bequeathed to her favorite endowments (Fig. 4.4).[33]

To remove any doubts about her standing in court, Tahmasp formally appointed her to be his main intendant (*Ishiq aqasi*).[34] Since she had to be around him at all times, she and her ladies-in-waiting took up horse riding and hunting and accompanied him on trips and campaigns. Their horsemanship

---

[28] For Hurrem Sultan see Chap. 1, for Anne of Beaujeu see Chap. 5.

[29] Dale, *The Muslim Empires*, 69, 88–91. Nazari, "Influence of Safavid Women," 15. Szuppe, "The Jewels of Wonder," 332. Szuppe, "Status, Knowledge, and Politics," 156.

[30] Membré, *Mission to the Lord Sophy of Persia (1539–1542)*, 80–81. Nazari, "Influence of Safavid Women," 6. See also Szuppe, "Status, Knowledge, and Politics," 144.

[31] Welch, "Two Shahs," 12. Mathee, "Safavid Empire," *Encyclopaedia Iranica*. It is interesting to note that while Tahmasp dedicated his sister to the twelfth Imam, he led the shift from the charismatic rule of Shah Ismail to a more routinized charisma, in which the shah himself was to be the earthly replacement of the Hidden Imam.

[32] Quoted in Birjandifar, "Royal Women and Politics," 45. See also Membré, *Mission to the Lord Sophy of Persia (1539–1542)*, 80–81.

[33] Szuppe, "Status, Knowledge, and Politics," 152. Szuppe, "La participation des femmes," Seconde Partie, 77. Beck and Nashat, *Women in Iran*, 152. Sotheby's Catalogue.

[34] Szuppe, "La participation des femmes," Seconde Partie, 67. The *ishiq aqasi*, formally *ishiq aqasi bashi-e divan*, was the senior adviser of the shah, held major political and economic power and was part of the divan. See Roger Savory, *Encyclopaedia Iranica*, "EŠĪK-ĀQĀSĪ-BĀŠĪ".

Fig. 4.4 Shrine of Ali Reza, Mashhad. Photo by Mostafameraji, 2017

was described by the traveler Michele Membré, who glimpsed Shahzada Sultanum on an outing with other ladies, and assumed it was a regular feature of the Safavid court:

> "*After more than half of the urdū [army] has gone by, the Shah's maidens pass on fine horses; and they ride like men and dress like men, except that on their heads they do not wear caps but white kerchiefs ... And I have seen that there were about 14–15 of those maidens, and they were beautiful, though their faces could not be fully seen. But what could be seen was beautiful and very fair. And sometimes they galloped and performed marvels with their horses, making them jump and do many other skillful tricks.*"[35]

Shahzada Sultanum and Hamida Banu Begum

In 1543, pursued by his enemies and deserted by his lieutenants, the Mughal Emperor Humayun had to flee from India with a tiny retinue. While staying in Sindh (today's Pakistan) he fell in love with the young Hamida, whose story was told in the previous chapter, and married her. Right after the wedding Humayun was informed that his own brothers had joined the forces and arrayed against

---

[35] Membré, *Mission to the Lord Sophy of Persia (1539–1542)*, 25, 31; See also Szuppe, "Status, Knowledge, and Politics, "142.

Fig. 4.5 Detail of a later-era wall painting describing the reception given by a sword bearing Shah Tahmasp (right) to the Mughal Emperor Humayun, seen here in a pose of supplication. Muhammad Mahdi Karim, dated to 1646–7, Chehel Sutun Palace, Isfahan. Photo: Muhammad Mahdi Karim

him, and had to keep running with his small entourage. Hamida's son, Akbar, born on the road two years later, was entrusted to the care of one of Humayun's relatives, and the band kept running. After a long and arduous journey, they crossed the border into the Safavid Empire and were warmly received by the Shah who had sent his three brothers, Princes Alqās, Bahrām, and Sām, to welcome the Mughal emperor and his retinue. Then, after a lengthy tour of the country, Humayun and Hamida were invited to spend time and hunt with the shah and his sister as their guests of honor. Tahmasp and Sultanum believed that in view of the rapid disintegration of the recently founded Mughal Empire, supporting the crowned emperor and helping him get back in the saddle would be a wise move. With the constant threat of Ottoman invasion from the west, it made good sense to have a strong ally on the eastern flank (Fig. 4.5).

In the *Humayun-name*, her detailed biography of her brother, Humayun's sister Gulbadan Begum devotes a chapter to this escapade, details of which she had heard mainly from her old friend Hamida: "*Shahzadeh Sultanum, the Shah's sister, used to ride on horseback, and take her stand behind her brother.*" Returning to his quarters one day, Humayun said, "*There was a woman riding behind the Shah at the hunt … People told me it was Shahzada Sultanum, the Shah's sister.*"[36]

---

[36] Gulbadan Begum, *History of Humayun*, 169–170. See also Zaman, "Instructive Memory," 689. Beck and Nashat, *Women in Iran*, 151.

Soon Shahzada Sultanum and Hamida Begum became close friends, spending much of their time in each other's company. Though only twenty-five years old, Sultanum was already an experienced stateswoman, used to meeting dignitaries and versed in the diplomatic etiquette of the time. Hamida, on the other hand, eight years younger, had no such experience. Here is an imaginary description of the first private meeting between the two:

> *It was early evening and Shahzada Sultanum was seated cross-legged on a dais inside the royal pavilion overlooking the pool. The light of the torches swayed in the breeze and was reflected in the water's ripples. Her latest work of art, a stylized Quranic calligraphy verse, lay half-finished beside her.*
>
> *Hamida, ushered in by the servants, wore a long silken dress and the wedding jewels she was given by Humayun. Her face, lit by the candles, was flushed and excited. She carried her head high as befits a royal wife but still seemed awed by the royal spectacle. The Safavid princess invited Hamida to sit and asked if she could take a closer look at her ruby necklace. Hamida immediately offered it as a gift, but Shahzada Sultanum adamantly refused. "I have too many jewels as it is," she laughed, "but this one is beautiful. Where did you get it?"*
>
> *Hamida then told her the story of her meeting with Humayun at his brother's court in Sindh, of his marriage proposal, and of her initial refusal to marry him. "I did not wish to marry a king who would always be distant and preoccupied", she said. "I hoped to marry someone who would be able to joke and laugh with me over the rice pilaf..." She left the sentence unfinished, but Sultanum had already heard the rumors and knew she was talking about Humayun's handsome younger brother, Hindal. "But you know kings" Hamida smiled modestly. "They get their way. Humayun kept insisting, sending me emissaries and presents, and I finally surrendered."*
>
> *The young woman was so candid and honest that Shahzada laughed out loud. The two then settled more comfortably, the servants brought figs and pomegranates, and Hamida recounted the hardships of their escape from India. "The padshah was betrayed by his closest allies, who made a pact with his enemies, and had to abandon the throne which was rightfully bequeathed to him by his father. We were married in Punjab and our son, Jalal ud-din Akbar, was born a year later. Then, to our surprise, my husband's treacherous brother, Kamran, also allied himself with his enemies and rose up against him. We had to keep running. But by the time we reached the mountain passes the weather was so cold that I couldn't risk taking the baby with us. I miss him so much," he eyes teared up, "but it had to be done".*
>
> *Her descriptions were so vivid and her analysis so intelligent that Shahzada suddenly realized: Hamida, not her husband Humayun, is the one that she and Tahmasp should depend on to secure their eastern front. Humayun may be the scion of an illustrious dynasty, and perhaps divinely ordained to rule, but he was also a pleasure seeker, too fond of opium, wine, and women to have the resolve needed to retake and govern his kingdom. Here was a woman who understood dedication and commitment, could think independently, and was prepared to carry the weight of the mission on her delicate shoulders. She vowed to help her.*

In the coming months the two couples—Tahmasp, Sultanum, Humayun, and Hamida—enjoyed hunting expeditions and picnics in tents pitched in the countryside, along with other men and women of the Safavid elite.[37] It was during one of those outings that the shahzada enlisted her other brother, Bahram, to help her, and together they convinced Tahmasp to assist Humayun in his quest to reconquer Hindustan.[38] Initially reluctant to offer his cavalry to a neighboring ruler, and a Sunni infidel at that, he was finally brought around by his sister.[39]

At the head of these well-trained troops, Hamida and Humayun returned to Kandahar, where Hamida was reunited with her young son, and later succeeded in defeating the rebellious brothers, and reestablishing the Mughal Empire in northern India. The Safavid's eastern front was now secure.[40]

Shahzada and Hurrem

While the Mughal couple was entertained at court, the Safavids were once more at war with the Ottomans, and both sides made use of their preferred tactics. The massive, disciplined Ottoman army sought victory on the battlefield, and the smaller and lighter Safavid troops, based on tribal cavalry and defending their home territory, relied on speed, shorter supply routes, tactical surprise, and scorched earth tactics. They tried to avoid open battle and attack where least expected. War waxed and waned for more than a decade until Tahmasp's brother, Alqas Mirza, rebelled against him and took refuge in Istanbul under the auspices of his archenemy, Sultan Suleiman.[41] Planning to overthrow his brother and take his place, Alqas Mirza promised Suleiman that he could raise a Qizilbash army in eastern Anatolia and lead it in battle against the reigning shah.[42] The Ottomans, hoping to finally get rid of Shah Tahmasp, install a Safavid prince who would do their bidding, and secure their eastern flank, declared war once again in 1548. Alqas was accompanied to the border by an army under the grand vizier Rustem Pasha and then sent forward with a small contingent to raise his own army. But he failed to deliver and was soon surrounded, along with a small group of loyalists, by his brother's forces. Finally, Tahmasp sent one of his father's wives, Khan-Begi Khanum, to negotiate with Alqas, and the rebel prince agreed to surrender in return for a promise of safe conduct and Tahmasp's solemn oath that he would not harm him in any way.

---

[37] Gulbadan Begum, *History of Humayun*, 170–171.
[38] Szuppe, "La participation des Femmes, Seconde partie," 77. Birjandifar, "Royal Women and Politics," 45. Zia-ud-Din, "Persians Serving Babur," 126.
[39] Birjandifar, "Royal Women and Politics", 45. Zia-ud-Din, "Persians Serving Babur," 127. Szuppe, "Status, Knowledge, and Politics," 156. Szuppe, "La participation des femmes," Seconde Partie, 77.
[40] The full story of Hamida and Humayun's Safavid sojourn is told in Chap. 3.
[41] This round of Ottoman-Safavid war began in 1532.
[42] For a more detailed description of Alqas Mirza's stay in Istanbul, the last bouts of Safavid-Ottoman war, and the signing of the peace treaty of Amasya, see Chap. 2 ("The Ottomans"). Peirce, *Empress of the East*, 254.

Following his surrender, Alqas Mirza was brought to the palace to discuss the future of their relationship. Shahzada Sultanum and Tahmasp finally concluded that the rebel prince was still contemplating disobedience and would always pose a threat to the stability of the dynasty. Bound by his promise not to harm his brother, Tahmasp asked his sister to give the order for his arrest and send him to Qahqaha, a prison castle in the north. A few months later, Alqas's dead body was found at the foot of the prison walls, probably pushed to his death on Tahmasp's or Sultanum's orders.[43]

It took yet another costly war in the early 1550s for Shahzada Sultanum and Hurrem, her Ottoman counterpart, to realize that the two Muslim empires were locked in a pointless cycle of conflict and that they must settle the dispute between them. On both sides the women co-rulers were deeply involved in moving the diplomacy forward and brokering the treaty, and in 1555 a peace agreement was finally signed in the city of Amasya. During and after the treaty, Shahzada Sultanum and Hurrem Sultan established an amiable stream of correspondence. Both had seen their states ravaged by war and wanted to make sure that the hard-won peace would not fail. Thus, as the inauguration of the great Suleimaniye mosque, of which the Ottoman sultan was very proud, approached, Shahzada sent Hurrem a letter of good intent complimenting her for her contribution to the peace agreement. Modestly omitting her own substantial contribution to the Amasya Treaty, she informed Hurrem that she was sending illuminated Quranic manuscripts and carpets handwoven by royal artisans for the new mosque and added that the people of Iran all prayed for the sultan and the success of his reign.[44]

In view of the enmity between the Shiite Safavids and the Sunni Ottomans, which in many ways resembled the ideological struggle that emerged at the same time between Catholics and Protestants in Europe, Shiites sending carpets and Qurans to adorn the greatest mosque of the Sunni world—and the Ottomans graciously accepting them—was not a run-of-the-mill royal exchange of gifts. It was an unprecedented gesture of religious reconciliation and an attempt at moderation, akin to what Catherine de Medici and Elizabeth Tudor tried to do a few years later in Europe (see Chaps. 6 and 7).

The treaty signed in Amasya guaranteed the peace between the two states for decades.[45] After Hurrem's death in 1558, Shahzada kept sustaining the

[43] C. Fleischer, "Alqās Mirza." *Encyclopaedia Iranica*, I/9, pp. 907–909 (https://iranicaonline.org/articles/alqas-alqasb-alqas-mirza-safawi). See also Mitchell, "Provincial Chancelleries," 487.

[44] Peirce, *Empress of the East*, 295. Peirce, *The Imperial Harem*, 221–222. Szuppe, "Status, Knowledge, and Politics," 154. Szuppe, "La participation des femmes," Seconde Partie, 62. Birjandifar, "Royal Women and Politics," 33, 43–45. Special thanks to Kathryn Babayan.

[45] In one of his books, the famous Ottoman traveler and diarist Evliya Çelebi mentions another, probably apocryphal, legend in this context. When he heard that the construction of Suleiman's great mosque was behind schedule, Tahmasp sent Suleiman a bag of diamonds, rubies, and other gems, ridiculing the sultan by offering financial help. Suleiman, enraged by what he saw as a gesture of charity toward a poorer relative, ordered the gems to be cut and buried in the masonry of one of the mosque's minarets. Since then, Istanbulites claim around that minaret, the gems sparkle in the sun.

peace by exchanging letters with her daughter, Mihrimah, who had taken her mother's place at Suleiman's side.[46] She continued to govern the Safavid state alongside her brother and, since she had no children of her own, oversaw the schooling of her young nieces in the harem, making sure to raise them as accomplished women, on a par in terms of education and experience with any of the kingdom's leading men.

On her deathbed, she bequeathed some of her vast estates to the royal princesses. Other properties, including collections of calligraphy and ceramics were donated to various religious endowments around the country and to some of her closest friends and advisors.[47] She died in 1562, fourteen years before her brother, and asked to be buried in the holy city of Karbala, where Husayn ibn Ali, founder of the Shia, was slain.[48] Two of her nieces—Parikhan Khanum and Zaynab Begum—were to become *de facto* rulers of Iran and played a major role in Safavid politics from the mid-sixteenth to the early seventeenth century.

PARIKHAN KHANUM

Tahmasp's daughter, Parikhan, or Pari Khan, Khanum (not to be confused with Tahmasp's sister of the same name) would become the first woman to formally govern the Safavid Empire as a sovereign queen.[49] Born in 1548 to Tahmasp's Circassian wife, Sultan Aga Khanum, she soon proved herself the brightest and most perceptive of the shah's children and became the apple of her father's eye.[50] From an early age she looked up to her aunt, Shahzada Sultanum, admired the way she governed the empire, and dreamed of following in her footsteps.[51] Like her aunt, she showed an aptitude for learning. Her father appointed a senior courtier, Afshar Khan, to be in charge of her upbringing and summoned the country's best teachers in science, jurisprudence, and literature to the palace, and she proved herself an avid and hard-working pupil.[52] She soon started composing her own poetry under the pen name *Haqīqī* ("the true one") and loved to spend time in the company of other poets, taking part in their contests and enjoying their sycophantic verses of praise.[53] One of her favorites, the poet Kashani, wrote a *qasida* enumerating her virtues:

---

[46] Beck and Nashat, *Women in Iran*, 154.

[47] Birjandifar, *Royal Women and Politics*, 39. Szuppe, "Status, Knowledge, and Politics," 152.

[48] Szuppe, "La participation des femmes," Seconde Partie, 67.

[49] Pari Khan, meaning "Fairy Queen," was a common name under the Safavids. See *Don Juan of Persia*, 129. Szuppe, "Status, Knowledge, and Politics," 146–147.

[50] Birjandifar, "Royal Women and Politics," 50–51. Golsorkhi, "Parikhan Khanum," 145.

[51] Szuppe, "The Jewels of Wonder," 332. Szuppe, "Status, Knowledge, and Politics," 156–157. Szuppe, "La participation des femmes," Seconde Partie, 77. Birjandifar, "Royal Women and Politics," 51–52.

[52] Like all Safavid princes and princesses, she was appointed a *lala*, guardian and mentor, in charge of their education and recreation. Szuppe, "Status, Knowledge, and Politics," 149.

[53] Golsorkhi, "Parikhan Khanum," 146–147. Birjandifar, "Royal Women and Politics," 35, 50–51.

The princess of all time and of the earth, the sun of the world
Who is as illuminating as Venus and as concealing as Maryam
Parī Khān who is the king of the angels and of mankind
Even Bilqays [the Queen of Sheba] learned kingship from her.[54]

And another:

Parikhan, whose command extends to the fourth throne of heaven. Worshipped on land and sea, her threshold is worn smooth, so often have khans and sultans politely touched their heads down upon it. Last night, a thousand kings of royal demeanour, came to touch the saddle cover of the least rider in her retinue.[55]

Fascinated by palace politics, she realized, like contemporary royal women in other countries, that to gain political clout, she needed to build a power base in society. The best way to increase her popularity was to contribute to public charity. She thus became known as a benefactress of "the poor and needy" and persuaded her father to contribute more to such causes.[56]

Before she was ten, Tahmasp and Shahzada had already promised her hand in marriage to her cousin Badi' al-Zaman, son of Tahmasp's deceased brother Bahram. The young man was recently appointed governor of Sistan in the south of the country, and the two were betrothed or maybe even officially married, but Tahmasp had no intention of letting his daughter join her husband. She was too valuable as a consultant, so she never left the capital, Qazvin, and the marriage was not consummated.[57] But one advantage her new status did afford her was some freedom of movement and a grand house of her own outside the palace. She kept a team of advisers, guards, and servants, which enabled her to act as an independent woman, allocate her money as she saw fit, and elevate her supporters, including her maternal uncle, Shamkhal Khan, who oversaw her protection detail, to senior military and governmental positions.[58]

Even when she was a young girl, her father enjoyed her wit and humor. But after Shahzada Sultanum passed away in 1562, the bereaved shah felt an acute need for someone like her to consult with. The fourteen-year-old Parikhan became her father's closest adviser, and although she was still a teenager, Tahmasp appointed her his lieutenant (*Sahib al-amr*). She took over all of her aunt's state responsibilities.[59] One contemporary chronicler, Natanzī, described

---

[54] Translated by Birjandifar, "Royal Women and Politics," 53. The third verse is a play on her name. Pari Khan means queen of the fairies. (Farsi is an ungendered language, so "khan" could be translated as king or queen).

[55] Translated by Paul Losensky, "Selections from the Poetry of Muhtasham Kashani," in Hani Khapipour (ed.), *The Empires of the Near East and India*, p. 411.

[56] Golsorkhi, "Parikhan Khanum," 147.

[57] Ibid, 146. Birjandifar, "Royal Women and Politics," 54.

[58] Szuppe, "Status, Knowledge, and Politics," 142, 143.

[59] Szuppe, "La participation des femmes," Seconde Partie, 78.

the connection between Tahmasp and his daughter at the time, claiming that even at that early date, she was the actual decider:

> *In spite of the presence of talented, worthy young princes and princesses ... the shah would act according to her advice and approbation in affairs minor and major, financial and administrative. All the important affairs of the shah, from politics and international relations to the rules and customs of monarchy, were carried out according to that wise and just queen's opinion and recommendation, and nothing was done without her knowledge and consent.*[60]

We do not have actual copies of letters that she exchanged with foreign kings and queens, yet it is clear from her own evidence that she was in charge of the kingdom's foreign relations. Her responsibilities included sending ambassadors to the empire's neighbors and receiving all emissaries from foreign lands to prepare them for work meetings with the government. In a famous letter she sent to her brother Ismail years later, under circumstances that will be discussed subsequently, she described some of her duties as co-shah: "*Not one of the ladies from the harems of the previous kings had the privilege of sending ambassadors to other kings ... [but] four of my ambassadors went to Anatolia, and every ambassador that was sent to the shah was received at my residences.*" From this circumstantial evidence we may conclude with almost absolute certainty that like her aunt, Shahzada Sultanum, she exchanged letters and gifts with Mihrimah Sultan and Nurbanu Sultan in Istanbul during the 1560s and 1570s.

Of Shah Tahmasp's reliance on her advice she writes: "*The only place that he was sure of was by my side. No other princess had this privilege, and my brothers also listened to me and welcomed my advice with an open heart.*"[61] It would make sense to assume that even when letters to foreign dignitaries were officially signed by the shah, it was Parikhan who dictated them and applied his seal (Fig. 4.6).

In 1574, Tahmasp fell seriously ill and was bedridden for almost two years. As his health deteriorated, tensions grew between the supporters of his son Ismail, who was suspected of treason and had spent the last twenty years imprisoned at Qahqaha castle, and his other son, Haydar, who resided close to the palace and was better positioned to replace his father. The rivalry between Ismail and Haydar was not just a personal one. Ismail was the champion of a Turkmen Qizilbash group of tribal leaders who saw him as an ally and linked their fortunes to his. Haydar, whose mother was Georgian, was backed by a small but powerful regiment of Georgian troops and by notables threatened by the Qizilbash. The third son, their older brother Muhammad Mirza Khodabanda,

---

[60] Quoted in Birjandifar, "Royal Women and Politics," 51. See also Babayan, *Aqāid al-Nisa'*, 353. Beck and Nashat, *Women in Iran*, 157. See also Manuchehr Parsadust, "Parikān Kānom," *Encyclopaedia Iranica*, https://iranicaonline.org/articles/parikan-kanom-1548-1578.

[61] Parikhan Khanum's letter to Ismail, in Birjandifar, "Royal Women and Politics," 103.

Fig. 4.6 Safavid princess, probably Parikhan, sixteenth century Persian miniature by Muhammadi

who was governor of Shiraz at the time, was almost blind and therefore not perceived as a serious candidate.[62]

Worried that Ismail's supporters might help him break out of prison and make a run for the crown, Haydar sent a secret letter from the palace to the master of Qahqaha castle and asked him to kill Ismail. But Parikhan, whose spies uncovered the plot, informed her father about it, and the ailing shah, who still cared about his imprisoned son, immediately sent a troop of loyal soldiers to ensure his safety. After this incident Tahmasp no longer trusted Haydar and passed on all his responsibilities to his beloved daughter.[63]

With Tahmasp incapacitated, Parikhan became acting shah, increasingly recognized by the courtiers as sovereign and making decisions on her own. She allied herself with Mirza Salman Jaberi, the shah's main minister, who now became *her* top adviser. Knowing the family intimately, Mirza Salman believed that Parikhan would be the best option in the Safavid family to replace Shah Tahmasp and supported her plans.[64] But although Tahmasp was on the brink of death and aware of the tensions at court, he refused to designate a formal

---

[62] Szuppe, "La participation des femmes," Seconde Partie, 79.
[63] Manuchehr Parsadust, "Parikān Kānom."
[64] Szuppe, "La participation des femmes," Seconde Partie, 65.

heir. Perhaps he realized that the Safavid elite was not ready to accept a female monarch. But believing that Parikhan would be the best choice for the dynasty, he hoped that, once he'd gone, she would find a way to nominate a male figurehead and keep pulling the strings behind the curtains. Parikhan may have also harbored such hopes but knew that it would be near impossible with three male sons vying for control. She finally concluded that a "real" shah should be appointed and vowed to assist the one finally chosen as best she could.[65]

When it became clear that the Shah was about to die, Parikhan had to decide which of the brothers to support. She opted for the imprisoned Ismail over the cocky self-assured Haydar. Perhaps she knew Haydar well, despised him, and believed that Ismail would make a better shah, or maybe she concluded that Ismail's Qizilbash supporters, who were closer to her own Circassian faction, would be the safer bet. She certainly believed that the ambitious Haydar, with his strong-willed mother and his Georgian clan, would prove a more dangerous rival once installed on the throne, and hoped that Ismail's gratitude for her help in releasing him from prison and crowning him, as well as his need for guidance in affairs of state, would enable her to maintain her influence at court. Little did she know.[66]

The Year of the Four Shahs

In May 1576, Tahmasp died, and Haydar began to prepare his own coronation inside the palace. He took the shah's crown and wore it and presented a letter signed and sealed by his father to the congregated members of the royal council as proof of his right of succession. Although it could not be proven, many believed that the letter was either a fake or signed under duress.[67] Rightly suspecting that his sister knew the truth and would oppose him, he threatened to kill or imprison her, but Parikhan appeased him with a promise of loyalty. "*Women are foolish creatures,*" she claimed according to one source. "*If, in my stupidity and short-sightedness, I have been guilty of any misdemeanor, I beg you to pardon me and spare my life. In that event, I will follow the path of obedience to you and will not deviate by so much as a hair's breadth from the course of conduct which is pleasing to your highness.*" She prostrated herself, kissed Haydar's feet, promised to assist him in conducting government business, and begged permission to leave the palace to bring his followers to the coronation. Reassured by her words, Haydar granted her permission to leave. But as soon as she was out of the gate, she gave the keys to her Uncle Shamkhal Khan and to a unit of Ismail's supporters, who on that day happened to be on guard duty around the palace walls. As they rushed into the palace, swords drawn, Haydar

---

[65] Babayan, *Aqāid al-Nisa'*, 352–353.
[66] Birjandifar, "Royal Women and Politics," 43, 56–61.
[67] Szuppe, "Status, Knowledge, and Politics," 149. *Don Juan of Persia* (pp. 130–131) tells a different story. According to him, Parikhan Khanum pretended to encourage Haydar to take the throne.

realized he was doomed. He took refuge in the harem and then tried to make his way out disguised as a woman, but his pursuers identified and killed him.[68]

After his death, Parikhan took over once again. She soon sent a contingent of soldiers to Qahqaha castle to inform Ismail of his brother's death and authorized the warden to release him and bring him to the palace to be crowned. But Ismail was in no hurry. It took him three weeks to arrive in the capital Qazvin, and even after his arrival he stayed outside the city for almost a month, basking in his newly gained freedom and waiting for his astrologer to decide on the most auspicious hour for his coronation. In the interim, Parikhan continued to run things. She convened the council at her house every day and took care of current affairs. To demonstrate that she was the actual sovereign, she increased the number of guards and chamberlains in her mansion and, knowing that as a woman she had to take extra care to make her status known to the public, instructed them to act in a special ceremonial way when accompanying her to the palace.[69] "*[T]hey arranged for more majestic rituals ... and ceremony ... and pomp ... than during the days of Shah Tahmasp.*"[70]

But after twenty years in prison, Ismail had no intention of letting anyone, let alone his baby sister, dictate anything. "*The meddling of women in the affairs of government,*" he declared, "*is not deserving of the kingdom's honor.*"[71] Probably following the advice of his new vizier, Mirza Salman Jaberi, who knew exactly when to shift his allegiance from Parikhan to Ismail, as soon as he ascended the throne he had Parikhan confined to her house, ordered all state officials to stop visiting her, confiscated most of her property, and, adding insult to injury, spread rumors about her infidelity to her husband.[72] A few weeks later, unsure of his hold on government, he executed dozens of his

---

[68] Golsorkhi, "Parikhan Khanum," 148–149. Birjandifar, "Royal Women and Politics," 43, 61–62. Manuchehr Parsadust, "Parikān Kānom." Szuppe, "La participation des femmes," Seconde Partie, 81. Olearius adds some details about the event: "*Eider [Haydar], who was but seventeen years of age, was so impatient to get into the throne, that he had the insolence to put the Crown on his head, and present himself, in that posture, before his Father, who was then near his death; and desirous to make his advantage of Ismael's absence and Mahomet [Khodabanda]'s refusal, made use of the interest which Periaconcona [Parikhan Khanum], his sister, had with the Grandees, to mount the Throne. The Princess, who had declar'd for the interest of the elder Brethren, considering with herself, that in their absence, Eider might commit such violences as might prevent her securing the Crown for Ismael, thought it not safe openly to oppose the pretensions of the younger Brother, but suffer'd him to assume the title of King, and he was acknowledg'd as such all over the Palace. But She had all the Avenues so well Guarded that it was impossible for Eider's friends to carry any tidings of it to the City. So that the young prince coming to distrust his sister's carriage, and apprehending it might be their design to sacrifice him to his Brother's ambition, conceal'd himself among the women, till such time as Schamal [Shamkhal], a Georgian, his uncle by the Mother-side, found him out and cut off his head.*" Olearius, *Voyages and Travells*, 257.

[69] Birjandifar, "Royal Women and Politics," 64–65. Babayan, *Aqāid al-Nisa'*, 353–355.

[70] The chronicler Iskandar Beg, as quoted in Babayan, *Aqāid al-Nisa'*, 354.

[71] The chronicler Munshī, as quoted in Birjandifar, "Royal Women and Politics," 64. See also Babayan, *Aqāid al-Nisa'*, 354.

[72] Golsorkhi, "Parikhan Khanum," 149–150. Babayan, *Aqāid al-Nisa'*, 353. Szuppe, "La participation des femmes," Seconde Partie, 84.

closest relatives and court officials, including most of the surviving Safavid princes. The only ones spared were his own baby son, Prince Shuja', his older full brother, Muhammad Mirza Khodabanda, who seemed helplessly blind, and the princesses whom he saw as too weak to present a threat.[73]

Scandalized by his cruelty, Parikhan wrote Ismail a long and angry letter. She said she had already donned her burial shroud (meaning she was mentally prepared to die) and castigated him for murdering his brothers and nephews. She denied all gossip indicating that she had conspired against him and claimed that she never had any intention of taking over. She also reminded Ismail that it was she who had him released from prison and brought to Qazvin. "*Women never wanted to rule,*" she wrote, "*and if I had wanted to, then when I was in charge, I would have chosen one of the princes whose mouth still smelled of milk, and I would have ruled without any problems.*"[74]

Perhaps misled by his own contempt for womankind, Ismail decided to spare his sister. This may have been a serious miscalculation on his part. In November of 1577, fifteen months after his coronation, Ismail was found dead outside the palace, in the apartment of his lover, Hasan Beg. A police investigation discovered that the two smoked opium together, drank wine, and fell asleep. The court physician suspected poisoning, and although proof was never found, it was commonly believed that it was murder and that Parikhan Khanum was behind it.[75]

As if to emphasize that earth-shattering events were taking place in the Safavid kingdom, a great comet, almost as luminous as the full moon, streaked through the sky over the horizon and remained visible for weeks. Everyone in the kingdom believed this was an omen sent from on high that had to do with current events, and they all wondered what it meant. Was it a sign of the Lord's disapproval of women's meddling in state affairs? Or was it, on the contrary, an affirmation of Parikhan's right to rule and of Ismail's deserved punishment? What did this bode for the future of the empire?

Parikhan waved these questions aside as superstition, just as Queen Elizabeth did in England at the same time, when she observed the comet from her palace window.[76] Restored to her former status as acting shah after Ismail's death and in charge once again, she had to plan her next move. In the absence of clear guidelines for succession in such a situation, and with Ismail's heir apparent, his son Prince Shuja', still in swaddling clothes, the royal council was summoned to decide who the next shah should be. Some of its members, mostly Qizilbash

---

[73] Manuchehr Parsadust, "Parikān Kānom." Rudy Mathee, "Safavid Dynasty," *Encyclopaedia Iranica*.

[74] Parikhan Khanum's letter to Ismail, translated in Birjandifar, "Royal Women and Politics," 103.

[75] Olearius, *Voyages and Travells*, 258: "Certain it is, he dy'd a violent death, on the 24 of November 1577. And that Periaconcona [Parikhan] was the Contriver and Instrument of it: but this was done so secretly, that it is yet not known, how Persia came to be rid of this tyrant." *Don Juan of Persia* (p. 132) suggests that it was a joint operation by the kingdom's nobles and Parikhan, and that the main motivation was Ismail's plans to convert to Sunni Islam.

[76] See Chap. 7.

Fig. 4.7 Palace in Qazvin, one of 274 vintage photographs, late nineteenth-early twentieth century. Brooklyn Museum, Purchase gift of Leona Soudavar in memory of Ahmad Soudavar, 1997.3.44

clan leaders, who admired Parikhan and believed she had their interests at heart, contended that she herself should rule as regent at least until Shuja' was old enough to ascend the throne. Others disagreed. Finally, once again declining the offer to be nominated shah, Parikhan decided to summon the only surviving senior male member of the dynasty, the blind Prince Muhammad Khodabanda. She sent envoys to invite him to come from Shiraz and take the throne.[77] This time, she hoped, with the weak brother on the throne, she would be able to continue running the state from behind the scenes.[78] Meanwhile she took command of the army and protected the throne along with the treasury and the other accoutrements of sovereignty "*as was necessary and proper ...*" (Fig. 4.7).

But Parikhan's spies, who had sent her reports about Khodabanda's situation, misled her once again, just as they had done in Ismail's case. Several of Ismail's former loyalists, who were afraid that Parikhan would avenge Ismail's

[77] Birjandifar, "Royal Women and Politics," 71–72. Szuppe, "La participation des femmes," Seconde Partie, 85.
[78] Birjandifar, "Royal Women and Politics," 71–72. Manuchehr Parsadust, "Parikān Kānom." Szuppe, "Status, Knowledge, and Politics," 157.

cruelty by imprisoning them, fled Qazvin. Most of them, including former Grand Vizier Jaberi, who seemed to figure out who the winner would be in every round and to jump horses just in time, joined the entourage of Prince Khodabanda in Shiraz and swore their allegiance. They soon found out that it was not the prince but his young wife, Mahd-i Ulya, who actually governed the province. They told her about Parikhan's political ambitions and claimed that the princess murdered Ismail to further her own interests. When the invitation from the palace arrived, it was already clear to Mahd-i Ulya that her first move should be to eliminate her sister-in-law.[79] As the new royal procession made its way to Qazvin, Mahd-i Ulya and Khodabanda sent ahead a detachment of soldiers to take control of the state treasury and prevent embezzlement. This message of distrust was, of course, a direct affront to Parikhan, who immediately understood that she had misjudged her opponents once again. When the couple finally arrived at the city gates, Parikhan came out to greet them. In a last-ditch effort to demonstrate power and authority, she asked to be carried in a dazzling gold-woven litter and escorted by dozens of special guards and courtiers. Here's an imagined description of their first and last meeting:

The way to the palace was strewn with jasmine petals; the horses' breath rose like smoke and lances glittered in the winter sun. Dressed in their finest livery, the entire palace staff waited at attention. The porters lay down Parikhan's litter and she rose from her seat, bowed deeply to her brother, the new shah, kissed the hem of his gown, and pledged her loyalty. As she stood up Mahd-i Ulya approached, smiling coldly, and kissed her hands. To the assembled courtiers this seemed like a gesture of appreciation, but Parikhan, who knew she was already planning her destruction, could not bring herself to reciprocate and bow to this woman. Mahd-i Ulya shook her head. There was fire in her eyes. She walked on without another word.

Life suddenly weighed heavily on Parikhan's shoulders. After this terrible period, from her father's illness and death, through the assassination of Haydar, to the long months of Ismail's cruel rule, she felt tired of this imperial rat race of death and survival. As the coronation ceremony drew to a close, she summoned her litter carriers. From the corner of her eye, she saw the new queen looking at her and whispering something to Mirza Jaberi, her own former vizier. She knew that her fate was sealed.

Mahd-i Ulya

Khodabanda's wife, Mahd-i Ulya, hailed from an ancient Marashi dynasty that traced its roots to the Prophet Muhammad and ruled the region of Mazandaran on the southern shores of the Caspian Sea for more than two centuries. She clearly saw herself as more deserving of royal privilege than the upstart Safavid family that she married into. Born in the 1550s as Khayr al-Nisa Begum, she was orphaned at a young age when her father, a provincial governor, was

---

[79] Manuchehr Parsadust, "Parikān Ḵānom." Babayan, *Aqāid al-Nisa'*, 356. Szuppe, "La participation des femmes," Seconde Partie, 88.

murdered in a dispute over power. She was then sent by relatives to the court in Qazvin.[80] Shah Tahmasp soon grew fond of the young woman and betrothed her to his son, perhaps to strengthen his ties with her aristocratic family. Not long after the marriage, however, Khodabanda fell ill, lost most of his vision, and was packed away to govern the province of Herat and later Shiraz. Once they got there, Mahd-i Ulya realized that her husband was not up to the task and took over the management of the province.[81]

Now that, in a weird quirk of fate, her husband—last in line for succession—was to be crowned shah, she read the situation clearly and understood that in order for her to govern unchallenged, her rival, Parikhan Khanum, had to be eliminated along with her powerful uncle, Shamkhal Khan. She planned carefully and carried out her plans meticulously on the day of their arrival. During the crowning ceremony she cynically ordered Afshar Khan, Parikhan's childhood mentor and one of the few people she trusted, to find and abduct her. As they made their way back from the ceremony, Parikhan and her guards were accosted by Afshar Khan's troops. A short scuffle ensued and the young princess—thirty years old at the time—was pulled off her litter, seized, carried away, and later strangled to death. On the same day another group of soldiers surrounded and killed her uncle. His head was brought to the palace and presented to the reigning couple. Ismail's baby son, Shuja', a potential future threat, was also murdered.[82]

Now, Mahd-i Ulya believed, all the obstacles to her absolute dominance were cleared. From that day on, while her husband spent his time praying, gambling, *"and diverting himself with the ladies,"* she became the real wielder of power.[83] Court chronicler Al-Qummi wrote: *"After kissing the feet of his highness [Shah Khodabanda] and of his son Hamzah Mirza, all the amirs and notables would go to her highness ... and nothing of importance could be carried*

---

[80] Szuppe, "Jewels of Wonder," 334. The name Mahd-i Ulya means "cradle of the greats" or "sublime cradle." Her previous name, Khayr al-Nisa', was originally the epithet of the Prophet Muhammad's first wife, Khadija. Mahd-i Ulya was a title first bestowed on Muhammad Khodabanda's mother (Tahmasp's wife Sultanum Begum).

[81] Szuppe, "Status, Knowledge, and Politics," 146. Szuppe, "La participation des femmes," Seconde Partie, 91.

[82] Birjandifar, "Royal Women and Politics," 80. Hani Khafipour, *The Empires of the Near East and India*, 179. Ambassador Olearius believed that it was actually Muhammad Khodabanda himself who demanded Parikhan's execution: "[H]e resolved to accept [the crown] that before he was oblig'd to make his entrance into Caswin, they should bring him the head of Peiraconcona, who had imbru'd her hands in the bloud of two of his Brethren, and in whose power it was in some respects to dispose of the Kingdom." Olearius, *Voyages and Travells*, 258. Don Juan of Persia claims that Parikhan was beheaded, and her head was displayed in public view "stuck on a lance point" (p. 135). On the affair see also Bekir Kötükoğlu, *Osmanli-Iran Siyasi Münasebetleri*, 13–16.

[83] Olearius, *Voyages and Travells*, 258. Szuppe, "The Jewels of Wonder," 332. Szuppe, "La participation des femmes," Seconde Partie, 81. Some of the sources describe him as a pious Muslim who spent most of his time in religious pursuits, others emphasize his gambling and womanizing tendencies. These pursuits were not necessarily mutually exclusive.

out without her consultation and approval."[84] She began to appoint her relatives and supporters to governorships and ministerial posts and installed her loyalists in the army.[85] Khodabanda was indifferent, but when reports about the weak and ineffectual shah spread, enemies within and without took advantage and pounced. Two decades after the signing of the Amasya Treaty, the Safavids had to fight once again on two fronts, against the Uzbeks in the east and against the Ottomans in the west, while at the same time contending with internal uprisings.

While Safavid forces held back the Uzbeks on the eastern front, the Ottomans made their way to Azerbaijan and the Caspian Sea, assisted by their allies, the Giray Tatars of Crimea. They occupied the provinces of Karabagh and Shirvan and threatened to invade the heart of the country. Frustrated by the army's lackluster performance, Mahd-i Ulya decided to ride up and join her forces in the north along with her twelve-year-old son and to lead them in the war against the Ottomans. Her arrival on the scene did make a change. After a few undecided skirmishes, her army, led by Qizilbash commanders, defeated their rivals and captured the commander of the Ottoman force, Adil Giray, brother of the Tatar khan.

Mahd-i Ulya's commanding presence made an impression on several English merchants who happened to be passing through the area at the same time, as they wrote in their account. "*[The] Queene of Persia (the king being blind) had beene with a great armie against the Turks that were left to possesse Media [Azerbaijan] and had given them a great overthrow... They gathered power together, and with the Queene of their country as chiefe, they entered the country of Media and overrane the same with sword and fire, destroying whatsoever they found.*"[86] Their words are echoed in a Georgian account of the episode, which describes Mahd-i Ulya as the leader of the army and credits her with its success.[87]

In an attempt to seal the victory and prevent another Ottoman attack, Mahd-i Ulya ordered the army commanders to keep pursuing the retreating Ottomans. But exhausted by the fight and drunk on plunder, the generals ignored the order and returned to their winter encampments. Furious at their disregard for her commands, she decided to leave the front and return to the capital, where she would make up her mind how to punish them. Crossing the snow-covered mountain passes, she reached Qazvin, followed by a small group of loyal troops (Fig. 4.8).[88]

Her feud with the Qizilbash emirs intensified later that year, when she ordered them to capture and execute Mirza Khan, a rebellious governor of

---

[84] Szuppe, "Status, Knowledge, and Politics," 159. Birjandifar, "Royal Women and Politics," 80. Szuppe, "La participation des femmes," Seconde Partie, 91.

[85] Banister and Duckett, agents of the Company of Muscovy in Astrakhan, quoted in Szuppe, "Status, Knowledge, and Politics," 153, 159. Szuppe, "La participation des femmes," Seconde Partie, 68.

[86] Szuppe, "Status, Knowledge, and Politics," 155. See also *Don Juan of Persia*, 149–151.

[87] Szuppe, "La participation des femmes," Seconde Partie, 65.

[88] Szuppe, "The Jewels of Wonder," 332. Szuppe, "Status, Knowledge, and Politics," 155.

Fig. 4.8 The Safavid Empire and its enemies, sixteenth century. Map by F. Dany (Fabienkhan)

Mazandaran whom she blamed for murdering her own father many years previously. The war they waged against Mirza Khan was long, costly, and arduous. The rebel found refuge in a castle which her forces besieged but were unable to break into. Finally, the Safavid commanders reached a compromise and gave Mirza Khan their word of honor that he would receive a royal pardon after submitting. Mirza Khan agreed, delivered the fort into their hands, and was sent to Qazvin with an escort. But unbeknownst to the army commanders, Mahd-i Ulya sent a detachment of soldiers to intercept the convoy, apprehend Mirza Khan, and kill him. When they found out that their promises of safe conduct were broken, the commanders were livid. They claimed that Mahd-i Ulya shamed them and justified the claims of their enemies.[89] As her relationship with the generals deteriorated, she added insult to injury by dismissing their ally, the governor of Kashan.

This was the last straw. In a letter to Khodabanda quoted by the chronicler Munshi, the furious generals demanded her immediate removal from power. The letter's misogynistic tone is exceptional even for this period: "*Your majesty well knows that women are notoriously lacking in intelligence, weak in judgment, and extremely obstinate,*" it began. Mahd-i Ulya mistreated them, they complained, and all their attempts to reach an understanding with her failed. The

---

[89] Birjandifar, "Royal Women and Politics," 85–93. Szuppe, "La participation des femmes," Seconde Partie, 95–96.

letter was carefully worded but included an explicit threat. "*In short, we do not consider it proper that word should spread among neighboring rulers that no member of the royal family still remains in the care of the Qizilbash because a woman has taken charge of the affairs of state and is all-powerful.*"[90] When these threats failed to spur the shah to action, the generals upped the ante, accusing Mahd-i Ulya of having an affair with her royal prisoner, the Tatar commander Adil Giray Khan.[91] Finally swayed, Khodabanda promised to send her away and stop her interference in affairs of state, but Mahd-i Ulya had no intention of leaving and refused to budge.

Running out of options, the officers decided to assassinate her themselves, probably with the shah's tacit approval. They carried out their plan in July 1579, eighteen months into her reign. Since assassination of royalty was a crime punishable by death, each Qizilbash faction was represented by one officer chosen to perform the act. On the agreed-upon date, the group of assassins burst into the royal harem, found Mahd-i Ulya, and strangled her, along with some of her guards and relatives. They then ransacked the harem, where, it was claimed, she hid stacks of gold. Her reputed lover, the prisoner Adil Giray, was also assassinated.[92]

After the queen's death, anarchy reigned for a while. The rest of Shah Khodabanda's reign—about seven years—was plagued with infighting between factions. The Ottomans and the Uzbeks attacked again, and wars with them continued until the 1590s. The Ottomans fought to take Georgia, Azerbaijan, and the province of Shirvan in the Caspian region and briefly conquered the city of Tabriz once again. The Uzbeks annexed large parts of the province of Khorasan. The shah's weakness also gave rise to several mutinies inside the army, and finally, in 1587, an uprising forced Khodabanda to abdicate.

Ascending the throne as an inexperienced seventeen-year-old boy, Khodabanda's son was crowned Shah Abbas I. Later known as "Abbas the Great," he would become one of the most successful Safavid shahs, but the road to greatness was long and arduous.

ZAYNAB BEGUM

Born in the early 1550s, Parikhan's younger half-sister, Zaynab, was the daughter of Tahmasp's Georgian wife Huri Khan Khanum. Like her sister, she received the best possible education and as a young kid was probably tutored by her aunt, the great Shahzada Sultanum. As she grew up, her father appointed his

---

[90] Szuppe, "Status, Knowledge, and Politics," 159. Szuppe, "La participation des femmes," Seconde Partie, 98. Birjandifar, "Royal Women and Politics," 94.

[91] *Don Juan of Persia*, 152. Don Juan claims that one of the reasons for killing Mahd-i Ulya and Adil Giray was the jealousy felt by Safavid nobles at the intimacy Adil Giray enjoyed with the shah and their fear that Adil Giray might come to have power in the country.

[92] Birjandifar, "Royal Women and Politics," 93–96. Jahandideh and Khaefi, Women's Status During the Safavid Period, 140. Szuppe, "Status, Knowledge, and Politics," 160. Szuppe, "La participation des femmes," Seconde Partie, 98.

commander of cavalry to oversee her educational and recreational needs.⁹³ Soon after Tahmasp's death, her brother, the cruel Shah Ismail II, promised her hand in marriage as a special favor to Ali-Qoli Khan, one of his senior officials. But on the day they were betrothed, Ali-Qoli Khan was appointed governor and sent to Herat with special orders to kill Khodabanda's son, Abbas Mirza. Shah Ismail did not think his blind brother himself would pose a threat to his reign, but his healthy six-year-old son was a potential risk, and Ismail wanted him dead.

While Zaynab, his young fiancée, remained in the palace to await his return, Ali-Qoli set out to begin his governorship in Herat. Upon arrival, reluctant to take the life of such a small child, he dilly-dallied for weeks, offering different excuses. Luckily, just as he was running out of pretexts, Shah Ismail suddenly died, and the child's life was spared. In the following weeks, even though the child's father was crowned shah, Ali-Qoli remained in Herat as young Abbas's guardian, defying orders to bring him back to Qazvin. The main reason was the situation in the capital, which still seemed unstable. At some point he was warned by the Shah that if the child was not brought to the capital immediately, he would be declared a rebel, but the governor refused to obey and kept the child in Herat. Seeing the anarchy that beset the state before and right after Mahd-i Ulya's death, Ali-Qoli rose up against the shah, aiming perhaps to replace him with his son. As the war escalated, the shah ordered the execution of the governor's own parents, and in response Ali-Qoli and his allies decided to declare Prince Abbas shah in Khorasan. They pledged allegiance to him in the traditional manner during the Friday sermon and minted coins in his name.⁹⁴ The angry Khodabanda then led his own army to quell the rebellion, but he failed and instead signed a truce offering amnesty to Ali-Qoli and his protégé, Abbas, in return for loyalty to the shah.

A few months later, Ali-Qoli himself was defeated in battle by another Qizilbash leader named Murshid Qoli Khan Ustajlu, who coveted the royal son. After killing Ali-Qoli, the victor managed to snatch Prince Abbas and take him to the city of Mashhad, where he kept him as a war trophy, a hostage, and a potential sovereign.⁹⁵

Meanwhile, in Qazvin, after Mahd-i Ulya's assassination, Tahmasp's oldest remaining daughter, Zaynab, was appointed head of the royal harem.⁹⁶ Lost without his strong-willed wife, Khodabanda soon sought her advice in all state matters. And as she took over the day-to-day running of the state, Zaynab understood that Khodabanda's days on the throne were numbered and invested

---

⁹³ Ghereghlou, "Zaynab Begum," *Encyclopaedia Iranica*. Babayan, *The Waning of the Qizilbash*, 91, n. 209.

⁹⁴ N. Savory, "ʿALĪ-QOLĪ KHAN ŠĀMLŪ," *Encyclopaedia Iranica*, I/8, pp. 875–876, available online at http://www.iranicaonline.org/articles/ali-qoli-khan-samlu-b. Ghereghlou, "Zaynab Begum," *Encyclopaedia Iranica*.

⁹⁵ Ghereghlou, "On the Margins of Minority," 17. Savory, "ʿALĪ-QOLĪ KHAN ŠĀMLŪ," *Encyclopaedia Iranica*, Ghereghlou, "Zaynab Begum," *Encyclopaedia Iranica*. Newman, *Safavid Iran*, 45.

⁹⁶ Szuppe, "La participation des femmes," Seconde Partie, 100–101.

in educating the one she believed would be his heir, his son Mirza Khan, preparing him for the throne. But her plans were dashed as Mirza Khan was suspiciously murdered during a campaign against the Ottomans in 1586.

After a period of unrest and ceaseless intrigue in the capital, Murshid Qoli Khan and his Qizilbash allies brought their seventeen-year-old royal captive over from Mashhad, forced Shah Khodabanda to abdicate, and installed the boy on the throne in October 1588. Murshid Qoli's plan was to remain in control and use Abbas as a puppet ruler to further his interests and those of his allies. But although the child, Shah Abbas, was totally powerless at this stage, he had no illusions about his Qizilbash masters. He witnessed their cruelty and infighting firsthand, and he never forgave them for assassinating his mother, Mahd-i Ulya, and for intentionally forsaking his beloved foster father, Ali-Qoli Khan.

Like his grandfather Tahmasp, the young shah was overwhelmed by the whirling winds of betrayal and conspiracy around him, and the only person he trusted was Aunt Zaynab. He soon reappointed her head of the harem and asked her to join the daily meetings of his cabinet.[97] Since the Qizilbash emirs were so disdainful of women and of bureaucratic matters in general, Zaynab quietly took over the cabinet step by step, by convincing Abbas to appoint her main advisor, Mirza Lutfallah Shirazi, to a senior ministerial post, with a right to affix his stamp to royal decrees.[98] Gradually she became the executive head of state, or, as another Italian visitor, Pietro Della Valle, described it, "*governor of the kingdom.*"[99]

Following her advice, Abbas made a show of complying with his Qizilbash masters' demands while slowly building up his power base. Emulating the Ottoman military slave system, he unobtrusively recruited and trained a new armed force made up of prisoners of war (*gholams*) who converted to Islam and pledged allegiance only to the shah. Such battalions existed in previous eras as well, but Abbas increased their number, gave them the finest training, and turned them into a professional army.[100] After discussions with the English Sherley brothers who visited Iran, and probably on Zaynab's recommendation, he sent a mission of diplomats and translators to Queen Elizabeth, the pope, the duke of Florence, and other European leaders, asking them to send him artillery and fortification specialists to bolster the power of his new troops. The duke of Tuscany, Ferdinand I, agreed to send the requested weapons and instructors, and gradually the *gholam* regiments grew in strength until they had enough power to face and defeat the Qizilbash tribal army.[101] Meanwhile, Abbas used subterfuge to get rid of the leaders who stood in his way, assassinating Murshid Qoli Khan and his cronies. By the end of the 1590s, he finally

[97] Babayan, *The Waning of the Qizilbash*, 91 n. 209.
[98] Szuppe, "La participation des femmes," Seconde Partie, 68.
[99] Quoted in Szuppe, "La participation des femmes," Seconde Partie, 101.
[100] See also Necipoğlu, "Framing the Gaze," 308.
[101] Babayan, *The Waning of the Qizilbash*, 42–45. *Medici Archives*, Vol. 4920, Fol. 23, 27 May 1589. See also Federici, "A Servant of Two Masters".

stood at the helm of the state as an independent ruler. The dynasty was no longer dependent on the Qizilbash.[102]

During all that time, Zaynab Begum acted as Abbas's guide and consultant, offering her wisdom and knowledge. In 1602, the shah officially promoted her to the post of Keeper of the Seal, with power to approve all royal decrees. As an added incentive, he entrusted to her the rich province of Kashan, which she held and governed by proxy until 1613. In addition, the shah awarded her the *Jizya* (the poll tax levied from non-Muslims) of the sizeable Zoroastrian population of Yazd, providing her with an independent source of funds. She used at least part of that money to construct buildings for the common good, including a famous inn—caravanserai—in the town of Ghamsar, on the main road from Isfahan to Kashan.[103]

All the while she kept heading the meetings of the *divan*, sitting with the ministers of state, giving her instructions, and speaking her mind.[104] It was common knowledge at the time that in order to get positions or ranks, members of the governing elite had to be interviewed by her, and when another war broke out with the Ottomans in 1603, she was directly involved in military planning, leading to one of the greatest Safavid victories. On the eve of the deciding battle, Shah Abbas lost his nerve and was on the verge of quitting the battlefield and retreating. Zaynab went over the plans with him, offered suggestions for improvements, and promised a victory. The next day, under his leadership, the Safavid army defeated a much bigger Ottoman force, changed the course of the war, and stabilized Safavid rule in much of the Caucasus.[105]

After the victory, Abbas sent a messenger to his neighbor, the Mughal Emperor Akbar, bearing a letter that described his military triumph, reiterated his peaceful intentions, and subtly warned Akbar against trying to attack. The emissary also brought a letter from Zaynab to Akbar's mother, the aging Hamida, mentioning her historic meeting with Shahzadeh Sultanum a few years before Zaynab herself was born and asking about her health.[106]

In 1613, as his confidence and power grew, Abbas ruthlessly assassinated all his perceived enemies inside the court, including some of his relatives. At the

---

[102] According to Olearius, Abbas himself took part in the assassination of Murshid-Koli Khan. Olearius, *Voyages and Travels*, 259. The Qizilbash were out of grace, but they became an internal enemy that dogged the state ever since.

[103] Ghereghlou, "Zaynab Begum," *Encyclopaedia Iranica*.

[104] Newman, *Safavid Iran*, 66. Ghereghlou, "Zaynab Begum," *Encyclopaedia Iranica*. Ghereghlou, "On the Margins of Minority," 17–18, 22. Birjandifar, "Royal Women and Politics," 39. Shah Abbas relied on her to such a degree that when an Uzbek high-ranking royal dignitary came for a crucial diplomatic visit, he put her in charge of the royal banquet. As Szuppe notes: "[L]e cas de Zeyneb Begom, tante et conseillère de Šâh Abbâs I, est très intéresant, par raport a ceux qui le précédent; il montre qu'une femme de sang royal pouvait exercer un grand pouvoir, même sous un souverain particulièrement fort." "La participation des femmes," 104.

[105] The Battle of Sufyan in Azerbaijan, 1605.

[106] Choksy and Hasan, "An Emissary from Akbar to Abbas I." Choksy and Hasan assume that "the aunt" who sent the letter was Shahzadeh Sultanum, but this, of course, is impossible since Mahin Banu died some forty years earlier.

Fig. 4.9 The young Shah Abbas I, engraving by Dominicus Custos, Atrium heroicum, Augsburg 1600–1602. Public domain

same time, to minimize needless killing of potential candidates for the crown, he decided to institute a new succession system adopted from his Ottoman rivals. From now on possible heirs to the throne would not be sent to govern provinces and would instead remain in a "cage" (*qafas*) inside the harem, controlled at all times by the royal family's women and the shah's servants. They were to be kept in this locked room until the shah died and one of them would be elected to take his place. By instituting this new system, Abbas hoped, based on his own experience, to curb the tendency of provincial leaders to challenge the reigning shah by using his sons as pawns. As official head of the harem, Zaynab took all the princes under her charge, ensuring the future of the dynasty (Fig. 4.9).

In 1618, Abbas rode in a triumphant parade into Isfahan, which now replaced Qazvin as the imperial capital. And although by that time horseback riding was no longer in vogue for royal women, and on those rare occasions when they did leave the harem they were mostly carried in closed litters or carriages, old Zaynab proudly led a procession of harem women, mounted on horseback, just as her predecessors had done, proclaiming once again that in the Safavid state women were men's equals.[107] Soon afterward, however, Abbas

---

[107] Szuppe, "Status, Knowledge, and Politics," 151.

quarreled with his aunt, perhaps because of rumors spread by the clergy, accusing her of meddling in religious affairs. In his wrath, the shah banished Zaynab from Isfahan to the old palace in Qazvin. Eventually, though, his anger subsided, and four years later, she was back in the royal palace and in 1627 had fully regained her status, once more becoming head of the harem and chief minister. Soon afterward, Shah Abbas fell ill, and Aunt Zaynab was at his bedside, overseeing his medical treatment until his death two years later.

Planning ahead as usual, she played a crucial role in convincing Abbas to declare his grandson, Sam Mirza, crown prince, and making sure that this time the transition would be smooth. Old and experienced, she saw too many tragedies unfold when no formal heir was declared. On Abbas's deathbed she convened an assembly of military chiefs and bureaucrats to endorse the new heir to the crown and to avoid another period of factional infighting, and obtained a testament signed by the shah, passing his crown on to his grandson. The eighteen-year-old Sam Mirza was then crowned Shah Safi in January 1629. But challenging her authority as acting head of state, the courtiers crowned him before she had time to arrive at Isfahan, and in another threat to her power, the new shah replaced Zaynab as head of the harem by his mother. Soon, however, it became clear that the shah and his mother would be lost in the labyrinth of internal politics without her guidance. Zaynab was invited to assume her old role and keep governing the country alongside the young monarch.[108] But although he showed signs of the same paranoia that had dogged his forebears, the new shah had little interest in the humdrum business of government, and after the initial excitement, Zaynab took charge of all administrative affairs.

Soon after Safi's coronation, another one of those interminable wars erupted between the Safavids and the Ottomans. Zaynab, now in her seventies, accompanied the shah to his army's encampment, giving marching orders to the troops and then, when it became clear that the Ottomans were threatening the capital, leading the royal harem to a place of safety. Once the Ottomans retreated and the war was over, Zaynab assisted the young shah in revalidating the old peace accords. This was the third time a Safavid queen helped affirm the Treaty of Amasya. This time she was aided on the Ottoman side by her counterpart Kösem Sultan, mother of Murad IV.

But soon Zaynab's topsy-turvy career took another hit. Recovering from an attempted poisoning, fearing another such attempt, and suspecting that other candidates for the throne were behind it, Shah Safi ordered the assassination of fifteen princes and their parents and of forty harem women. Zaynab was not among the victims but was banished once again to Qazvin. She only returned to Isfahan in 1640, right before her death. She was buried in the shrine of Ali Reza in Mashhad, the same one that her aunt, Shahzada Sultanum, loved so

---

[108] Babayan, *The Waning of the Qizilbash*, 92, 96. Ghereghlou, "Zaynab Begum," *Encyclopaedia Iranica*.

much.[109] Zaynab's death, as Kathryn Babayan points out, marked a great shift in Safavid queens' political power.

Two major changes were apparent. First, Shah Safi's recent killing frenzy notwithstanding, the new cage system introduced by Abbas left most of the princes alive. Whereas in previous eras the princes would be sent out to the provinces, often on their own (as was the case with Tahmasp, Ismail II, and Abbas I), now they were to stay in the harem with their mothers hovering over them. This gave mothers greater influence over their sons and over court politics. Sisters, wives, daughters, and aunts, on the other hand—as Shahzada Sultanum, Parikhan Khanum, Mahd-i Ulya, and Zaynab Begum were to the ruling shahs—would no longer play major roles on the political scene, and what remained of female power was the exclusive domain of mothers. By that time, however, the mothers themselves were bound by the strict rules of a royal etiquette that had become highly stylized and regulated.

The other great shift, directly connected to the first, was visibility. In the first century of Safavid rule, women were often seen in public, riding horses to the hunt with their faces uncovered, participating in formal ceremonies, entertaining diplomatic missions, and even accompanying their male co-rulers to the battlefield. Now they were relegated to the harem. They could still exert influence on the course of events, but they had to do it from within the palace, hidden from public view, with impaired contact with the males operating in the outside world.[110] Although in theory female family members could still inherit the throne, they never did. To make sure they would have no claims on royal power, some of the possible heiresses were blinded, just like their male kin.[111]

Through the centuries the visibility of women was reduced. Vincenzo D'Alessandri, an Italian who visited the city of Qazvin well into the Safavid era, witnessed the period of transition. "*The women sometimes have permission from the King to come out of the palace; those, indeed, who have children, under the pretext of seeing them when they are ill. And I saw the mother of the Sultan Mustafa Mirisce, who was slightly indisposed, come out with her face covered with a black veil, riding like a man, accompanied by four slaves and six men on foot.*" Sometimes their faces were uncovered, too, he claimed. "*[The women in Qazvin] wear robes of silk, veils on their heads, and show their faces openly. They have pearls and other jewels on their heads, and on this account pearls are in great demand in these regions.*"[112]

This growing marginalization of women could also be seen as a side effect of the gradual shift from a largely heterodox Turko-Mongol style of government to Islamic orthodoxy, with the shah becoming both its lay and religious leader. In this strictly segregated atmosphere, women's participation in public

---

[109] Babayan, *The Waning of the Qizilbash*, 92. Ghereghlou, "Zaynab Begum," *Encyclopaedia Iranica*.

[110] Babayan, *The Waning of the Qizilbash*, 100.

[111] Babayan, *Aqāid al-Nisa'*, 352.

[112] Quoted in Szuppe, "Status, Knowledge, and Politics," 143. D'Alessandri visited the kingdom in 1572.

life was deemed a transgression. Their marginalization came into sharper focus at the end of the century, with an edict by the last Safavid ruler, Shah Sultan Husayn, which forbade music and dance in weddings and enforced the wearing of the veil in all circumstances. From now on women were forbidden to linger in the streets and bazaars, to stroll in gardens on their own, or to go on walks with anyone but their legal guardians (usually a father or husband). They were allowed to move out of the harem only with their guardians' permission and protection.[113]

Although he points out that in other segments of Safavid society, including villages and the lower classes, women did not lose public visibility to the same extent, Rudi Matthee sums it up:

> *There is little doubt that, over time, royal women experienced a decrease in public visibility and saw themselves increasingly relegated to the private palace. The image of women of the court entourage riding on horseback in full view of males, even foreign visitors, is a far cry from the female seclusion of the quruq, and the transformation epitomizes the dramatic changes that took place in Safavid Iran over a period of two centuries, from the freewheeling days of Shah Ismail, via the female-only entertainment decreed by Shah Abbas I, to the restrictive, some would say suffocating, ambiance of Shah Sultan Husayn's reign. Taken together, they appear to confirm greater strictures on female attire and comportment. It is probably true that, as the society became unmoored from its tribal roots and increasingly became urban-centered and as the influence of the clerical forces increased in the second half of the Safavid period, pressure on women grew and more restrictions were imposed on them.*[114]

Dr. John Fryer, who visited Iran in 1677–78 and knew nothing about the autonomous and commanding Safavid women of yore, could dismiss royal women as uneducated and confined to the harem:

> *[T]he women of this country are in a bad State, where Jealousy reigns with such a sway ... They were not brought up "in those Principles from their Youth which should fit them to become prudent matrons." They were not permitted to meddle in "Matters of State," and were not allowed to go outside their homes unattended and unveiled. It seemed "as if they were created only to be idle Companions" for their husbands.*[115]

Szuppe points out that as long as they stayed behind the curtain women could still be recognized as major political actors, but once they tried to install themselves in or near the throne, in full public view, as Parikhan Khanum and

---

[113] Edict of 1694–5, Babayan, *Aqāid al-Nisa'*, 357–358. Rudi Matthee, "From the Battlefield to the Harem."

[114] Matthee, "From the Battlefield to the Harem," 110. Quruq was the edict that banned the presence of any males over the age of six along the road through which the Shah would pass with his harem.

[115] Dr. John Fryer, who visited Iran in 1677–78, quoted by Ferrier, "Women in Safavid Iran," 384.

Mahd-i Ulya did, they encountered fierce male resistance.[116] She also ascribes this shift in the status of women to the gradual strengthening of sedentary Irano-Islamic tradition and the weakening of the more egalitarian nomadic Turko-Mongol heritage, which accepted women as equal partners in government.[117]

This shift is certainly an important factor, but since we see a concurrent trend—diminution of women's power in ruling elites—in most other Eurasian societies, other causes could have been at play. There seems to be no single cause for the fading of queendom in Mughal India, Safavid Iran, and Ottoman Anatolia. The reasons for the decision of the Ottoman *valide*, Turhan Sultan, to give up her political power and hand it over to the viziers may have been very different from the hedging in of female family members by male rulers in Safavid Iran or from the surprising disappearance of Mughal queens from the political arena after the greatest memorial to a queen that the early modern world had ever known was erected. Yet in all three Muslim empires, in the space of less than two decades, queendom simply vanished.

In the following chapters, we shall see that a similar process was at work in western Europe. There, too, queendom developed in the early 1500s and disappeared almost completely until the middle of the following century.

---

[116] Szuppe, "La Participation des femmes," 105.
[117] Szuppe, "Status, Knowledge, and Politics," 162. Szuppe, "La Participation des femmes," 102.

CHAPTER 5

Queens of the Jews

If the sun is superior to all other planets, it is because its powers bring greater benefits to all that grows on our earth. Which of the lofty luminaries of our people can deny similar superiority to you, most illustrious lady? Though their powers have been trained on the farthest province of the earth, you have done more than all of them to bring forth into the light the fruit of the plants that lie buried in its darkness.
Samuel Usque's dedication to Dona Gracia Consolation for the Tribulations of Israel, *Ferrara, 1553*

Jokes about domineering Jewish mothers aside, there were no Jewish queens in the early modern world, and while the dark hues through which their history is depicted in that period tend to be exaggerated, Jews *were* persecuted almost everywhere in Europe. They were banished from their main life center on the Iberian Peninsula and dispersed in all directions, mainly to the Muslim world. A chapter on Jewish queens in a book on sixteenth-century queendom might thus sound a bit fanciful. Yet after the Spanish and Portuguese deportations in the late fifteenth and early sixteenth centuries, the Jewish and Crypto Jewish (Marrano) community—mostly merchants, bankers, physicians, and writers—were integrated into a power grid that underpinned and connected monarchies and dukedoms in East and West alike.[1]

This emerging network and its crucial importance for monarchies around the world were perhaps best described by Hillary Mantle in her novel *Wolf Hall*. The protagonist, Thomas Cromwell, meets with young Henry Percy,

---

[1] Marranos was a derogatory term used to describe Jewish converts to Christianity who secretly continued to practice Judaism ("Judaizing" was the term used), or at least stayed in touch with Jewish relatives and communities. The term "Marrano" has dubious etymology. Its source may be the Portuguese verb *marrar*, meaning "to force," or the same verb in Spanish, meaning "to err." Some claim its source is the Arabic word *muharram*, meaning 'forbidden'.

Earl of Northumberland, in 1532. Cromwell asks him to back out of his half-baked betrothal to Anne Boleyn, so the king will be able to marry her. Percy refuses, and Cromwell, who knows that the earl owes huge sums to moneylenders across Europe, threatens to set the bankers on him. Percy doesn't seem to grasp the gravity of the issue. How can I explain to him? thinks Cromwell, *"The world is not run from where he thinks. Not from his border fortresses, not even from Whitehall. The world is run from Antwerp, from Florence, from places he has never imagined; from Lisbon, from where the ships with sails of silk drift west and are burned up in the sun. Not from castle walls, but from countinghouses, not by the call of the bugle but by the click of the abacus, not by the grate and click of the mechanism of the gun but by the scrape of the pen on the page of the promissory note that pays for the gun and the gunsmith and the powder and shot."*[2]

The Jewish-Marrano network, which included some extraordinary women, spread from the Middle East and Europe to the New World, and their close connections with royal houses enabled the female rulers of the world during those years to get a clearer picture of other polities, customs, and aesthetic preferences and to create a rudimentary connecting grid between them. Describing the emergence of this interconnected web and its leading women as an outcome of the expulsion from Spain would also serve as an introduction to the European royal scene and its connection to the Muslim world from a different vantage point.

QUEEN ISABELLA OF CASTILE AND THE EXPULSION OF THE JEWS

In January 1492, the decades-long campaign for the conquest of Andalusia ended. Queen Isabella of Castile and her husband King Ferdinand II of Aragon brought the Muslim kingdom of Granada to its knees and sent its royal family into exile. For Ferdinand and Isabella, taking Granada and placing the entire peninsula under the power of the Church after seven centuries of Muslim rule was final proof of Christianity's triumph over all other religions and, in a sense, retribution for the conquest of Constantinople by the Ottomans four decades earlier.

Isabella presented a unique model for early modern Europe. Born in 1451, third in line for the crown that her half-brother, the incompetent Henry IV of Castile, inherited, she finally took the throne after a series of battles with internal rivals, shrewd political alliances, and the practical unification of her realm with Ferdinand's kingdom of Aragon.[3] With vision and remarkable personal courage, she crushed rebellions and led her armies to victory over her enemies. She soon repaired the damage wrought on the country by her brother, appointed a

---

[2] Hillary Mantle, *Wolf Hall*, Kindle Edition (New York, Macmillan), p. 349.

[3] Isabella's marriage to Ferdinand did not amount to a formal unification of Castile and Aragon. Officially, Spain was only unified under their great grandson, Philip II, but since that marriage the two kingdoms were governed by the same family. Courtney Herber, "Katherine of Aragon: Diligent Diplomat and Learned Queen," in Woodacre et al., *The Routledge History of Monarchy*, 41–45.

capable finance minister, an experienced Jewish banker who helped refill the treasury that had been bankrupted by Henry's careless squandering; appointed professionals of the lower nobility and the bourgeoisie to the Royal Council; established a direct line of contact with her subjects through a system of formal complaints; created a special police force, *La Santa Hermandad*, to fight criminal activity; and sponsored Columbus's daring trip to discover a new route to India.

Her impressive rule, economic and military successes, personal courage, and daring exploits impacted royal women long after her death. Among them were her daughter Katherine of Aragon, who married Henry VIII of England, her granddaughter, Queen Mary I, and many ruling women in France, the Habsburg Empire, and other monarchies in Europe. It would not be a stretch of the imagination to assume that queens such as Bona Sforza in Poland or Catherine de Medici in France almost a century later still looked up to her as a model of queenship (Fig. 5.1).

But Isabella was also a deeply religious queen. Her victory, depicted as Catholicism's triumph over other religions, gave rise to a special vision of purity: to cleanse her realm of those who still refused to acknowledge the Lord's truth, and mainly of the stubborn Jews, a substantial, influential, and well-integrated community in Spain, whose members refused to convert

Fig. 5.1 Ferdinand and Isabella on the throne. The youth on their right is almost certainly their son, Don Juan Prince of Asturias. Author unknown

despite enjoying special privileges.[4] Three months after the *Reconquista*, sitting in the throne room of the great Alhambra palace in Granada, the victorious royal couple issued a decree calling on all Jews to embrace the one true religion immediately. Those who refused to do so were given four months to get their affairs in order and leave the country.

As Columbus and his captains prepared for their voyage in the harbor of Palos de la Frontera, the Jews who refused to convert boarded adjacent boats to their new destinations. Many tried their luck in the flourishing city-states of Italy or in the Netherlands, where the dreaded Inquisition had not yet set foot. Others crossed the Strait of Gibraltar to Morocco along with some of their Muslim neighbors. A large group sailed to the Ottoman Empire whose sultan, Bayezid II, saw them as a boon to the realm and invited them to settle and contribute to its economy. Many, perhaps the majority, consented to be baptized and thus keep their homes and workplaces. Some of them truly converted, became ardent believers, and even joined the clergy. One influential group went further and joined Ignazio Loyola's newly founded Society of Jesus (later called the Jesuits), traveling to the farthest corners of the world as missionaries to help convert others. But most of the newly baptized Christians went through a semblance of conversion, biding their time in the hope of returning to the old faith in the future.

Suspecting precisely this kind of fake conversion, Isabella unleashed the full force of the Spanish Inquisition, headed by the Dominican friar Tomas de Torquemada—himself from a family of converted Jews—on the dissemblers. With the holy investigators snapping at their heels, the Crypto Jews now had three options: remaining in Spain, giving up Judaism and truly embracing Christianity; leaving the country and trying to reach the few destinations in which they were allowed to freely identify as Jews; or holding on to their fake conversion but moving to other European states in which the Inquisition had no authority.

This third group, ostensibly Christian but secretly retaining its Jewish heritage, gradually spread from the Iberian Peninsula to the rest of Christian Europe and sparked intellectual, commercial, and industrial activity that reinvigorated early modern Christian culture. Often referred to in Europe as "New Christians", they benefitted from their families' long experience as advisers, financiers, doctors, and scientists under more lenient Muslim and Christian monarchs. As Christians they were now allowed to study medicine, philosophy, and law in elite universities that refused to accept Jews and could engage in professions and types of commerce forbidden to their former coreligionists. But as José Tavim rightly noted, even when they truly embraced Christianity, the designation "New Christians" was applied for a reason. There was a clear

---

[4] Muslims in the newly conquered territories were still considered too powerful and too valuable as a taxable resource to challenge until much later.

religious boundary between old Christians and new. Their conversion was always unfinished, their devotion forever suspect.[5]

What distinguished this group of Marranos most of all from other Christians was their internal cohesion. They stood at the intersection of Christianity, Islam, and Judaism, and for all three religions they were the other within. Not fully trusted as Christians by European sovereigns, they were still suspected by Muslim rulers of harboring Christian sympathies. Even their former Jewish coreligionists who knew that many of them kept the faith in secret were hesitant to trust them. Yet internally they were a tight-knit community. They married within the group, the better to hide their true beliefs, and they made use of society's rejection to connect to other Marranos across spatial, political, and ideological boundaries. Jewish royal physicians in the Ottoman Empire were closely connected to their Marrano cousins in Poland, Italy, France, England, and North Africa. Marrano ladies corresponded across continents and oceans and made use of their acquaintance to promote commercial and political interests. Even those who felt safe enough in their places of exile to return to Judaism adhered to their old bonds with New Christian relatives. Marrano jewelers, physicians, bankers, and merchants often allied themselves with royalty to enhance their own influence. Quite a few women in this group attached themselves as confidantes to women in positions of power and created a kind of female synergy that played a crucial role in the emergence of a female international grid.

This chapter focuses on four women who led fascinating lives as independent women and leaders of Jewish and Marrano communities in the sixteenth century: Dona Gracia Mendes (née Beatrice de Luna), Benvenida Abrabanel, Esther Handali, and Esperanza Malchi. The narrative will shed light on their contribution to the emerging female leadership network.

Gracia Mendes

Many of the families who refused to convert in 1492 crossed the border into nearby Portugal, which at the time was not under the Inquisition.[6] Most of the newcomers paid the Portuguese monarchy a tax of eight *cruzados* per adult, for which they were given temporary permission to stay. Rich families were offered permanent residency for payment of one hundred *cruzados* per person. But five years later, to demonstrate his Catholic bona fides in anticipation of marrying Isabella's daughter and allying himself with powerful Spain, the king of Portugal emulated Isabella and Ferdinand's decree. In a declaration of his own, he called on the Jews in his realm to choose between conversion and exile. Many emigrated once again, but almost all the families that outwardly converted remained

---

[5] Jose Tavim, "Portuguese New Christians in the Turkish "Carrefour" between the Mediterranean and the Indian Ocean in the Sixteenth Century: Decentralization and Conversion," Journal of Early Modern History 17.5-6 (2013)," 562.

[6] The Inquisition in Portugal was authorized by the pope only some forty years later.

in Portugal and kept performing Jewish rites in the privacy of their homes. Among those was the aristocratic de Luna family.

The life story of Beatrice de Luna (later Dona Gracia Mendes), who was born in Lisbon in 1510, moved to Antwerp, Venice, and Ferrara, and ended her life in Istanbul, offers a different perspective from which to examine the amazing cluster of women who governed the European and Ottoman worlds for more than a century. Her extraordinary life story made her a major hub of the emerging feminine royal network.[7]

Early Years in Lisbon

From a very early age Beatrice knew that her family was different. Complex ties connected her father's family to her mother's, and she soon worked out that all the different family names she heard in her childhood—Mendes, de Luna, Miques, and Benveniste—were branches of one big extended clan so inextricably entangled that the names could be used interchangeably. Her family inhabited an imposing house overlooking Lisbon's harbor. She knew that her parents' families came from Aragon in Spain and that they were originally Jewish. Her great-grandfathers, Abraham Benveniste and Alvaro de Luna, were high-ranking ministers in the governments of Castile and Aragon before the expulsion.[8] She grew up with a younger sister, Brianda, who was to accompany her through all her wanderings across Europe, and two brothers. One of them, Agostinho Miques, taught medicine at the University of Lisbon and was soon appointed physician to the royal court of Portugal. Beatrice received a good education, as was common for women in her class. Private tutors taught her languages, philosophy and (Catholic) religion, music, handicrafts, and perhaps also basic accounting practices.

On Sundays and holidays the family went to mass at the main city cathedral, but there was always a sense of uneasiness about these rites. Her parents had their own private set of ceremonies: lighting candles on Friday before sunset in one of the inner rooms, eating different foods, and clandestinely celebrating other festivals. Her parents told her not to talk about these customs outside the house, and when she was ten, they revealed the secret that she had already known in her heart. At home, hidden from view, they still kept the old faith. Her Hebrew name, they said, was Hanna, or Gracia in Portuguese, but she should keep that to herself.

Being a precocious girl, Beatrice easily adapted to this double life, Christian in public and Jewish at home. For a while she may even have enjoyed playing the

---

[7] Since the choice of name has to do with questions of identity, I use the name most often used in each phase of Beatrice/Gracia's biography. She is referred to as Beatrice (Beatriz, Beatrix) until the early 1550s and began to use the name Gracia (Grazia) when in Ferrara, under the local duke's protection.

[8] Birnbaum, *The Long Journey*, 3/24. (Page numbers in Birnbaum are given according to the Internet version of the book: https://books.openedition.org/ceup/2135). Roth, *Dona Gracia*, 6–8, 14.

game. But as time went by, keeping these worlds apart became increasingly difficult. The reports coming from Spain were alarming. Encouraged by the militant Catholicism of Charles V, Spain's new king and now emperor of the Holy Roman Empire, the Inquisition renewed its persecution. With the Lutheran movement blazing a trail of sedition through northern Europe and challenging the foundations of Catholicism, Charles was adamant that all forms of heresy be rooted out. On a visit to Valencia in 1528, he even attended an *auto-da-fé*, a burning of heretics at the stake, staged in his honor.[9] In addition, King João III of Portugal, seeking to prove his mettle as a true Catholic and to placate the emperor's sister, Margaret, whom he had recently married, requested the pope's approval for bringing the Inquisition to his country as well.

Right after her eighteenth birthday Beatrice was married to her maternal uncle, Francisco Mendes-Benveniste, who was thirty years her senior. Francisco's ancestors served the kings of Aragon as physicians, tax collectors, and financiers for generations and arrived in Portugal with much of their sizeable capital intact. His family, like Beatrice's, outwardly converted to Christianity during the harsh years at the end of the previous century but continued on as Crypto Jews. Since the crime of apostasy was punishable by death, arranged marriages within the group were deemed essential for the safety of the community. They allowed families to keep their faith at home and minimize the risk of exposure by maintaining the outward appearance of being devout Christians. A sumptuous wedding ceremony took place in 1528 at Lisbon's municipal cathedral, attended by members of royalty and nobility. Later, a Jewish wedding was probably quietly celebrated at home. Soon the couple had a daughter, whom they publicly christened Brianda, like Beatrice's sister, and privately called Reina, most likely a translation of the common Hebrew name Malka (queen).[10]

The Indian Spice Trade

Even before the wedding, Francisco and his brother Diogo (known as Meir inside the family) realized the enormous potential of the new Asian trade routes. At the time, spices, mainly pepper, were not just exciting additives to improve the taste of food. In the absence of effective refrigeration in summer, they were crucial for the preservation of food and therefore a sought-after commodity that brought immense profits.

In 1497, as the two brothers were growing up, Vasco da Gama embarked on his first trip around the tip of Africa, in search of a route bypassing the barrier imposed by the Muslim kingdoms and their accomplice, Venice, to the importation of spices from Asia. His success came at a great cost in men and capital. Two of his four ships sank, and only a third of his crew members returned to Portugal at the end of the journey. But a mere six years later, Portuguese ships laden with spices from India were already unloaded in Antwerp, to huge

---

[9] Birnbaum, *The Long Journey*, 3/30.
[10] Ibid, Chap. 1. Roth, *Dona Gracia*, 14.

acclaim. "*The first cargo was sold at so tremendous a profit that the famine feared in Portugal was averted*," wrote Cecil Roth.[11] Soon a dispute arose between Portugal and Venice over control of the spice trade. Venice imported the same spices mostly overland through the Ottoman empire, and thence on Venetian ships to Europe. It saw the Portuguese trade as unfair competition—and Don Isaac Abrabanel, a former Spanish statesman who settled in Venice, was asked to negotiate the terms of trade between the two commercial empires. He finally declared that there was enough spice in India for everyone and enough demand for it in Europe to enrich both, and there was no need to restrict quantities.[12] Venice continued to profit from the import of Indian spices overland for some two centuries, but the costs of Portuguese ocean travel were soon sharply reduced and those who invested in it amassed great wealth. The Mendeses therefore shifted the focus of their family business from the importation of gems to international trade in pepper and other spices.

Ocean voyages to India were now made with growing frequency, and the Mendes wealth grew in proportion.[13] Between 1517 and 1534, Francisco Mendes is listed in Portuguese treasury records as "the highest depositor of silver in Lisbon's mint." Before the establishment of an international banking system, depositing silver in the mint was the surest way of protecting one's wealth, and the huge amounts of precious metal that Francisco accumulated implied that he was the richest merchant in the land during this period.[14] Although Portugal's royal house, entitled to twenty-five percent of all profits, also enriched itself, it gradually became more dependent on the Mendeses for funding its global trade and colonial expansion.

As its Asian and African trade flourished, Lisbon became a thriving port city, but its northern rival, Antwerp, was still the main European hub of international trade. Ships from the Far East, the Americas, the Mediterranean, the Baltic, and the North Sea weighed anchor in its great natural port at the mouth of the Scheldt River. The city, governed along with the rest of the Lowlands by the Habsburgs, became the trade capital of the entire world. It was clear that the Mendes firm needed an office there, and in 1512 Francisco's brother, Diogo, was entrusted with the mission. The young Portuguese merchant soon became one of Antwerp's leading spice traders.[15] To hedge their investments in the hazardous trips to India—corsairs, enemy war ships, gale winds, and stormy seas still presented a grave risk—the Mendes brothers joined the world's biggest spice trade consortium. Along with other famous trading companies such as the Italian Affaitati of Cremona, and the German Hochstetters, Welsers, and

[11] Roth, *Dona Gracia*, 21.
[12] *Ibid*. See also Brummett, Ottoman Seapower, pp. 149–151.
[13] Roth, *Dona Gracia*, 14, 22. Klooster, "Sephardic Migration," 125. Mauro, "Merchant Communities," 263. Goldstone, "Trends or Cycles?", 113. De Castro, *The Pepper Wreck*, 13.
[14] "Salomon and Leoni," p. 141, fn. 14. During the sixteenth century royal mints served as virtual banks, the only safe vaults for merchants' assets. The profits were exchanged, most often for silver, and the silver deposited under the merchant's name in the royal mints.
[15] Andrade, "A Senhora e os destinos," 89.

Fuggers of Augsburg, they exported copper and other European commodities to Asia and brought back spices and textiles. From 1525 on, the consortium led by Diogo Mendes purchased Portugal's entire volume of pepper imports—more than a million tons per year—for distribution in Europe.[16]

Meanwhile in Lisbon, Beatrice joined Francisco in running the local branch of the family's firm. Diligently studying harbor politics and Portuguese bureaucratic practices, the young bride soon became an indispensable asset to the firm. Her intelligence and intuition helped expand the Lisbon end of the business. The firm's great wealth and their transactions with the royal court allowed Francisco and Beatrice to firmly establish themselves as high Portuguese nobility. In appreciation of their contribution to the monarchy, King João III and his wife, the Habsburg Queen Catherine of Austria, had given a special charter to Francisco, their friend and banker, "*one of the most important merchants of my India trade*," granting him privileges and immunities "*for services rendered me and my late father [King Manuel I].*"[17] Soon Francisco became a regular guest at the royal court. His substantial loans, credit guarantees, and sound economic advice helped defray expenses and pay for Portugal's rapidly growing naval empire. Beatrice, who in addition to being Francisco's wife was also the royal physician's sister, was an honored guest in her own right. She was entertained by Queen Catherine, only three years her senior and, just like her, newly married. The two young women must have had a lot to talk about. Through these interactions Dona Beatrice learned how to conduct herself as a highborn Portuguese lady.

Ironically, even as he lavished praise on his Crypto Jewish friends, the Portuguese king was in negotiations with Pope Clement VII to allow the Inquisition to operate in Portugal and expose the secret apostates in its midst. No one publicly suspected the Mendes family of heresy, but Francisco clearly did not relish the idea of investigations on Portuguese soil. To counter the move, he conducted his own secret negotiations with the pope through his emissary in Rome, Senõr Duarte de Paz, and to prevent the arrival of the Inquisition, he sent precious gifts and donations to the pope and the cardinals.[18] His efforts were successful for a few years, but in December 1531 he realized that they were destined to fail. The aging pontiff was about to concede, and Francisco decided to change tactics. Instead of trying to delay the Inquisition, he acquired a brief of protection from the pope, granting him and his family immunity from any future accusations of heresy.[19]

---

[16] Roth, *Dona Gracia*, 23–24. Salomon and Leoni, 139, 141–142. Thomas, "Indian Pepper and German Copper," 319–322. Birnbaum, *The Long Journey*, 3/33-4. Grunbaum-Ballin, *Joseph Naci*, 28. Brummett, *Ottoman Seapower*, 149–153.

[17] Salomon and Leoni, 141.

[18] Segre, "Sephardic Refugees in Ferrara," 175–176. Roth, *Dona Gracia*, 15. Tavim, "Portuguese New Christians," 569.

[19] Salomon and Leoni, 180–181. The original wording of the Latin brief was: *"Quare Franciscus Memendus et Beatrix ac aliis exponentes prefati nobis similiter supplicari fecerunt ut eis in premissis de opportuno remedio iustitie providere de benignitate apostolica dignaremur."*

But then, just as Beatrice and Francisco got their papal papers and felt secure, Diogo was suddenly arrested in Antwerp and accused of a series of crimes, including "Judaizing" (that is, secretly practicing Jewish rites while posing as a Christian), establishing a secret underground route for Marranos to leave Spain and Portugal, and monopolizing the pepper trade. It is difficult to know whether this arrest was retribution for Francisco's success in bribing the pope, part of a new offensive of religious fervor by Emperor Charles and his sisters, or motivated by simple greed. It is clear, however, that the arrest alarmed the king of Portugal, who immediately wrote to the emperor, his brother-in-law, praising the Mendeses in the warmest terms and begging him to release Diogo.

The king's wife, Queen Catherine, wrote her own letter to her brother, describing Francisco and Diogo as cherished friends and diplomatically requesting "*an investigation into [Diogo's] case so that his rights are fully respected with no account taken of any unfavorable report concerning him, and his case dispatched promptly.*" According to some sources, King Henry VIII of England, still friendly with the emperor at this time, also sent a letter in appreciation of Diogo Mendes's support for the English crown, although no such letter has been found in the archives. In any case, the heavy barrage of support letters finally convinced the Habsburg emperor to write to his other sister, Mary, queen-governor of the Netherlands, asking her to release Diogo on bail. Later the charges against him were dropped.[20]

Things got back on track for a while, but three years later, in 1534, Beatrice's husband suddenly died, leaving his young widow in charge of his enormous inheritance. This was soon followed by the death of his protector, Pope Clement VII. The new pope, Paul III (Alessandro Farnese), relented to the Portuguese monarchy's pressure and finally gave it permission to establish the Inquisition in Portugal. Despite the Papal Brief of Protection that she had in her hands, Beatrice understood that Portugal would no longer be safe for her and her family. She decided to leave and join her brother-in-law in Antwerp.[21] Her resolve strengthened when she found out that King João and Queen Catherine, eyeing Francisco's riches, intended to declare themselves legal guardians of her daughter Brianda, to bring the young girl up in the palace as their protégé, and to marry her off to a member of the nobility, making a nice profit on her dowry.[22]

In a move that characterized her throughout her career, Beatrice made a quick decision. She immediately sent emissaries and promissory notes to her brother-in-law in Antwerp, packed her most precious belongings, and left instructions to her underlings in Lisbon. She then set out with her daughter,

---

[20] Viaud, *Lettres des souverains portugais*, 192–193. "Salomon and Leoni," 141–148. For the text of King João and Queen Catherine's letters see ibid., 183–5. Roth, *Dona Gracia*, 34–6. Grunbaum-Ballin, *Joseph Naci*, 29–30. Adelman, "The Venetian Identities," 14–15.

[21] Andrade, "A Senhora e os destino," 96–7.

[22] Salomon and Leoni, 148–149. Andrade, "A Senhora e os Destino," 90.

her sister, and her two orphaned nephews, João and Bernardo Miques, sons of her late brother Agostinho, the court physician. João, who would become famous in the Ottoman sultan's court in later years as Don Joseph Nasi, Duke of Naxos, was twelve years old at the time. Fearing an attempt to prevent her from leaving, she secretly boarded a company ship that took the family to England, where they stayed until final arrangements were made for their settlement in Flanders. Diogo, now one of Antwerp's patrons, asked the mayor and town elders of the city to send a letter to Thomas Cromwell, Henry VIII's adviser, to let him know that a grand lady is on her way *"and should be accorded respect."* He also asked an English friend of his, the chief butler of England John Hussey, to make sure that the family was taken care of during its sojourn in England.[23] At the time of Beatrice's arrival, the island kingdom was rocked by the scandals of Henry VIII's divorce from Katherine of Aragon, Isabella's daughter, and by his marriage to Anne Boleyn in defiance of the pope. We do not know whether Beatrice met with any members of the royal family during her stay.

Antwerp

Meanwhile, Diogo's palatial mansion in Antwerp was made ready to receive the family.[24] Upon her arrival, Beatrice reunited with many of her acquaintances from the Marrano community who found refuge in the city, including her family friend Amatus Lusitanus (also known as João Rodrigues de Castelo Branco/ also known as Haviv Ha-Sephardi), a famous doctor and author who became the Mendeses' personal physician.[25] Soon after their arrival, Diogo married Beatrice's sister, Brianda, at Antwerp's cathedral, in another May–December wedding meant to preserve both the property and the family's secret faith. Their daughter, Beatrice la Chica, was baptized in 1540 with Diogo's Italian friend and business partner, Gian Carlo Affaitati, as her godfather.[26]

While Brianda raised her baby daughter, the in-laws joined forces to expand the firm, merging Diogo's possessions with Beatrice's investments. Business blossomed again, and the nephews, João and Bernardo, were sent to study at Leuven, one of the most prestigious universities in Europe. João is mentioned in the university's list of alumni as a member of the aristocracy (*Dominus*

---

[23] Grunbaum-Ballin, *Joseph Naci*, 31. Roth, *Dona Gracia*, 16. Birnbaum, *The Long Journey*, 3/53. Harozen (Reznik) *Don Yosef Nasi*, 12–14. Beatrice's decision to leave Portugal also hinged on a new edict by Emperor Charles allowing New Christians to settle in the Low Countries.

[24] Twenty years later, when residing in Venice, Beatrice sold the house for some 3000 gold ducats (interestingly, the huge sum loaned by Shylock to Bassano in *The Merchant of Venice*). See Segre, "Sephardic refugees in Ferrara," 179, n. 66.

[25] "Amatus" is a Latin translation of his Jewish name, Haviv. He is credited with discovering the function of the valves in the heart and blood vessels. He later served as Professor of Medicine in Ferrara and as physician in the Vatican.

[26] Andrade, "A Senhora e os destino," 96–97. Note that Beatrice named her daughter Brianda, and Brianda named her daughter Beatrice, indicating good relations between the sisters at that time.

Johannes Micas Lusitanus intitulatus in specie nobilis).[27] Beatrice soon became part of the local elite and was frequently hosted by Mary of Hungary, Emperor Charles's sister. Mary was formally subservient to her brother, but for all practical purposes she ruled the Netherlands and Flanders as an autonomous queen, and Charles treated her as an equal. In Mary's palace, Beatrice hobnobbed with other royalty from northern Europe, including Princess Christina of Denmark, Mary's niece and protégé. Beatrice and Mary discussed loans to the treasury and gossiped about Mary's younger sister, Queen Catherine of Austria, whom Beatrice knew well from Lisbon.[28]

Although Diogo was declared innocent of the crimes he was previously charged with, the emperor's suspicions about his clandestine activities had a basis in truth. While posing as upright members of the Catholic aristocracy, Diogo and Beatrice operated a clandestine underground route to sneak Crypto Jews out of Portugal under the watchful eye of the Inquisition and bring them to Antwerp or send them over the Alps to Italy. In this venture, they were assisted by Daniel Bomberg, a Christian humanist from Antwerp who established a printing press in Venice and was the first to print books in Hebrew.[29] Their operations were speeded up with a sense of urgency when persecution began in Antwerp as well and Christians suspected of Judaizing were imprisoned, tortured, and executed. Part of their operation was predicated on the friendship struck between Beatrice, Diogo, and Ercole II d'Este, Duke of Ferrara in Italy. A courageous defender of his Jewish subjects, the duke promised them that he would shelter the Jews and Marranos sent southward and provide them with lodging. It was clear to the Habsburgs that someone was financing these expensive getaways, and their informants pointed to the involvement of the Mendes family.[30]

Then, in July 1543, another crisis shook the family. In the midst of these underground operations, Diogo fell ill and died. According to his will, all his company's assets were to be bequeathed to Beatrice, his talented sister-in-law. His wife was formally allotted half of the inheritance, but this part was also to be managed by her sister, with Brianda receiving just an annual stipend. This was to prove a bone of contention between the sisters for years to come. Meanwhile, the assets inherited from Diogo, combined with her own, made Beatrice one of the richest people in the continent, probably richer than most monarchs.[31] Although she was a young woman on her own, with no male to front her business, Beatrice kept leading the firm's international business, buying loads of pepper and other goods in India, distributing them in Europe, and exporting European produce to the Far East.[32] At the same time, she kept

[27] Birnbaum, *The Long Journey*, Chapter III.
[28] Geoffrey Parker, *Emperor: A New Life of Charles V*.
[29] Birnbaum, *The Long Journey*, 3/40.
[30] Leoni, "Manoel Lopez Bichacho," 79–81. Segre, "Sephardic Refugees in Ferrara," 170.
[31] Birnbaum, *The Long Journey*, 3/74–76.
[32] Roth, *Dona Gracia*, 39–40. Birnbaum, *The Long Journey*, 3/65. Segre, "Sephardic Refugees in Ferrara," 169 n. 31. Birnbaum, *The Long Journey*, 68.

running the clandestine people-smuggling operations, although she had to shift the relay point because of repeated imperial edicts forbidding the settlement of New Christians in Antwerp and constant demands for bribes from Governor Mary and her courtiers.

As news of Diogo's death spread, vultures began to circle around the family once again, just as they did in Lisbon after Francisco's death. Many hoped to lay their hands on Beatrice's legendary fortune. The most insistent was a certain Don Francisco of Aragon, an illegitimate son of Charles V, who promised his Aunt Mary vast sums of money for arranging a marriage between him and Beatrice's young daughter, Brianda. Knowing Beatrice well, the queen said she would try to convince her but doubted the lady would play along.[33] She was right. Reluctant to give her daughter in marriage to this gold digger (or to any other Christian for that matter) and bearing a deepening grudge against Habsburg greed and their persecution of the Marranos, Beatrice dilly-dallied for as long as she could. This imperial pressure was now added to the constant danger of herself being exposed and tried for heresy. Clear-sighted and resolute as always, she made up her mind to move once again. But this time she wanted to distance herself as much as possible from the clutches of the Habsburg family. A few years later, her fears proved justified when the emperor expelled all the Portuguese New Christians who settled in Antwerp in the previous seven years.[34]

Beatrice knew that leaving would not be that easy this time around. One idea she contemplated was to claim that she would be returning to Portugal. Such a move would seem legitimate to the Habsburgs and would allow her to justify liquidating her business venture in Flanders. In a letter sent by a Medici agent in Antwerp to the Duke of Florence in 1545, the writer reported that this was indeed Beatrice's *declared* intention but added excitedly that in his conversation with her, she inquired specifically about moving to Pisa in Tuscany, suggesting that it was a "convenient location for trading with Spain, Portugal, Naples and Rome." The agent recommended keeping the negotiations secret. It appears from the letter that his patron, Duke Cosimo de Medici, was eager to convince the family to move its business to his domains (Fig. 5.2).[35]

Beatrice considered other possibilities but finally decided to transfer the family and the firm in their entirety to the Most Serene Republic of Venice. She knew that the move would annoy Emperor Charles and his sister Mary, who might suspect, with just cause, that Venice is merely a steppingstone on the way to the Ottoman Empire.[36] To the humiliation of letting the family escape and return to Judaism would then be added that of the Mendes riches serving the Habsburgs' archenemy, Sultan Suleiman. The family's real destination had

---

[33] Grunbaum-Ballin, *Joseph-Naci*, 34–7. Birnbaum, *The Long Journey*, 3/77–80. Andrade, "A Senhora e os destino," 110.
[34] Leoni, "Manoel Lopez Bichacho," 77.
[35] *Medici Archive*, Vol. 1170a, Fol. 455 Recto. October 26, 1545.
[36] Beatrice's plan was apparently to move to the Ottoman Empire from the outset. See *Medici Archive*, Vol. 1172, Fol. 83 Recto.

Fig. 5.2 Gracia Nasi the Younger by Pastorino di Giovan Michele de' Pastorini. Source: The Jewish Museum, New York

therefore to be kept secret for as long as possible. It was a complex maneuver for one of the biggest trading companies in Europe, and months of careful preparation preceded the move.

The first step was obtaining a safe-conduct document from Pope Paul III, permitting her to take her family and retainers to any papal-related territory and specifically exempting them from persecution on the grounds of "*heresy or Judaism*."[37] In the following months the departure was planned like a military operation. The firm's assets had to be gradually siphoned out. She entrusted considerable sums of money to the Affaitatis of Italy and to other international trading houses in return for a promise of reimbursement across the Alps. Some of the assets were given to her comrade-in-arms Daniel Bomberg to send on, and the rest was advanced to monarchs and princes across Europe as loans, to be collected later. In a brazen move, Beatrice offered a loan of 200,000 ducats to Governor-Queen Mary, in order to allay her suspicions and reassure her that the family had every intention of remaining in Habsburg territory. She knew that the chances of recovering this sum were slim.

To assist with these transactions, Beatrice recruited her nephew João Miques, who by that time graduated from Leuven. At school, João spent his nights drinking with Prince Maximillian, heir to the Habsburg throne, who soon

---

[37] Salomon and Leoni, 153. In this period "heresy" usually meant Lutheranism or one of its offshoots.

became his jousting and hunting partner. Hobnobbing with many of Maximillian's royal friends, João became a regular guest at Europe's royal courts.[38] At Beatrice's behest, he traveled to France to invest some of the firm's money there and used his connections to offer loans to its king, Henry II, and to other local rulers. During his stay, the young entrepreneur also tried his hand at a business venture: an investment in silkworms and silk production in Lyons.[39]

But when all the pieces were in place, a flare-up of religious wars inside Europe and a series of new restrictions imposed on the New Christians of Portugal forced Beatrice to delay her exit. In 1544, twenty people were found guilty of Judaizing in Lisbon and burned at the stake. In June that year, an imperial decree forbade the settlement of New Christians in the Low Countries and confined those who had arrived at its ports to a local jail. They were to be interrogated and tried for heresy. In a final push to assist the persecuted, Beatrice sheltered those who got away in her houses, and young Don João was frequently sent to Mary's court to request that those arriving be allowed to stay under house arrest rather than in prison. The detainees were finally released upon payment of a bail of more than 20,000 guilders. Although this monetary arrangement allowed them to settle in the Netherlands, many opted to leave once again and resettle outside Habsburg-controlled territory. It is estimated that about three hundred New Christian families left Antwerp for Italy at that time, carrying with them some four million ducats in gold.[40]

Yet, as Don Francisco of Aragon's determination to marry her daughter grew, Beatrice decided she could no longer wait. Her next move in this hard-nosed chess game against the Habsburgs was to send Reina to Venice with a group of trusted servants, to make sure that whatever happens, her daughter would be out of danger. She herself left a few months later, in early 1545, with her sister Brianda, her employees, and a detail of armed guards. Even with most of her capital safely tucked away, a caravan of such magnitude—in addition to the people and household items, Beatrice's convoy carried 300,000 gold coins, gems, and pearls—was bound to draw attention. To add to the confusion, she announced that her only intention was to spend some time at the healing spa of Aix-la-Chapelle (today's Aachen in Germany) a few days' ride away.[41]

The procession had indeed gone in this direction, making a long stopover at Brussels and spending a couple of weeks "taking the waters" at Aix-La-Chapelle. She had then succeeded in eluding the surveillance of imperial authorities and, exploiting a short pause in the interminable wars between France and the Habsburgs, crossed the border and continued at a leisurely pace

---

[38] See also Harozen (Reznik), *Don Yosef Nasi*, 20–21.
[39] Salomon and Leoni, 152. Birnbaum, *The Long Journey*, 3/65, 3/84. Roth, *House of Nasi*, 5. Andrade, "A Senhora e os destino," 99, 111.
[40] Birnbaum, *The Long Journey*, 3/74. See also a translation of the section of "Consolations for the tribulations of Israel" in Roth, *Dona Gracia*, 77.
[41] Birnbaum, *The Long Journey*, 3/81. Grunbaum-Ballin, *Joseph Naci*, 36–37. Salomon and Leoni, 154–5. Roth, *Dona Gracia*, 44–45.

on to Lyons.⁴² France's monarchs, Henry II and his wife Catherine de Medici, recently granted New Christians permission to settle in France, and Beatrice felt more secure going through their domains than through Habsburg territories.⁴³ When her deception and getaway were finally discovered by the authorities, the frustrated emperor ordered an embargo on all her real estate and on forty chests full of valuables, still kept in Antwerp. Negotiating for return of these assets would be João's next assignment.⁴⁴

We do not have a full record of Beatrice's year-long trip to Venice, but her journey took her through Lorraine, Alsace, and Burgundy, and we may surmise that during the journey, she met with other dukes and princes, including Princess Christina of Denmark, her old acquaintance from Antwerp, who traveled the same route from Brussels at the time to be crowned regent of the Duchy of Lorraine.⁴⁵ Then, after a short layover at Besançon, the procession stopped at Lyon, France's bustling industrial and commercial center. Based on the connections that João made in his earlier foray, Beatrice collected debts, renegotiated loans, cut new deals for imports, and made investments in commercial ventures.⁴⁶ Lyon was now designated as the Mendes family's new business headquarters, and João was put in charge as Beatrice and her entourage continued on to Venice. It is not known whether she met with any of France's royal family during this time, but she may have met with Diane de Poitiers, Henry II's beloved concubine and his partner in government. A few years later, Duke Ercole II of Ferrara, Beatrice's personal friend, would send a letter to Madame de Poitiers on Beatrice's behalf.⁴⁷ In any case, France's monarchs received another hefty loan from the Mendes firm.⁴⁸

The caravan then snaked across the Alps to Turin and continued on to Milan, the seat of the Sforza family, where some initial connections may have been established, and thence on to La Serenissima, the Republic of Venice, where Beatrice finally settled. During the entire trip and the first months in Venice, messengers went back and forth between Beatrice and her nephew, who took care of business up north. João traveled to Antwerp and Regensburg, where the indignant Emperor Charles held court, to demand release of the Flanders property. This may seem like an act of defiance against one of the most powerful kings of the period, but as Beatrice knew well, the Habsburg Empire's huge new territorial expansion in Mexico (then called "New Spain") and Peru and its constant wars with France and the Ottomans necessitated a steady flow of money loans. Charles and his sister Mary were therefore careful not to lose the trust of the banking community—the Fuggers, the Affaitati, and others—who resented any royal attempt to confiscate property and supported João's

---

⁴²Roth, *Dona Gracia*, 45.
⁴³Segre, "Sephardic Refugees in Ferrara," 169, 178.
⁴⁴Birnbaum, *The Long Journey*, 3/81.
⁴⁵Cartwright, *Christina of Denmark*, years 1544–1545.
⁴⁶Roth, *Dona Gracia*, 61 (French ambassador letter).
⁴⁷Segre, "Sephardic Refugees in Ferrara," 172, n. 45.
⁴⁸Ibid., 178. Birnbaum, *The Long Journey*, 4/1.

claims. The emperor had to walk a fine line between his sister's fury at Beatrice's escape, his own anger and greed, and his total reliance on Antwerp's trading community. João drove a hard bargain, and at some point, with the promise of another loan, even recruited the local cardinal, Dausburg, to convince Princess Mary to let go of the Mendes property. With typical audacity, as part of the negotiations with Emperor Charles the young man also elicited a formal knighthood rank—*Capitaine de la cavalerie*.[49]

Finally, in July 1546, the emperor caved and informed his sister Mary in a short personal note in his peculiar French—a treat to lovers of the language—that an agreement was reached and that in return for payment of a lump sum and an interest-free loan, the properties in Antwerp and Aix should be returned to the Mendes family:[50]

> *Madame ma bonne sour, Jehan Micas, facteur des vesve et filles de feuz Francisco et Diego Mendis, s'est icy trouve devers moy et apres plusieurs communications l'on a finablement traicte et conclud avec luy ce que vous verrez par la copie dudit traicte que je vous envoie cy-joint lequel ferez observer de poinct a aultre selon sa teneur et desarrester tous les deniers, biens et aultres choses de quelque qualite qu'ils soyent qui a l'occasion de leur absence sont este arrestez[.]*[51]

Mary refused to acknowledge the agreement and threatened to appeal to the royal council to annul it. Their coffers were empty, she protested, and the Mendes properties would greatly improve the empire's financial situation. But the emperor insisted that he gave his word and signed the deal, and finally his sister had to let go.[52]

Venice

Business-wise, relocation to Venice turned out to be a smart move. After a slow decline at the beginning of the century as a result of the discovery of new trade routes, in the 1540s Venice's trade with India picked up again, almost eclipsing that of Portugal. It may have been caused by the new threat posed to Portuguese

---

[49] Roth, *Dona Gracia*, 47. Grunebaum Ballin, *Joseph Naci*, 37–38. Harozen (Reznik) *Don Yosef Nasi*, 35.

[50] Salomon and Leoni, 155, 193. Grunbaum-Ballin, *Joseph Naci*, 37–38. Roth, *Dona Gracia*, 47. Jacob Reznik, *Le Duc Joseph de Naxos* (Paris, 1936) 52–72, presents *in extenso* the transcription (including two facsimiles) of the correspondence between Emperor Charles V and his sister Queen Mary of Hungary, governor of the Netherlands, extending from April 6, 1546, to July 3 1547, culled from BAGR, PEA, 4, Reg. 55–59.

[51] "Salomon and Leoni," 193. ("Madame my good sister, Jehan Micas, the agent of the widow and daughters of Francisco and Diego Mendes, has presented himself here before me, and after many communications we have finally agreed and concluded with him that which you will see in the copy of the said treaty, which I send in attachment, and which you shall follow from one point to the next according to its content and release all the goods and other things of whatever quality, which have been confiscated on the occasion of their absence.")

[52] Harozen/Reznik, *Don Yosef Nasi*, 40–41.

trade by the newly arrived Ottoman Indian Ocean fleet, or by "*the reputedly inferior quality of Portuguese commodities, whose aroma, according to connoisseurs, was diminished by the long sea voyage.*"[53] The Portuguese pressured the Indian producers to sell at low prices, and by paying slightly more, the Venetians reserved the best products for themselves. As a shrewd businesswoman, Beatrice may have noticed the turning tide earlier than others and chose Venice as her next abode over other cities.

By that time Jews were permitted to live in Venice if they resided inside the Ghetto—the quarter specifically designated for their use—but, hanging on to her Christian identity, Beatrice rented a palazzo on the Grand Canal in the best area, near the state mint (*zecca*) and the ducal palace. To the outside world the Mendes family led "*a flamboyant social life*" with frequent parties, but behind the scenes Beatrice managed to make the house a temporary center for Marrano refugees passing through Venice on their way to the East.[54] The wealthy lady soon became an object of fascination and gossip in town, and one might assume she met with the current doge, Francisco Donato, and with his wife, Alicia Giustiniani, who at the time was busy overhauling the glass industry on the island of Murano. In the elegant parties she threw in her palace, partly to cover her underground smuggling operation, Beatrice would have met the future dogaressa, Zilia Dandolo, who was the city's leading female aristocrat and power broker.[55] A few years later, in 1557, when Zilia's husband, Lorenzo Priuli, was elected doge of Venice, Zilia herself was crowned in an unprecedented ceremony. Beatrice may have also entertained the next dogaressa in line, Cecilia Contarini, whose family members were frequently elected doges and ambassadors to the Ottoman Empire and who enjoyed the same exceptional honors as her predecessor. Years later, already settled in Istanbul, she continued to correspond with these aristocratic Venetian women.[56]

Although life in Venice was comfortable and most of the property was recovered by her competent nephew, Beatrice planned to move on to Istanbul. There were several reasons for the move. First, she was tired of constantly posing as a Christian, but living as a Jew, even in Venice, was still fraught with danger. In the Ottoman Empire, in contrast, the leadership welcomed Jews and had no qualms about letting them keep their faith. They were trusted in the Ottoman "well-guarded domains" more than Western Christians, and they often served as a necessary cultural link between the two civilizations. The advantages of moving East were even greater for Marranos. Though despised in many Christian states, Jews were allowed to subsist. Those who wished to return to Judaism *after* conversion, on the other hand, were perceived as apostates, hunted down, and sometimes burned at the stake.

---

[53] Braudel, *The Mediterranean*, 545.
[54] "Salomon and Leoni," 155. Roth, *Dona Gracia*, 52.
[55] Crawford, *Catherine de Medici*, 655. At the time Zilia's brother, Matteo Dandolo, was Venice's ambassador to Rome and to France.
[56] Staley, *The Dogaressas*, 254–266, 277–278.

Second, with Sultan Suleiman and his wife Hurrem at the helm, the state was clearly a rising global power, commercially as well as politically. A few years earlier they had conquered Egypt and Syria from the Mamluks, taken Mesopotamia from their Safavid rivals, expanded their rule deep into the Caucasus, advanced westward to Hungary in central Europe, and even besieged Vienna. These territorial gains gave them full control of all land routes to India and East Asia and even threatened Portuguese supremacy in the Red Sea and the Persian Gulf. After the decisive Ottoman victory over the combined Habsburg-Genoese fleet at Preveza in 1538, the Ottomans were well on their way to dominating the central Mediterranean as well. From a business point of view, then, it made sense for the Mendes trading house to ally itself with the sultan's court, while hedging its bets by maintaining the maritime Indian trade through their agents on the Atlantic seaboard.

Once again, the move had to be prepared in secret, and, fearing arrest at the last moment, Beatrice sought the sultan's protection. The Venetians were the Ottomans' political and business rivals in the eastern Mediterranean but were always in awe of their military power and did their best to maintain cordial diplomatic relations. She sent letters and presents to her allies in Istanbul and cultivated a relationship with Moshe Hamon, royal physician to the Sultan, and with the *kira*, Esther Handali, Hurrem Sultan's assistant. The first Ottoman request to the Venetians to allow Beatrice and Reina to leave for Istanbul was made in 1549. Later, when this request was ignored, Hamon raised the issue with Suleiman and Hurrem, who expressed interest and agreed to help.[57]

But a year earlier, as Beatrice's allies in Istanbul laid the groundwork for the move, Brianda, jealous of her sister's fortunes and vexed at having no part of the company, glimpsed an opportunity. Now that Beatrice was on the cusp of moving to the enemy's camp, she decided to sue her in a Venetian court. Diogo's inheritance, she claimed, was to be divided equally between them, but Beatrice was proclaimed legal guardian of her niece (Brianda's daughter) in Antwerp and, therefore, given control of her sister's part as well. Now that circumstances have changed and the family moved to Venice, she demanded her share as mother and widow. She also insinuated that Beatrice was Judaizing in secret. Brianda believed that when the Venetian Senate learned of Beatrice's plans to defect to the Ottoman side and disavow her Christianity, its members would side with her.

As always, Beatrice was one step ahead. As soon as the trial began, she asked her friend Duke Ercole II d'Este for a permit of safe conduct to Ferrara. The duke willingly complied. In December 1548, when the court in Venice demanded that she deposit half of her assets in the city's mint in anticipation of a final verdict, she understood that a ruling in favor of Brianda was the most likely outcome. In the still of the night, she and her household left the city and

---

[57] Roth, *Dona Gracia*, 56–57. Heyd, "Moses Hamon," 159–160.

moved to the duchy of Ferrara, seventy miles to the south.[58] Her old physician, Amatus Lusitanus, and some of her assistants were already settled there waiting for her.[59]

Ferrara

When Beatrice arrived, Ferrara's court was one of the most refined in Italy, a model of Renaissance taste and budding humanism. Duke Ercole II d'Este was a nephew of Isabella d'Este, known as "the first lady of the Renaissance," and in his youth was acquainted with the period's greatest artists, including Leonardo Da Vinci, Michelangelo, Raphael, and Giovanni Bellini, and with famous writers and thinkers such as Baldassare Castiglione, author of the famous *Book of the Courtier* and one of the great advocates of women's education. Ercole and his wife Renée, daughter of King Louis XII of France, also supported learning, protected their Jewish and Marrano subjects, and were excited about the lady's arrival. As soon as Beatrice arrived, the duke's secretary, Bartolomeo Prospero, offered her his family's palatial villa in the Giovecca district, and she rented it for the significant sum of 200 scudi for two years. The rental document describes it as a two-story building made of marble, with painted ceilings in the living rooms, orchards, vineyards, cold-storage rooms, bakeries, and even "two marble columns both carrying a statue of Hercules of fine metal" in the garden.[60]

Before settling in, there was one more order of business to take care of. In anticipation of the negative outcome of the court case between the sisters in Venice, the duke signed a legal decree confirming Beatrice's executive powers in the management of the inheritance and reaffirming the terms of Diogo's will. The "*splendidissima domina Beatrix ex Luna nobilis Lusitanie*," he announced, was entitled to hold on to her property, issue power of attorney to her agents in Portugal, Spain, Antwerp, and Lyons, and run all company affairs, including in the name of her young niece.

In 1548, Ferrara was an important center for Iberian Jews. The head of the community at the time was Dona Benvenida Abrabanel. Benvenida's late husband, Samuel, was the son of Don Isaac Abrabanel, the minister who was asked to arbitrate the spice dispute between Portugal and Venice all those years ago. The family settled in Naples, which, although under Spanish rule at the time, was free of the Inquisition. The Abrabanels had such high standing that the Spanish viceroy, Don Pedro de Toledo, entrusted the upbringing of his daughter Eleonora to Benvenida and Samuel. But in 1541, under pressure from Emperor Charles, the Jewish community was expelled from Naples, and although the Abrabanels were given permission to stay, they decided to leave

---

[58] "Salomon and Leoni," 156. Segre, "Sephardic Refugees in Ferrara," 169–170. Roth, *Dona Gracia*, 54–62.

[59] Andrade, "A Senhora e os destino," 110.

[60] Segre, "Sephardic Refugees in Ferrara," 181. One scudo weighed more than 20 grams of silver.

Fig. 5.3 Map of the Duchy of Ferrara in the sixteenth century, copper engraving by Joan and Cornelius Blaeu, c. 1640. Koninklijke biblioteek, The Hague

along with the other members of the community. Hearing about the expulsion, Duke Ercole asked his secretary about Abrabanel, and Prospero described him as "*the king of the Jews from the Kingdom of Naples.*" The duke invited the entire community to settle in Ferrara (Fig. 5.3).

Even though they never renounced their Judaism, the Abrabanels conducted themselves as royalty. They held court in their Ferrara mansion, handed out charity and alms to the poor, and invested in the arts and sciences.[61] Their reputation reached Beatrice long before she arrived in Ferrara, and she was impressed both by their adherence to Judaism in the face of all obstacles and by their commitment to the community. If Samuel Abrabanel was king, his wife Benvenida, whose story will be told below, was the undisputed queen of Italian Jewry, reigning supreme long after her husband died.[62] Dona Benvenida was both a model and a challenge for Beatrice. A meeting between the two was arranged soon after her arrival. This is an imagined description of this first meeting:

Although Benvenida saw herself as an Italian Jew, and was suspicious of the immigrants from the Iberian Peninsula who still embraced their Christianity, she admired

---

[61] Usque, *Consolation*, 209–210.
[62] Griffi, "Documenti Inediti," 28.

Beatrice both for her business acumen and for the long years of clandestine work smuggling Jews from Portugal and Flanders, many of whom arrived in Ferrara. Beatrice, of course, already heard stories about the aristocratic Abrabanel family as a child and had some dealings with them even before her arrival in Italy. She was a guest in town, and since Benvenida was still officially in mourning, she came to pay her respects.

They met in an elegant drawing room lined with books. Dressed in black, Benvenida embraced Beatrice, greeted her in Spanish and Hebrew, and invited her to sit. Servants offered wine and small dishes, and the two exchanged polite small talk. Gracia thanked Benvenida for her hospitality, and told her about the circumstances of her arrival. Then she talked about her sister's betrayal, which Benvenida had already heard about in detail from the duke. Soon the discussion turned to business. Both families had banking and trade ventures, and the widowed Benvenida asked Beatrice for advice. Beatrice offered her experiences of Venice, Lyons and the industrial development of France, and Benvenida told her about her special relationship with her foster daughter Eleonora di Toledo, now married to Duke Cosimo de Medici. The two women decided to join forces and use their banking networks to their mutual benefit.

Warming up to each other, they shared stories of persecution and exile, and Beatrice said she always wanted to renounce her Christianity and return to Judaism but that at every turn this posed insurmountable problems for her business and her loved ones. Benvenida assured her that in Ferrara, under Duke Ercole, she could safely return to the faith.

At the end of the visit Beatrice decided to take the jump. From now on, she said, everyone should refer to her by her Jewish name, Dona Gracia.

Soon Beatrice/Gracia was introduced to Eleonora, who maintained a close relationship with Benvenida even after she married in 1539 and became Duchess of Tuscany.[63] The Mendes company already had commercial ties with the Florentine banking houses of Antinori and Salviati since the 1530s, and these ties were further developed in 1549, when Cosimo granted Dona Gracia and her firm license to dwell and trade in Tuscany. But they were considerably strengthened during Gracia's stay in Ferrara.[64]

There were rumors of enmity between the two women, but for Dona Gracia, taking her first hesitant steps as a Jew in plain sight, Benvenida was mainly a role model of Jewish nobility. She was not just a leader of the community, but also a donor and benefactor who sponsored many works of art and letters. Emulating her, Gracia also began to support Jewish learning and publication during her short stay in Ferrara.[65] In 1553, the author Samuel Usque dedicated his famous book *Consolation for the Tribulations of Israel* to "the great senora" Dona Gracia, his old friend and patroness who financed its publication. But in

---

[63] Roth, *Dona Gracia*, 66–68. Griffi, "Documenti Inediti," 29. Birnbaum, *The Long Journey*, 25.
[64] Segre, "Sephardic Refugees," 174–177.
[65] Birnbaum, "Jewish Patronage in Sixteenth Century Ferrara," 139. Segre, "Sephardic Refugees in Ferrara." Roth, *Dona Gracia*, 63–64. Birnbaum, *The Long Journey*, 23–25.

the book, as we will see below, he spares no praise for Benvenida and Samuel Abrabanel, a clear indication of the warm relationship between the two women.

With Benvenida's assistance Gracia set up a charity for the needy.[66] During her stay she also sponsored the publication of the famous Bible of Ferrara, which was printed in two versions: Ladino for the Sephardic Jews and Spanish, dedicated to the Duke of Ferrara, for the Christians. The translation to Ladino was made by Yom Tov Athias (also known as Jerónimo Vargas) and Abraham Usque (Duarte Pinhel). But it was the translation into Spanish that was really revolutionary. In Western Europe, up to the sixteenth century, the Christian Bible could only be copied or printed in Latin. Those who translated it into vulgar languages such as English, French, or Dutch were arrested and often executed for blasphemy. Now for the first time, speakers of Spanish who could not understand Latin were able to read the Bible in their own language.[67]

In 1551, Gracia returned to Venice to settle the dispute over her family's remaining property with the city's tribunal and move on to Istanbul. Several months earlier, realizing that her sister had gotten the best of her once again, Brianda accepted her defeat and joined Beatrice in Ferrara.[68] In the following year, the duke (who was promised a special fee by Brianda) worked hard to settle the dispute between the two sisters. They finally signed a notarized agreement in his palace in July 1550.

Returning as an apostate to the city that she left amid a rancorous trial was a risky move. Gracia was indeed arrested, but this time, as she knew well, she had the formal backing of the sultan, whose shadow loomed ever bigger in recent decades.[69] In early 1552, Suleiman himself sent a letter to the doge of Venice, Francesco Donato, demanding that "the two widows," which he claimed were relatives of his royal physician, Moshe Hamon, were under his protection and should be allowed to emigrate to Istanbul with their family members. Since the trial was not yet officially over, and decisions were complicated by Brianda still insisting on being a Catholic, the sultanic messenger (*çavuş*) was asked by the doge to delay his mission, and his return had reportedly enraged the sultan and his ministers. Dona Gracia was eventually released and returned to Ferrara for a while, but the story did not end there.[70] A few months later the Ottoman messenger was sent again, but this time he was formally received by the Venetian senate. Despite being under Ottoman protection, and thus able to leave Venice

---

[66] Cook, "A Pilgrimage to a Personality," 154.

[67] Cook, "A Pilgrimage to a Personality," 154. Roth, *Dona Gracia*, 72. See also Alberto Manguel, *A History of Reading*, 69.

[68] Segre, "Sephardic Refugees in Ferrara," 170, n. 34. Roth, *Dona Gracia*, 61–62 (French ambassador letter).

[69] Roth, *Dona Gracia*, 79–81.

[70] Heyd, "Moses Hamon," 159. See also *Medici Archive*, Vol. 2968, Fol. 351 Recto; Vol. 2968, Fol. 363 Recto. The author, a Florentine in Venice, recounts that the Ottoman Ciaus (çavus) was ostensibly sent to reassure Venice about Ottoman friendship, but his real purpose was to accompany Dona Gracia and her family to Constantinople. In the second letter, the author seems to believe that João Miques, the proposed bridegroom of Gracia's daughter, is the son of Suleiman's doctor.

in splendor, thumbing her nose at the Venetian authorities, this time Dona Gracia did not return to the city. She had her agents take care of the property in Venice and left Ferrara in August 1552 for the port of Ancona.

Accompanied by many other conversos seeking to escape Christianity, she and her retinue boarded a ship to Ragusa, a semiautonomous island republic on the other side of the Adriatic Sea. Ragusa (today's Dubrovnik) served as a commercial exchange zone between Venice and the Muslim world.[71] Its port provided an ideal point of transit for commodities going to and from Europe and Asia. Understanding its importance as a commercial hub, Gracia rented a large warehouse on the waterfront for her merchandise and negotiated with the Ragusan authorities a generous customs contract for the great volume of trade passing through the port. While there, she also prepared notarized letters formally ending her partnership with four agents who remained in Italy, including her nephew João Miques and Tomaso Gomes. Now that she openly embraced Judaism, she felt it was necessary to sever such formal ties in order to protect them from interrogations by the Inquisition and confiscations of property.[72]

The Ragusans were in a bind. The deal with the lady was tempting, but business with the Italian states was their lifeline, and authorities in the mainland might be furious about the Mendes fortune slipping through their fingers and passing into infidel hands. In their ire, the Venetians were liable to accuse the Ragusans of aiding and abetting an apostate. Fearing punishment, they dithered on her offer to make use of their port for transit. Finally, in November 1552, her agents upped the ante, promising a special bonus of 500 ducats up front, and the authorities agreed to the deal.[73]

By that time her caravan was on its way to Istanbul through the city of Salonica (Thessaloniki), which had become a hub of industry, commerce, and learning for Spanish-speaking deportees even before the 1492 expulsion. Over more than a century, those who arrived from the Iberian Peninsula brought with them new sophisticated textile and metallurgy techniques, which they combined with Ottoman craftsmanship to transform the city's artisanal manufacturing. Salonica became a thriving source of exports to Europe and the Middle East.[74] Ladino, Spanish, and Portuguese were more common in its streets than Greek or Turkish. It was a vibrant city in which Jews and others moved freely and could reside anywhere without hindrance.[75] A few years

---

[71] Roth, *Dona Gracia*, 85–87. Roth assumes she had arrived in Ragusa at the beginning of 1553, but she was there already in the summer of 1552. See Miović and Severović, "Gracia Mendes in Dubrovnik," 68–69.

[72] Heyd, "Moses Hamon," 159. Miović and Severović, "Gracia Mendes in Dubrovnik," 67–68. On the Jewish merchants of Raguza/Dubrovnik, see also Metin ZIya Köse, *Osmanli Devleti ve Dubrovnik Ilişkileri, 1500–1600*.

[73] Miović and Severović, "Gracia Mendes in Dubrovnik," 67–75.

[74] Braude, Benjamin. "The Rise and fall of Salonica Woollens, 1500–1650: Technology transfer and western competition." *Mediterranean Historical Review* 6.2 (1991): 216–236. Minna ROzen.

[75] Roth, *Dona Gracia*, 86–87.

later, perhaps remembering her initial amazement at this lively Jewish center, Dona Gracia founded a synagogue in Salonica with an adjoining rabbinic academy.

Istanbul

When the convoy passed through Edirne Gate in early 1553, Istanbul was a proud imperial capital. Rushing through the streets, Dona Gracia's four carriages must have impressed those who watched them, but she also felt a sense of awe riding through this thousand-year-old imperial center. With a population of more than half a million Turks, Greeks, Armenians, Arabs, and Jews and a sizable community of foreign diplomats, merchants, and adventure seekers, all vying for space in its crowded and colorful streets, Istanbul was truly a cosmopolitan city. Lisbon, Antwerp, and even Venice, numbering around 100,000–120,000 inhabitants each, were mere villages in comparison.

Although she was relieved to reach this haven at the end of her long and grueling trip, she probably felt somewhat disoriented. With its minarets, wooden houses, and winding streets, this was a very different place from the European cities she was accustomed to, and her nephew João, her pillar of strength, was far away. But she was attracted to the city's bustling commerce, to the dozens of ships from the Black Sea and the Mediterranean in the Golden Horn harbor, to the heavily laden camel and donkey caravans moving through the streets, and to her coreligionists' communities with their synagogues in full view: Romaniotes, Castilians, Granadans, Portuguese, and Ashkenazis of all kinds bickering as usual about every point of law. Even the European diplomats in Galata felt different. They were a comforting sight, part of the familiar cultural world she grew up in.

Known in the West as "the Magnificent," and in his own domains as "the Lawgiver," Sultan Suleiman had been on the throne for 33 years when she arrived, and his experience on the world stage was matched only by that of his wife, Hurrem Sultan, and his hated rival, Emperor Charles V Habsburg. Taxes and tributes flowed into the sultan's treasury from all the provinces and vassal states, along with taxes and customs duties on trade between Asia and Europe. Even the welfare of Venice depended on his good will. Some Jews, including Istanbul's chief rabbi (*haham başı*) Elija Capsali, who died a couple of years before her arrival, believed that the great sultan is the redeemer who will deliver them from the yoke of "wicked Rome" and lead them to the promised land. Others were just thankful for a state in which they could profess their religion without fear of persecution.[76]

But 1553 was a difficult year, and despite the tributes arriving from all the provinces, imperial resources were stretched. After twenty years of border skirmishes, war with the Safavid Empire was again imminent, and Suleiman ordered

---

[76] Roth, *Dona Gracia*, 87–88. On Catherine de Medici, see Chap. 6.

his grand vizier, Rustem Pasha, to equip and lead his armies against Shah Tahmasp. A couple of months later Suleiman himself followed suit. At the same time, bound by his treaty with France, he had to send his Mediterranean fleet to assist its invasion of Spain-occupied Corsica. Things took a turn for the worse in October of that year. On his way to the eastern front, Suleiman was informed that his eldest and most talented son, Prince Mustafa, who was expected to join the war with his troops, was instead planning a coup against him. When Mustafa came to his headquarters to pay his respects, Suleiman's guards seized and killed him, causing an uproar in the ranks. Anatolia was in disarray, and for a while the sultanic throne—and Hurrem's standing in court—seemed to teeter on the brink. Order was only restored after Mustafa's coffin was brought to Istanbul and buried in state.[77]

Dona Gracia must have known about these events, but initially she did not involve herself in royal politics. Her servants had prepared a mansion in Galata for her when she arrived, right across the Golden Horn from the Topkapı palace.[78] The new house *"reproduced on the banks of the Bosphorus the domestic manners of a patrician family of Lisbon, Antwerp, or Venice,"* but much like the one on the Grand Canal, it also served as a transit station, sheltering Jews and Marranos who came into the empire from Europe and needed a place to stay. Soon Gracia also established a local charity for the community. It was said that every day eighty paupers ate at her table. To members of the ex-Iberian community, she became known as "La Señora."[79]

There were two people she was especially anxious to meet as soon as she arrived. The first was Moshe Hamon, the royal physician who sponsored her attempts to obtain the sultan's support. By that time Hamon was also involved in diplomacy, helping the sultana and her daughter Mihrimah to fashion the empire's policies vis-à-vis Europe and the Balkans. But for Dona Gracia the physician also represented a delicate dilemma. She knew that one of his reasons for investing so much in bringing her over was his wish to have his son marry her daughter. But Gracia had decided long ago that Reina should marry her cousin João/Joseph in order to keep the family's assets intact. There must have been a few awkward moments in her first meetings with Hamon, but she finally made it clear to the doctor that he stood to gain from their partnership in many other ways. They remained friends throughout their lives.[80]

The second person Gracia asked to meet as early as possible was the sultana's *kira*, Esther Handali, whose story will be told below. She was the only person

---

[77] Andrea, "Women and Islam," 18. Szabari, "The Crescent Moon," 1. Busbecq, *Turkish Letters*, 43. For a dramatic description of Mustafa's execution see Clot, *Suleiman the Magnificent*, 158–159.

[78] Birnbaum, *The Long Journey*, 60, 47–58. See also Galante, *Esther Kyra*, 6. Although there are no records of any connection before 1565, Galante believes Esther Handali assisted Dona Gracia upon her arrival in Istanbul.

[79] Roth, *Dona Gracia*, 103–104. Birnbaum, *The Long Journey*, 64. The variants "Señora," "senhora," and "Signora" were all used by different communities in the empire.

[80] Birnbaum, *The Long Journey*, 62.

outside the palace at the time with direct access to Hurrem Sultan.[81] And as the sultana's jeweler, clothier, and personal envoy to diplomats and courtiers outside the palace, she was in a position to influence Ottoman policymaking. Dona Gracia wanted to thank her for her assistance but also to find the quickest inroads into the core of Ottoman power. It was Esther Handali and Moshe Hamon who introduced her to the Ottoman governing elite and created contacts with the sultana and her husband, Sultan Suleiman.

As described in the first chapter, the Ottoman governing elite in the sixteenth century was composed in large part of former Christians culled from villages inside the empire. They were recruited in a process called *devşirme*, (literally, "gathering") and formally proclaimed "slaves of the gate." The most impressive ones were brought to the sultan's palace, converted to Islam and trained for several years to fill positions of leadership. Others in the elite came from prominent Muslim families, but to join the governing circle, they too had to accept a formal servile status. The most successful ones became the sultan's closest aides—army commanders, governors, and his personal retinue. It was a system built on merit and personal excellence, but it also ensconced the palace and the harem in an almost impenetrable shell. Few outsiders could interact directly with the sultanic family. To advance her business and politics, Dona Gracia needed the goodwill of this inner circle, and she knew that Esther would be an important conduit. Hans Derschwam, the Fugger House representative, who clearly saw her as competition, was envious of her rapid integration into the Ottoman elite. "*She claims that she had left a great fortune in Europe and that it will soon reach her here,*" he wrote, "*but with their expenses, it will soon shrink, since she richly pays the pashas, and has given several thousands of ducats to the Jewish hospital and has distributed money among the poor.*"[82]

Gracia was already a very wealthy woman, but there seemed to be so many new opportunities that it was difficult to decide what to do first. The Ottoman Empire had been growing at a very fast pace in recent years. The Middle East, Hungary, Moldavia, Transylvania, the Caucasus, parts of the Persian Gulf, and the coasts of North Africa were new conquests. The Black Sea and the Eastern Mediterranean were dominated by Ottoman navies. Soon Gracia took over a chunk of the European trade in pepper and grain through Venice, Ancona, and Tuscany and imported quantities of textiles from Europe. "*The operations were on such a scale that Dona Gracia had her own ships to carry the goods; and it was said that she even built them.*"[83]

But this trade needed the empire's protection, and the key was the Topkapı palace. Gracia soon convinced Esther *Kira* to introduce her to Hurrem Sultan, who immediately saw the potential of having this entrepreneurial woman as an

---

[81] Galante, *Esther Kyra*, 6. Uriel Heyd, "Moses Hamon," 159–160. Roth, *Dona Gracia*, 102–108.
[82] Birnbaum, *The Long Journey*, 64.
[83] Roth, *Dona Gracia*, 112. Birnbaum, *The Long Journey*, 58.

ally. Having traveled all over Europe, Gracia understood continental politics better than most people, and she used her connections to develop trade and diplomatic relations with Venice, Ferrara, and Tuscany. This trade allowed her agents in Italy, Agostino Enriques and Duarte Gomez, to amass such great wealth that they themselves became part of Venice's patrician society. It was a natural next step to employ the Mendes factors all over Europe as diplomatic go-betweens and as an intelligence gathering service. Soon Gracia's network provided crucial information, which in many instances was delivered to the harem even before it reached the sultan.[84]

The three women—Hurrem Sultan, Dona Gracia, and Esther Handali—assisted by Gracia's network tried to reshape the neighborhood. They conspired with the community of traders in the Portuguese "Estado da India," many of them New Christians of Jewish origin, to hand their colony over to the Ottomans and thereby enable them to monopolize the entire spice trade.[85] But, trading under the Portuguese flag and protected by its strong navy, the India traders were disinclined to cooperate with such a dubious plan, especially when it seemed that there was no real military backing for it. Other schemes were more successful. During the Ottoman-Safavid war, the Habsburg court saw an opportunity to reclaim Hungary and pressured Princess Isabella, widow of the Ottomans' Hungarian vassal, King John Zapolya, to marry a Habsburg prince and relinquish her son's claim to the Hungarian throne. Dona Gracia backed and financed the attempt made by Hurrem and her daughter, Princess Mihrimah, to convince Isabella to refuse the Habsburg proposal and stay on as regent on behalf of her young son under Ottoman tutelage. The Habsburgs understood the Ottomans' commitment to Isabella and trod carefully until Suleiman's return from his Persian campaign (Fig. 5.4).[86]

In 1554, Gracia was joined in Istanbul by her nephew João, by now a thirty-year-old European aristocrat, who soon after his arrival formally reconverted to Judaism and changed his name to Don Joseph Nasi. A few weeks later he married Reina, his cousin and playmate ever since they both played hide and seek on the decks of the boat that took them from Lisbon to England. Soon after his arrival his aunt introduced him to the sultan and to Prince Selim. The gallant young man regaled the royal entourage with tales about his meetings with Emperor Charles in Augsburg and with King Henri II in Paris, and joked about his university drinking mate, Prince Maximillian, who was to become Holy Roman Emperor a decade later. He soon joined Selim's retinue, hitching his fate to that of the next sultan.

---

[84] See, for instance, Gürkan, "Espionage in the 16th Century Mediterranean," 4–7. Roth, *Dona Gracia*, 106–107.
[85] Tavim, "Portuguese Jewish Communities," 569–570.
[86] Tracy, "the Road to Szigetvar," 19–20. Peirce, *Empress of the East*, 251–252. See the details of this episode in Chap. 1.

Fig. 5.4 Dona Gracia on an Israeli stamp issued in 1992

The Ancona Boycott

Two years later, the friendship Gracia had built with Hurrem, and her financial support of the empire's campaigns, were put to the test. In 1555 the newly elected pope, Paul IV, published an antisemitic edict known as "*Cum Nimis Absurdum*," named for its opening words: "*Since it is absurd and utterly inconvenient that the Jews, who through their own fault were condemned by God to eternal slavery...*" The edict declared the necessity of subduing the Jews and restricting their economic, social, and geographical mobility. It proclaimed the establishment of a special quarter in Rome (Ghetto, named after the Venetian enclosure) enclosed by a wall with one gate, required the Jews to wear distinctive clothes and yellow hats in order to be immediately recognizable on the street, allowed them to have only one synagogue, destroying all others, and limited the occupations they were allowed to practice to the sale of secondhand clothing and preparation of food. Paul IV had a particular loathing for the New Christians, whom he saw as traitors to the faith that had welcomed them. In the same year, he ordered the arrest of a group of people in the port city of Ancona suspected of performing Jewish rites and prayers in secret. Many in this group were merchants who had settled in Ancona only after receiving specific guarantees from the previous pope that they would not be persecuted for their religious beliefs. Breaking his predecessor's promise, the new pope had twenty-four of them indicted for heresy and burned at the stake in the town's main square. Some of the others paid bribes and managed to save their lives, but most of those who weren't executed were sentenced to serve as oarsmen in the galleys, which was practically a death sentence as well.[87]

Dona Gracia was livid. Ancona was one of her main trade depots, some among those executed were her agents and factors, and others she knew personally and helped escape from Portugal. She felt responsible for their fate.[88] As soon as she received news of their arrest, she contacted her allies at court—Esther *Kira*, Moshe Hamon, and the sultana—and requested an audience with the sultan. After hearing the report, Suleiman sent an envoy to Ancona to demand the release of all those he could formally claim were Ottoman subjects under his protection. Using the services of the French ambassador, he even sent a personal letter to the pope, claiming that this action was financially damaging, requesting an immediate solution, and threatening to take similar measures against Christian envoys in the Ottoman realm. As rumors spread about the sultan's involvement in the Ancona matter, ships bound for this and other papal destinations changed course and sailed to Venice instead. Ancona's non-Jewish merchants, fearful of the sultan's reprisal, begged for mercy, but the pope was adamant. He only agreed to release those who were registered as subjects of the sultan and properties belonging to Ottoman merchants. The trials of heresy continued, and the pope refused to pardon Jacob Mosso, Dona Gracia's chief agent in town. He was burned with others in mid-June 1556.

Following the suggestion of a group of Jews who had escaped from Ancona and found refuge in nearby Pesaro, some forty miles to the north, Dona Gracia proclaimed a boycott of the port of Ancona. She demanded that all merchandise be diverted to Pesaro. With the Sultan's backing and the support of most of the Ottoman Jewish business community, the boycott was successful for eight months. Imports dwindled and export merchandise rotted on the docks. But some rabbis feared that Ancona's ancient Jewish community, which was humiliated by the edict but was not persecuted as part of the aggression against the Judaizing Marranos, would also be punished as a result. Eventually, a few months later, after a long struggle inside the community, Gracia had to lift the boycott, and trade with Ancona was resumed, although she stubbornly refused to send her own ships to any of the papal states ever again.[89]

She finally had her revenge that same year when Emperor Charles V threatened Pope Paul IV's sovereignty on the Italian peninsula. "*He believes the world must be his*," the pope seethed. We would have listened respectfully if places that had already fallen into his hands benefitted from his rule, he argued, but after his conquest they all remained miserable, impoverished, and starving. The frustrated pontiff planned a crusade against Habsburg rule in Naples and Sicily.

---

[87] Birnbaum, *The Long Journey*, 82–83. "Salomon and Leoni," 164. Segre, "Sephardic Refugees," 173.
[88] Roth, *Dona Gracia*, 134–178.
[89] Roth, *Dona Gracia*, 134–175. Segre, "Sephardic Refugees," 173–174.

The idea was to make an alliance of the papal state with France and certain German principalities, coordinate it with the Ottomans, and wrest these Italian territories from Habsburg hands. When one cardinal claimed that the Germans would not back the pope in this venture, Paul IV cried, "*The Turks will not fail us!*"[90] But despite the intense animosity between the Ottomans and the Habsburgs, and even though the pope dispatched envoys to France to plead with the Ottomans for cooperation, his plan failed, and a year later his forces were routed by Charles's Spanish troops.

Dona Gracia continued to exert influence in court even after Hurrem died in 1558. A year later the Habsburg ambassador to the empire, Ogier Ghiselin de Busbeck, recounted that he had asked to meet her because she was an intimate of Suleiman's daughter, Princess Mihrimah, wife of Grand Vizier Rüstem Pasha. Gracia chatted with him in Spanish as they discussed Ottoman and European state affairs.[91] In the early 1560s, she received from Suleiman a vast land grant in Tiberias and its surroundings on the Sea of Galilee, which she intended to make into a safe haven for the persecuted Jews of Europe. She invested much of her wealth in rebuilding the town, reconstructing its walls, and preparing the land for agriculture. Her dream was to make Tiberias her final destination. She would pack her bags once more, take along her most loyal servants, and live in a house overlooking the lake. She never reached the Holy Land. She died in 1569 and was buried in Istanbul.[92]

But she did live to see her nephew become one of the empire's leading statesmen. Sultan Suleiman had died three years earlier. Soon after Selim's accession he appointed Joseph Nasi, Duke of Naxos. Selim needed Don Joseph's counsel and perspicuity and, it is said, appreciated the wines he procured even more. In 1570, following the duke's advice, the Ottoman navy invaded Cyprus and captured the island from Venice at the end of a long and tortuous campaign. But the costly war and the defeat at Lepanto a year later diminished Don Joseph's influence in court. Soon, following Selim's death in 1574, he fell out of grace and died a few years later, in 1579. He had continued the Hebrew printing press established by Gracia, and after his death his wife Reina, Gracia's daughter, kept it going.

Benvenida Abrabanel

Like the Mendeses and de Lunas, the Abrabanels were an old aristocratic family boasting roots going back hundreds of years on the Iberian Peninsula, and perhaps even further. The family claimed descent from the Royal House of David in ancient Judea. In contrast to the Mendeses, who made most of their fortune as New Christians, the Abrabanels refused to convert and remained Jewish through many travails and expulsions.

---

[90] Isom Verharen, "Allies with the Infidel," 43–44.
[91] Heyd, "Moses Hamon," 165.
[92] Roth, *House of Nasi*, 116.

Benvenida's uncle, Don Isaac Abrabanel, was finance minister to King Afonso of Portugal in the 1470s. After Afonso's death, he was accused of treason and had to flee the country. He settled in Toledo and was soon invited by Queen Isabella to be her finance minister and secure funds for the continued conquest of the Iberian Peninsula. When Isabella and Ferdinand published the Alhambra Decree calling for the deportation of the Jews in 1492, Don Isaac fought in vain for its cancellation. Even though he and his family received royal permission to stay, when he realized that the deportation would not be called off, they joined the other deportees, left Spain, and settled in Spanish-controlled but Inquisition-free Naples. Here he was received with open arms by the viceroy, who recognized his talents and gladly appointed him finance minister. Soon, however, persecution caught up with him. He was forced to uproot his family once again, this time to Sicily and Corfu, and finally to Venice, where he died.[93]

His niece, Benvenida, was born in Spain in the 1470s and moved to Naples with the family. She was educated by the best teachers in the community and married off to her cousin Samuel, Isaac's son, a brilliant scholar who soon became the leader of the Italian Jewish community. This is how Salomon Usque describes him in his *Consolation for the Tribulations of Israel* a few years after Samuel's death: "*Among the notable Jews in Naples was a man of esteem, a dignified elder of the Spanish nation, the foremost and most distinguished man among the Spanish Jews. He had earned the accolade of 'Trismegistus,' thrice great, as the Greeks say. He was a great sage in the law, eminent in Noble society, and philanthropic with his wealth, which he generously used to alleviate the tribulations of his brethren.*"[94] Benvenida was his match in every respect. Her family's chronicler, Immanuel Aboab, described her as "*one of the noble and high-spirited matrons who have existed in Israel since the time of our dispersion ... a pattern of chastity, of piety, of prudence and of valor.*"[95] She gave great sums to charity and ransomed hundreds of Jewish captives held by pirates.

An order for the expulsion of the Jews of Naples was published in 1510, and most of the Jewish families had to leave, but a group of 200 families agreed to pay a hefty sum for permission to stay.[96] During that time, Samuel befriended one of the local grandees, Don Pedro De Toledo, who several years later became the Spanish viceroy. Don Pedro was so impressed with the atmosphere of learning and arts in the Abrabanel household that he asked Dona Benvenida to take his second daughter, Eleonora de Toledo, the future duchess of Tuscany, under her wings.[97]

Like many other Jews of the mid-sixteenth century, Benvenida believed that she was living in messianic times. The earth-shattering discoveries, the Ottoman

---

[93] Although they never converted, the title "Don" was recognized for the Abrabanel family, at least in Ferrara. See Segre, "Sephardic Refugees," 172.
[94] Usque, *Consolation*, 209–210. See also Griffi, "Documenti Inediti," 28.
[95] Birnbaum, "Jewish Patronage," 139.
[96] Griffi, "Documenti Inediti," 28. Segre, "Spanish Refugees," 165.
[97] Griffi, "Documenti Inediti," 29. Birnbaum, "Jewish Patronage," 139.

conquest of the Holy Land, and the tribulations that Jews suffered in recent decades around Europe were all interpreted as "pains of the coming Messiah," indicating that redemption was nigh.[98] Thus, when two young and charismatic Jewish dream weavers, David Reuveni and Shlomo Molcho (Diogo Pires), arrived in Italy and obtained an audience with Pope Clement VII, she truly believed that they were messianic forerunners, that there really was a secret Jewish kingdom behind the roiling Sambation River deep in Asia, and that it would help liberate the Holy Land and redeem her people. She embroidered a silk banner with Bible verses and the symbol of the Ten Commandments, and sent it to Reuveni along with a Turkish-style golden gown. The pope was impressed and promised to help, but after interviewing the couple a few years later, Emperor Charles dismissed the whole thing as a scam, ordered Molcho to be burned at the stake for apostasy, and sent Reuveni to prison in Spain, where he sank into oblivion. It broke her heart when her expectation came to naught (Fig. 5.5).

In 1533, after a short period of prosperity, the emperor ordered his viceroy to expel the remaining Jews of Naples, but the exile was deferred thanks to the intervention of Benvenida's protégée, Eleonora di Toledo. Only eleven years old at the time, Eleonora pleaded on their behalf with the emperor. This gave the community a short respite, but seven years later Charles published an edict that required the Jews of Naples to wear distinctive clothing and restricted their freedom of movement. Appalled, the community decided to leave. The Abrabanels were once again offered an opportunity to stay, but they decided to leave with the rest of the community. They found refuge in the Duchy of

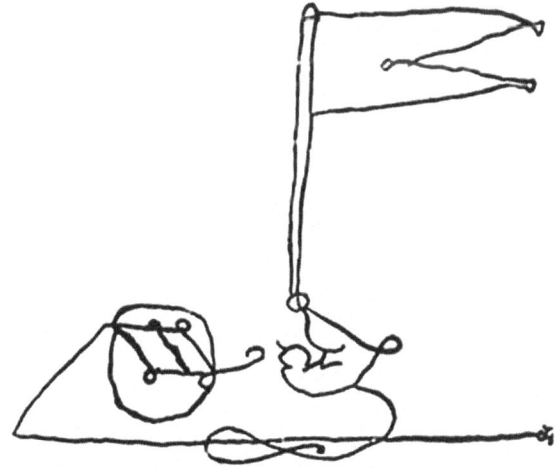

Fig. 5.5 Shlomo Molcho's signature. Source: Jewish Encyclopedia (1901–1906)

[98] Based on Isaiah 26: 17.

Ferrara, whose ruler, Ercole II, offered protection for the Jews and New Christians in his domains. The Abrabanels soon regained their previous status.[99]

Benvenida, who entered her marriage with a sizable dowry, conducted business and was involved in state affairs even while her husband was alive. In 1544, she traveled to Florence to meet her beloved goddaughter Eleonora, the duchess. While chatting with her, Duke Cosimo de Medici joined and the conversation developed into a fascinating open discussion of faith and theology. The duke later gave Benvenida permission to open five banking establishments in Tuscany.[100] It appears that one of Dona Gracia's relatives, Ferdinando Mendes, was a close friend of Eleonora's brother, who also resided in the Medici court. Ferdinando later became a senior public official in Tuscany.[101]

Samuel died in 1547, a year before Dona Gracia's arrival in Ferrara, and bequeathed all his assets to his wife. Benvenida now owned the entire wealth of the family, including real estate, banking establishments, and trading companies.[102] While she was still in mourning and making up her mind which of her multiple ventures to keep running and which to sell or transfer to her sons, Dona Gracia arrived in the city. Despite the age difference—Benvenida was some thirty years older—the two women became close friends during that short period. Benvenida was impressed by Gracia's effective management of a great trading house and a network of agents spanning Europe, the Middle East, and India. Although we have no definite proof, we can surmise that they used each other's contacts in Europe and the Orient to expand their commercial and social networks.[103]

Among other things, Benvenida developed her financial operations in Florence, the foremost financial center of Europe at the time, bringing in Jews from Spain and Portugal to run the banking establishments. In 1552, she sent two of her sons, Isaac and Jacob, to establish a branch of the bank in Lyons.[104] In consultation with Gracia, she sent a considerable monetary gift to the Genoese noble Teodoro Spinola, who was close to Charles V, asking him to intercede with the emperor to allow a hundred Jewish households to return to Naples, presumably to revive the trade that had gradually declined there since they left. Perhaps the real purpose was to allow Jewish businessmen who already worked in Naples surreptitiously to come out of hiding and resume their public lives.

The date of Benvenida's death is not known, but according to some sources, she survived into the 1560s. In the next century, when Jewish life in Amsterdam was revived, several of her descendants became pillars of the community there. The Russian post-impressionist painter Leonid Pasternak and his son Boris, author of *Dr. Zhivago* for which he won the Nobel Prize in 1958, claimed descent from Benvenida's family.

---

[99] Segre, "Sephardic Refugees," 169.
[100] *Medici Archive*, 1171/434 R. Segre, "Sephardic Refugees," 174.
[101] Segre, "Sephardic Refuges," 175. Griffi, "Documenti Inediti," 30.
[102] Segre, "Sephardic Refugees," 183–184.
[103] Birnbaum, "Jewish Patronage," 139.
[104] Segre, "Sephardic Refugees," 177.

The *Kiras*: Esther Handali and Esperanza Malchi

During the sixteenth and seventeenth centuries, almost all women in the sultans' harem—those who would become the rulers' favorites and queen mothers, as well as domestic servants and administrators—were bought in slave markets or taken captive in war. The only exceptions were the sultans' daughters, who were, of course, free born. Initially the slaves remembered their mother tongues, but most were brought to the palace as illiterate young girls, then resocialized and reeducated to finally emerge as accomplished Ottoman ladies. When they rose to greatness, some claimed aristocratic European descent in order to connect to governing elites in their native lands. Nurbanu and Safiye, for instance, two of the greatest queen mothers, claimed descent from Venetian nobility. But in truth they knew little about the world around them, and when they rose to positions of power, they needed assistance.

The most efficient way to become acquainted with the outside world, get its news, and figure out the political scene was to be informed by the group of women who entered the harem as purveyors of jewelry, textiles, cosmetics, and other accessories.[105] For slaves in the royal harem such items of luxury were not just a way to adorn themselves and dress elegantly. They were crucial insignia indicating rank and status. The higher a woman was in the hierarchy, the bigger her daily stipend and the more she could spend on clothes and jewels, which she then displayed just as an army officer would wear his uniform. Since non-Muslim women, particularly widows, were free to come and go as they pleased, they were most often tasked with purchasing such items. This, alongside the fact that Jews were the main importers of such luxury items from Europe at the time, may explain the large number of Jewish women among the *kiras*.

As trust developed between the royal consorts and their *kiras*, they often discussed world politics with them and employed them as envoys to the outside world. The fact that most of them were educated and spoke European languages made them a natural choice for carrying secret verbal messages, writing letters on behalf of their mistresses, and communicating in other ways with ambassadors and consuls outside the palace.[106] As women gradually took over the government of the empire starting in the 1520s, the *kiras* rose in importance alongside them.

During the sixteenth century, the harem moved to the Topkapı palace, and it became even more difficult to reach this inner sanctum in the third court of the palace. Only a few hand-picked women were allowed through the first two gates to supply the harem's needs. The first such woman that we know of was a Karaite lady named Strongilah or Stranhilla, daughter of a certain Eliyah

---

[105] For an explanation of the term *kira*, see Chap. 2.

[106] For a detailed description of the harem and the ruling women of the Ottoman Empire, see Chap. 2.

Gibor.¹⁰⁷ Employed by Hafsa, Suleiman's mother, she first sold jewelry to the ladies of the harem and bought precious stones from them, but she was soon asked to perform tasks of a different nature. She converted to Islam and became known as Fatma Hanım (Lady Fatma), giving this position its initial shape. In 1526, she was sent by Suleiman's worried mother to the Venetian ambassador to get information on the state of his campaign in Hungary and gradually became the main conduit for messages between the sultan's mother and officials inside and outside the palace.¹⁰⁸ We may surmise that by Suleiman's time there was already a small, hierarchically ordered contingent of *kiras* serving the hundreds of concubines, princesses, and female servants in the royal palace.

Hurrem Sultan inherited the elderly Fatma Hanım from Hafsa but soon chose Esther Handali, a younger, more energetic woman, to be her *kira* and confidante. Esther and her husband Eliyahu arrived in Istanbul in the 1520s from Jerez de la Frontera in Spain and started a small cosmetics business. This was Esther's initial inroad into the harem, but her star really began to rise after the death of her husband. The young widow became an indispensable assistant to the Sultana, carrying her messages and conducting her business affairs. Since the palace authorities were reluctant to allow male doctors into the harem, she even doubled as a medical expert to the ladies.¹⁰⁹ Esther kept this position for several decades, from the 1530s until her death in 1592, serving in turn Hurrem, her daughter Mihrimah, and her successors, Nur Banu and Safiye. She also worked closely with Grand Vizier Rustem Pasha, Mihrimah's husband.

In 1533, when Sultan Suleiman flouted custom and married Hurrem, her power in the palace grew considerably. Esther soon learned to make use of those extraordinary powers, and her influence and riches increased in direct proportion. She was now the main point of contact between Hurrem, who gradually emerged as the epicenter of palace rule, the governing elite, and the foreign diplomatic community. Every aspiring pasha seeking a position in government or a bigger salary as governor sought Esther's intercession. Every ambassador who needed strings pulled at the palace willingly paid for her services.¹¹⁰ As one rabbi wrote about her: "*In Constantinople there is an eminent woman sitting on the doorstep of the king of Turks ("melech ha-tugar" in Hebrew), and all ministers kneel and bow to her, and anyone appealing for a measure of authority from the king comes and goes by her word.*" The bribes and presents she received gradually corrupted her, and she began using her influence to transfer state-held estates (*timars*), which were supposed to be awarded to deserving *sipahi* (cavalry) officers on a merit basis, to profit seekers who paid her. This led

---

¹⁰⁷ Karaaites (or *Kara'im* in Hebrew) were a sect that split away from Rabbinic Judaism in earlier centuries, claiming their only source of law was the Holy Scriptures and refusing to recognize the authority of later rabbinic sources such as the Talmud.
¹⁰⁸ Peirce, *Empress*, 113, 140–141. Rozen, *History of the Jewish Community*, 204–205.
¹⁰⁹ Uriel Heyd, "Moses Hamon," 153.
¹¹⁰ Galante, *Esther Kyra*, 3–6. Maria Pia Pedani-Fabris, "Veneziani," 68 n. 3.

to resentment in military and judicial circles and finally led to her cruel murder and the desecration of her body by officers of the cavalry in 1592.[111]

But until that gory end, the *kira* enriched herself and her community and had a hand in state politics as well. She and the royal physician, Moshe Hamon, often worked in tandem. Their familiarity with their states of origin, and a network of Jewish and Marrano acquaintances around the continent, provided them with invaluable information, which they often used to their advantage, deftly steering the sultana and her husband toward their own goals. In 1541, for instance, they assisted the deposed *voivoda* (military governor) of Moldavia, now an Ottoman province, to recover his authority, in the hope of improving the lives of the province's Jews. But the scheme failed and the reinstated *voivoda* continued to persecute the Jews in his domains.[112] Judging by their actions, their main strategic purpose during Suleiman's lifetime was to curb the power of the Habsburgs as much as possible and check their advance into the Balkans. Charles V, already reigning over Spain, Central Europe, the Netherlands, and the rapidly growing colonies in the Americas and East Asia, was Suleiman's great nemesis. But he also zealously persecuted Jews and Marranos in Europe and used them as a scapegoat. Many of Esther *Kira's* stratagems were meant to derail his plans of expansion.

A case in point was the Hungarian monarchy crisis. In the early 1540s, John Zapolya, King of Hungary and Governor of Transylvania, died, and his widow, Isabella Jagiellon, was voted in as regent for his minor son. Hungary, a constant tug of war between the Ottomans and Habsburgs, was attacked by Charles's brother, Ferdinand, and the widowed Isabella was pressured to sign an agreement that would deliver Transylvania into Habsburg hands. But with encouragement from Hurrem, Hamon, Handali, and Dona Gracia, Suleiman decided to back Isabella's claim for Hungary's throne. The sultan acted forcefully. He arrested the Habsburg ambassador Giovanni Malvezzi and made Temeşvar (Timişoara), Transylvania's main city, into the capital of an Ottoman province, thereby formally annexing the territory. A decade later, when war broke out between the Ottomans and the Safavids in Iran, Ferdinand saw another opportunity to seize Isabella's queendom. He once again pressured her to cede the lands she held as regent, but when Suleiman returned from his Persian campaign, in 1554, he threatened to invade Hungary. Esther and Hurrem made sure that Isabella, whom Hurrem viewed as her own protégée, was recognized as sovereign of Transylvania.[113]

Esther also assisted Hurrem and Grand Vizier Rustem Pasha in their efforts to support Isabella's mother, Bona Sforza, Queen of Poland, and secure her hold on the throne in the face of Habsburg encroachment. They made sure that Bona's son, Sigismund Augustus, would be crowned King of Poland and

---

[111] Galante, *Esther Kyra*, 8–11.
[112] Roth, *The House of Nasi*, 33.
[113] Tracy, "The Road to Szigetvar," 19–20.

Lithuania.[114] Years later, with the next *kira*'s assistance, another court physician, Solomon Ashkenazi, would once again intervene in Poland's politics as he promoted the election of the French Prince Henry de Valois (later Henry III of France) to the Polish throne.[115]

When Gracia arrived in Istanbul in 1553, the symbiotic relationship between royal consorts and their *kiras* was at its zenith. Now their activities were fueled by Gracia's finances and by her intelligence network. Following the capture by French privateers of a ship carrying two Ottoman ladies, who were then employed in the French court, the *kiras* initiated an exchange of letters between Princess Mihrimah and Catherine de Medici, Queen of France.[116] Their goal was to improve relations and to increase goodwill and cooperation between the Ottomans and the French, against the Habsburgs. Later, they focused on England, which, in view of its King Henry VIII's rift with Catholicism and the annulment of his marriage to Katherine of Aragon, they perceived as a natural ally against Spain.

When Hurrem died in 1558 and Prince Selim's favorite consort, Nurbanu, became the leading woman, Esther persisted as envoy to the European diplomatic missions in Istanbul and Galata. But around that time another *kira* began her ascent in the harem. Esperanza Malchi, born in Italy, immigrated to Istanbul with her family. She was probably introduced to the palace by Esther herself as part of the small contingent of trading women in the service of the *valide* and the consorts. Safiye, one of many female slaves at the harem, befriended Esperanza, and the two developed a strong relationship. In later years, especially after Nurbanu died and Safiye became queen mother, Esperanza ascended to the position of leading *kira*. She and Esther must have competed for the top position at least until Nurbanu's death in 1583. But where it mattered, they knew how to cooperate and work closely. Minna Rozen rightly points out that Esther and Esperanza were so alike that they were often conflated in consular reports and confused with each other.[117]

By that time Esther was more experienced than anyone else in the Ottoman harem, including the sultanas. In Nurbanu's service, she corresponded with Queen Catherine de Medici and with the doges of Venice.[118] On one occasion, for instance, Safiye asked Esther to carry messages to the Venetian ambassador and request the release of a ship taken by pirates with the wife of Algiers' governor on board. On another, perhaps as part of her struggle for influence against her rival, Esperanza, Esther herself informed the Venetians about letters exchanged between Safiye Sultan and Queen Catherine de Medici concerning a request to send the Ottoman navy to threaten Spain. In their report the

---

[114] Peirce, *Empress of the East*, 224–225, 251–252.
[115] Roth, *House of Nasi*, 197. Gurkan, *Espionage*, 450. Rothbard, "Queen Bona Sforza," 47. *Medici Archive*, 4727/227. See Chaps. 2 and 6 for more details.
[116] Peirce, *Empress of the East*, 296. Tavim, "Portuguese Jewish Communities," 569–570, 582.
[117] Rozen, *History of the Jewish Community*, 206–207.
[118] Ergin, "Ottoman Royal Women," 94.

Venetian ambassadors also included a paragraph about the very close relationship between the *valide* and Esther.[119]

In her last decade, Safiye employed a Venetian woman who had converted to Islam and entered the harem service taking the name Fatma. At one point, Fatma, actually a Venetian spy, sent a handwritten note to the ambassador to warn him that Esperanza *Kira* was forcefully trying to convince the sultan that Venice was siding with the Habsburgs in their war against the Ottomans. "*I do not know what the Jews have found out about Venice's actions, but they agitate greatly the sultana who is full of fire, and from what I have heard this Jewish woman ... says that the Venetians are traitors. Other particulars I really don't know, except that she [Esperanza] is making every effort to damage Venice's reputation.*"[120] The ambassador reported that "*this situation eventually boiled over into a heated argument in front of the sultana between Fatma and Esperanza.*"[121]

The *kiras* also cooperated to strengthen the sultana's (and their own) political network. In 1578, for example, assisted by the royal physician, Salomon Ashkenazi, they arranged a marriage between one of the sultan's daughters and the son of Aleppo's governor. According to some of the sources, having agreed with her partners that they should make the governor, a high-ranking pasha, their ally, Esther suggested the idea to the *valide*, Nurbanu, who warmed up to it and brought it up with her son, Sultan Murad III. The sultan declined at first, claiming that by custom a sultan's daughters should be wed to former palace slaves who were recruited from Christian villages, converted, and educated in elite institutions, rather than to members of second-generation Muslim aristocracy, but he later changed his mind and agreed.[122]

After the Spanish armada was defeated in 1588, England was recognized as a major player on the global stage, and an alliance with it seemed like a good idea.[123] In 1599, Esperanza corresponded in Safiye's name with Queen Elizabeth of England. She wrote one letter on behalf of her patroness and another in her own name, confessing her admiration for Elizabeth and asking her to send cosmetic products. (The letters are discussed in two other chapters of this book: once from Safiye Sultan's vantage point in Chap. 2 and another from Queen Elizabeth of England's in Chap. 7).

Like her predecessor, Esperanza exploited her proximity to the sultana to demand bribes from senior officials, who in their turn blamed her for meddling in state affairs, for corruption in the ranks, for the poor state of the cavalry, and even for the devaluation of the currency. They complained to Safiye Sultan, and when she ignored their pleas, they acted themselves. They dragged Esperanza out of her house and stabbed her to death. Her body was then carried to the

[119] Galante, *Esther Kyra*, 7. Peirce, *Imperial Harem*, 226.
[120] Durstetler, "Beatrice Fatima," 368–369.
[121] Pedani, "Safiye's Household," 27.
[122] Pedani, "Safiye's Household," 29.
[123] Skillier, "Three Letters." Adler, "Auto da Fe and Jew," 701. Peirce, *Imperial Harem*, 224–225. Roth, *Dona Gracia*, 107.

central hippodrome square (*At meydanı*) and left to rot. There were reports that after her death enormous sums of money were retrieved from her house.[124] Her killing was followed by pogroms against the Jews of Istanbul, who were all seen as her accomplices.[125] Yet Edward Barton, the joint representative for England and France at the end of the sixteenth century, lamented her murder: "*Because my selfe cannot come to the speech of the Sultana, and all my busines passe by the hands of the said Mediatrix, loosing her friendshippe, I loose the practick with the Sultana* ..."[126]

The position of *kira* continued to the next century, but it never regained the power it acquired in the sixteenth century under Esther Handali and Esperanza Malchi.

Jewish Ladies as a Bridge to European Queendom

Dispersed around the Mediterranean when their families were driven out of the Iberian Peninsula in the late fifteenth and early sixteenth centuries, Jewish and Marrano women became the basis of a network that spanned East and West and may be described as the connecting tissue of female rule. Thus, through her travels from Lisbon to Antwerp, Venice and Ferrara, and finally to Istanbul, Dona Gracia herself connected many of these queens simply by meeting them and conveying news, gossip, and oral messages. Benvenida Abrabanel, close friend of the Spanish viceroy in Naples and foster mother to his daughter Eleonora, Duchess of Florence, added her set of royal connections. Finally, the *kiras* connected the sultanas of the Ottoman Empire to their peers in the West, conveying their messages and interpreting their intentions.

By following the lives of exiled Jewish women during this period, we are introduced to the realities of sixteenth-century Europe. There are several major trends that we can point to. One is the new sea routes to Africa, Asia, and the Americas that changed the global economy, enriching some, impoverishing others, and creating opportunities for new, dynamic entrepreneurs and rulers. A second major trend was the internal rift between Catholics and Protestants, which became violent almost from the first day. This rivalry was the main determinant of European politics in the sixteenth and early seventeenth century and directly impacted East-West relations. It also had an effect on Christian-Jewish relations. Catholic efforts to eradicate heresy and the fear of losing positions of power drove a persistent effort to dispossess, deport, and execute Jews and New Christians suspected of favoring (or being favored by) Protestantism. This is what drove many Jews to find refuge in the Islamic world, mainly in the Ottoman Empire and Morocco, and enabled them to create a bridge between the worlds.

---

[124] Rozen, *History of the Jewish Community*, 207.
[125] Galante, *Esther Kyra*. Holmberg, "Jews of all Trades," 39.
[126] Ergin, "Ottoman Royal Women," 95.

A third powerful driving force of the century, pulling in an opposite direction, was the Renaissance, and in our context the humanist movement that emerged from it. It was this humanist spirit that opened up for women such as Gracia Mendes and Benvenida Abrabanel the opportunity to become leaders of their communities inside Europe and independent businesswomen. As we shall see in the next two chapters, these same winds of change opened the way for royal women to rise to leadership positions in the Western world.

CHAPTER 6

Queens of France

> *Even Solomon in his great light of wisdom would not have comported himself more wisely than you have comported yourself in pursuing and conducting the desired deliverance of the king's person, in which you have demonstrated profound prudence, a durable and skillful experience, unparalleled conduct and marvellous deftness.*
> Brinon, French ambassador to England, quoting Cardinal Wolsey in a letter to Louise of Savoy, 14 February 1526[1]

In 1328, King Charles IV of France died a young man leaving no male heirs, and his sister's son, King Edward III of England, saw an opportunity. He insisted that since he was Charles's closest male relative, the crown should go to England.[2] In their desperate attempt to deny England's claim, the French blew the dust off an ancient feudal rescript called the Salic Law, according to which land could only be inherited by male children. Being a woman, they claimed, Edward's mother was legally barred from inheriting the crown, and therefore Edward would not inherit it, either. The monarchy was passed on instead to the dead king's cousin, and this dispute between England and France finally led to what came to be known as the Hundred Years' War. Long after the reasons for the war had been forgotten, the Salic Law was used in France as a reason to deny women the right to rule.[3]

---

[1] Gilbert Jacqueton, *La politique extérieure de Louise de Savoie: 1525–1526* (Bouillon, 1892), 431 (my translation).

[2] Charles IV's daughter, Marie, was one year old when he died, and she herself died as a child. Another, Blanche, was born two months after his death. She was the only one to survive to adulthood.

[3] Crawford, "Catherine de Médicis and Political Motherhood," 645. The Salic Law is mentioned by Shakespeare in the first act of *Henry V* as the reason for the Hundred Years' War. Derek Whaley, "From A Salic Law to The Salic Law," 443, in Woodacre et al., *The Routledge History of Monarchy*.

© The Author(s), under exclusive license to Springer Nature Switzerland AG 2024
D. Ze'evi, *Queens Around the World, 1520–1620*,
https://doi.org/10.1007/978-3-031-58634-7_6

French women's long and arduous road to return to positions of power began some eighty years later. In 1405, Christine de Pizan, the educated daughter of France's court astrologer and a successful author in her own right, published a pathbreaking study she entitled *The Book of the City of Ladies*. It was a survey of great women in history from the Queen of Sheba to the medieval queens of France. The book was written as a dialogue of the author with three virtues personified as women—Reason, Rectitude, and Justice—who offered her examples of virtuous women who could help her build a city consecrated to ladies. In her book, de Pizan refuted the common claim that women were sinful and devoid of reason by nature. Instead, she attempted to instill a sense of self-worth and faith in the future:[4]

Consider all the evil kings in various countries, disloyal emperors, heretical popes, and other unbelieving prelates filled with greed—and you will find that men should really keep quiet and that women should bless and praise God who placed their precious souls in feminine vessels. I will be quiet about all of that. In order to refute with examples the comments of these men who have called women so weak, I will tell you about several very strong women, whose exemplary stories are wonderful to hear.[5]

De Pizan's book eventually became a bestseller throughout Europe, but her literary success arrived at a time of great distress. Although by now few could remember exactly why it broke out, the long war between England and France for the crown continued to drag on, with countless dead lying on the battlefields and the two economies ruined. In 1420, in the wake of Henry V's famous victory at Agincourt, his army captured Paris itself and France's troops were demoralized. Two years later, in 1422, both Henry V and his French rival, Charles VI, died, and Charles's son, the future Charles VII, still referred to as the Dauphin, fled Paris and found refuge in the small city of Bourges. The situation seemed hopeless (Fig. 6.1).

Broken-hearted, Christine de Pizan also left her Paris apartment and moved to a nunnery outside the city. But then, in 1427, as the French troops were on the verge of collapse, a sixteen-year-old girl named Joan (Jeanne in French) from the village of Domrémy in northern France insisted on meeting the king. She claimed that she knew how to win the war. Finally given an audience with the acting monarch, she told him that she had visions of saints and angels who entrusted her with a mission: to lead France's armies against their foes and to save the kingdom. The king consulted with his advisers, and after deliberations

René Langlois, "Comparing the French Queen Regent and the Ottoman Validé Sultan" in Woodacre et al. *A Companion to Global Queenship*, 271–272.

[4] 1364–1430. De Pizan and Richards, *The Book of the City of Ladies*, 170. See also de Pizan, *The Book of the City of Ladies* (trans. Rosalind Brown-Grant). De Pizan was influenced by several previous authors, chief among them the Italian author Boccaccio. The concept of "the city" harks back to Augustine's comparison between the earthly city and the heavenly city. On the way women themselves read and memorized books empowering women, see Alberto Manguel, *A History of Reading*, 117.

[5] De Pizan and Richards, *The Book of the City of Ladies*, 170.

Fig. 6.1 Virtuous ladies building their city. Meister, Illustration from *The Book of the City of Ladies*, 1410. Bibliothèque nationale de France

they finally suggested that the young woman, later known as Saint Joan of Arc, be put to the test.[6] If she succeeded in lifting the English siege on the city of Orléans, she would receive the king's blessing and lead the army.[7]

Dressed in shining armor astride a royal charger and carrying the French banner, the maiden's appearance on the battlefield (and the rumors about her divine mission) galvanized the French army and heartened the besieged population. After a series of successful French counterattacks, the siege was lifted, and from that point on Joan led the French forces from victory to victory, regaining much of the territory occupied by the English.

Less than two years later, her chain of victories was cut short. She was betrayed, captured by collaborators, and delivered to the English commanders. In May 1431, she was tried for heresy and burned at the stake in the city of Rouen. But even after her death, the legend of the armor-clad cherubic saint, sent by God to save the righteous, drove the French forces to push England out of most of the territory it had gained on the mainland.

[6] The name Joan of Arc emerged only several centuries later. Her place of birth was the village of Domrémy in northern France, but apparently her father's name was Darc and in later centuries it was mistaken for d'Arc (of Arc), a place of origin.
[7] Taylor, *The Virgin Warrior*, Chap. 3.

One woman in particular was responsible for Joan of Arc's lasting reputation as the savior of France. In 1429, upon hearing about her victories on the battlefield, Christine de Pizan published an epic poem praising the maiden's courage, patriotism, and devotion and emphasizing her gender and young age. A year later Christine de Pizan died, but Joan's legacy, immortalized in her work, echoed in French homes and palaces for decades. De Pizan's *Book of the City of Ladies* and her verses about the holy maiden, translated into Spanish, Flemish, and later into English, became very popular around Europe. In France itself they began to dismantle the barriers constructed under the Salic Law.[8]

ANNE OF FRANCE

But even after the heroic exploits of Joan of Arc and the defiant writings of Christine de Pizan, it took forty years for significant changes to occur. The first real chink in the male shield was Princess Anne of Beujeu—better known as Anne of France—daughter of King Louis XI. Anne's father was a controversial king, but one with an eye to modernizing and centralizing the kingdom. Upon his death in 1483, his favorite daughter was appointed regent for her minor brother, Charles VIII.[9] The twenty-two-year-old Anne held this position for eight years and carried out her duties so successfully that the Royal Council asked her to continue to govern even after her brother reached legal maturity.

Blocking attempts by other male members of the family to usurp the crown, she astutely read the political map of the continent. In the deteriorating Wars of the Roses between the houses of York and Lancaster in England, Anne of France allied herself with England's new claimant to the throne, Prince Henry Tudor, financed his campaign, and equipped him with troops that helped him win the civil war. As soon as the prince, now crowned Henry VII, secured his hold over England, she pushed both sides with patience, wisdom, and tenacity to sign the Treaty of Etaples that officially ended the Hundred Years' War. Detecting another threat to the crown of France, she sent her army to fight a decisive battle against the united troops of Brittany and Orléans and forced them to remain under French suzerainty. She lowered taxes for the common people and, as a final official act, convinced her brother, King Charles, to marry the Duchess of Brittany, adding her territories to those of the French crown.[10]

After the king's wedding, Anne left the palace and withdrew to the autonomous duchy of Bourbon in central France, where for the next two decades she made use of her knowledge as a veteran politician to advance the cause of women in politics. Based on her experience, she wrote a book of lessons for her daughter, which she entitled "*The Teachings of Anne of France, Duchess of Bourbon and Auvergne, to Her Daughter Susanne of Bourbon.*" The book developed some of the main themes in de Pizan's *City of Ladies* and, more

---

[8] McCartney, "The King's Mother and Royal Prerogative," 125.
[9] Crawford, "Catherine de Médicis and Political Motherhood," 648.
[10] Zum Kolk, "Household of the Queen," 8, 20–21.

practically, expounded the most important guidelines for heading a great household and being an independent lady.[11] She soon became the educator of choice for many daughters of Europe's aristocracy, including the future queens Louise of Savoy and Margaret of Austria, who were to follow in her footsteps.[12]

Although French insistence on the provisions of the old Salic Law had seemingly turned maleness into a *sine qua non* for sovereignty, doubt began to creep into the public's mind. The lives and works of these three women—Christine de Pizan, Joan of Arc, and Anne of France—suggested that there was always another option: with courage and wisdom, and with the right kind of education, women could be as successful as men in leadership roles, and perhaps even better. Other historic examples of ruling women, such as the beatific Blanche of Castille, reappeared in public discourse and became popular examples of womanhood. Blanche gained fame more than two centuries earlier as regent and guardian of France when her husband Louis IX, later known as Saint Louis, was taken prisoner during the ill-fated eighth crusade. Suddenly the prospect of a woman ruling France did not sound so preposterous.

Louise of Savoy

When her mother died in 1483, the seven-year-old Louise, daughter of the duke of Savoy, was sent to Anne of France's court to be educated. There she met and befriended Margaret of Austria, aunt of the future Emperor Charles V Habsburg, with whom she would sign an unprecedented peace treaty almost four decades later. When she was twelve, her father agreed to her betrothal to the king's cousin, Charles of Angoulême. A short while later he pulled her out of school and married her off to Charles, with whom she shared a love for books and culture. Still a teenager, she had one daughter, Margaret/Marguerite, and one son, Francis/François. But before her twentieth birthday, her husband suddenly died; she was now Duchess of Angoulême, but also a widow with two young children.

But history had other plans for her. Having no male children of his own, France's king at the time, Louis XII, named his second nephew, Louise's son Francis, his heir apparent. To learn the ways of the court, the boy was invited, along with his mother and sister, to reside in the royal palace. A novice in state affairs, young Francis relied on his mother's knowledge and sagacity to guide him through the palace's intricate politics.[13]

---

[11] The full title is *Les Enseignements d'Anne de France, duchesse de Bourbonois et d'Auvergne, a sa fille Susanne de Bourbon.*

[12] Thompson, "Anne de Beaujeu," *Encyclopedia of Women in the Renaissance*, 42–44. Wellman, *Queens and Mistresses*, 114, 190. On debates about the education of women at the time see also Manguel, *A History of Reading*, p. 73.

[13] Crawford, "Catherine de Medici and Political Motherhood," 649. Tracy Adams, "La Prudence et la formation des femmes diplomates," Brioist et al., *Louise de Savoie*, 29–38. (https://books.openedition.org/pufr/8358#bodyftn4). Zum Kolk, "Household of the Queen," 13. Robin et al., *Encyclopedia of Women*, 332–332.

On January 1, 1515, the king suddenly died, and Louise's twenty-one-year-old son was crowned Francis I. Right after his coronation the ambitious young monarch announced that he would head to the Italian peninsula to take back his dominions in Lombardy, which had been invaded by the Habsburgs. Trusting no one else at court, he wished to appoint his mother to govern the kingdom in his absence. But despite Anne of France's recent guardianship for her minor brother, there was no formal legal definition of female regency in the king's absence. Francis had to write a letter to the parliament explaining why he had no choice but to appoint his mother. To soften the impact, the letter included a proviso instructing the queen mother to seek the advice of senior parliament members in all matters of state and a promise to appoint a special council of (male) court members to oversee her actions. The meandering style of the letter offers some insight into the difficulty of officially appointing a woman:

> [C]onsidering that all the princes and lords of our blood follow and accompany us in the above said enterprise, having given this charge and power to our very dear and very well-loved lady and mother, the duchess of Angoulême and Anjou, as one in whom we have total and perfect confidence and which we know certainly that she will know to fulfill this [task] wisely and virtuously by her prudence, for the great and singular love and zeal which she carries for us and this our realm; to the aforesaid dame and mother we leave good and notable company and good, great and virtuous personages of all estates...[14]

Although Francis took the royal seal of government along with him and did not officially confer the title of regent on his mother, the move was endorsed by the powerful pope, Leo X (Giovanni de Medici), whose attempts to block the Habsburg incursions into his realm made him an ally of France.[15] Louise held the reins of government efficiently until her son's return and performed the king's ceremonial duties faithfully, ignoring the grumbling of Parliament members, who believed that government was not a proper vocation for women. Luckily, Francis returned victorious from the war, and in retrospect his victory became an additional justification for having appointed his mother.

Like her contemporary Aisan Daulat Begum, mother of Emperor Babur in the distant Mughal kingdom, Louise used this success to set the stage for her role as co-ruler. Upon hearing of her son's victory, she commissioned a special book to commemorate the triumph, harp on the rare connection between her and King Francis, commend her love for the country and her careful running of the state, and praise the king for wisely putting his trust in her.[16] From that point on, mother and son ruled the country together and formed such a

---

[14] Crawford, "Catherine de Médicis and Political Motherhood," 650. See also Cédric Michon, "Le rôle politique de Louise de Savoie," in Brioist et al., *Louise de Savoie*. McCartney, "The King's Mother," 126.

[15] McCartney, "The King's Mother," 126.

[16] McCartney, "The King's Mother," 126–127. Broomhall, "Issuing from the Great Flame," 67.

compact couple that it was difficult to tell which decision was made by whom.[17] Letters and decrees published by the monarchy habitually ended with the signature "*Le Roi et Madame.*"[18]

In 1519, Francis put forward his candidature for the crown of the Holy Roman Empire. The empire was in fact a late-medieval conglomerate of central European principalities and duchies, presenting itself as the rightful heir to the long-gone Roman Empire and the medieval Carolingian kingdom. Each time their emperor died, the princes and nobles would come together to elect a new one, which would most often be the highest bidder among the candidates. Francis' offer was rejected, however, and the peers elected his rival, King Carlos of Spain, of the House of Habsburg, whose grandfather was the previous emperor. They later crowned him Emperor Charles V. By adding this central European chunk of territory to their vast domains, which already included Spain, the Lowlands, Austria, and parts of Italy, the Habsburgs completely surrounded the French kingdom. This humiliating failure would haunt Francis throughout his life and make him and Charles mortal enemies (Fig. 6.2).

Realizing that the political situation had changed and that they now had to contend with a hostile power on their northern, eastern, and southern borders, Francis and Louise attempted to redress the balance by signing a treaty with their country's other traditional rival, England. But the resplendent and

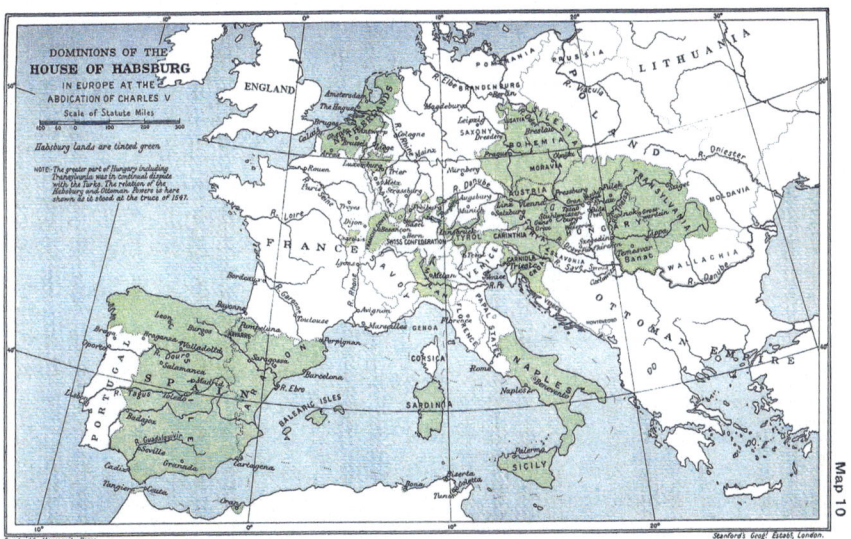

Fig. 6.2 Map of the Habsburg Empire during Charles V's reign. Source: *Cambridge Modern History Atlas*, 1912

---

[17] Michon, "Le rôle Politique de Louise de Savoie."
[18] Brioist et al., *Louise de Savoie*, Introduction.

dramatic meetings between Francis and his cocky young counterpart, England's Henry VIII, which took place in the summer of 1520 in two regal pavilions at a countryside location known as The Field of the Cloth of Gold (*Camp du Drap d'Or*), ended in failure. Too many issues were hanging in the balance, not least England's continued occupation of parts of the French coast and its claims to other parts of the mainland. Instead of seriously debating the issues and reaching a conclusion, the two royal roosters tried to outshine each other. A few years later, under circumstances described below, Louise would make another attempt and reach a successful treaty with England.[19]

But in 1525, frustrated with the failure of his talks with England, bored by the tedious day-to-day running of the state, depressed by the premature death of Claude, his wife and mother of his children, and longing to make up for all of it by another shining victory on the battlefield, the king decided to return to Lombardy. He was determined to take back the lands that, he believed, were stolen once again by the Habsburgs and their allies after his glorious victory at Marignano. As he prepared to set out with his army, he again officially appointed his mother regent of France. This time she was authorized to exercise the full powers of government, including issues that were formerly reserved for the king, such as pardoning criminals and filling vacant positions at court. Now that Louise's leadership qualities and popularity among the populace were evident to the aristocracy, these sweeping powers became a constant source of friction. Fearing loss of their executive powers to a woman, members of Parliament fought tooth and nail against her appointments and decisions.[20]

But soon these petty squabbles had to be put on the back burner because a much more serious crisis loomed over the kingdom. Dashing the king's hopes for a quick victory, the Italian campaign faltered, and in a battle outside Pavia, in the region of Milan, the French army was overwhelmed by its enemies. In the heat of battle, Francis and his small retinue of bodyguards were cut off from the main force and surrounded, and the king was taken prisoner. After a short detention in Italy, he was delivered into the hands of his enemy, Emperor Charles V, who was in Spain at the time. It was time for Louise to prove her mettle.

The king's captivity sent shock waves around Europe. In a moment of panic, fearing that Louise was not up to the task, the French Parliament demanded that she be replaced by the king's closest male relative, Charles de Bourbon. But the queen refused to budge and fought back. Finally, threatened by Louise, or perhaps realizing that she would handle the crisis better than he could, Bourbon declined the request. The Parliament and the judicial court then came up with the claim that Louise's sovereignty should not be recognized since *they* drew their authority from the king himself, while according to the old Salic Law Louise had no autonomous standing. The queen brushed these

---

[19] For a fascinating, if literary, description of the meeting, see Hilary Mantel, *Wolf Hall*, 312–384.
[20] McCartney, "The King's Mother," 131. Michon, Ibid. Tracy Adams, "Louise de Savoie, la prudence et la formation des femmes diplomates vers 1500" in Brioist et al., *Louise de Savoie*, 29–30.

claims aside, arguing that her powers derived from her appointment as regent and from her legal standing as royal mother and so were inseparable from those of the king and superior to any claim by the court.

Hoping to resolve the matter quickly and bring her son home, Louise sent her daughter Margaret to Spain to negotiate his release, but to no avail. When this initial effort failed, she realized that a more radical approach would be required and decided to recruit other sovereigns and request their assistance. One of her first destinations was Sultan Suleiman. An infidel he might be, and the scourge of Europe, but extreme situations called for extreme measures, and the powerful Muslim monarch would make an ideal ally on the Habsburgs' eastern flank. As her emissaries made their way to Istanbul, she also sent messengers to the kingdoms of Poland and Hungary, asking for their support. If the Habsburgs surrounded France, she thought, her alliances would create a similar situation for Charles, with powerful armies arrayed against him on all sides.

Her first envoy to the Ottomans, who traveled with a train of servants and expensive gifts, was ambushed and killed in Bosnia, and all his possessions, including her letter, were stolen. She then sent a more experienced courier, the Croatian-born Jean Frangipani, who chose to travel incognito and arrived safely in Istanbul, hiding Louise's letter in the sole of his shoe. There is no record of Frangipani's meeting with the sultan, but he returned with an encouraging reply and was immediately sent back to Istanbul with an offer of alliance. His mission turned out to be the first step in a long-term relationship between France and the Ottoman Empire initiated by Louise.

Writing about France's missions to the Ottoman Empire, De Lamar Jensen claimed that Francis directed the operation from prison: "*Interpolating from the activities of Antonio Rinçon, the French agent in Poland, and from the letters exchanged by Francis I with Sigismund of Poland and John Zapolya of Transylvania that culminated in the Franco-Hungarian alliance of 1528, it appears that Francis hoped to build up a broadly based anti-Habsburg eastern front.*"[21] But in this case Francis probably receives undue credit. It was his mother Louise who acted boldly to save her son and protect the realm, and she did so with the assistance of two other prominent women.

The first to respond positively to her request was the young Queen Bona Sforza of Poland, who relished the opportunity to ally with France against the Habsburgs. Queen Bona also sent emissaries to the sultan's new favorite, Hurrem, who was still taking her first steps in international politics, and convinced her that supporting France against a common enemy would benefit all three countries. The coalition tying together Louise of Savoy in Paris, Hurrem Sultan in Istanbul, and Bona Sforza in Krakow initiated a joint strategy that pressured the Habsburgs to release the captive king (Fig. 6.3).

---

[21] Jensen, "The Ottoman Turks in Sixteenth Century French Diplomacy," 453.

Fig. 6.3 An allegorical painting depicting Louise of Savoy as a winged woman holding the rudder of the ship of state and talking to the Ottoman Sultan Suleiman, lying at her feet. Source: Etienne Leblanc, Frontispiece of Geste de Blanche de Castille, c. 1520–1522. Bibliothèque nationale de France

While her envoys were busy securing the eastern front and building a coalition against the Habsburgs, Louise acted decisively to recruit allies on her western flank as well. She approached Cardinal Wolsey, Henry VIII's mentor and main advisor, and offered, once again, to settle the outstanding territorial issues between France and England that her son had failed to resolve in the meeting at the Field of the Cloth of Gold. Her patience, negotiating skills, and sensible suggestions opened the way for a new alliance, the Treaty of the More, which she signed with King Henry in 1525. Cardinal Wolsey was full of admiration for the French queen.[22]

---

[22] Tracy Adams, "La Prudence et la formation des femmes diplomates," Brioist et al., *Louise de Savoie*, 29–38. Michon, Ibid.

When her envoy, Frangipani, returned to France from his second mission to Istanbul, Francis was already out of prison and on his way back to Paris after signing an agreement later known as the Treaty of Madrid with Emperor Charles. In it he ceded some of the kingdom's land in Italy as well as the Duchy of Burgundy to the Habsburgs and, to guarantee his good intentions in the future, also pledged to send his two sons, Princes Francis and Henry, to Madrid as hostages. He then sent a note to his mother notifying her about the deal and asking her to bring his sons to the agreed-upon site for the transfer.

Sad and dejected, Louise accompanied her grandsons, still young children, to the border and delivered them into the hands of wardens who would take them to Madrid in exchange for her son. But realizing that the constant threat to his sons' safety hanging above his head would only paralyze France, Francis soon decided to repudiate the agreement, claiming that it was signed under duress and therefore illegal. Instead, he sent envoys to Istanbul with offers of a fully-fledged military alliance against Charles V, and the Ottomans consented. Just months later, Francis and Charles were once again at each other's throats. As the children languished in their Madrid prison, the emperor's forces sacked Rome and held the pro-French Clement VII prisoner, while France's army invaded Milan and Naples. At the same time, Suleiman's imperial infantry and cavalry prepared to attack from the east and besiege Vienna.[23]

While Francis's and Suleiman's armies fought Charles's troops again, Louise looked desperately for a way to stop this madness. She felt that the constant wars were sapping France's strength and yearned to bring her grandsons back home. In 1529, she found her opportunity when her childhood friend Margaret of Austria wrote her a letter suggesting peace negotiations. Margaret, Louise's sister-in-law by marriage to her brother Philibert, was also emperor Charles's aunt and now Habsburg governor queen of the Netherlands. Both fondly remembered their happy days together at Anne of France's house, where they were sent as young girls to be educated and enjoyed each other's company. And both realized that a meeting between them might be the only chance for the two empires to sign a true peace treaty and prevent further bloodshed. Too proud to negotiate themselves, Charles and Francis authorized the negotiations realizing, just like their Ottoman, Safavid, and Mughal male contemporaries, that letting the ladies negotiate in their stead was a way to save face if the negotiations failed. And were the ladies to succeed, they could always write it off as their own achievement.

Margaret of Austria, who trusted Louise, waived her advisers' fears of entrapment and crossed the border accompanied only by several ladies-in-waiting and a small contingent of archers, more for show than for real protection. For three weeks the town of Cambrai on France's northern border bubbled with excitement as the ladies met and argued the fine points of a deal, until they finally

[23] Jensen, "The Ottoman Turks in Sixteenth Century French Diplomacy," 452–453.

hammered out an agreement, which they celebrated by praying together in the local cathedral.[24] Signed by the two queens and endorsed by Louise's daughter, now Queen Margaret of Navarre, the historic Treaty of Cambrai became famous in Europe as the "Peace of the Ladies" (*La paix des dames*). According to its terms, Emperor Charles would recognize France's claim to the duchy of Burgundy, and in return France would relinquish some of its territorial claims on the Italian Peninsula. Finally, after a heavy ransom was agreed, Charles promised to send back the children he held hostage. In the spirit of reconciliation, Francis agreed to marry Eleanor, Charles's older sister.[25]

Saying that Francis was not happy about this marriage would be an understatement. He already knew Eleanor from his time as captive in Charles's palace. She visited his cell on occasion and apparently fell in love with the gallant French monarch. He flirted with her, perhaps in an attempt to gain her support, and even pledged to marry her in the future, but Eleanor took his promises more seriously. Four years later, when the Peace of the Ladies was negotiated, she made sure that her aunt Margaret would include the marriage to Francis as one of the treaty's conditions. Louise and Margaret saw this as another way to guarantee the treaty, a marriage that would seal the alliance between Europe's two great empires, and Francis reluctantly agreed.

Immediately after signing the treaty Louise fell gravely ill, but she still insisted on traveling the long way to Bayonne, on France's southern border, to receive her grandsons who were sent north from Madrid along with Eleanor, the eager bride. The two delegations met on the French border, and Francis himself joined them there a few days later. His official wedding with Eleanor was celebrated in Bayonne's cathedral in July 1530, and the king hurried back to Paris for urgent business. The new bride was then taken to Bordeaux to prepare for her official grand entrance into the capital. Several weeks later, when her procession made its way through the streets of Paris and approached the palace, Francis made a public show of his disregard for her by standing at an open window with one of his mistresses. Eleanor was officially crowned queen of France sometime later, but Francis practically ignored her after that (Fig. 6.4).

Once her grandchildren were back home, Louise could die peacefully. In her ten years on the throne at Francis's side she etched herself in the collective memory as a wise and far-sighted lady-monarch. Through her bold and decisive actions, she succeeded in breaking, or at least shaking, the hold of the Salic Law on French politics and her reign blazed the trail for the most influential queen of France in the sixteenth century.

---

[24] Robin et al., *Encyclopedia of Women*, pp. 331–332.

[25] The peace treaty received as good news by the king and queen of Portugal: Viaud, *Lettres des souverains portugais*, 147.

Fig. 6.4 The opening page of a tract by Jean Thibault, the royal astrologer, with the three signatories of the Peace of the Ladies: Louise of Savoy, Margaret of Austria, and Margaret of Navarre

Catherine de Medici

At the age of six Prince Henry and his older brother Francis were taken to the Spanish border to serve as hostages for their father's good behavior, accompanied by their grandmother (their mother, Queen Claude, died two years previously). The kids had no idea that they would be away from their families for four long years. Before they were handed over to the Habsburg soldiers, the two kids were hugged and kissed by Louise, and one of her ladies-in-waiting, Diane de Poitiers, held them tightly to her bosom. This embrace by the beautiful Diane ignited the love that Prince Henry felt for her in the coming years. As he languished in his distant cell, her golden hair and deep blue eyes became the embodiment of love and tenderness.[26]

[26] Leonie Frieda, *Catherine de Medici*, 35. Wellman, *Queens and Mistresses*, 186–188.

Like Louise and Margaret, Diane was a graduate of Anne of France's school. Like them, she was taught the skills needed to govern a noble household and take part in politics. At fifteen she was betrothed to the fifty-six-year-old Louis, a gentleman of higher noble status who was personally related to the royal family. Despite the huge age difference, the marriage was successful, and for seventeen years the two lived in harmony. Diane bore her husband two daughters, and the couple stayed most of the time in court, where Louis served as Francis's master of the hunt and Diane as Louise of Savoy's lady-in-waiting. At the age of thirty-one, when both her husband and Louise died, Diane remained in the royal palace and was tasked with taking care of the princes who had just returned from captivity and seeing to their needs.

During the first year of their imprisonment in Spain, while their father still adhered to the treaty with Emperor Charles, Francis and Henry were treated as part of the royal household. They were entitled to keep books and toys, were looked after by their own servants, and were visited regularly by the French ambassador. But once King Francis abrogated the terms of the agreement, they were treated more harshly. Locked up in a dusky cell, their meals were downgraded, their servants sent to the galleys as oarsmen, and the ambassador barred from visiting them. Four years later, when they were sent back to France, they were scarred by the trauma that shook their young lives. Matteo Dandolo, a Venetian ambassador to the French court, described the returning Henry as "morose" and claimed that few people had ever heard him laugh.[27] He became a rough boy, devoid of social grace, and spent most of his time honing his fighting skills. His only soft spot was his beloved Diane de Poitiers. In a tournament to celebrate their return, the two kids were dressed as knights in armor and participated in mock jousts. While the older one, Crown Prince Francis, announced that he would fight in honor of his late mother, Henry chose to wear Diane's colors and publicly professed his admiration for her.[28]

Motherless, and neglected by a father who doted on his elder brother and had no patience for this gloomy second son, Henry must have felt lonely. Diane took the eleven-year-old child under her wings and groomed him to be a prince of the realm. She taught him manners, had special clothes made for him, and finally convinced him to marry Catherine of the Florentine House of Medici, who also happened to be her second cousin. By marrying a daughter of the Medici, she explained, Henry would acquire their legendary wealth and their territories in Italy and become related to Catherine's uncle, Pope Clement VII. She also hinted that getting access to papal authority would enable him to launch a new crusade and liberate the Holy Land, which the romantic teen still saw as his mission in life.

Although he accepted her advice and consented to marry Catherine, Henry fell even more desperately in love with Diane, daydreaming about her and writing these awkward and very revealing verses:

[27] Leonie Frieda, *Catherine de Medici*, 32–48. Wellman, *Queens and Mistresses*, 196–197.
[28] Wellman, *Queens and Mistresses*, 194–198.

How many times I wished
To have Diane as my only mistress
But I feared that she, who is a goddess
Would not want to abase herself,
To value me who, without her esteem
Would have no pleasure, joy or contentment.[29]

Diane also had an ulterior motive in promoting the marriage to Catherine. An ardent Catholic, she pushed for an alliance with the pope against the growing power of the Protestant movement in and around France. The marriage, she believed, would be an important link in an alliance connecting King Francis and the pope.[30]

French high nobility, still holding on to the medieval ethos of a military-based aristocracy, regarded the Medicis of Tuscany as merchant upstarts, but marrying them was not unprecedented. In 1518, Lorenzo de Medici, Catherine's father, married Madeleine de la Tour d'Auvergne, a countess related to the French royal family. The marriage received the French monarchy's blessing, mainly for financial reasons. Unfortunately, Lorenzo, who was syphilitic and suffering from tuberculosis, soon infected his wife. When their daughter Catherine (whose full name was Caterina Maria Romola di Lorenzo de Medici) was born on April 13, 1519, her mother added a postpartum infection to her list of ailments. The couple's worsening medical condition enabled their local rivals, the Della Rovere family to defeat them and take Florence. A short time later both parents died, and the orphaned baby was sent to her uncle, Pope Leo X, in Rome.

The pope immediately saw the advantages of using the girl as a pawn in the political chess game between the Habsburg Emperor Charles, who happened to be her uncle, and her mother's relative, King Francis.[31] Yet the first ten years of the orphan girl's life was a roller coaster of hope and despair. Before she was two, Pope Leo had died and was replaced by Adrian VI, a Dutch professor of theology who detested the flashy Medicis and favored his former student, the ascetic Emperor Charles. Catherine was packed off to a strict nunnery near Florence. But less than two years later, Pope Adrian himself died and another uncle of hers, Cardinal Giuliano de Medici, was elected by the Curia, taking the title Clement VII. Clement overturned his predecessor's policy and resumed Pope Leo's anti-Habsburg approach, and Catherine was summoned back to Rome. Then, in the wake of the terrible defeat of the French army at Pavia and the capture of King Francis in 1525, the victorious soldiers in the service of Habsburg allies raided and sacked the city of Rome. The pope was incarcerated in Rome's Castel Sant'Angelo and forced to sign a humiliating treaty with Emperor Charles, while the eight-year-old Catherine was once again confined

---

[29] Ibid., 199.
[30] Ibid., 194–198.
[31] De Lamar, "Catherine de Medici and her Friends," 57. Wellman, *Queens and Mistresses*, 226–227.

to a convent. She only rejoined her uncle Clement once again when he was reinstated after the Treaty of Madrid and after the Medici family took Florence back from the Della Rovere family a few years later.

This time, when Catherine arrived at the pope's residence, Rome was being redesigned by the greatest talents of the Renaissance. Architects, sculptors, painters, poets, and scholars were frequent house guests, and she was thrilled by the new artistic trends. Some observers who saw her then described a skinny girl, not very pretty but vivacious, with bulging, curious eyes. Antonio Vasari, the famous artist and biographer who painted her picture, said, *"I was so affected by her particular qualities and by the affection she showed, not only to me, but to my whole country, that I adore her as one adores the saints of paradise."*[32]

Eager to cement Rome's alliance with France, the pope wrote to King Francis, offering Catherine's hand in marriage to his second son, Prince Henry, and promising a dowry of one hundred thousand écus and vast territories in Italy's northwestern regions. Although Catherine was an orphan, Francis agreed to the wedding, both because Henry himself did not seem like much of a catch and because the pope's offer was lucrative. Besides, Catherine's mother *was* his close relative, which gave her a French royal connection of sorts (Fig. 6.5).

Three years after Henry's return from captivity the negotiations were concluded. Catherine and Henry, both fourteen years old, were formally engaged and Catherine was invited to France. She landed in Marseilles that October with an impressive procession headed by her uncle the pope and accompanied by a group of ladies on richly caparisoned horses. The retinue was trailed by a detachment of soldiers dressed "a la Turca" in multicolored fabrics. King Francis and Prince Henry met them there for the celebration. The streets of Marseilles were festooned with rich fabrics, a series of festivals ensued, and, finally, Pope Clement officially wedded the couple. Eager for the marriage to produce offspring, the king and pope waited up and peeped into the newlyweds' chambers, and Francis remained awake all night to ascertain that the two youngsters were doing what they were expected to do. *"They had shown valor in the joust,"* the proud king declared the next morning.[33]

But love did not strike. Although Catherine was quite taken with the sullen boy, Henry was still in love with Diane, and when the initial excitement wore off, he lost all interest in his new bride. The spurned young woman found consolation in joining her father-in-law's hunting expeditions, and Francis enjoyed chatting with the bright, quick-witted girl, who knew so much about Renaissance art, philosophy, and architecture. She also used her free time to study languages, literature, and mathematics with the king's sister, Margaret, who was famous for her intelligence and broad education. There was no love, but life at the French court was bearable.

---

[32] Frieda, *Catherine de Medici*, 23–25. Wellman, *Queens and Mistresses*, 227.
[33] Wellman, *Queens and Mistresses*, 229. Frieda, *Catherine de Medici*, 43–45.

Fig. 6.5 Young Catherine de Medici, sixteenth-century painting. French School, Galleria Palatina di Palazzo Pitti, Inv. 1890 n. 2448

In September 1534, Pope Clement died and, devoid of her papal connections, the still-childless Catherine held little value for the French crown as a pawn in the political game. She was increasingly ignored at court, not least by her husband, who by that time had made Diane his official mistress. There was even talk of annulment of the marriage, but there was no reason to rush things. Henry was not slated to be the future king, and the ménage-à-trois even had some advantages for all three. Catherine's presence provided cover for the illicit affair between Henry and Diane, and the continuation of the marriage was therefore in Diane's interest. In turn, she gave Catherine the support she needed to stay married and helped her navigate France's political and court labyrinths.[34]

But two years later, in another twist of fate, Henry's older brother, Francis, died unexpectedly. The death of the adored crown prince, apparently of heart failure after a tennis game, was a shock to all, not least to his father, who much

---

[34] Wellman, *Queens and Mistresses*, 230–231.

preferred him to his uncouth and taciturn brother. Henry had become the Dauphin, heir apparent, and although Catherine's daily routine had not changed much, she was suddenly pampered as a future queen. At this point her loyalty to France was also questioned. Although her mother was French and she hardly had any connection to the current Duke of Tuscany, Cosimo de Medici, many in France suspected Catherine of favoring the interests of Florence above those of France. The detractors remembered that Medici rule in Tuscany was restored with the consent of Emperor Charles, that since then Florence sided with the Habsburgs in their wars against France, and that the emperor forbade Duke Cosimo to send an ambassador to France. Catherine needed to prove her credentials as a full-blooded French patriot.[35]

As France's next queen, the pressure to produce heirs for the throne was even greater than before. England's King Henry VIII's annulment of his marriage to his first wife, Katherine of Aragon, ostensibly because she produced no sons, was fresh in Catherine's mind. So was the recent execution of Henry's second wife, Anne Boleyn, who also failed to bear him a male heir. Both were glaring examples of the dangers that awaited her should she fail to give birth to a son. She took every available cure in an effort to conceive, including a steady regimen of drinking mule urine in the morning, but only succeeded in getting pregnant eight years later, in 1544, when she was twenty-six. Yet once the dam broke, the pregnancies kept coming. Despite Henry's frequent affairs with other mistresses, she had nine more children, three of whom would become kings of France. Diane, who worried that if there were no male issue, Catherine would be replaced by a more attractive young wife, was most pleased with the birth of the new royal princes.[36]

In 1547, King Francis died and Catherine's husband was crowned Henry II. As king, he continued to neglect his wife and bestowed precious gifts on his beloved Diane, including Chenonceau, a lovely palace in the Loir Valley. He also gave her a role in running the state and often asked her to represent him in official tasks that were customarily the queen's prerogative. But although Catherine clearly disliked Diane, she hid her frustration well and bided her time. Her first glimpse of real power came when Henry attacked the Habsburgs in 1552, in another attempt to recapture the former French domains in Italy. State precedent, set by Louise of Savoy thirty years earlier, obligated Henry to appoint his formally recognized consort as regent in his absence. Reluctant to leave all power in Catherine's hands, he dictated that the role should be filled jointly by Catherine and by the keeper of the royal seal, who happened to be Diane's appointee. Catherine played her part as required and frequently sent the King detailed reports on events and goings-on in the capital, but Henry often ignored her and wrote back to Diane instead.[37]

---

[35] De Lamar, "Catherine de Medici and her Friends," 58. Wellman, *Queens and Mistresses*, 230.
[36] Wellman, *Queens and Mistresses*, 231–232.
[37] Ibid., 232–233.

In 1557, Henry's army suffered a humiliating defeat at the hands of the forces of Philip II of Spain and his wife, Queen Mary of England.[38] The French army was routed, many soldiers died in the crucial battle, and thousands were taken prisoner, including the military commander, the Duke of Montmorency. The army was shattered, in urgent need of resupply and fresh soldiers. The combined Spanish-English army advanced to a mere forty miles from Paris, and there was almost no organized force to stop them. With the enemy at the gates, Catherine summoned all her oratory powers and delivered an emotional speech to convince Parliament to allocate the necessary funds required for a recruitment drive and the refurbishment of the army. The nobles were so moved by her appeal that they approved the funds immediately. The army was quickly resupplied, the Spanish advance was blocked, and France was saved. Overnight her star rose as a leader, a patriot, and a competent stateswoman in her own right.

Meanwhile, a serious new threat arose. Protestantism was rapidly spreading across Europe. At first, most people were not certain what the new faith consisted of. Did it constitute a reform in Catholic Christianity or a radical departure from it? Should it be perceived as conversion, heresy, or simply a different style? The devout Henry tried in vain to check Protestantism's rise by threatening apostates and heretics with execution. But unlike her husband, Catherine was receptive to new ideas and not obsessively opposed to Protestantism. As a gesture of silent resistance to her husband's policies, she owned and often read a Bible in the forbidden French translation, even though the Catholic clergy insisted that this was a sin punished by excommunication.

Like her younger contemporary, Princess Elizabeth of England, she prayed for reconciliation between Protestants and Catholics, but her relatively tolerant attitude was ahead of its time. Both sides of the religious divide insisted on a zero-sum game: If one side wins, the other loses. Meanwhile, the Reformation grew so powerful in France and the Low Countries that it endangered the monarchy. And with Elizabeth's ascension to the throne in 1558, the papacy was in retreat even in England. Only a year earlier, under Queen Mary and her husband King Philip of Spain, England was believed to have become, once again, a bastion of Catholicism but now the danger of a Protestant takeover was palpable. In a precarious balancing act that would be the hallmark of her style of government throughout her life, Catherine suggested a rapprochement with Catholic Spain. Her intention was not to destroy Protestantism but rather to check its advance, and especially that of its militant Calvinist faction. Henry, who distrusted the Spaniards since his imprisonment there and loathed them even more after his army's defeat the previous year, was reluctant at first. But once he agreed to talks with Spain, he impetuously went too far and signed the Treaty of Cateau-Cambrésis, in which he relinquished hard-won territories.

Cateau-Cambrésis was actually a set of two agreements, one signed with England's Elizabeth, the other with Philip II of Spain. The latter was also approved

---

[38] For details of Philip and Mary's joint ventures see Chap. 7.

by Philip's uncle, Emperor Ferdinand I of the Habsburg Empire.[39] According to its terms, France ceded to Spain many of its territories in the Pyrenees and in Italy. Other territories were promised to the Duke of Savoy. To seal the treaties, Catherine's daughter, Elizabeth of Valois, was to marry Philip of Spain, widowed since the death of his wife Mary. Her other daughter was to marry the Duke of Savoy. England, for its part, agreed to give up its claims to Calais.

Catherine, who only sought a short respite from continuous war, was appalled by the extent of Henry's concessions and begged him not to ratify the treaty. She angrily blamed Diane de Poitiers for what she saw as a shameful French surrender, and it is said that when Diane walked in on her shortly after the agreement and asked what she was reading, Catherine angrily replied, "*I have read the histories of this kingdom and I have found in them that, from time to time at all periods, whores have managed the business of kings.*"[40] But the deed was done and the treaty was ratified on April 3, 1559.[41]

That same year, tragedy struck again. During Philip II's wedding to Catherine and Henry's daughter, the French king decided to demonstrate his prowess and challenged a young nobleman to a jousting match on horseback. It was supposed to be a harmless sparring exercise, but during the contest, his opponent's wooden spear broke, and a splinter passed through the slit in Henry's facial armor and penetrated his eye. The king was seriously wounded, and the startled Catherine suddenly remembered a quatrain by the enigmatic seer Nostradamus, which seemed to make no sense until the event:

> *The young lion shall overcome the old one*
> *On the field of combat in a single battle*
> *He will pierce his eyes through a golden cage*
> *Two wounds made one, then he dies a cruel death*

Indeed, the king died in agony ten days later, and Catherine, who took to wearing black from that day on, truly grieved for her husband. Yet almost instantly she became the new linchpin of French sovereign power. "*She is not beautiful,*" wrote Contarini, the Venetian ambassador, "*but she possesses extraordinary wisdom and prudence. There is no doubt that she would be adept at governing, even though she is neither consulted nor considered to the extent she deserves to be, being that she is not of a blood equal to the king.*"[42] It was specifically her carefully nurtured public image as the perpetually black-clad widow and mother that allowed her unprecedented freedoms and increased her political sway from that point on.[43]

---

[39] After Emperor Charles V abdicated in 1556, his empire was split into two parts. Philip II received Spain, the Low Countries, Naples, Sicily, and Sardinia, and Ferdinand I became ruler of the central European empire that included Germany, Austria, northern Italy, and parts of the Danube region into the Balkans.

[40] Frieda, *Catherine de Medici*, 169. Wellman, *Queens and Mistresses*, 232.

[41] Frieda, Ibid., 168–178. Wellman, Ibid., 237.

[42] Wellman, *Queens and Mistresses*, 234.

[43] Ibid., 235–236.

6 QUEENS OF FRANCE

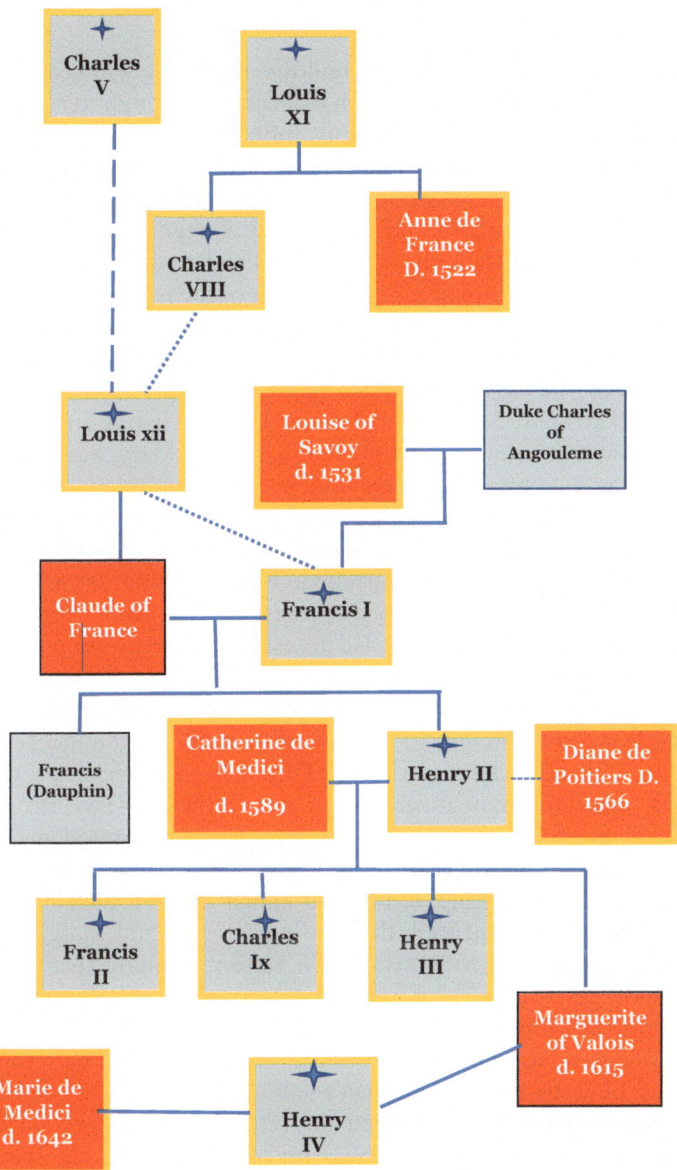

Lineage from Anne de France to Marie de Medici

Mother of Francis II

Sickly, frail, and suffering from tuberculosis, Catherine's fifteen-year-old son was now crowned Francis II. Although formally old enough to rule by himself, the young king was under the grip of his ambitious teenage wife, Mary, daughter of the French Marie of Guise and King James V Stewart of Scotland. Mary's father died right after she was born, and her mother remained in Scotland to rule in his stead and be officially recognized as regent. At five, the ginger-haired tot was sent to Catherine's household and was soon betrothed to her son. Once Francis was crowned, Mary's uncles of the powerful Guise clan took control of the state, shoving Catherine aside. The queen, still in her first year of mourning and newly introduced to the Guises' aggressive style of power politics, recognized Mary as the new queen, gave her the crown jewels, and receded into the background. Mary, on the other hand, behaved arrogantly to her mother-in-law, muttering at one time that while she, Mary, was of royal blood, Catherine was merely a Florentine shopkeeper's daughter. As she and her uncles steered the young king to support their militant Catholic faction, their French Protestant rivals—the Huguenots—who hoped that Catherine would embrace their cause, were disheartened. French Protestantism was cruelly repressed, leading to a failed coup by Protestant extremists who tried to take the palace by force. This episode led to even more repression and a never-ending cycle of violence.[44]

Catherine, who still had access to her son's ear, sought to restore balance and provide a counterweight to the emerging Catholic dominance. Her idea was to renew France's alliance with the Ottomans, who were Spain's enemies and, hence, pro-Protestant at base. A few years earlier, in 1557, these relations suffered a blow when two high-born Ottoman women captured in a piracy raid were presented to Queen Catherine. Although their families demanded their return to the Ottoman Empire, the two joined the queen's entourage, converted to Christianity, and took the names Catherine and Margaret. Initially, Sultan Suleiman refused to demand their return, claiming that once they've become apostates, there was no point, but the women's family gained the support of Princess Mihrimah, Suleiman's daughter, and of her husband, Grand Vizier Rustem Pasha, who issued an official demand to send back the women.

Another blow to French-Ottoman relations came when the sultan's close friend, Don Joseph Nasi, demanded the return of the huge sum of money loaned to the French crown by his aunt, Dona Gracia. His demand was rebuffed, with the French government quoting laws against apostasy (Don Joseph, previously João Miques, was a Marrano who reverted to Judaism). At Don Joseph's request, the Sultan ordered that all French ships carrying merchandize to the empire be stopped and searched and part of their cargo confiscated to repay the loan. These two issues became sticking points in the

---

[44] Frieda, *Catherine de Medici*, 42, 127, 184–186. Some historians claim that there was no real coup, and the entire episode was cooked up by the Duke of Guise in order to further repress the Huguenots.

relationship. Catherine sent three envoys to Istanbul to settle the issues, and although the negotiations initially stalled and failed to produce concrete results, they succeeded in reestablishing diplomatic ties between the two countries.[45]

She quickly found a way to use this renewed relationship to France's advantage. In July 1560, in a joint raid, the Ottoman admiral, Piyale Pasha, and his ally, the corsair Torgut, defeated the Spanish fleet off the island of Gerba near Tunis and captured the Spanish military base on the island. Among the many officers and sailors taken prisoner was the garrison's commander, Don Alvaro de Sande, an experienced and decorated soldier. Catherine, who in her signature stabilizing policy sought an opportunity to improve relations with Spain even as she courted the Ottomans, sent her representative, the Italian Salviati, to Istanbul to negotiate the release of the high-ranking prisoner. Salviati was ordered to discuss the matter with the sultan's daughter, Mihrimah, who replaced her mother as chief adviser to her father and, if possible, with the sultan himself. Don Joseph, who received information about Salviati's mission from his spies even before the emissary reached Istanbul, advised the sultan and his daughter to grant the French their wish. Eventually, the one who succeeded in ransoming Don Alvaro and sending him back to Spain was the Habsburg ambassador Ogier Ghiselan de Busbecq. But the French envoy's negotiations with the sultan and his daughter served as a basis for renewed French-Ottoman diplomatic activity and opened a lively dialogue. Soon things were patched up and new economic agreements were signed.[46] The Ottomans were once again a force to be reckoned with on the European chessboard, and Catherine succeeded in her balancing act.

Then, two years after Francis II's accession, just as things started to look up, at least on the international front, the ailing teenage king died. Next in line for the throne was Catherine's second son, a ten-year-old boy crowned Charles IX. Francis' ambitious Scottish wife, Mary, became a widow at seventeen, and her uncles, the duke and cardinal of Guise, who had become *de facto* monarchs during Mary's reign, lost their hold on power. No longer willing to be pushed aside, Catherine elegantly maneuvered them out of the new king's sphere of influence and made sure that *she* would be declared regent, with full sovereignty during his minority. Angry and frustrated, the Guises became a vocal opposition to her rule and accused her of favoring their Huguenot enemies.

The Guise family did not give up easily on its efforts to push Catherine aside and rule France. Even before Mary's official mourning period was over, they started looking for another royal match. One prospective husband was Don Carlos, the cruel and mentally unstable son of Philip II. Another was Archduke Charles, son of the Austrian Emperor Ferdinand. Both of these matches threatened Catherine's position. With either Philip or Ferdinand as an in-law, the Guise clan would become even more powerful in French politics and in the

---

[45] Nathan Michaelewitz, "Franco-Ottoman Diplomacy," 178–182. Roth, *House of Nasi*, 24–27.
[46] Roth, *The House of Nasi*, 32–33. De Lamar, "Catherine de Medici," 61.

Catholic League. Also, if she were to marry Don Carlos, Mary might push aside Catherine's own daughter, Elizabeth, who was married to his father Philip, just as she had done to Catherine herself. Catherine did everything in her power to thwart the marriage proposals, including offering her other daughter, Margaret, as bride to Don Carlos (which, luckily for Margaret, Philip courteously declined). Finally, Mary herself refused both marriage offers and instead boarded a ship bound for Scotland to take its crown, and then fight for England's as well. She left France in August 1561. Catherine could now breathe more easily and act as an autonomous sovereign with full monarchic powers. To remove any doubt about the actual locus of government, she appointed herself "Governor of France" and restructured the Royal Council to include her devotees.[47]

Around that time, Gabriel Bounin's play *La Soltane* was staged for Catherine and must have struck a deep chord in her soul. With a protagonist loosely based on Hurrem/Roxelana, beloved wife of Suleiman the Magnificent, the play dwelt on the sultana's alleged conspiracy to have Prince Mustafa, son of another consort, assassinated. Her aim, the play suggested, was to find a way for her own sons to inherit the Ottoman throne. In the play, the (despised) protagonist, named Rose, is in cahoots with Grand Vizier Rustem Pasha, thinly veiled as Rustan, and the two trick the sultan into believing that his son had rebelled against him. Bounin's intention was to write an allegory for the French crisis, with its two rival religious factions—Catholics and Huguenots—mirrored by a struggle inside the Ottoman royal family. Some critics identified the executed prince with a French claimant to the throne (Bourbon Prince of Condé) and Rose and the vizier, Rustan, with members of the Guise family. The play was intended to depict Catherine de Medici as the savior of the realm who would overcome these religious challenges.[48]

La Soltane was not a good piece of theater. In his attempt to create a land that was France and Turkey at the same time, Bounin blended together Islam, Old Testament stories, Greco-Roman mythology, and Christianity into an impossible concoction. One could never be sure who the heroes of the story were and who its evil characters. But, as often happens in literary depictions, the play's impact on spectators wasn't exactly what the author had intended. While Bounin presented the sultana as a scheming usurper, Catherine may have seen her in another light altogether. She may have sympathized with the innocent Prince Mustafa, assassinated at his father's command, as other spectators did, but she must have had an eerie feeling that her own dilemmas were played back to her by the actress who played Rose. If she had any misgivings about the role she would play henceforth on France's national stage, *La Soltane* dispelled them. Like the play's Rose, a foreign girl who rose to power, she would do everything necessary to protect her own sons, pave their way to the throne, and

---

[47] Frieda, *Catherine de Medici*, 219.
[48] Szabari, "The Crescent Moon," 1–3.

pull strings behind the scenes to get rid of their enemies and lead the dynasty forward.[49]

Not long after watching the play, she decided to write to the current sultana, Nurbanu, Hurrem's daughter-in-law, and propose a renewal of the special relationship between the two states. Perhaps she was reminded of the messages sent by Louise of Savoy to Hurrem Sultan to save her son.[50] In her negotiations she was aided by Pétremol, the French ambassador in Istanbul, who pushed for a renewal of France's position as sole representative of all western European states. Although the Ottomans were in favor of such a relationship, it presented a problem for the sultan. France at the time was still formally allied with Spain, and as long as that alliance existed, the Ottoman court could not fully trust France.[51]

Mother of Charles IX

In consideration of the new king's tender age, and still under the pall of his brother's premature death, Charles's coronation was a subdued affair. This time Catherine made sure that during the ceremony she would be front and center. Like Khanzada's throne set side by side with that of Emperor Humayun at the Mughal mystic feast in Agra, she had her chair placed in line with her son's throne, at exactly the same height (although the mother was substantially taller than the child), so that they would be seated as equals on the elevated stage. After the coronation she convened the Royal Council and carefully studied the business of governing the kingdom.

She began a move for reconstruction but soon realized that drawing power from her position as regent presented a problem of authority. Centrifugal religious forces were tearing the state apart, her hold on power encountered growing resistance, and a minor on the throne commanded little respect. In August 1563, therefore, even before Charles reached his fourteenth birthday, and although she knew well that he was not up to the task, she insisted that he be declared "of majority," ending her role as regent and formally making him sovereign with full powers. This was duly done in an official ceremony, but at the end of the announcement, in a carefully rehearsed act, her son came over to where she stood, bowed, kissed her, and announced that she would "govern and command as much and more than before."[52]

As Leoni Frieda writes: "*Catherine set about creating the national symbols of authority reflecting her new position. As for a new monarch, she had a huge seal specially created for her as 'Gouvernante de France'. It depicted Catherine standing, holding the sceptre in her right hand with her left hand raised and index finger pointing upwards in a gesture of command. Upon her head sat a crown*

---

[49] Ibid., 1–5. Andrea, *Women and Islam*, 19.
[50] Spagni, *Una sultana veneziana*. Andrea, *Women and Islam*, 18, 21.
[51] Nathan Michaelewitz, "Franco-Ottoman Diplomacy," 176–177.
[52] Frieda, *Catherine de Medici*, 220–247.

with her widow's veils clearly visible. The following legend was inscribed around the edge: 'Catherine by the grace of God, Queen of France, Mother of the King'."[53]

Soon tensions between Catholics and Huguenots surfaced again and ignited clashes in all parts of France. In an effort to bring unity to the realm, Catherine decided to take her son on a tour of his domains, accompanied by a huge retinue of armed guards, servants, and attendants. Her purpose was to make the majesty, power, and justice of the monarchy palpable by presenting it to the public in all its magnificence and by adjudicating local grievances on the spot. Catholics and Protestants were to be treated equally and a sense of security under the crown imparted to all subjects. To demonstrate the new Christian harmony, in many of the towns on their itinerary, a procession of Catholic and Protestant children walking hand in hand was prepared to welcome them.

The mother and son's traveling convoy set out in 1564 with dozens of chariots and coaches and stayed on the road for more than two years. In its course, Catherine met several foreign leaders. In Lyons, she discussed European affairs with Emmanuel-Philibert, Duke of Savoy, and with Alfonso d'Este, Duke of Ferrara, all the while corresponding with her cousin, Cosimo de Medici, and keeping him abreast of her itinerary. She was so happy, she wrote, to meet such obedience and loyalty toward the monarchy, growing from one day to the next.[54] Later on, in the city of Bayonne, she was scheduled to meet King Philip II of Spain and his wife, her daughter Elizabeth, whom she had not seen for several years. One of her goals was to improve relations and promote further royal marriages between Spain and France; but on the way to the meeting, she received word that Philip decided to stay away because he heard that Catherine had met with an envoy of the Ottoman sultan. He also learned that France intended to send a military force to settle the colony of Florida in America, which was occupied by Spain at the time.[55] Philip consented to his wife's meeting with her mother, but only on condition that "no Huguenots will contaminate the gathering." Elizabeth did arrive to meet her mother, but although Catherine tried to impress the Spanish delegation with her art treasures and riches, during the meeting Philip's emissaries made clear that Spain strongly disapproved of Catherine's policy of toleration.

In the southern town of Salon, she finally met the seer Nostradamus, whose prediction of her husband's death proved so chillingly accurate. She asked the old sage to predict the fate of her young son, King Charles, but he hesitated and then was only willing to promise, half-heartedly, that the child king would outlive her chief of staff, General Montmorency, who was already in his seventies. Nostradamus was mostly intrigued by another young man in the entourage, Prince Henry of Navarre, who at the time was only sixth or seventh in line

---

[53] Ibid., 208.

[54] Palandri, Eletto. *Les Négotiations Politiques et Religieuses*, 105. See also René Langlois, "Comparing the French Queen Regent and the Ottoman Validé Sultan" in Woodacre et al. *A Companion to Global Queenship*, 275.

[55] Frieda, *Catherine de Medici*, 248–270.

for the throne. The seer talked to him for a while and to Catherine's dismay prophesied that he would one day become king of France. At the time this seemed almost impossible.

Upon her return to the capital, Catherine faced a spate of new problems. One of them was Thomas Norris, a special envoy sent by Queen Elizabeth of England, who demanded the return of the city of Calais, claiming that France violated the treaty by taking it. Catherine dictated to her son the answer that he was to give Elizabeth: "*Since the Queen has broken the peace herself by taking Le Havre, she should renounce Calais and be content to keep the natural boundaries of her kingdom.*"[56]

The tour succeeded in offering France's inhabitants a sense of nation, pride, and respect for the king and the queen mother, but it failed to ease tensions between Catholics and Huguenots. Despite her tolerance toward the Protestants, Catherine openly displayed her own Catholic faith during the grand tour. Moreover, in an attempt to mend fences with her son-in-law Philip after the botched meeting in Bayonne, she supported his repression of the Protestant rebellion in the Low Countries. These actions disillusioned the Huguenots, made the monarchy's Catholic leaning clear, and, despite her efforts to present a tolerant face, marked her as an enemy of the Protestant movement. The growing tension led to an uprising in France itself, which was led by the young Prince Henry of Navarre and his mother, the Protestant Jeanne d'Albret, who was queen of this small kingdom in the Pyrenees. Fearing a Huguenot coup, Catherine advised her son to declare war against the rebels, and France was plunged into a civil war that rapidly escalated.

Two years later, in 1570, after several bouts of bitter fighting between their forces, the two queens, Catherine and Jeanne d'Albret, decided to stop the bloodshed and resolve the crisis. They met at the palace of Chenonceau, which had previously belonged to Diane de Poitiers, and although the puritanical queen of Navarre hated the chintzy baroque palace that felt like a den of promiscuity, and although she claimed that Catherine acted haughtily toward her, they reached an agreement. The Treaty of Saint-Germain-en-laye, named for the palace in which it was finally signed, promised the Huguenots freedom of worship and liberty of conscience. As usual, it was sealed with the promise of a future wedding, this time between Catherine's daughter Margaret and Jeanne's son, Henry of Navarre. Perhaps Catherine was not altogether oblivious to Nostradamus's prophesy that Henry would one day be king.

Following the treaty's ratification, the Venetian ambassador Corer wrote that Catherine believed she was buying time for her son. This peace treaty would afford the country a period of peace, and maybe "*the obedience of the people to the king would increase with the age of the king.*" But the treaty was soon breached. Huguenots who hoped that it would make them equals in the

---

[56] Frieda, *Catherine de Medici*, 282.

land felt deceived, and many Catholics, not least the powerful Guises, resented the queen for not being ardent enough in her commitment to the Church.[57]

Catherine was sufficiently open-minded, and perhaps cynical enough, to play both sides, but, driven into a corner by Huguenot threats of an uprising and fearing for her family, she sided with the Catholic militants, sometimes ruthlessly. To buttress her government, she arranged another marriage, this time between her son, King Charles, and Elizabeth of Austria, the sixteen-year-old daughter of Holy Roman Emperor Maximilian II. The marriage was celebrated with great pomp and circumstance in November 1570. For the festivities Catherine commissioned a telling sculpture, in which she was portrayed as a Greek goddess surrounded by four great women of antiquity, including her favorite, Artemisia, devoted wife of King Mausolus, who had built the Mausoleum at Halicarnassus to commemorate him.[58] But even as the church bells were ringing for the wedding, which was celebrated as a symbol of France's unshakeable ties to the Catholic Church, Catherine was busy setting the stage for another balancing act. In a gesture that had by now become her clearest political hallmark—an attempt to offset the forces arrayed against her—she made new overtures to the Ottomans, sending the sultan a small fleet of battleships and a dozen fine hunting falcons. The ships were lost by the Ottomans later that year in their greatest naval defeat, the Battle of Lepanto, but the friendship (and the falcons) remained.[59]

The second wedding, that between Margaret and the Huguenot Henry of Navarre, finally took place in August 1572 amid growing distrust between the factions. Four days after the wedding, on St. Bartholomew's Day, the chief of staff and leader of the Huguenot delegation to the wedding, Gaspar de Coligny, was shot and badly wounded on the street. Almost certainly committed on orders of the Guise family, the act was meant to disrupt the marriage and break the peace. Claims were made later that Catherine was in on the plan, but this is unlikely and no proof has ever been presented. In the wake of the incident, rumors spread that the Huguenots were planning to topple the monarchy or to abduct the king. Trying to forestall another civil war, the Royal Council met, this time in the presence of the king and his mother. It decided to make a move against the leaders of the Protestant party, although it is not clear whether the plan was simply to arrest them or to go further and assassinate them. The instructions may have been left moot on purpose.

On August 24, some of the king's sentinels, incited by the Guises, broke into the wounded Coligny's house, murdered him, and displayed his severed head to the public. In the following hours, other Huguenot leaders were killed or captured. Catherine may have believed that there was indeed a plot against the monarchy and that killing the plot's leaders would stop it, but the acts of violence got out of hand and unleashed a murderous frenzy. For more than a

[57] Wellman, *Queens and Mistresses*, 245–248. Frieda, *Catherine de Medici*, 221–223.
[58] Frieda, *Catherine de Medici*, 320.
[59] Ibid., 318.

week Parisian Catholics slaughtered thousands of Huguenots. Despite Catherine's persistent attempts to find a middle ground between Catholics and Protestants, when push came to shove her political decisions led to the infamous slaughter, and St. Bartholomew's Day massacre became a terrible stain on France's monarchy and specifically on her own reputation.

As France sobered in the wake of the great tragedy, Catherine knew she had to make amends to leaders around Europe who supported the Protestant cause. Her first concern was Elizabeth of England, whose sympathies lay with the Huguenots. In her letter to Elizabeth, she claimed that the assassinations of Huguenot leaders were necessary to stop an attempted coup and safeguard the state. Once again trying her hand at political matchmaking, she proposed a marriage with her much younger son Francis Hercule, believed to be a Protestant.[60] She went even further in her juggling act and, contrary to her previous policy, expressed support for the rebellion of the Protestants against Spanish rule in the Netherlands. There may have been an ulterior motive here. As part of an emerging dream of creating a Valois Empire ruled by her children, Catherine hoped that a successful Protestant rebellion would end up crowning Francis Hercule King of the Netherlands.[61]

But while showing support for Protestants abroad she still pushed for the destruction of their bastions in France and sent her third son, Henry de Valois, to lay siege to the Huguenot-held fortress of La Rochelle on the Atlantic coast (later the scene of Alexandre Dumas' *Three Musketeers*). This action soon pegged Henry as the leader of the anti-Huguenot faction, and plots for his assassination sprang up across the country. Henry's deliverance came from an unexpected source. King Sigismund Augustus of Poland died in 1572 with no male heir, and Catherine came up with the idea of suggesting him as a candidate for the Polish-Lithuanian throne. This, she believed, would keep him safe from death threats at home and at the same time incorporate another country into the dream empire, which had been gradually taking shape in her mind.

Though intrigued by the idea of a French royal candidate for their throne, the Polish nobles had many doubts. The advantages were clear. The major threat to the Polish-Lithuanian Commonwealth at the time came from the Habsburgs, who claimed they had a hereditary right to the Polish throne. An alliance with Queen Catherine of France would act as a bulwark against these claims and those of the Russians. But would it be enough? And how would the Ottomans react to the idea of a neighboring country ruled by the French? To allay the fears of the Polish nobility, Catherine once again initiated dialogue with the Ottomans. Knowing that Sultan Selim was inebriated most of the time, she sent her ambassador to his wife, Nurbanu, and her daughter, Ismihan. The sultanas discussed the matter with the palace physician Solomon Ashkenazi, an old hand in European state affairs who was previously physician to the Polish

---

[60] Francis was named Hercule when he was born. He changed his name to Francis when confirmed as Duke of Anjou, in honor of his dead brother.
[61] Wellman, *Queens and Mistresses*, 260.

monarch. Ashkenazi approved of the idea and, at the sultanic family's behest, lobbied the Polish nobility, assuring them that the Ottoman Empire supported the appointment. Convinced by the combined efforts of the French envoy, Monluc, and the Ottomans, the Polish Sejm elected Catherine's son Henry King of the Polish-Lithuanian Commonwealth.

In February 1574, Henry arrived in Poland and was crowned in Krakow but, with no experience in eastern European politics, almost immediately got into trouble. A group of hawkish Polish nobles convinced him of the need to capture Ottoman-held Wallachia, and although Henry barely knew where Wallachia was, he gave his permission. Their plans were leaked, however, and the sultan—meaning his wife—was offended by what he saw as betrayal by an ally. The alliance between France and the Ottomans was once again in danger of crumbling.

But a mere four months later, in May 1574, Henry's older brother, the ailing King Charles IX, died of tuberculosis and Henry was asked to return and be crowned in his stead. Catherine's envoys to Krakow arrived just as Ottoman troops started gathering on Poland's southern border, and to prevent the crisis from deteriorating further, she wrote to Sultan Selim II, informing him of the French predicament and asking him, in a sincere tone, "*to continue toward this kingdom the same affection that has always been there.*" Her letter to Selim was sent even before formal letters were dispatched to her son-in-law King Philip of Spain and to the pope, to inform them of Charles's death and the request to Henry to take his place. The Ottomans, however, were hard to convince, and it took all of Catherine's diplomatic skills to reestablish a modicum of trust between the countries.[62]

To make his coronation more palatable to the Huguenots, who had marked him as an enemy, Catherine had to perform another delicate juggling act while Henry made his way to France. She clandestinely approached the Ottomans once more, this time to ask them to open a second front against the Habsburgs and support the uprising of the Dutch Protestants against Spain. Such assistance, she insisted, would benefit both France and their empire, create a safe haven for the Huguenots, and rid France of this trouble. She wrote to Safiye, the new sultana, and simultaneously sent her ambassador to request an audience with the sultan. She also consulted with her advisor, Alvaro Mendes (Solomon Abenaish), an experienced Marrano statesman who knew the Ottomans and had high-level contacts in Istanbul. Mendes promoted the renewal of the French-Ottoman alliance and perhaps even suggested to Safiye a way to assist the Dutch insurrection without getting directly involved. Convinced by his consort and the grand vizier, the sultan, Murad III, sent his fleet to engage the Spaniards in battle and capture Tunis, forcing them to divert forces from the rebellion in the Low Countries. At the same time, he instructed his friend and banker, Don Joseph Nasi, to use his contacts to put the Dutch insurrectionists in touch with the Spanish Moriscos (Muslims

---

[62] Michaelewitz, "Franco-Ottoman Diplomacy," Dissertation, 216–218.

forcibly converted to Catholicism), who had also rebelled against their Spanish overlords. Although in this round the plan failed to achieve its final goals (it took several more decades before the Dutch were finally rid of Spanish rule), Safiye was so impressed by Alvaro Mendes's acuity and network that she lured him from Catherine's service, invited him to Istanbul, and had him appointed Duke of Mytilene (Lesbos).[63]

Mother of Henry III

In a letter to her relative, Duke Cosimo de Medici in Florence, the thrice bereaved mother wrote: "*Once [Charles] gave up the fight and let go of the miseries of this life, he left me with the pain, which naturally a mother may have after the loss of the thing she holds most dear and precious, which makes me want to give up and to dispose of all business to seek some tranquility of life. Nevertheless, [since] I am obligated by the plea he made to me to embrace this office for the sake of this crown, to which I recognize myself held by all that God granted, I was forced to accept the said load, hoping that God will thank me...*"[64] She then informed the duke that her third son, Henry, was on his way from Poland to bear the crown of France.

The handsome youth, Henry of Valois (so named to set him apart from his rival and successor, Henry of Navarre), was Catherine's most beloved child, and she often called him "*chers yeux*" (precious eyes). Even during his short and unsuccessful reign in Poland, he had gained some government experience and, unlike his two sickly older brothers, was healthy and self-assured. A man of good taste and learning like his grandfather Francis, he was also extravagant, sometimes vain, and arrogant. He surrounded himself with a group of male favorites (often referred to as *mignons*), which infuriated the royal family and made it difficult for anyone outside this circle to reach him. He distanced himself from the network of powerful women who bound the monarchy to the aristocracy and, once settled on the throne, tried to wrest power from the nobility and govern as an absolutist monarch. Meanwhile, the country was in disorder and the Huguenot challenge to its legitimacy gained strength. Soon placards appeared on the streets mocking "*Henry, by the grace of his mother, apathetic king of France, imaginary king of Poland, concierge of the Louvre.*"[65]

In July 1585, after long years of mistrust and frequent clashes with Protestant forces, Catherine was once again worried that her domains would fall into alien hands. Henry of Navarre, a descendant of the House of Bourbon with a legitimate claim to the throne, and by now Margaret's husband, was gaining strength. The queen was even more fearful of a takeover by his ultra-Catholic

---

[63] Roth, *House of Nasi*, 201, 205. Galante, *Esther Kyra*, 7–8. See also Krstić, "Moriscos," 130, 135–136.

[64] Medici Archive, Vol. 4727, Fol. 227. On her developing relationship with Cosimo see Frieda, *Catherine de Medici*, 232, 234–235.

[65] Wellman, *Queens and Mistresses*, 259.

Guise rivals. To block the prince of Navarre and simultaneously appease the Guises, Catherine sought an agreement with their political instrument, the militant Catholic League. She consented to the League's demands, presented by the Cardinal of Bourbon and the Duke of Guise, that all Huguenots either convert to Catholicism or leave France's soil at once.

By signing this agreement, she hoped to curb Catholic agitation and to secure the kingship for her son, but its effect was just the opposite. By agreeing to their demands, Catherine lost her ability to divide and rule and ceded part of the monarchy's power to the League, which immediately started to persecute the Huguenots, initiating a wave of crises with France's neighbors. The consent given in 1587 by Queen Elizabeth to execute her cousin, Mary Queen of Scots, a dedicated Catholic and a scion of the Guise family, was in part retribution for the Catholic League's violence. In a vindictive mood, Elizabeth also decided to fund a unit of German and Swiss Protestant soldiers to help defend the Huguenots in the Netherlands. That October, the Protestant army and Elizabeth's paid soldiers, led by Henry of Navarre, won a decisive victory against the Catholics.[66]

Tired and ailing, the sixty-seven-year-old Catherine tried once again to preserve some kind of equilibrium and prevent war, but her son Henry, riled by the Protestant insurrection and goaded by the Catholic League, no longer deferred to her. He ignored her advice and dismissed the ministers she appointed. Given an ultimatum by the Guises in 1588, and without the Huguenots as a balancing force, he negotiated from a position of weakness. He gave amnesty to Catholic militants who fought against his rule, and recognized Cardinal Charles of Bourbon, the Guise candidate for the throne, as his heir apparent, practically losing his hold on the reins of power. Trapped in a corner and still ignoring his mother's political advice, Henry opted for violence again and decided to kill the Duke of Guise and his brother. The assassination orders were carried out on Christmas day of 1588, but instead of bolstering his position, this act only enraged the other Catholic leaders, who decided to rebel and depose him. On her death bed, Catherine failed to appease the new leader of the League, the Cardinal of Bourbon. She died a few days later, on January 5, 1589, in the midst of the bloody uprising.

In August of that year, a Catholic monk avenged the murder of the Duke of Guise. He entered the king's quarters posing as a messenger delivering papers and assassinated Henry III. After another bout of internal struggles, the king was succeeded by his cousin and brother-in-law Henry of Navarre, who narrowly escaped death himself in the St. Bartholomew's Day massacre. Henry, now Henry IV, whose ascent to the throne Nostradamus had predicted so many years ago, had finally reached his goal.

Having devoted her entire career as queen to finding the golden path between Catholics and Huguenots, Catherine ended up hated by both sides. In Paris, the angry members of the Catholic League who saw her as a traitor to

[66] Ibid., 260–265.

their cause threatened to snatch her body from the funeral procession and drag it through the streets. She was thus buried in the city of Blois outside Paris, not in the royal chapel of Saint Denis, which she had constructed for her family's burials. Her bones were exhumed and reinterred in Saint Denis only twenty years later.[67]

To appease the Catholic majority that refused to acknowledge a Protestant monarch, Henry agreed in 1593 to formally convert to Catholicism. He became one of France's most successful kings.

Marie de Medici

Henry and Margaret's wedding, four days before the St. Bartholomew massacre, did not bode well for the couple or the country. Queen Margot, as she was later known, did her best to reconcile her Protestant husband with her Catholic mother and brother. At Catherine's request she undertook several diplomatic missions, including a failed attempt to convince the Dutch to appoint another brother, Francis Hercule, king of the Netherlands.

Margot was also a patroness of arts and learning who, like the Mughal Gulbadan, wrote her own memoirs and hosted a literary salon in which many of France's intellectuals, including quite a few pioneering women, participated. But over time her relations with her husband soured. Henry's many mistresses added to the tension created by the religious divide and by her continuous failure to produce an heir. Margot reacted to his philandering by taking lovers of her own and flaunting them in public, to the dismay of clerics and self-righteous courtiers. Her decision to act independently and maintain an active sex life, though a mirror image of her husband's, shocked the period's chroniclers, who portrayed her as a nymphomaniac and her actions as scandalous. In 1614, the year before she died, she published a book called *The Learned and Subtle Discourse*, in which she countered these claims of promiscuity and also contended, astonishingly for her time, that women were superior to men in every respect: "*One must say that ... the world was created for Man, man for woman, and woman for God.*"[68]

Rejected by her brother Henry III and later shunned by her husband, Henry IV, she finally abandoned the royal court and lived in practical seclusion for twenty years, fomenting Catholic rebellion against the monarchy. She went through a series of escapes, insurrections, and imprisonments. Toward the end of the century, with no prospect of bearing children, she agreed to an annulment of her marriage to Henry. His hold on the French throne was finally

---

[67] Ibid., 266–268.

[68] *Laurent Angard, "Marguerite de Valois et 'La querelle des femmes,'"* 134: "*Par quoi, il ne faut plus dire le monde avoir été fait pour l'homme, et l'homme pour Dieu, mais il faut dire le monde avoir été fait por l'homme, et l'homme pour la femme, et la femme pour Dieu.*"

secure and he desperately sought an heir to his crown. The annulment was endorsed by Pope Clement VIII in 1599.[69]

Henry then sought a second wife and finally settled on the Italian Marie de Medici. Though only distantly related to Catherine, there is a great resemblance between the careers of both. There are also many similarities between Marie's career and those of Kösem Sultan and Nur Jahan, her Ottoman and Mughal contemporaries in the early 1600s. All three represent the last stage of female-dominated monarchy. They brought female power to its apogee in their respective realms and were, in a sense, responsible for terminating the century-long stretch of female rule.

Marie de Medici's father was Tuscany's Grand Duke Francesco, and her mother was Joanna of Austria, whose lineage included both the Austrian and Spanish branches of the Habsburg dynasty. Born in 1575, she lost her mother at three, made an orphan at twelve when her father died, and was raised by her uncle Ferdinando, who replaced her father as grand duke. She was still given the best education available and turned out to be a talented pupil, interested mostly in science, music, and the arts. At this stage, perhaps to offer the lonely girl some company, the duke brought in a slightly older girl of Jewish origin named Dianora Dori. Dianora, who later changed her name to the more elegant sounding Leonora and bought for herself the respectable surname Galigai, would become Marie's most trusted companion and closest adviser.[70]

By that time—the 1590s—the Medicis were the richest family in Europe, and many of Europe's royal houses offered lucrative marriages, but when a proposal arrived from the king of France, it could not be ignored. Henry's decision to propose was motivated mainly by financial need. The grand duke had previously lent him more than a million ecus to finance his struggles against internal and external enemies, but after long years of Catholic-Protestant infighting, the state's coffers were empty. Taking heed, other money-lending institutions were reluctant to advance more credit to the French monarchy, and the danger of bankruptcy was imminent. Marrying Marie was the best way to erase the debt and enrich the king's private treasury by another six hundred thousand gold ecus, part cash and part credit.[71] Henry wasn't thrilled about the prospect of marrying a relative of Catherine de Medici who, as he said, "*harmed France so much, and me in particular.*" But she sent him a portrait in which she looked very pretty, and the dowry was simply irresistible.[72]

The terms of the contract were finally agreed, and the marriage announcement was celebrated for several days in Florence in the king's absence, followed by a wedding at the Cathedral of Santa Maria del Fiore, in which Henry was represented by his delegate, the Duke of Belle Garde. Henry's mistress, Henriette d'Entragues, who still hoped that Henry would marry him, was livid.

---

[69] Sluhovsky, "History as Voyeurism," 195.
[70] Batiffol, *Marie de Medicis*, 1–5.
[71] Paiter, "Toscani alla Corte," 83.
[72] Ibid. Batiffol, *Marie de Medicis*, 9.

She ridiculed Marie at court, calling her "the fat banker," and insinuating that she was of a lower class.[73] Others were more forgiving. The aging Queen Elizabeth of England penned a letter to Marie in her native Italian, congratulating her on the marriage and accepting her into the royal fold.[74]

After the wedding, Marie sailed from Livorno to Marseille with an entourage of two thousand people and thence to Lyon, where she met Henry. The king was not disappointed. As one observer wrote, she had a *"fine figure, full and well developed, a little coarse, perhaps, but with beautiful eyes and complexion ... unmarred by paint, powder, or other vain devices."*[75] Clearly excited, Henry admitted that he had not reserved a room for the night at the hotel and asked her permission to stay with her. The two spent the night together and for a short time afterward seemed to be in love. The king was even heard to say that he loved her *"not only as his wife but also as his mistress."*[76] She probably conceived on the night of that first meeting because almost exactly nine months later, in September 1601, their son, the future Louis XIII, was born. The king was elated. Then, in quick succession, Marie gave birth to five more children, two sons and three daughters. There was no longer a problem of succession, and Henry's reign seemed more stable (Fig. 6.6).[77]

But when the initial excitement died down, the marriage settled into the old recognizable pattern. Marie continued as wife but was not officially crowned queen, and her husband seldom visited her quarters, spending most of his time with his paramours. At this stage, Marie had little interest in politics, ignored court intrigues, and enjoyed raising her children and indulging her artistic pursuits. Although she disliked Henry's mistress, Henriette, who often humiliated her, Henry's trysts did not bother her as much as the fear that, out of jealousy or paid by one of the other princes in line for succession, one of his mistresses might poison her children.[78]

In May 1610, setting out to participate in the European War of the Jülich Succession (in today's Germany), Henry had to appoint a regent in his absence, and his spouse was the choice required by law. She was therefore duly crowned in a ceremony at the courtyard of Notre Dame Cathedral in preparation for the mantle of regent.

But as fate would have it, the next day tragedy struck again. While laboriously making its way through streets thronged with people who had come to witness the coronation, Henry's open carriage was stalled. Suddenly a Catholic zealot, furious at Henry's tolerant views of Protestantism, jumped up and stabbed him. He died on the spot. Later that same day, with the country still in shock, his nine-year-old son was crowned Louis XIII, and Marie's regency was

[73] Batiffol, *Marie de Medicis*, 15, 117.
[74] Felix Pryor, *Elizabeth I: Her Life in Letters*, 247–248.
[75] Batiffol, *Marie de Medicis*, 6–7, 17.
[76] Ibid., 17.
[77] See also Ya'arah Bar-On, '*A Jewish Witch*' *at the court of Louis XIII* (Hebrew), 24–31. Paiter, "Toscani alla Corte," 83.
[78] Silard, "Continuity and Identity."

Fig. 6.6 Peter Paul Rubens, Marie de Medici's portrait presented to Henry IV by the gods of love (detail). At Henry's back, the helmeted "France" urges the smitten king to propose. Part of the 24-painting series known as the "Marie de Medici Cycle" commissioned by the queen in 1622 (now in the Louvre) (see René Langlois, "Comparing the French Queen Regent and the Ottoman Validé Sultan" in Woodacre et al. *A Companion to Global Queenship*, 273)

confirmed. She could scarcely hide her joy at finally being in a position to have things her own way.[79] One of the most famous paintings made by Peter Paul Rubens shortly afterward in his famous cycle of Marie's paintings was "The Death of Henry IV and the Proclamation of the Regency," a huge canvas that depicted her sovereign power. As Henry is being hauled up into heaven, Marie, sitting on the throne in funerary black, is adored by a group of mythological goddesses and heroes, musketeers, and angels.

Even though, following Catherine's lead, Marie meticulously dressed as the grieving widow, and though she had a grand statue of Henry cast in Italy and erected on the Pont Neuf in Paris, soon after her appointment conspiracy theories began to swirl in town about her possible involvement in the assassination. There was no truth to the rumors, but people readily believed them, perhaps because Italian internal politics were known for their cutthroat violence. These rumors would mar her reign going forward (Fig. 6.7).[80]

Just before Henry died, his mistress Henriette was involved in a plot to murder both him and Marie's son, the dauphin Louis. Hatched by some members of the nobility with Spanish support, the plan was to crown Henriette's own son, Henry's illegitimate child, instead. James I of England, who caught wind of this conspiracy, alerted Henry, and Henriette was apprehended and

---

[79] Batiffol, *Marie de Medicis*, 21.
[80] *Medici Archive*, Vol. 4729a, Fol. 614, Doc. 17718.

Fig. 6.7 Assassination of Henry IV

thrown in jail along with her entire family and other conspirators. Later, the king pardoned them, but Marie did not forget. After the king's assassination, Henriette flung herself at Marie's feet, begging for mercy. Marie and Louis graciously offered her a ten-thousand-franc annuity but banished her from court forever.[81] Many of Henry's other courtiers followed suit.

Marie ruled France formally as regent until her son's majority four years later, *"applying herself to affairs with unexpected steadfastness and purpose."*[82] She decided not to stray from Henry's tolerant religious policy, reconfirming his Edict of Nantes that accorded religious tolerance to France's protestants. On the other hand, as a scion of the Habsburg dynasty, she shifted from France's by-now-traditional anti-Spanish policy and allied herself with Spain,

---

[81] Batiffol, *Marie de Medicis*, 119.
[82] Ibid, 26.

raising tensions with her former allies, England, Savoy, and the Ottoman Empire, and with France's Huguenots, who saw Catholic Spain as the great Satan. The new treaty was sealed with the marriages of Marie's daughter Elizabeth to Philip III's son, and of her son, King Louis XIII, to Philip's daughter. After the marriages she tried, with partial success, to imitate the sinister, formal, and imperious Spanish court etiquette in France's royal court.

When Henry IV was crowned, he decided to cut the expenses of the royal household, and one of his main decisions was scaling down the queen's expenditures, which were greatly expanded during Catherine de Medici's time. The number of ladies in waiting, ladies of the chamber, and other servants was cut in half. But Marie, the rich party in the marriage, had different ideas and gradually increased their number. In 1606 her own household numbered four hundred and sixty salaried women, and after Henry's death that number was almost doubled. In addition, a host of men occupied various positions, including physicians, apothecaries, cooks, and grooms. Marrano Portuguese doctors were special favorites of the queen, including Philter Montalto, the head physician.[83]

Political power arrived quite suddenly, and Marie applied herself with panache. Her first hurdle was the palace itself. She had no network of trusted courtiers to work with, apart from her childhood friend Leonora Galigai who accompanied her to Paris, and Leonora's husband, a deceitful Italian named Concino Concini. The tragicomic couple of crooks, reminiscent of the Thénardier innkeepers in Victor Hugo's *Les Misérables*, gobbled up state power when Marie was confirmed as regent. Concini was soon made the queen's "First Gentleman in waiting" and with the huge sums bestowed on him by the queen bought the title of Marquis d'Ancre. A short while later, Marie conferred on him the governorships of Amiens, Normandy, and several other provinces, and he bought for himself the title Marechal de France, becoming the most powerful person after the queen. Concini continued to embezzle the royal treasury unashamedly, becoming the most hated man in France, and his corruption also stained Marie's reputation. She tried desperately to improve her popular image by making lavish donations to charity, publicly washing the feet of poor girls and providing young women with marriage trousseaus, offering doles to sick soldiers, paying the debts of some convicts and releasing them from prison, and giving annuities to scholars and Jesuit priests, but to no avail. She was still branded a corrupt monarch.[84]

Many in France were infuriated by the conduct of her corrupt protégés. The first to rise up against her was Henry II of Bourbon, Prince of Condé, a relative of the dead king who believed that regency over Louis XIII should have been given to him. Condé surrounded himself with other disgruntled nobles, threatened the monarchy and, to prevent rebellion, had to be placated by huge bribes and admission into the Royal Council. But in 1616, when an opportunity arose, he was arrested by Concini and sentenced to prison. His arrest

---

[83] Batiffol, *Marie de Medicis*, 76, 87. Zum Kolk, "Household of the Queen of France," 11–20.
[84] Batiffol, Ibid., 34.

precipitated a war between two camps of aristocrats, which ended with a temporary power-sharing agreement between the queen and the Prince of Condé.[85]

Meanwhile, the young king, Louis XIII, came into his own and began to resent his mother's and Concini's constant meddling. He relied more and more on his close friend, Charles, the Duke of Luynes, who served as commander of the Louvre palace contingent, and in 1617 Concini was finally assassinated when he crossed the moat bridge to the Louvre. Once he was moved out of the way, the king reasserted his rule, helped by Luynes and by Marie's former protégé, Cardinal Richelieu, another fast-rising star in French politics. They organized a coup d'état against his mother, banishing her to the castle at Blois, south of Paris. Leonora Galigai was arrested, convicted of witchcraft, and summarily burned at the stake.[86]

But Marie had no intention of relinquishing her hold on power. Jehanne Medici, a Turkish slave whom she had emancipated, baptized, and made a member of her own family, became her close confidante. Jehanne may have apprised her of developments in the Ottoman Empire, including the latest details on the reign of her contemporary, Kösem Sultan, who had to contend with similar problems.[87] Two years after her banishment, the resolute Marie tricked her guardians at Blois castle, slipped out, scaled a forty-meter wall with a rope ladder, escaped to her allies in the palace of Angoulême in southwestern France, and incited an uprising known in French history as "the war between mother and son" (*guerre de mère et du fils*). After a failed first attempt at reconciliation, orchestrated by Richelieu, the war flared up again, and only eighteen months after it broke out, in August 1620, did the king and his army manage to overcome the rebellion. But the actual result was a truce. The king forgave his mother and her loyalists and, following Richelieu's advice, admitted her back into the Royal Council. She regained some of her political clout and began constructing a new palace, the elegant Palais du Luxembourg in Paris. On its portal she sought to place statues of great mothers in history such as Saint Helena, mother of Emperor Constantine, and the mother of Alexander the Great. She also tried to convince those she believed to be her allies, including Spain's King Philip IV and the Austrian Habsburgs, to come to her assistance against Luynes and Richelieu, but to no avail.[88]

In 1630, failing to notice the shifts in European politics and the immense political power that Richelieu had garnered at court, Marie confronted her son and demanded that he dismiss the cardinal from office. The king, who had no such intention, soon lost patience with his mother once again. He banished her to the northern Chateau de Compiègne. But this time, assuming that the queen would try to escape once again, he and Richelieu set a trap. They feigned

---

[85] Silard, "Continuity and Identity."
[86] Ya'arah Bar-On, *A Jewish Witch*.
[87] *Medici Archive*, Vol. 4729a, Fol. 354, Doc. 17709.
[88] *Medici Archive*, Vol. 4949, Fol. 702, Doc. 7744. René Langlois, "Comparing the French Queen Regent and the Ottoman Validé Sultan" in Woodacre et al., *A Companion to Global Queenship*, 274.

a removal of the guard detail and opened the way to escape north, to Spanish-controlled Brussels. Marie jumped at the opportunity but then, stranded in the Lowlands, found herself banished from France altogether, losing her income and forced to beg her relatives for financial help.

This exile could be seen as the symbolic end of French queendom. For several years Marie de Medici toured Europe as a vagabond ex-queen. She visited the new Dutch Republic, where, being the first royal to recognize the new independent state, she was still received with great fanfare. She then paid a visit to her daughter Henrietta Maria, who was married to Britain's King Charles. But gradually the hubbub around her died down. She lost her assets and became a nuisance even to her closest relatives and friends, who turned her away. In 1642, she wrote to the grand duke of Florence, her relative Ferdinand II, begging him to take her in. She died on her way from Cologne to Italy.

As in the Ottoman Empire after Kösem Sultan, or the Safavid after Zaynab Begum, the female space painstakingly carved out for queens by Anne of France, Louise of Savoy, and Catherine de Medici was sharply diminished after the disastrous last years of Marie de Medici. It was taken over by the king's chief ministers, first Richelieu and then Cardinal Mazarin. France's next queen, Anne of Austria, wife of Louis XIII, turned her attention elsewhere, and her husband kept her away from affairs of state. When he died and her famous son, Louis XIV, the so-called Sun King, was still a minor, she insisted on being named regent in contravention of her husband's wishes, but this feeble attempt to capitalize on the gains women had made in the previous century did not last long. She soon handed over the government to Cardinal Mazarin.

CHAPTER 7

Queens of the British Isles and Ireland

> *To promote a woman to beare rule, superioritie, dominion or empire aboue any realme, nation, or citie, is repugnant to nature, contumelie to God, a thing most contrarious to his reueled will and approued ordinance, and finallie it is the subuersion of good order, of all equitie and iustice.*
>
> John Knox, The First Blast of the Trumpet against the monstrous regiment of Women *(1558)*

In many of the cases described in the previous chapters, women held actual political power in their hands, but it was rarely official. In all these cases, women's faces loom over the shoulders of their male kin who were the public site of sovereignty. They were regents waiting for their minor sons to come of age, widowed wives asked to oversee the transition of power, or simply mothers, sisters, daughters, aunts, and nieces who proved capable enough to stand in for incompetent or reluctant monarchs. But they were never recognized as sovereigns in their own right. England and Scotland were the exception. Apart from Spain, they were the only places in Europe where women could be recognized by law as legitimate rulers in the sixteenth century. But whereas Spain had no sovereign queen since the end of the fifteenth century, no less than four women held *formal* sovereignty in the British Isles during the period examined in this book.[1]

Female sovereignty was made legal in England precisely to counter what made it *illegal* in France. As mentioned in the previous chapter, the Salic Law was enacted to thwart the attempt by England's King Edward III—the son of the French king's sister—to take over the French crown in the early fourteenth century. The archaic law maintained that only men could inherit titles and

---

[1] The first appearance of the term *British Isles* in English as a name referring to what is today the entire U.K. and Ireland dates to the early eighteenth century.

© The Author(s), under exclusive license to Springer Nature Switzerland AG 2024
D. Ze'evi, *Queens Around the World, 1520–1620*,
https://doi.org/10.1007/978-3-031-58634-7_7

estates, and since it prohibited King Edward's mother from inheriting the crown, her son was to be barred from it as well. England refused to recognize the Salic Law, and the entire Hundred Years' War, from the mid-fourteenth to the mid-fifteenth century, could in fact be described as a war to determine whether women had the right to hold sovereign power. So even though all its male sovereigns made the utmost effort to bestow the crown on a son rather than a daughter, England had to uphold this right.

The four women who would become sovereigns in the British Isles during the sixteenth century—Mary I, her half-sister Elizabeth I, their cousin Mary Queen of Scots, and Gráinne Ní Mháille, better known to English readers as Grace O'Malley, who ruled western Ireland—were born to riches and splendor. They should have fared better as young girls than slaves such as Hurrem and Nurbanu, who were abducted, enslaved, brought in chains to Istanbul, and sent to the royal harem, or than the persecuted Marrano Dona Gracia, who had to hide her religion and flee the Inquisition across Europe. But their way to the throne was just as precarious, fraught with danger and paved with constant struggle.

KATHERINE OF ARAGON AND THE RISE OF QUEENDOM IN ENGLAND

In December 1485, seven years before the conquest of Granada, a daughter was born to Isabella of Castile and her husband Ferdinand of Aragon, the youngest of five surviving children. She was named Catalina. While her mother and father conquered Granada and established the rule of the Cross over all of the Iberian Peninsula, deported the Jews, and sent Columbus on his audacious journey, the child grew up in the royal palace in Madrid. She was taught law, mathematics, history, philosophy, and theology, as well as Spanish, French, German, Castilian, Latin, and a bit of English, by the famed Italian Renaissance scholar Alessandro Geraldini and his assistants.[2]

Beautiful and precocious, she would have made a good match for any prince in Europe. But being the youngest, last in line to inherit the throne, and having English maternal great-grandmothers, her parents decided to offer her hand in marriage to Arthur, son of King Henry VII and England's heir to the throne.[3] For the parvenu Tudors, a marriage with Spain's royal houses was an impressive coup. At the beginning of the sixteenth century, Spain was the greatest power in the Christian world, and the House of Tudor, which had taken over just a few years earlier and was considered illegitimate by many of Europe's monarchs, was in dire need of this seal of approval. In 1501, at sixteen, she arrived

---

[2] Courtney Herber, "Katherine of Aragon: Diligent Diplomat and Learned Queen," in Norrie et al., *Tudor and Stuart Consorts*, 41–43. On Isabella of Castile and the *reconquista* see also Chap. 5.

[3] Katherine of Aragon's maternal great-grandmother was Philippa of Lancaster, daughter of John of Gaunt Duke of Lancaster and Blanche of Lancaster. She was the sister of King Henry IV. Her other maternal great-grandmother was Catherine of Lancaster, also a daughter of John of Gaunt by his second wife, Constance of Castile.

in England, where her name was rendered as Katherine, and married Prince Arthur, who was one year younger.[4]

But six months after the wedding ceremony, Arthur suddenly died of a mysterious illness, perhaps the disease known at the time as "the sweating sickness." The question whether the marriage was consummated, that is, whether Arthur and Katherine had penetrative sex before he died, would divide the country and lead to an international crisis some thirty years later.[5] But meanwhile, since the dowry promised by Katherine's father was so substantial, and since only part of it was already paid, King Henry VII refused to send her back home. She stayed in London, a virtual prisoner, notwithstanding Spain's remonstrances. In 1507, as a partial settlement of the diplomatic impasse, she was appointed Spain's ambassador to England (the first female ambassador in European history). Finally, after an avowal that her marriage to Arthur had never been consummated, she was betrothed to his brother, Henry, who was six years younger than the beautiful widow and deeply in love with her. The wedding took place in 1509, two weeks before he was crowned Henry VIII (Figs. 7.1 and 7.2).[6]

Henry and Katherine were an efficient power couple, although they did not succeed in having children in the first few years. Katherine miscarried in 1510 and a year later bore a boy, Henry, who died less than two months after birth. In 1513, Henry led his army to war against France, leaving his wife in charge of the kingdom with full monarchic powers under the title 'Regent and Governess of England, Wales and Ireland'. While he was away, war broke out between England and Scotland. Heavily pregnant once again, Katherine oversaw the recruitment and training of another military force. She took part in preparations for the campaign, and under her astute leadership, the English forces defeated their Scottish rivals. Scotland's King James IV was killed on the battlefield, and the victorious Katherine sent a piece of his bloodstained coat to Henry in France, reassuring him that the kingdom had overcome this hurdle and suggesting that he use it as a flag to rally his soldiers to battle. Soon Spanish circles reported that, despite her pregnancy, she led the army, clad in full armor, just like her conquistador mother. Although these reports had no basis in truth, they circulated around Europe. Yet she did not come out unscathed. Under the stress of war, Katherine once again lost her baby, the third in a row.[7]

Only in her fourth attempt did she succeed. Her daughter, Mary, born in 1516, survived. Then, two years later, she became pregnant once more. Henry's high hopes for a male heir were dashed again when the child, a daughter, was stillborn. But despite his clear disappointment, Katherine's importance for the English royal court grew. In 1519, her nephew, Charles, was crowned Holy Roman Emperor, gathering under his rule great swaths of Europe. When the young emperor briefly visited England a year later, Katherine tried to

---

[4] Richards, "Gender Difference and Tudor Monarchy," 34.
[5] Courtney Herber, "Katherine of Aragon: Diligent Diplomat and Learned Queen," in Norrie et al., *Tudor and Stuart Consorts*, 46.
[6] Ibid., 50.
[7] Ibid., 52–53.

Fig. 7.1 Young Katherine of Aragon as the Magdalene. Painting by Michael Sittow (late fifteenth or early sixteenth century), oil on oak panel. Detroit Institute of Arts, Founders Society Purchase, General Membership Fund, 40.50

convince her husband to ally himself with the Habsburgs against France, but Henry was suspicious of Charles and too excited about the coming meeting with his French counterpart, King Francis, which was to take place in the Field of the Cloth of Gold.[8] Despite her ties to the Habsburgs, Katherine decided to support Henry's (failed) attempt to reach a settlement with France. Years later, as relations with France deteriorated further, England once more contemplated an alliance with the Holy Roman Empire, and as part of the deal Katherine suggested offering Charles the hand of her daughter, Mary. But the relationship between the countries was too volatile. and nothing came of it.

Meanwhile, having been taught and influenced by humanist Renaissance authors, Katherine decided to make her own contribution to the world's changing attitudes toward the education of women. Her ally in this venture was Juan Luis Vives, a famous Humanist scholar from a family of converts, whose parents were executed for Judaizing. Vives himself fully embraced Catholic Christianity and, having studied philosophy and scholastic disputation

[8] See Chap. 6.

Fig. 7.2 Young Henry VIII. Attributed to Meynnart Wewyck, about 1509. Denver Art Museum: Gift of the Berger Collection Educational Trust, 2021.29. Photography courtesy Denver Art Museum

at the Academy of Valencia and the University of Paris, was appointed professor at the University of Leuven. Katherine had invited him to England to serve as tutor to Princess Mary, and at her behest he wrote his famous book, *De Institutione Feminae Christianae* (translated into English in 1529 as *Education of a Christian Woman*), which he dedicated to Queen Katherine. Despite the obvious sycophantic tone, it is clear that Vives truly admired Katherine and used her as his model.

> *I dedicate this work to you, glorious Queen, just as a painter might represent your likeness with utmost skill. As you would see your physical likeness portrayed there, so in these books you will see the image of your mind, since you were both a virgin and promised spouse and a widow and now wife (as, please God, you may long continue), and since you have so conducted yourself in all these various states of life that whatever you did is a model of an exemplary life to others. But you prefer that virtues be praised rather than yourself. Although no one can praise female virtues without including you in that same praise, I shall nonetheless obey you, provided that you know that under the rubric of excellent and outstanding virtues other women similar to you may be mentioned by name, but it is you always, even if tacitly, who are spoken of. For virtues cannot be extolled with praise without commending those who, though unnamed, excelled in those virtues. Your daughter Mary will read these recommendations and will reproduce them as she models herself on the example of your goodness and wisdom to be found within her own home. She will do this assuredly and,*

unless she alone belie all human expectations, must of necessity be virtuous and holy as the offspring of you and Henry VIII, such a noble and honoured pair. Therefore, all women will have an example to follow in your life and actions, and, in this work dedicated to you, precepts and rules for the conduct of their lives. Both of these they will owe to your moral integrity, by which you have lived and through which I have been inspired to write. Farewell.[9]

Translated into many languages, Vives' book became an instant bestseller in Europe. Although it still emphasized attributes such as chastity, serenity, and support for the husband, it advocated education for all women and argued that they were intellectually equal or even superior to men and that women's education was essential for the advancement of society.[10]

His book helped set the stage for formal schooling of girls, at least for well-off families, but in England it was Thomas More, one of the greatest philosophers of the period, who actually demonstrated how it could be done in the absence of educational facilities, by educating all the women, young and old, in his own household. More believed that the purpose of education should be spiritual, and therefore he emphasized morality and modesty in his teaching.[11] His ideas were developed two decades later, when Robert Vaughan's *Dyalogue Defensyve for Women, against Malycyous Detractours* was published. Vaughan presented his claims in the form of a dialogue between two birds, a pye (magpie), speaking as a detractor of women, and a falcon as their supporter. In one of the dialogues the falcon says, astoundingly:

> *That to knowledge and virtue, women apt be*
> *And yf of theyr lyves comparison thou make*
> *More godly than men, they seme*
> ....
> *If women in youth had suche educacyon*
> *In knowledge and lernynge, as men use to have*
> *Theyr works of theyr wyttes, wolde make full probacyon*
> *And that of men councyll, they need nat to crave.*[12]

These contributions in support of women's education and, perhaps even more importantly, women's sense of self-worth may have prepared Princess Mary for eventual queenship, but they did not change her father's craving for a male heir. As Katherine got older, and her chances of getting pregnant diminished, Henry became desperate. The House of Tudor had only gained the throne one generation earlier, in the wake of the bloody Wars of the Roses between the Houses of York and Lancaster. There were still some in England who cast doubts on the Tudors' right to rule, and Henry may have feared that

---

[9] Vives, *The Education of a Christian Woman*, 50. See also Herber, "Katherine of Aragon," 53–54.
[10] Attreed and Winkler, "Lessons in Statecraft," 971–972.
[11] Benson, "Invention of the Renaissance Woman," 157–158.
[12] Ibid., 157–158, 206–207, 209.8.

his lineage would not survive if there were no male heir to succeed him.[13] He blamed Katherine for the failure to produce a son, turned away from her, and started flirting with other courtiers.

Soon, he set his sights on Anne Boleyn, a charming young lady-in-waiting, and planned to marry her. As a Catholic, he was prohibited from divorcing his wife and marrying another, but then, perhaps with the encouragement of his top adviser, Thomas Cromwell, and his new mistress, came up with the idea of *annulling* the marriage to Katherine, a practice recognized by the Church when one of the parties has failed to fulfill the essential conditions of a binding union. Henry claimed that Katherine lied about her marriage to his brother Arthur and that, contrary to her testimony, she did have sex with him and was not a virgin when she married Henry. His matrimony, he argued, was therefore unlawful according to the Bible (Leviticus 18 and 20). He famously declared that having only a daughter was his punishment for marrying his brother's wife and for living in sin. Katherine denied the allegations and as proof of her innocence produced a letter that she wrote to her parents immediately after Arthur's death, in which she told them that she did not consummate the marriage. The issue was then referred to Pope Clement VII, the highest authority in the Catholic Church, but despite Henry's efforts to convince him, the pope, who was a virtual hostage in the hands of Katherine's nephew, Charles V, refused to annul the marriage and forbade Henry to marry his mistress.[14]

Finally, in 1531, Henry could no longer bear the frustration. Even though the matter was not settled by the religious authorities, he banished Katherine from the palace and a year later married Anne Boleyn in a secret ceremony, perhaps hoping to get authorization after the fact. Finally, when his emissaries came back from Rome with another refusal to annul, he realized that the pope would never approve this marriage and decided to sever his ties to the Catholic Church. Instead, he asked the archbishop of Canterbury, an acquaintance of the Boleyn family and now the senior cleric in England, to declare his marriage to Katherine null and void, defying the pope's verdict. Once the archbishop consented, Henry's daughter Mary was declared illegitimate and taken away from Katherine. Mother and daughter could only correspond secretly with the help of sympathizers who carried letters and word of mouth between them.

Katherine of Aragon's first contribution to government by women in England was simply her provenance. Coming from the powerful Spanish royal house, in terms of lineage as grasped by the era's elites, she was Henry's superior. And even as Arthur's widow, before she married Henry, she broke new ground by being appointed the first ever female ambassador in England and successfully representing her empire of origin. After the marriage, her triumph in the war with Scotland in 1513 was etched in English memory as a great

---

[13] Lauren R. Browne, "Elizabeth of York: Tudor Trophy Wife." Catherine James, "Bogus or Bona Fide."

[14] Richards, "Gender Difference and Tudor Monarchy," 35, 38.

victory. Finally, her patronage of Juan Louis Vives and Thomas More, major promoters of female education, laid the ground for Mary to access the throne and for Elizabeth's long successful reign.

Anne Boleyn

Anne, born in the first decade of the sixteenth century, was the daughter of Thomas Boleyn, an English aristocrat and diplomat in the service of the Tudors. During her childhood her father was sent as ambassador to the Low Countries, where he met and befriended the governor queen, Margaret of Austria, whose court, mirroring that of her own tutor, Anne of France, was "an important training ground for the European elite." Soon Anne Boleyn was invited to Margaret's household as a maid of honor and from there went on to the service of Queen Claude of France, wife of Francis I. During this period, she may have made the acquaintance of Margaret, sister of Francis I and later Queen of Navarre (and mother of Queen Jeanne d'Albret), an independent thinker who supported the translation of the Bible from Latin into French and English, a kind of precursor to Protestantism. Margaret educated her about the necessity of religious reform.[15]

Pretty, dark haired, and olive skinned, she was a graceful addition to court life. She arrived in England in 1522 and a short time later may have been secretly engaged to her relative Henry Percy, son of the Earl of Northumberland. At the time, her sister was the king's mistress, but soon Henry VIII had met the young Anne and fell in love with her. Probably to enable the romance, Cardinal Wolsey told Percy's father that his son and Anne were involved, and in a fit of rage, Northumberland insisted that the engagement be broken. Meanwhile, Anne flirted with the king and even promised to marry him if his marriage to Katherine were dissolved. Conscious of the Reformation now in vogue in northern Europe, it is plausible that Anne pushed Henry to dissociate himself from the papacy and thus be able to annul the marriage to Katherine.[16]

While Katherine sided with her nephew Charles Habsburg, Anne rooted for the French side in the endless European wars and persuaded Henry to make another attempt at coming to terms with King Francis. The English-French summit, which she is said to have had a hand in orchestrating, finally took place in Calais in 1532 and ended in agreement. During the meeting, despite his formal allegiance to the pope (and the ongoing negotiations for the betrothal of the pope's niece, Catherine de Medici, to his son, Prince Henry), King Francis expressed support for Henry's marriage to Anne. The impatient Henry, who believed that Anne would finally give him the male heir he yearned for,

---

[15] Fairbanks and Lane, "Anne Boleyn: Traditionalist and Reformer," in Norrie et al., *Tudor and Stuart Consorts*, 61.
[16] Ibid, 62.

could wait no longer and married her secretly on the way to England, even before the annulment of his marriage was officially announced. He made her Marquess of Pembroke and lodged her in Queen Katherine's old quarters in the palace. Soon she informed him that she was pregnant, and another wedding, public this time, was hastily prepared. It took place in January 1533. The Archbishop of Canterbury, Thomas Cranmer, provisionally the senior religious authority of the land, declared the marriage valid.[17]

King Henry may have hoped that the pope would endorse his marriage now that it was a done deal, but even before the wedding, perhaps under pressure from Emperor Charles, Pope Clement VII threatened the couple with excommunication. A short time later, the defiant Henry took over the Church of England. Although most of the English public was still in shock by the looming breakup with Rome and viewed Henry's new marriage as a travesty, Anne was crowned Queen in Westminster Abbey a month later. The official promulgation of excommunication only took place under Pope Paul III five years later, in 1538.

But Henry's hopes for a son were dashed again. In September 1533, to his chagrin, another daughter was born, and her mother named her Elizabeth after Henry's own mother. King Francis, who was invited to attend the celebrations and prepared himself to be the boy's godfather, was notified that the celebrations in honor of the baby boy were cancelled. The birth was duly celebrated, but festivities were subdued, and once they were over Elizabeth was sent, along with her wet nurse, to Hatfield House in the country. She was joined by Katherine's daughter, Princess Mary, whose punishment for refusing to recognize Henry's marriage to Anne Boleyn was to wait on the baby princess.

Soon Anne was pregnant again, and the court was alive with excitement, but the baby was stillborn and Henry, in a foul mood, mulled the possibility of divorce. The couple reconciled, but then, on January 29, 1536, Anne, who was pregnant for a third time, panicked when Henry fell unconscious during a tournament and miscarried five days later. From this point on events moved quickly. The king had a new mistress, Jane Seymour, one of Anne's ladies, and Thomas Cromwell was ordered to find a way to get rid of the queen, who, ironically, was instrumental in his own rise to power. They finally accused her of adultery with several lovers, including her brother George, some members of the privy chamber, and one of her musicians. Later she was also accused of high treason. In May 1536, less than three years after her coronation, she was locked away in the tower and promptly beheaded (Fig. 7.3).[18]

[17] Ibid., 67.
[18] For all theories concerning the reasons for her execution see ibid., 76–77. See also Bernard, "The Fall of Anne Boleyn," mainly pp. 584–585. Walker, "Rethinking the Fall of Anne Boleyn," 1–29.

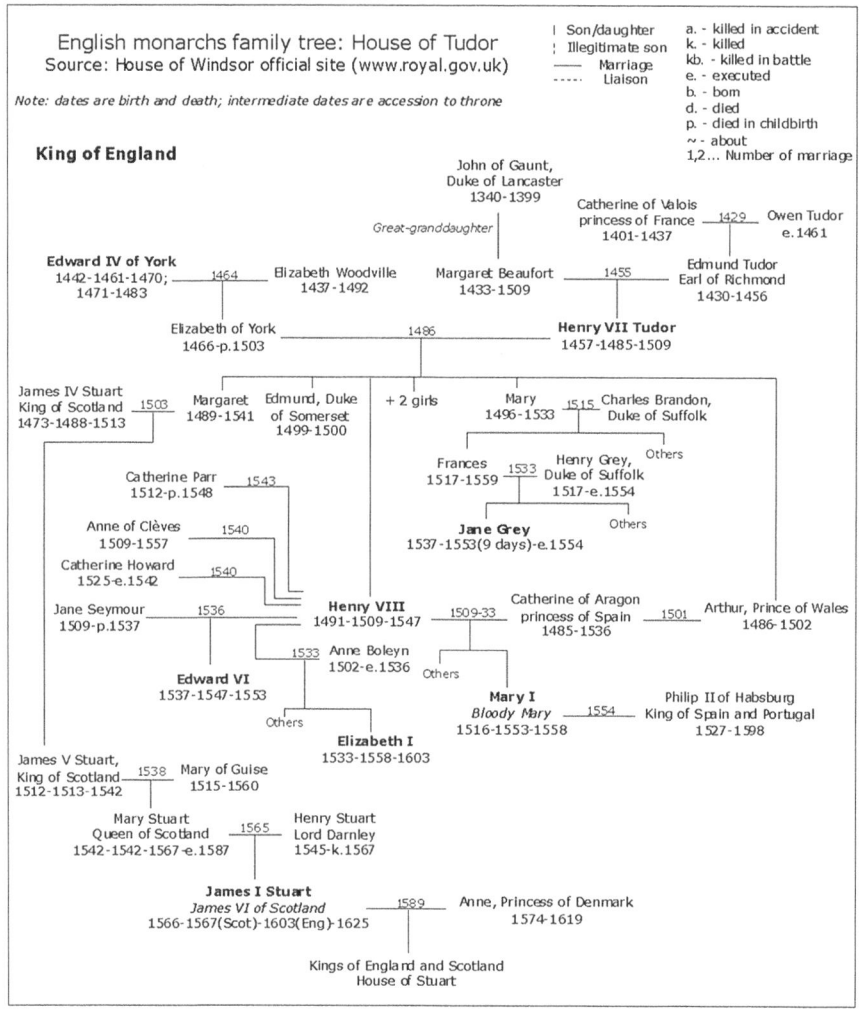

Fig. 7.3 House of Tudor family tree, by Muriel Gottrop (enwiki)

Mary I

Henry went on to have four more wives. He married Jane Seymour, then the German Anne of Cleves, Catherine Howard, and, finally, Catherine Parr. With Jane Seymour he finally had a son, Edward, in 1537. Jane died soon after the birth from postnatal complications, but as soon as Edward was born, Henry's disposition began to change. He became kindlier toward his two daughters, and the twenty-one-year-old Mary was invited to serve as Edward's godmother at his christening. Elizabeth, aged four, was also invited to the celebration but later sent back to Hatfield House.

In 1547 Henry died, and his nine-year-old son Edward ascended the throne. Shortly before his death, Henry realized that his chances of having more offspring were slim and worried that if he died with his two daughters still unrecognized by the state, next in line for the throne after Edward would be another Mary, the daughter of King James V of Scotland and granddaughter of his sister Margaret. And if that Mary, who at that point in time was engaged to France's crown prince, should inherit the English crown, France would once again rule England. His dynasty would be wiped out and the Tudor name forgotten. He therefore decided to restore his daughters to the order of succession. If something were to happen to Edward, he decreed, his daughter Mary was to rule after him, and Elizabeth after Mary. Henry's last wife, Catherine Parr, who acted as foster mother to all his children, was instrumental in reaching this arrangement.

Edward, the child king, was put under guardianship of his uncle, Edward Seymour, Duke of Somerset, who headed a council of regents and soon became the monarchy's sovereign for all practical purposes. But two years later, feeling that the crown was already within his grasp, Seymour overplayed his hand and tried to make his position official. He was imprisoned for a series of purported crimes of mismanagement and later executed. Another member, John Dudley, now upgraded to Duke of Northumberland, took his place as leader of the council and tried to act in concert with the other members. Unlike his predecessor, he was loath to start new wars and strove to reach agreement with Scotland and France. Yet he seems to have had other plans for Edward's succession.

In 1553, Edward fell ill and was soon moribund. Having no offspring of his own and unwilling to leave the kingdom in women's hands, he tried to find male alternatives. Under the influence of John Dudley, he wrote a document bypassing his sisters and naming his cousin, the sixteen-year-old Lady Jane Grey, queen. Since Jane was already married to Dudley's son, it was clear to all that her husband would be the actual monarch. Their successors, so the dying king hoped, would also be male.[19]

Edward died at fifteen, and Dudley attempted to keep his death a secret until his sisters would be under his control, perhaps locked up, but Mary had gotten word of her brother's death from her own sources on the council. Suspicious of Dudley's motivations and, like many among the public, riled by the dead monarch's militant anti-Catholic reforms, she refused to accept Jane Grey as her liege. She left her home to organize resistance, proclaimed herself the lawful queen, demanded homage from the nobles—who mostly hesitated, waiting to see where the wind would blow—and encouraged the people of England to rise up.[20] An able commander, like her mother and grandmother, she divided her followers into fighting units, inspected their encampments, and

---

[19] Richards, "Gender Difference and Tudor Monarchy," 32–33, 38. Richards, *Elizabeth I*, 24–25. Duncan, *Mary I*, 12–13, 37–38.
[20] De Guaras, *The Accession of Queen Mary*, 89–92.

gave heart-bracing speeches. When Jane Grey was proclaimed, her forces began to make their way southward to London. A civil war was in the offing.

Trying to save his monarchic wager, John Dudley ordered the royal navy's ships to block any possibility of Mary crossing over to the Spanish Netherlands and recruiting a Catholic army. He hastily gathered a cavalry unit to meet and defeat her. But as he was making his way northward, he learned that the navy mutinied and that the Privy Council in London, facing the public's wrath, quickly backpaddled, dismissed Jane Grey, and proclaimed Mary Queen. Northumberland had no choice but to give up and pledge allegiance to the new queen.[21]

On August 3, 1553, the thirty-six-year-old Mary rode into London at the head of a dazzlingly resplendent convoy. The Earl of Arundel rode before her bearing a sword, and another noble carried the train of her dress. Eight hundred loyal nobles and officers rode behind her, "*the least of whom wore a velvet suit and chains*," as one Spanish merchant wrote, and ten thousand horsemen followed the royal train.[22] Such splendor was to be a hallmark of her reign, setting the stage for her sister Elizabeth, who proudly accompanied her on her way to the throne and was in close attendance during her coronation.[23] Two weeks later, John Dudley, Duke of Northumberland, was tried and executed. For the time being, Lady Jane Grey were spared.[24]

Red haired, with piercing eyes (though apparently nearsighted), of small stature but toughened by separation from her mother and her strict upbringing, Mary was a bright and keen student. As a child she could already speak and write English, Latin, French, and Spanish. Although she was never formally given the title Princess of Wales as befitted an heiress to the throne, in her tenth year she was tacitly acknowledged as such by her father and sent to Ludlow Castle to preside over the Council of Wales and the Marches. But by then Henry was already looking for ways to annul the marriage to Katherine, and soon Mary was declared illegitimate and sent away. She spent five years at Hatfield House before being quietly reinstated to the court after Anne's execution.[25]

This was the first time in recorded history that a woman officially sat on England's throne, and there were no guidelines for such an event. In the fifteen centuries since the reign of Queen Boadicea during the Roman invasion of the island, only one woman reigned by herself over England: Matilda (or Maude), daughter of Henry I, in the mid-twelfth century. But although she governed

---

[21] De Guaras, *The Accession of Queen Mary*, 92. A detailed description of Lady Jane's short reign and Mary's accession can be found in Nichols, *The Chronicle of Queen Jane*, written by a cleric during the period.

[22] De Guaras, *The Accession of Queen Mary*, 100.

[23] Nichols, *The Chronicle of Queen Jane*, 14. Richards, "Gender Difference and Tudor Monarchy," 33, 40. Richards, *Elizabeth I*, 28.

[24] Edwards, *Mary I*, 113.

[25] Report of Giovanni Michiel to the Venetian Senate, quoted in Medvei, "The Illness and Death," 768.

England and Scotland for 209 days, she was never crowned, and therefore no legal precedent existed. Could a woman govern on her own, or would she be required to marry? And if she *were* to marry, should the husband then become king, governing the country as a man was expected to govern his wife? This issue was especially acute since many of Mary's detractors denounced women's rule as a sign of the devil and Mary herself as a bastard and, therefore, officially not Henry's daughter.[26]

Seeking to understand what the Church had to say about female rule, the pious Mary found some guidance in the writings of Henry Parker Lord Morley, a Catholic humanist, who knew her as a child and presented her with his book after the coronation. Seemingly a compendium of religious faith, perhaps to disguise its true purpose, *An Account of the Miracles Performed by the Holy Eucharist* actually offered examples of women in leading roles. Focusing on her paternal great-grandmother, Margaret of Beaufort, who orchestrated the rise to power of the Tudor dynasty, Parker set her as an exemplary model. He also presented other examples of strong women from the Old Testament and ancient history. The book suggested that England's economic woes during Mary's first year—a long period of incessant rain and poor harvests—was the consequence of heresy taking root and that the "golden world" of true religion must be restored.[27]

Parker enumerated the issues in which a queen should be involved and the way she should conduct herself in such affairs. One part she was fond of reading was Lady Margaret's distress over the Ottoman advance into eastern Europe and her effort to unite all Christians in a crusade against them. Margaret expressed her willingness, Parker claimed, to be a laundress and wash the clothes of the knights who joined such a crusade. She was said to be generous to the poor, setting up tables for them on holidays, and to have visited the sick and dying, personally contributing to burial expenses. Margaret also understood the importance of education, founding two of Oxford's most famous colleges. Morley may have intended to present her as a model of balance and temperate behavior, forgiving and tolerant, but Mary adopted mainly what she understood to be her key traits of character: piety, faith-based justice, and a willingness to sacrifice everything for one's true belief. She believed they were vital to all the actions of a female monarch.[28]

Marriage to Philip of Spain

The leading issue of her first year on the throne was the question of marriage. With England as her potential dowry, there was no dearth of suitors. Even as a princess, before her mother fell from grace, she was first promised to Prince

---

[26] Sarah Betts, "What's in a Name? Dynasty, Succession and England's Queens Regnant," in Woodacre et al., *The Routledge History of Monarchy*, 481–482.
[27] Attreed and Winkler, "Lessons in Statecraft," 979–981.
[28] Attreed and Winkler, "Lessons in Statecraft," 981–983.

Francis, son of King Francis I of France, and then, at the age of eight, to her cousin, Emperor Charles V. Both offers were retracted as relations between England and these monarchies soured. But when she became queen, the issue of marriage was foremost on her mind for several reasons. First, throughout her youth, Mary stayed loyal to the Catholic Church. When she finally acceded, what she most wanted was to reverse her father's and brother's policies and return to the true Church. Although her relations with her sister were not altogether negative, she suspected (rightly) that Elizabeth harbored Protestant sympathies. She therefore had to find a husband immediately, both in order to produce an heir who would block Elizabeth's way to the throne and to help her bring the country back to the papal fold. She soon accepted Emperor Charles's suggestion that she marry his son, Prince Philip of Spain, who was almost ten years younger than she was and poised to inherit his father's huge empire. Philip seemed like a good option, but in the absence of a clear precedent for England, this could be a dangerous move. If English common law were to be followed to the letter, Philip would be crowned king and England would become just another outlying province of the sprawling Habsburg Empire.[29]

This fear of a Spanish takeover soon led to an attempt to depose Mary and crown Elizabeth in her place. But the uprising was crushed and its leaders captured and executed. Although she was not suspected of supporting the rebellion, Lady Jane Grey, who was already a prisoner in the tower and whose father had joined the rebels, was also beheaded. The public was so volatile that a special law had to be enacted in Parliament, a "marriage act" accepting Philip as King of England on equal terms with Mary, but barred from acting inside the country without her consent and from appointing foreigners to positions of government. Mary herself was also conscious of the problem that such a marriage, subordinating her by law to her husband, would present to the crown of England, and she pushed for a clear definition of her autonomy as a ruler. It was finally agreed that the arrangement granting Philip monarchic powers in England was to be valid only during Mary's lifetime, after which the crown was to return to England exclusively. Furthermore, it was decided that the native integrity of the realm would be preserved and that Philip would be prevented from removing his wife, or any children he might have, from England.

Once the Parliament's conditions were accepted by Emperor Charles, the marriage contract was signed. To elevate his son to the same rank as Mary's, Charles abdicated his titles of King of Naples and titular King of Jerusalem and bestowed them on Philip. It was understood that these titles would also devolve to Mary after the wedding. When the two were married a year later at Winchester Cathedral, Mary entered the church preceded by a sword bearer, symbolizing England's sovereignty, while Philip, officially still a prince, had no sword.[30] Soon, new "double-faced" coins were minted bearing Mary's and Philip's

---

[29] Duncan, *Mary I*, 40.
[30] For a detailed description of the wedding see Nichols, *The Chronicle of Queen Jane*, 167–172.

profiles facing each other "almost nose to nose." Mary's sister, Elizabeth, suspected of Protestant heresy, was not invited to the wedding.[31]

Few in England were thrilled about this marriage. Many feared an eventual takeover by the Habsburgs, and rumors spread that the archbishopric of Canterbury was to be given to a Spanish cleric, raising tensions again and perhaps contributing to a new uprising.[32] But the many lords who still belonged to the Catholic faction were reassured that the break with Rome would be healed in due course and the Reformation banned.

False Pregnancies and Catholic Reform

Shortly after the wedding Mary stopped menstruating. She was believed to be pregnant, but although preparations were made for great celebrations and festivities, no child was born. Mary, who had already dictated announcements to be sent to the pope, Emperor Charles, and the king of France, informing them of the successful delivery, now had her letters destroyed. It was most probably a false pregnancy, and the remedies offered by her doctors, which included frequent bleeding, harmed her health even more.[33]

Meanwhile, the queen was busy reversing her father's and her brother's secessionist policies and hunting down sympathizers of the religious reform. Since she inherited her brother's role as head of the Church of England, she had the authority to rule in such matters.[34] First she had the Parliament declare her mother's marriage retroactively valid and, hence, herself a legitimate daughter. In consequence, all the other marriages of Henry VIII until Catherine's death—including, of course, the one to Anne Boleyn, Elizabeth's mother—were declared invalid. She then imprisoned the bishops appointed by her predecessors and abolished most of their religious reforms.[35] While Catholics breathed a sigh of relief, many devout Protestants, troubled by the country's retreat to Catholicism, fled abroad. Those who remained and insisted on holding on to their beliefs were prosecuted for heresy. Hundreds were burned at the stake, including Cranmer, the Archbishop of Canterbury who was appointed by her father. Before his execution, Cranmer recanted and swore allegiance to the pope, but then, after it was clear that Mary had insisted on putting him to the stake, he repudiated his recantation on the last day. Mary's harsh rule gave rise to anti-Catholic sentiments and growing sympathy toward the Protestants and earned her the title "Bloody Mary."

---

[31] Attreed and Winkler, "Lessons in Statecraft," 976–977. Nichols, *The Chronicle of Queen Jane*, 169. Sarah Betts, "What's in a Name? Dynasty, Succession and England's Queens Regnant," in Woodacre et al., *The Routledge History of Monarchy*, 490–491. Richards, *Elizabeth I*, 36. Duncan, *Mary I*, 78–81. Cook, "Like Philip and Mary on a Shilling."
[32] Nichols, *The Chronicle of Queen Jane*, 82.
[33] Medvei, "The Illness and Death," 767–768.
[34] Richards, "Gender Difference and Tudor Monarchy," 30.
[35] Ibid, 36.

In early 1557, she expressed her intention to recruit an army and join her husband's war against France, but the Parliament refused to authorize the war, citing economic hardship. War broke out anyway a few months later, when an insurgent English force allied with the French invaded English soil in another attempt to depose Mary. A disastrous short campaign followed, at the end of which England lost Calais, her only remaining foothold on the continent, handing another blow to Mary's prestige. A decade later Elizabeth would try to regain a foothold in France, but she would fail again.[36]

Later that year Philip visited England once more, and after his departure Mary was again convinced that she was pregnant. But in a repeat of the previous false pregnancy, although her abdomen was swollen, no child was born. Modern medical knowledge suggests that her condition may have been caused by her terminal illness: ovarian cancer or prolactinoma. Be that as it may, her health deteriorated rapidly. Since her days were clearly numbered, she now had to decide on the line of succession. In her final days, she considered removing Elizabeth and moving up the next woman in line, her cousin, the Catholic Scottish-French Mary. But Mary had just married Francis, the French dauphin, and the queen's spies in France informed her that her cousin had already signed over Scotland and England to the French crown. It was clear that with so many years of enmity between England and France, and after the crushing defeat that the French army dealt England in Calais, the English public would be loath to accept a French king as co-sovereign. Furthermore, Philip, still formally king of England, was opposed to crowning Mary Queen of Scots for fear that it would strengthen the influence of his nemesis, the king of France, in the English court and turn him against Spain. So even though he was aware of Elizabeth's Protestant leanings, he preferred her to her relative.

Mary died in November 1558, at the age of forty-two, knowing that her efforts to bring England back to the Catholic fold were bound to fail. She is usually depicted as a tragic figure who had to contend with long years of terrible crops and a failing economy, tried desperately and unsuccessfully to have a child that would succeed her, failed in the attempt to return her country to the Catholic Church despite the wholesale burning of Protestants, and lost England's last foothold in France. While all her actions could be subsumed under the heading "getting England back into Europe," she inadvertently pointed England in the other direction, away from the continent. But despite all these failures, her reign was an important turning point. By creating the legal framework for a woman as the nation's sovereign, she had paved the way for her sister's accession.

[36] Richards, *Elizabeth I*, 58.

7 QUEENS OF THE BRITISH ISLES AND IRELAND 229

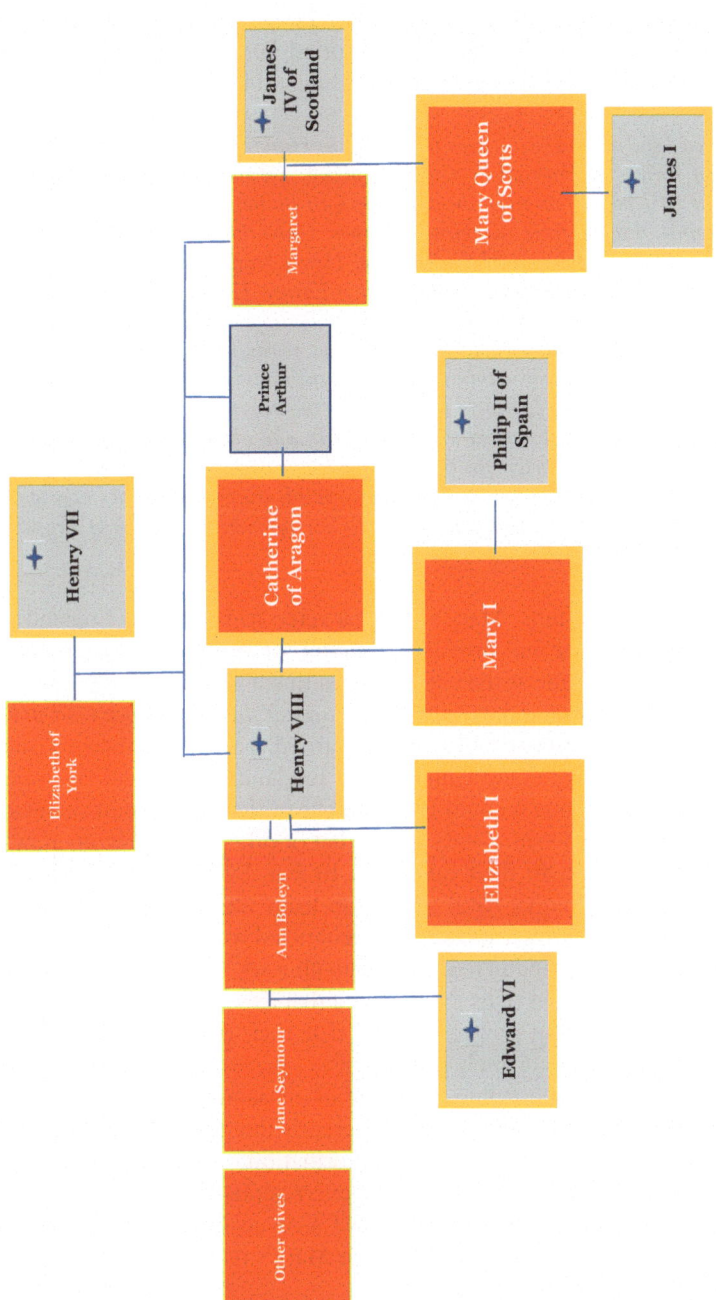

Elizabeth I

In an insightful paragraph in his book *The Perspective of the World*, part of his trilogy *Civilization and Capitalism*, historian Fernand Braudel claims that it was only at the end of Mary's reign that England became a nation unto itself:

> *Between 1453 and 1558, between the end of the Hundred Years' War and the recapture of Calais by François de Guise, England, without realizing it at the time, became (if I may be forgiven the expression) an island, in other words, an autonomous unit, distinct from continental Europe. Until this turning point, despite the Channel, the North Sea and the Straits of Dover, England had been bodily linked with France, the Netherlands, and the rest of Europe. Her long conflict with France during the Hundred Years' War ... had, as Philippe de Vires rightly says "taken place at a more or less provincial level." In other words, England acted as a province (or a group of provinces) within the Anglo-French unit which was in its entirety, or virtual entirety, both battlefield and prize in the interminable struggle. For many years, over a century, England was enmeshed in and absorbed into the huge field of operations in France, before the two sides gradually disentangled themselves.*
>
> *Thus England was late in developing its own identity: she engaged in the temptation, or rather dangers of gigantism until, having been driven out of France, she found herself back home.*[37]

In spite of all its faults, Mary's five-year reign had prepared England for the accession of her sister and provided a model for women's kingship. The laws enacted during her time at the helm ensured that a woman's sovereignty should be equal in authority and power to "*the kynges of thys realme her most noble progenitours*," and that this would apply to married as well as unmarried queens.[38] The provision curbing Philip's authority in England was particularly important. It made clear that women could be monarchs in the full sense of the word and separated a queen's personal status from that of other married women, who, by law, were subservient to their husbands. In fact, by doing so, the Parliament transformed gender-equal royal succession from vague theory into law. Mary also insisted that crowned queens be recognized as having the power of the healing touch and the ability to cure certain illnesses, which had previously been the domain of male kings only. Recognizing that female rulers could be endowed with God-given healing powers implied that their rule, just like that of their male counterparts, was divinely ordained.[39]

This claim of women ruling by divine dispensation was anathema to many men who believed that females were inherently inferior to males but was most bitterly criticized by adherents of the Reformation camp, who saw it as part of a Catholic ploy to subdue England. The overzealous and misogynistic Scottish preacher John Knox, who studied with Calvin in Geneva, wrote a scathing diatribe against the rule of women during Mary's reign, which he entitled *The*

---

[37] Braudel, *The Perspective of the World*, 353.
[38] Richards, "Gender Difference and Tudor Monarchy," 38.
[39] Richards, "Gender Difference and Tudor Monarchy," 40–43.

First Blast of the Trumpet Against the Monstrous Regiment of Women. Having Mary in mind he described *"the monstiferouse empire of women"* as repugnant to God, scripture, and nature. While men could use cold and balanced reason, he claimed, a woman was guided by emotions. Moreover, by having women in power, England would come to resemble Catholic Spain. Appealing to both anti-Spanish and antisemitic undercurrents in English culture, he claimed, *"The Spaniardes are Iewes [Jews] and they bragge that Marie of England is of the roote of Iesse* [Jesse, father of King David, meaning that she is a Jew as well]."[40] Knox's deeply held belief that women's government is a travesty was supported by many Protestants at the time, including Calvin himself, who claimed that women's rule was against the "proper order of nature."[41] Yet when the pro-reform Princess Elizabeth was crowned, most of them changed their tune. Even Knox exempted her from his harsh judgment, claiming that, unlike her predecessor, Elizabeth was a righteous queen *"by a miraculous dispensation of God."*[42]

Elizabeth's Upbringing

Elizabeth's life and reign were studied perhaps more than those of any other English monarch, and arguably more than those of any other female monarch before the nineteenth century. Although its basic outlines will be given here, the purpose of the following section is not to offer yet another biography of "the Virgin Queen" but rather to focus on her contribution to the changing attitude toward women rulers and to describe some of her relations, in letters, through emissaries, and in personal meetings, with other female rulers.

Soon after her birth Elizabeth was proclaimed "the high and mighty princess of England" and sent to the elegant Hatfield House, north of London, where she was raised with a household of her own, superseding her older sister Mary as the royal princess for a couple of years.[43] But she was still a baby when her mother, Anne Boleyn, was imprisoned in the Tower of London and then beheaded. Even though Anne was accused of adultery (which legally meant that she had sexual relations with another man *after* having consummated marriage), her marriage to Henry was retroactively declared invalid and annulled. By implication, Elizabeth became an illegitimate child, and the pecking order was reversed once again, with Mary becoming the leading princess. Yet, although the impetuous Henry behaved cruelly toward his estranged daughter, sometimes refusing to see her, he still loved Elizabeth, could not bring himself to ignore her completely, and made sure she would take part in special celebrations. Her situation improved somewhat at the age of ten, when Henry

---

[40] John Knox, *The First Blast of the Trumpet*, 6–7, 35–36. John Guy, *The Life of Mary Queen of Scots*, 141–2, 176–7.
[41] John Guy, *The Life of Mary Queen of Scots*, 176–177.
[42] Knox, ibid. Richards, *Elizabeth I*, 41.
[43] Richards, *Elizabeth I*, 12–13.

married his sixth (and last) wife, Catherine Parr, a motherly type who doted on all three of Henry's children and saw to their education.[44]

Elizabeth proved an exceptionally intelligent and hard-working pupil, who zealously studied ancient languages, history, philosophy, theology, rhetoric, and science, became fluent in French and Italian, and played several musical instruments. Her main teacher was the Cambridge-educated scholar Roger Ascham, who later served as a diplomat and secretary to Queen Mary and to Elizabeth herself. In his notes, Ascham commended her in glowing terms, revealing his own misogynist bias in the process: "*Her mind has no womanly weakness. Her perseverance is equal to that of a man, and her memory long keeps what it quickly picks up.*"[45] She studied the principles of the English Reformation during her father's and brother's reigns but always reserved judgment about religious truth, was open to doubt on questions of faith, and kept her views mostly to herself. Although inclining to Protestantism, as part of her reforms after accession she reintroduced some Catholic rites and reemphasized, for understandable reasons, the figure of the Virgin Mary. Being wise beyond her years, she foresaw the futility of the deadly fight between the Protestants and Catholics and steered clear of it as much as she could.[46]

At fifteen she was falsely accused of taking part in a plot hatched by Sir Thomas Seymour, who married her stepmother Catherine Parr after Henry VIII's death. Thomas, a charmer who often flirted with the teenage Elizabeth even when his wife was alive, was accused of planning to marry her and to initiate a rebellion against King Edward in order to become king himself. Elizabeth was taken into custody and interrogated about her involvement but insisted on her innocence, kept her poise, and was cleared of suspicion. Thomas Seymour was executed. His foiled plot, and her subsequent interrogation, made clear to Elizabeth just how precarious her life would be as long as her siblings were on the throne.

Under Mary

This sense of impending danger became even more acute once Mary was crowned and married Philip II of Spain. Elizabeth did her best to reassure Mary of her loyalty, but her letters (rendered here in modern English) convey her apprehension:

> *Good Sister, though I have good cause to thank you for your oft sending to me, yet I have more occasion to render you my hearty thanks for your gentle writing, which how painful it is to you, I may well guess by myself; and you may well see by my writing so*

---

[44] Ibid, 17–18. Susan Doran, *Elizabeth I and Her Circle*, 16–17.

[45] See Hamill, "Her mind has no womanly weakness."

[46] Simon Adams, "The Succession," 42–48. Richards, *Elizabeth I*, 23. New research claims that Elizabeth's accomplishments were overstated.

oft, how pleasant it is to me. And thus I end to trouble you, desiring God to send you as well to do, as you can think and wish, or I desire or pray.[47]

To no avail. Although few people knew exactly where Elizabeth stood on matters of religion, many believed that she—the remaining scion of Henry VIII—would be their only chance to rid England of "Bloody Mary," crown a reform-minded queen, and get the Reformation back on track. Some took it a step further and rebelled against the reigning queen. As the obvious beneficiary of such plots, even if Elizabeth had nothing to do with them, she was in constant danger of arrest and interrogation. In February 1554, in the wake of one such uprising, she was indeed brought to Mary's court and after three weeks of house arrest was sent to the tower until May 19 of that year.[48] Afraid that she would end up beheaded for treason like her mother, she insisted on writing a letter to Mary even before she was taken to prison, pledging her full allegiance and denying any knowledge of the rebellion:

> [...] *I protest before God (Who shall judge my truth, whatsoever malice shall devise), that I never practiced, counselled, nor consented to anything that might be prejudicial to your person anyway, or dangerous to the state by any means. And therefore I humbly beseech your Majesty to let me answer afore yourself, and not suffer me to trust to your Councillors, yea, and that afore I go to the Tower, if it be possible; if not, before I be further condemned.*[49]

After long and arduous interrogations, the investigators were satisfied she had nothing to do with the plot. Her life was spared, and she was later released.

Elizabeth's Accession

Ironically, when Mary died the public was just as elated as when she acceded to the throne five years earlier. Most had had enough of the vengeful queen, and although the Catholic nobles had apprehensions about the younger sister, many had hoped that she would bring healing and relief to the country. During her coronation procession on January 14, 1559 which was just as lavish as her sister's *grande entrée* into London, she gave a first indication of her religious leanings by picking up and kissing an English-language Bible presented to her by a girl in a pageant. By this simple act she overturned Mary's decree banning

---

[47] Elizabeth to Princess Mary, October 27 (?), in Harrison, *Letters of Queen Elizabeth*, 16. Note that some of these letters are quoted verbatim, with all the quirks of sixteenth-century English, while others have been "corrected" and presented in modern-day language.
[48] Loades, *Elizabeth I*, 101–110.
[49] Elizabeth to Queen Mary, March 16, 1554, in Harrison, *Letters of Queen Elizabeth*, 19. See also Richards, *Elizabeth I*, 34–35.

the use of Bibles not printed in Latin and made clear to the public that she was not opposed to the Reformation.[50]

From the first days of her reign Parliament pressured Elizabeth to get married, threatening to vote against the laws she proposed as long as she stayed single. It was hoped that she would govern independently for a short period, "*to quench her thirst for rule,*" and then marry an aristocrat, handing the reins of government to a man. Despite their fears of foreign interference after their experience with Philip of Spain, many conservatives believed that *any* man would be better at governing than a woman. To counter their claims, Elizabeth's advisors touted an idea that was first toyed with in Mary's time. The theory of "the two bodies" held that once on the throne, a woman's mortal body was changed by a kind of alchemical reaction. Her female parts would be fused together with "the body politic," an embodiment of the state, to produce a genderless perfect ruler. This theory probably strengthened her hand in the struggle to refrain from marrying and to rule without interference. But from the start she made clear that it would be *her* choice whether to marry or not, as she said in her address to Parliament:

> "*I maye saye unto yow, that from my yeares of vnderstandinge, syth I first had consideration of my self to be borne a servitor of almightie god I happelie chose this kynde of life in which I yet lyve. Which I assure yow for myne owne parte, hath hitherto best contented my self and I trust hath bene most acceptable to god.*"

The Virgin Queen

From that moment on, marriage negotiations with foreign leaders notwithstanding, Elizabeth was presented to the public as "the virgin queen."[51] This concept of hallowed celibacy—which developed and grew throughout her reign as the likelihood of marriage faded—struck several chords that went right to the heart of her people. One, of course, was the association of virginity with the Mother of Christ, who though slightly marginalized by the Reformation still had an emotional hold over the public. Another was the idea of a queen wedded to her beloved people rather than to alien kings (a later version depicted her as a mother devoted to her people). Finally, this insistence on celibacy and virginal purity was a welcome change after Henry VIII's scandalous liaisons and Mary's awkward marriage. An added advantage was the flexibility that not being bound by marriage afforded her in foreign relations and the ability to continuously juggle alliances and obligations to her benefit.[52]

Still, Elizabeth was well aware of the advantages of marriage or, to be more precise, of the political advantages of having suitors and considering marriage

---

[50] Richards, *Elizabeth I*, 42–45.

[51] The first time this title was formally mentioned was during Elizabeth's progress to Norwich in 1578.

[52] Heisch, "Elizabeth I and the Persistence of Patriarchy," 45–49. King, "Representations of the Virgin Queen".

proposals. A successful marriage would strengthen at least one alliance and offer a united front against enemies. And there was no shortage of such proposals. England had come a long way since the beginning of the century and was now considered a coveted prize for any royal house. For a short while she was courted by the widowed Philip II, who still hoped to win England back for the Catholic Church; then by Eric XIV, King of Sweden; by Francis Hercule, Duke of Anjou and Alençon, whose mother, Catherine de Medici, continuously pressed her for a wedding; and by quite a few others, including a host of high-born English nobles. She may have fallen in love with Robert Dudley, the Earl of Leicester (and son of the previous Duke of Northumberland, who conspired to put Lady Jane Grey on the throne), but even her affair with him, if there was one, was never taken to the next level. As she got older and the question of succession was brought up more often, the pressures on her to marry, from Parliament and the lords of the realm, mounted, but she kept refusing.[53]

She seems to have been taken with her youngest foreign suitor, Catherine's son Francis Hercule, who was twenty years younger and spent a considerable amount of time courting her. Francis was presented by his mother as a defender of the Protestants of the Netherlands, and by having him marry Elizabeth she believed she would be able to restore the balance she always sought between Catholics and Protestants and perhaps protect her realm from Spanish encroachment. But it wasn't just politics. Elizabeth actively flirted with the young duke, naming him "my frog" and treating him as both a son and a suitor. Perhaps she believed that, unlike her other suitors, who by marrying her hoped to rule England, this naïve lad would pose no danger. They spent long hours together, chatting and amusing each other with funny anecdotes, and when he left for France in 1581, it seemed that a wedding was in the offing. Yet, strongly opposed by several of her closest advisers, the marriage did not take place, and a short while later the duke died of malaria. Heartbroken, Elizabeth wrote a heartrending and clearly undiplomatic letter to Catherine de Medici:

> *If the extremity of my misfortune had not equaled my grief for his sake, and had not rendered me unequal to touch with a pen the wound that my heart suffered, it would not be possible that I had so greatly forgotten to visit you with the fellowship of regret that I afford you, which I assure myself cannot exceed mine; for, although you were his mother, yet there remain to you several other children. But for myself, I find no consolation if it be not death, which I hope will make us soon to meet.*[54]

In hindsight, it may be said that England gained more from *negotiations* of marriage than it would have had she settled for one of those suitors. The

---

[53] Heisch, "Elizabeth I and the Persistence of Patriarchy," 47. See also Harrison, *Letters of Queen Elizabeth*, 42. Felix Pryor, *Elizabeth I Her Life in Letters*, 66–69. Richards, *Elizabeth I*, 59–62, 99–100, 104.
[54] Elizabeth to Catherine de Medici, July 1584, in Harrison, *Letters of Queen Elizabeth*, 162–163. The original letter was written in French. See also Susan Doran, *Monarchy and Matrimony*, 154–194. Carol Levin, *The Heart and Stomach of a King*, 60–65.

constant parade of potential grooms, each one representing different sets of alliances and enmities, also helped her play factions vying for influence at court against each other. Yet Elizabeth was always aware of the grave problem her persistent refusal to marry presented. Without an heir—a son or a daughter of her own—the Tudor dynasty would come to naught. Her siblings were all dead and childless, she was the last living descendent of Henry VIII, and if she were to die childless, next in line to the throne was her cousin, Mary, Queen of Scots. Since Mary was a staunch Catholic with a French mother, her coronation as Queen of England would bring back all the tensions of the previous queen's reign, which Elizabeth did her best to overcome.[55]

Left to govern as she pleased, Elizabeth turned out to be an excellent administrator and a fearless leader. She expected counsel rather than flattery, allowed her ministers to speak freely, and appointed the best people to be ministers and envoys. She often procrastinated, and yet, when push came to shove, knew how to decide, sometimes with cold-hearted calculation. In 1559, she was declared by Parliament Supreme Governor of the Church. It refused to grant her the title Supreme Head of the Church since its members could not accept a woman as head. But Elizabeth shrugged it off, saying that in fact the title "head" belongs to Christ alone, and continued to lead the Church.[56] She restored her father's and brother's reforms and moved cautiously to ingrain a new version of Christianity in the local parishes: an English translation of the Bible, a new hymnal, novel liturgical forms, and an independent church hierarchy. She did not hunt down Catholics, but disliked Puritans of all kinds and was not tolerant of those who challenged her religious settlement. She used threats to demand obedience to her rules and made allegiance to her religious reforms a condition for government and Church appointments.[57]

Elizabeth's attitude changed drastically in 1570, when was excommunicated by Pope Pius V. The pope, who pronounced her a "usurper and pretensed queen of England," intended to capitalize on the northern rebellion of 1569, which, he hoped, would lead to Mary's return to the throne of Scotland. In practical terms, the pope's proclamation amounted to a call for insurrection. It meant that Elizabeth's Catholic subjects no longer owed her allegiance, that Rome would excuse all resistance to her rule, and that support for her rival, Mary, would be an act of faith. In response, the English Parliament passed a series of laws defining any claim that Elizabeth was not the legitimate queen as treason and making it illegal to even carry the Papal Bull proclaiming her excommunication. Although Rome's gamble failed and the people of England remained loyal to their queen, tensions between Catholics and reformists spiraled from that time on, and the queen had to resort to the same executions and burnings that made her sister so unpopular. This ongoing fear of a Catholic coup, which was manifested in a series of conspiracies, including those known

---

[55] Heisch, "Elizabeth I and the Persistence of Patriarchy," 48–49.
[56] Carol Levin, *The Heart and Stomach of a King*, 14. Loades, *Elizabeth I*, 132–138.
[57] Richards, *Elizabeth I*, 51–54.

as the Ridolfi plot and then the Babington plot, was also one of the reasons for the Queen of Scots's execution in 1587.[58]

And yet Elizabeth came into her own as a great monarch mainly in the second decade of her reign. In November of 1577, almost twenty years after her accession, the great comet that traced a path around the world was observed in England, and like all other astronomers and astrologers of the period, from Peru to Denmark, English ones believed it should be interpreted as an omen and wrote tracts trying to divine what the Lord had intended to convey by placing this comet in the heavens. The most crucial question on everyone's mind was what the comet portended for government by women.

Perhaps the most popular of these texts was one written by Thomas Twyne, an amateur scientist and star gazer. Twyne published a pamphlet called "A view of certain wonderful effects, of late dayes come to passe and now newly conferred with the presignyfications of the comete, or blasing star, which appered in the Southwest."[59] Drawing an astrological map, Twyne saw in the comet a symbol of the union of Queen Elizabeth with the Anglican Church and the prediction of a long life. His rationale—which must have made sense to other astrologers—was that the comet was dominated by Venus with the anticipation of Mars, rather than Saturn. In the pamphlet's seventh section, he compared the prosperity and happiness that England experienced under her rule with the scarcity and war that befell other countries. The joys of the English public were due, he pointed out, to the administration of God's chosen queen (Fig. 7.4):

> [I]t both not only portends the inseparable coniunction and marriage, as it were, of our most true and natural souveraigne Queene Elizabeth, with the holy Church and gospel of Jesus Christ, indissolubly united: but also of sutch ordinancies, leagues, and confederacies, as she hath taken, or meaneth to take, eyther within her owne dominions, or abroade with foreign Princes, for the maintenance therof, and assurance of those that professe the same. And moreover, I am of this opinion contrary to the trayterous iudgments of some hollow harts, that the lengthening of her Maiesties long life and prosperouis reigne over her Realmes, is hereby most effectually signified.[60]

Elizabeth's Foreign Relations

Throughout her reign, Elizabeth's main concern was keeping at bay her two great continental rivals, France and Spain. Both saw England as a rising threat and at the same time as a great prize in their struggle for Catholic dominance.

---

[58] Guy, *The Life of Mary Queen of Scots*, 463–470, 481–484. Roberto Ridolfi was an international banker and double agent who was behind a plot, organized and financed in 1569, with inside help, including that of Thomas Howard, the Duke of Norfolk, to depose Elizabeth and crown Mary. Babington, a young Catholic Englishman, acted on behalf of an exiled Spanish ambassador to foment rebellion against Elizabeth in 1586. His communications with Mary Queen of Scots were intercepted by Elizabeth's agents. See also Carol Levin, *The Heart and Stomach of a King*, 105.

[59] Twyne, "A View of certain wonderful effects."

[60] Twyne, "A View of certain wonderful effects," Section 6. See also Hilary Mantel, *Wolf Hall*, 290.

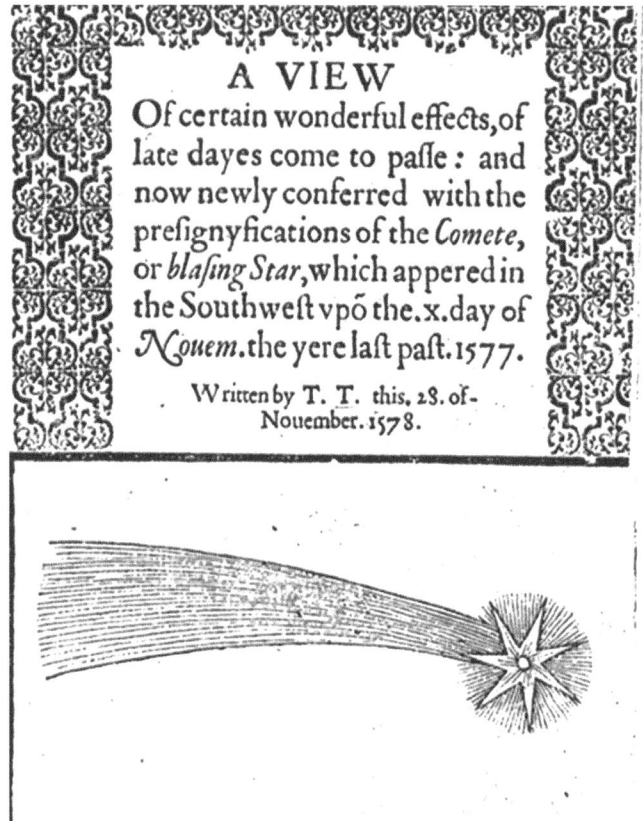

Fig. 7.4 Cover of the pamphlet "A View of certain wonderful effects," by Thomas Twyne, 1578

But she also had other issues on her mind. Her sister Mary had left the kingdom's economy in a disarray that had to be dealt with immediately, and inflation, created by the constant influx of spices, gold, and silver brought by her rivals from the Americas and from India, was jacking up prices and creating shortages in imported foodstuffs and materials. One of her first goals, therefore, was to strengthen England's presence in markets abroad and, specifically, in the three fastest growing ones—India, North America, and the eastern Mediterranean. In the Atlantic, she secretly encouraged a group of privateers, supported by the crown and led by Sir Francis Drake and Sir Walter Raleigh, to attack and raid Spanish ships on their way from North America to Spain. When the Spanish ambassador lodged formal complaints, she claimed that she had no control over these private ships roaming the ocean. Yet through them England established a foothold in the Caribbean and in North America. In 1577 Drake even circumnavigated the world, crossing over to the Pacific through the Strait of Magellan and visiting the east Asian Maluku Islands.

As regards the eastern Mediterranean and India, the English government had very vague ideas. In 1562, the English merchant Jenkinson arrived in Qazvin, the Safavid capital. Better known for his part in establishing relations between England and Russia, Jenkinson carried a letter—in English with copies in Hebrew and Italian—from Elizabeth to the "Great Sophy of Persia," referring to him as "the emperor of the Persians, Medes, Parthians, Hyrcanes, Caramanians, Margians," most of whom were long forgotten biblical states or had ceased to exist as nations centuries ago. He was given an audience with Shah Tahmasp, who was annoyed, according to Jenkinson's report, by this ignorance and the fact that the letter was presented in three unfamiliar languages. "We have no neede to have friendship with the unbeleevers," he dismissed the Englishman. Later missions from England did not achieve any great breakthrough.[61]

To develop trade with East Asia in the wake of Drake's enormously successful trip around the world, the queen encouraged traders to develop Indian connections and later supported the founding of the "Governor and Company of Merchants of London Trading into the East Indies," which later became the East India Company. She gave the company a formal charter in 1600. She also strove to improve trade with the Ottomans. Until the late 1560s, Elizabeth did not know much about the Muslim empire in the eastern Mediterranean. Some of what she had heard had to do with the scandal that shocked Europe at the time: the execution of Prince Mustafa by his father, Sultan Suleiman, in 1553. Like Catherine de Medici, Elizabeth may have read about it in works of fiction, notably Nicholas Moffan's book in Latin, or its English translation *The horrible acte, and wicked offence of Soltan Soliman Emperour of the Turkes, in murtheringe his eldest sonne Mutapha, the year of our Lorde 1553*, which blamed the death of Mustafa on the manipulations and wiles of "*the adulterous harlot*" Roxolana.[62] Like Catherine de Medici, Elizabeth may have read the stories with a ruling woman's eye, realizing that there must have been a feminine angle to the story.

By the early 1580s, she further encouraged trade with Venice and the Ottoman Empire, subsumed under the Venice Company and the Turkey Company. Bound by the capitulation agreement recently ratified with France, the Ottomans initially demanded that all European trade with the empire be carried out under the French flag. Having no other option, Elizabeth agreed to this stipulation, but both sides acknowledged that this was a problematic arrangement. When France and England were at odds, English trade with the Levant was hampered, and the same was true for periods of tension between the Ottomans and the French. Such incidents occurred, for example, when the French refused to return the sums loaned to King Henry II by Dona Gracia. At her nephew's behest, the sultan ordered his navy to stop and search all ships sailing under a French flag, confiscating part of the merchandise on board as compensation for the loan.

Elizabeth wanted to shake off this French tutelage, establish independent relations, and sign trade agreements directly with the empire. She also saw this as a possible avenue for a strategic alliance against Spain and other common enemies. On the Ottoman side, her excommunication by Pope Pius V was seen as a positive sign. It was an indication that she would not be part of the enemy camp

[61] Subrahmanyam, *Three Ways to Be Alien*, 84–86.
[62] Andrea, *Women and Islam*, 18–19.

led by the Catholic Habsburgs. In establishing relations with the sultan, she was probably guided by her physician, Rodrigo Lopez, whose cousin Solomon Abenaish was a favorite of the Ottoman Sultana Nurbanu. In 1579, she sent her emissary, a seasoned merchant and negotiator named William Harborne, with a letter to Sultan Murad III. In the letter she introduced herself and her kingdom, stressed the ideological commonalities between Protestants and Muslims, requested the release of captured Englishmen who were sent to serve as oarsmen in Ottoman galleys, and offered a commercial treaty.[63]

Once she received the sultan's positive response, Harborne was sent to Istanbul once more. This time, she also suggested a treaty against Spain. Harborne took his time and began his negotiations in the sultanic court only four years later. By then he must have realized that the most important figure at court was not the sultan but the woman at his side. Although she was still young and inexperienced, Safiye came into her own as Sultan Murad III's chief consort and governed the harem and the palace. Harborne's success in his mission owes a great deal to his contacts with her through her main ally, Grand Vizier Mehmed Sokollu, and her adviser Solomon Abenaish. It is very likely that these contacts were also encouraged and maintained by the *kira*, Esperanza Malchi, who was Safiye's messenger and carried the ambassador's gifts to Sokollu in the late 1570s. Although the French ambassador remonstrated and did his best to obstruct the signing of a separate treaty, Safiye was intrigued by the queen of England and promoted the relationship. Harborne was granted trade privileges, and Elizabeth received a welcoming reply from the Sultan. To allay French fears, the Ottomans claimed that the privileges were not granted *carte blanche* to all English traders, but only to specific ones. Yet in principle everyone could apply for a permit. After his success, Harborne was appointed England's first ambassador to the empire, and the volume of England's trade with the Levant grew rapidly.[64]

But by that time, the 1580s, dark clouds appeared much closer to the English shore. It was clear that Spain could no longer tolerate Elizabeth's audacity. Philip's colonies in America were plundered and threatened, his gold-laden ships constantly attacked on the high seas by the queen's pesky privateers, and English-funded "volunteers" supported the Dutch rebels. He had had enough. With his help, he believed, there was still hope of a Catholic insurrection inside England. In 1586, he ordered the construction of an 'Armada', an enormous fleet with which he intended to invade England, decimate her small standing army, take over the land, and bring it back to the Catholic fold.

Two years later, after many preparations, the Armada set sail for Flanders, where it was to take on board an invasion force and land in England.[65] As the English army prepared for its landing, Elizabeth addressed her soldiers in Tilbury on the Thames and famously claimed that, although she had "*the body*

---

[63] Horniker, "William Harborne," 297–298. Andrea, *Women and Islam*, 26.

[64] Horniker, "William Harborne," 289–292. Andrea, *Women and Islam*, 19. For Sultan Murad's letter, see Oxford University, *Bodleian Library*, MS.Eng.hist./c.477/fol.94.

[65] Richards, *Elizabeth I*, 118–121, 137.

of a weak and feeble woman," her heart and stomach were those of a king. Though not recorded at the time, the quoted text of the speech is probably close to the original and reveals her way of thinking as it developed over the years.[66] She thought of herself as a woman in appearance but the equal of any man in her inner essence. Her words are sometimes used, anachronistically, to prove that she was no feminist, that even though she was a reigning queen, she still believed that men had more power. But this was not what she really felt. Her claims of female frailty, in speeches and letters, and the frequent association she made between courage and manliness, like similar claims of weakness by other powerful women around the world at the time, could best be described as tropes, a way of speaking to a world ostensibly governed by men, in which men still thought of themselves as superior to women. Rather than argue that women were their equals, Elizabeth believed that men would do her bidding more readily if she were to stroke their male egos and reassure them of her physical frailty. She may have also believed that the "two body theory," this union between a female body and a male heart, gave her a halo of sanctity, setting her apart from other men and women.[67]

Led by the Duke of Medina Sidonia, the huge cumbersome ships of the Spanish Armada were first beset by bad weather, and when they reached the English Channel in the summer of 1588, they were attacked by smaller and faster English ships that decimated part of the fleet. Then a storm destroyed some of the remaining ships and pushed the rest northward into the North Sea. The invasion ended as a humiliating defeat for Spain and a huge victory for Elizabeth. It was immediately interpreted by Protestants as a sign of God's grace.[68]

As the victory was announced (and quickly reported to the Ottomans through the Marrano network), ambassador Harborne returned to England and left behind his assistant, Edward Barton, who soon found a way to reach Safiye Sultan's ear.[69] Through Barton and Esperanza *Kira*'s mediation, Elizabeth and Safiye established contact, exchanging gifts and letters (described in detail in Chap. 2), and strengthening relations between the Ottoman Empire and England. As Andrea points out, their letters not only established a connection between sovereign women but also recognized and elevated women's power, in contravention of the Ottoman custom, which tended to re-gender women rulers as male. By 1595, Safiye's husband was dead and she was already royal mother to the next sultan, Mehmed III. In her letters from that period, Safiye refers to Elizabeth as "*the model of Christian womanhood*" and "*she who is obeyed by princes.*" Perhaps recalling her own Christian ancestry, she also mentions Mary, mother of Jesus, as a model.[70] Elizabeth's inclusion of her own

---

[66] Ibid., 143. Carol Levin, *The Heart and Stomach of a King*, 1, 143–144. See also Heisch, "Elizabeth I and the Persistence of Patriarchy," 53.

[67] Heisch, "Elizabeth I and the Persistence of Patriarchy," 51–54.

[68] Richards, *Elizabeth I*, 140–143.

[69] Horniker, "William Harborne," 311.

[70] Andrea, *Women and Islam*, 25–26. Although Christ is not believed by Muslims to be the son of God, he is still considered one of the prophets, and his mother, Mary, is also respected.

portrait—of the kind usually sent to male suitors—among the gifts sent to Safiye was intended as a prop for female bonding. *"[W]e may conceptualize Elizabeth and Safiye's exchange of gifts and letters as the means whereby these sovereign women negotiated the patriarchal contradiction of women's rule without negating either term of this shared cultural oxymoron."*[71]

ELIZABETH AND MARY, QUEEN OF SCOTS

As Simon Adams rightly claims, with the exception of the Habsburgs, who were always a close-knit family, *"relations within the royal family, whether among immediate siblings or all those with a claim to the throne, are the key to the politics of the monarchies of late medieval and early modern Europe."*[72] Elizabeth's successes and her caution in religious matters did not spare her the anger of Protestants, who saw her reforms as partial and inadequate, nor of Catholics, who were still persecuted and openly rebelled against her from their strongholds in the north of England. Catholic uprisings and attempted coups often revolved around Mary, Queen of Scots, who believed herself, and was believed by many in Europe, to be the rightful queen of England.

When Mary was less than a week old, her father, King James V of Scotland, had died in battle with no other heir. At that point, her mother, Marie de Guise, took over the government of Scotland, and five years later sent Mary to the Guise household and later to the French royal court. Since her paternal grandmother, Margaret Tudor, was Henry VIII's older sister, Mary and many of her Catholic loyalists believed that in addition to Scotland, she had a stronger claim to the English throne than Elizabeth, whom they saw as illegitimate. Her claim was supported by France's king, Henry II, who considered Elizabeth a heretic and a threat to France, and encouraged her to add England's emblems to her coat of arms. Meanwhile, the young girl grew up in France's court, under the watchful eyes of Queen Catherine de Medici.[73]

But at seventeen she suddenly received a bigger prize than Scotland, and perhaps even England. She was betrothed to the sickly fifteen-year-old French dauphin, who was crowned Francis II in 1560. Mary became queen of France and in view of her monarchic prospects soon agreed to sign a treaty with her cousin, Queen Elizabeth. In the treaty, she consented to relinquish her claim to the English crown by stopping her usage of the English coat of arms and by withdrawing French forces from Scotland. The treaty was crafted in Edinburgh and signed in principle, but then, just as suddenly, two years after his coronation, Mary's husband died. His brother Charles was crowned, and in one fell swoop the childless Mary no longer had any official standing in the French court. The ratifying ceremony did not take place.[74]

---

[71] Andrea, *Women and Islam*, 27. See also p. 28.
[72] Adams, "The Succession," 43.
[73] Richards, *Elizabeth I*, 55. Guy, *The Life of Mary Queen of Scots*, 13–17.
[74] Guy, *The Life of Mary Queen of Scots*, 101–105. For a more detailed description of Mary's time as France's queen, see Chap. 6.

Feeling they have been cheated out of the French crown, and in an attempt to improve their chances of taking over again, Mary's Guise relatives tried to find a new royal match for her, but she rejected all offers. Since her mother, died in Scotland the previous year, she decided to board a ship and take over her kingdom, which she also saw as a springboard for taking over England and returning it to the Catholic orbit. In August 1561, three years after Elizabeth acceded to the English throne, she was crowned Queen of Scotland.[75]

Elizabeth saw Mary as a dangerous rival but also remembered that she was her closest relative and a potential heir, as she told William Maitland, Mary's secretary, in a beautifully spelled report: *'sche [Mary] is of the blude of Ingland, my cousing and nixt kynnswoman, so that nature must bind me to luif hir dewlie'* (She is of the blood of England, my cousin and next kinswoman, so that nature must bind me to love her duly).[76] She wrote to Mary demanding that she commit to the treaty signed—but not ratified—between them:

> *For we required no other thing of you but to perform your promise whereunto you are bound by your seal and your bond. For the refusal whereof we see no reason alleged can serve, specially considering we covet but that which is in your own power as Queen of Scotland, that which yourself in words and speech doth compass, that which your late husband and our good brother's Ambassadors and yours concluded, that whereto your own nobility and people were made privy, that which indeed made the peace and [amity] betwixt us, without which no perfect amity can continue betwixt us.*[77]

Despite Mary's ongoing attempts to foment rebellion against her, Elizabeth treated her with patience. Remembering her own constant fear of the other Mary, her older sister, she maintained a modicum of civility between them even as news arrived of Scottish war preparations, and there was no certainty as to Mary's intentions. "*We assure you,*" she wrote, "*that whatsoever we can imagine meet for your honour and surety that shall lie in our power, we will perform the same that it shall and will appear you have a good neighbour, a dear sister and a faithful friend.*"[78] There was another motivation at play. Elizabeth always remembered that her brother Edward and her sister Mary died childless and that there were no other serious Tudor contenders for the English crown. If she, Elizabeth, were to end up childless as well, Mary would of necessity be next in line.[79] Her idea was to suggest a marriage between Mary and Elizabeth's favorite, Robert Dudley, an act that would integrate her into the English aristocracy.[80] Mary ended up marrying another English (and Scottish) noble, Lord Darnley. Their son, the future James VI of Scotland and James I of England, was born in 1566.

[75] See Ken Follett, *A Column of Fire*, p. 30.
[76] English in Elizabeth's time was still very loose in its spelling of words. The laws of spelling as we know them today were set mainly by the introduction of Tyndale's translation of the New Testament, the King James Bible, and Shakespeare's plays.
[77] Elizabeth to Mary Queen of Scots, August 15, 1561, in Harrison, *Letters of Queen Elizabeth*, 33.
[78] Elizabeth to Mary Queen of Scots, June 23, 1567, in Harrison, *Letters of Queen Elizabeth*, 51.
[79] Simon Adams, "The Succession," 44.
[80] Simon Adams, "The Succession," 44.

Not long after the wedding, Darnley was murdered, and Mary was ousted by the Scots and remanded to custody in Loch Leven castle. Her son, James, was formally crowned in her place and brought up under a tutor in Scotland. Catherine de Medici, worried about the fate of her daughter-in-law—and probably about the fate of the Catholic monarchy in Scotland as well—wrote to Queen Elizabeth, who promised her, in a response letter, to do the utmost to protect Mary:

> *Having learned by your letter, Madame ... your honourable intention, and that of the King, my brother, on the part of my desolate cousin the Queen of Scots, I rejoice me very much to see that one Prince takes to heart the wrongs done to another ... I promise you, Madame, that even if my consanguinity did not constrain me to wish her all honour, her example would seem too terrible for neighbours to behold, and for all Princes to hear.*[81]

By 1568, seven years after her coronation, Mary's rule in Scotland ended completely. She was driven out of the north and stayed as a guest/prisoner in England. Yet despite Elizabeth's attempts to demonstrate sisterly compassion and forgiveness, it was rumored that Mary, who had fallen ill and worried about her own succession, decided to bequeath her right to the throne of Scotland and her place in the English succession to the French king and his heirs. Upon hearing this, although she realized that her cousin still held the keys to the continuation of the Tudor dynasty, Elizabeth totally lost her patience with the Scottish queen. "*Pray do not give me occasion to think that your promises are but wind*," she wrote.[82] Mary denied these allegations and Elizabeth, in an elegant analysis of the situation and a barely disguised threat, informed her that even though she—Mary—may not have promised it outright to the French king, some of her servants probably had, and winking thus to France might at some point in the future be used by its monarchs in their attempt to claim England:

> *[P]erhaps some relative, or rather some Ambassador of yours, having the general authority relative, of your signature to order all things for the furtherance of your affairs, had adjusted this promise as if it came from you, and deemed it within the range of his commission. Such a matter would serve as a spur to a courser of high mettle; for, as we often see a little bough serve to save the life of a swimmer, so a light shadow of claim animates the combatants. I know not why they consider not that the bark of your good fortune floats on a dangerous sea, where many contrary winds blow, and has need of all aid to obviate such evils and to conduct you safely into port.*

Despite these suspicions and the ominous host of mixed metaphors, Elizabeth prevaricated and seemed willing to recognize Mary as her successor. Things came to a head in 1570, when Pope Pius V excommunicated Elizabeth and implicitly gave the green light to a Catholic uprising. A year

---

[81] Elizabeth to Catherine de Medci, October 16, 1567, in Harrison, *Letters of Queen Elizabeth*, 51–52.

[82] Elizabeth to Mary Queen of Scots, June 30, 1568, in Harrison, *Letters of Queen Elizabeth*, 52–53.

Fig. 7.5 Mary, Queen of Scots, by François Clouet (1558–1560) Royal Collection Trust

later, Mary was implicated in the infamous Ridolfi Plot, which aimed, with the Spanish king's assistance, to assassinate Elizabeth and replace her. Many members of Parliament called for the death sentence. Still, Elizabeth gave her cousin the benefit of the doubt and refused to order her execution (Fig. 7.5).[83]

Tensions rose especially after the St. Bartholomew's Day massacre of the Huguenots in France.[84] Elizabeth did her best to remain above the fray between Catholics and Protestants, but finally, after more pressure from her council, as enmity between England and Spain grew, and as another pope, Gregory XIII decreed that the world should rid itself of the sinning queen, she agreed to assist the Dutch rebellion against Spanish rule. In 1585, she sent a small contingent of soldiers to help the rebels. Meanwhile, conspiracies swirled around her, Jesuits were executed for secretly infiltrating England, spying, and fomenting dissent, and more schemes were uncovered. Elizabeth's spies discovered that Mary was deeply involved in several of them. Mary was judged, convicted, and sentenced to death, but for three months Elizabeth could not bring herself to sign the death warrant. Even after she did, she asked Davison, the man tasked with

[83] Loades, *Elizabeth I*, 259–260.
[84] See Chap. 5.

getting her signature not to deliver the order, but he took it straight to her secretary, Baron Burghley. Along with other members of the Privy Council, Burghley decided to go on with the execution. In contravention of her instructions, he did send his messenger, and Mary was finally beheaded in 1587. On the night before her execution, she wrote a final letter to King Henry III of France:

> *I am to be executed like a criminal at eight o'clock in the morning. I haven't had enough time to give you a full account of all that has happened, but if you will listen to my physician and my other sorrowful servants, you will know the truth, and how, thanks to God, I scorn death and faithfully protest that I face it innocent of any crime...*[85]

Elizabeth, who was already prepared to dangle the prospect of the English crown before Mary's son, James VI of Scotland, washed her hands of the execution and even wrote and begged him not to blame her *"for that miserable accident which, far contrary to my meaning, has befallen [her]."*[86] But this was merely a rhetorical ploy. Had she really wanted to, she could have stopped the execution.[87]

Some fifteen years after Mary's death, her son, "legally and lawfully descended from Margaret Tudor, daughter of Henry VII," was proclaimed James I of England, thereby fusing its crown with that of Scotland and putting an end to 50 years of rule by women.[88]

ELIZABETH AND GRACE O'MALLEY (IRELAND)

The United Kingdom—Britain—did not yet come into being, but perhaps uniquely during Elizabeth's reign three major parts of that future political entity—England, Scotland, and some of Ireland—were ruled by women.[89] Elizabeth was crowned in 1558, Mary took the Scottish crown in 1561, and at the same time an Irish woman, Gráinne Ní Mháille, known in England as Grace O'Malley, ruled western Ireland. Since there is no record of her in the Irish archives, most of the information we have about her comes from English sources, and mainly from a record of her meeting with Elizabeth.[90]

Based in Claire Island off the coast of County Mayo, the Ó Máille family ruled much of Connacht Province on the Atlantic shore. They built a fleet of ships and engaged in piracy on the high seas. Grace, born to this rebel family around 1530, must have had some formal education, since she spoke Latin with Elizabeth during their meeting. When her father, Eóghan Ó Máille, died, she became head of the clan. She married Dónal O'Flaherty, scion of a

---

[85] Guy, *The Life of Mary Queen of Scots*, 495–501. See also Richards, *Elizabeth I*, 132–133.
[86] Pryor, *Elizabeth I*, 93.
[87] Guy, *The Life of Mary Queen of Scots*, 476–477. Richards, *Elizabeth I*, 136.
[88] Guy, *The Life of Mary Queen of Scots*, 503.
[89] The fourth part, Wales, was annexed by England in the thirteenth century, long before the Welsh-born Henry VII and the House of Tudor took over. But in the mid-sixteenth century it was formally and finally incorporated into the kingdom by law.
[90] Grace O'Malley's biography is based on Chambers, "Ireland's Pirate Queen."

powerful family in Connacht Province, and the couple had three children. Widowed in 1565 when Dónal was killed in an ambush, and having to protect her realm against other powerful Irish families, she returned to her base on Claire Island and fortified it. She then went on the attack against her enemies, taking over their castles and property. Later she got married again, this time to Risdeárd (Richard) Bourke, another local warlord.

With her fleet of ships and an army of several hundred fighting marines, she became notorious in English navy circles as a pirate queen, operating her fleet, sometimes in the service of others, lying in wait on sea lanes to Spain, France, and England and looting the ships. Her pirates pillaged Toledo steel, wine, salt, silk, and alum, filling her coffers and rousing the enmity of city traders and English lords. An army sent against her lay siege to her castle but had to retreat after 21 days.

Suspecting King Philip II's plans to invade England and fearing an attack from the west side aided by the rebellious Irish, England moved deeper into Ireland in the 1580s, attempting to bring its independent western territories to heel. Elizabeth appointed Sir Richard Bingham, a professional soldier, to oversee the operation. Combining threats and promises, Bingham tricked one of Grace O'Malley's sons into an ambush and killed him, taking over his castle and expanding British rule over Connacht Province. While Grace was not set against cooperation with the much stronger English state, she rebelled against Bingham's cruel regime and was caught in a spiral of violence with his English troops. Her mutiny increased in intensity when her second son decided to side with Bingham against her.

As the struggle became even more violent and her two other sons were captured, Grace decided to petition Queen Elizabeth. After answering a set of questions sent to her, she sailed to England, and while there is no positive proof that the two women ever met, the description of a meeting at Greenwich palace soon became one of the most powerful stories told about Grace O'Malley.[91] As the story goes, defiant as ever, Grace came to the meeting hiding a small dagger in her formal dress, which Elizabeth's guards found and confiscated, but the meeting went on as planned after she explained that she always carried this knife for self-protection. She also refused to bow, claiming that Elizabeth was not yet queen of Ireland and they were therefore equals. The two leaders spoke Latin since O'Malley knew no English and Elizabeth no Gaelic. To the surprise of all present, they soon found common ground and reached an agreement. Elizabeth would release O'Malley's son, relieve Bingham of his position, and return the confiscated property, and in return the Irish queen would stop supporting the rebellion and discontinue her piracy against the English (although raiding all other ships would be okay). According to Elizabeth, Grace promised "*to employ all her power to prosecute any offender against Us ... and fight in our quarrel with all the world.*"[92]

---

[91] See Brandie R. Segfried, "Notorious: Gráinne Ní Mháille, Graven Memory, and the Uses of Irish Legend," in Levin and Stewart-Nuñez, (eds.) *Scholars and Poets*, 234–236.

[92] Grace O'Malley's biography is based on Chambers, "Ireland's Pirate Queen."

Fig. 7.6 Meeting between Elizabeth (right) and Grace O'Malley. Illustration from Anthologia Hibernica, 1793

Bingham was indeed called back, but the confiscated property was not returned, and Grace once again supported the rebellion until her claims were settled and she became an ally of England. Like Elizabeth, Grace O'Malley died in 1603 (Fig. 7.6).

After the crowning of Mary's son James VI of Scotland as James I of England, the creation of Great Britain took shape in hesitant steps. But from that moment on, women receded into the background and only men were crowned as sovereigns. It took almost a hundred years for another woman, Mary, to rule, alongside her husband, the Dutchman William of Orange (William III). The couple reigned jointly for five years, from 1689 to 1695. Another decade passed until Mary's sister, Queen Anne, acceded to the throne on her own and reigned for twelve years. Next in line was Queen Victoria, the second great female monarch in the British Isles, who was crowned in 1837, two hundred and thirty years after Elizabeth.

CHAPTER 8

The Three Phases of Sixteenth-Century Female Rule

Like the great comet, this era of female government glowed over the historical horizon for a century or so before men took over once again and restored the "natural" order of things. It is true that women such as Catherine the Great in Russia or Queen Anne in England, flickered in positions of power in later centuries, but the dense and influential latticework of women rulers that dominated the sixteenth century was never replicated. This book attempts to solve the riddle that this period poses: how did it come about? What was different about this time in human history? And how and why did it end?

In previous chapters, we discussed many cases of female rule but did not attempt to analyze the phenomenon as a whole. While we looked at some of the best-known examples, others were mentioned only in passing, or not at all. Thus, the sequence of Habsburg women that governed the Netherlands and Flanders from the early sixteenth century to the mid-seventeenth was discussed only through their interactions with other protagonists of this book. This is also true of Bona Sforza, the Italian-born queen of Poland, and her daughter Isabella, who governed Hungary and Transylvania under shifting Ottoman and Habsburg suzerainty. Another sixteenth-century queen was known to her subjects as *Al-Sayyida al-Hurra*.[1] Scion of a family of Andalusian refugees, she reigned over large swaths of northern Morocco in the mid-sixteenth century, leading a fleet of pirate ships against the Spaniards and Portuguese. Her fascinating adventures were only mentioned here in passing. The Hindu Queen Rani Durgavati, ruler of the state of Gondwana, who resisted a takeover and fought bravely against the Mughal army, was mentioned briefly. And finally, there was no mention of great African female rulers such as Queen Nzinga of Ndongo and Matamba in the region of modern Angola, who resisted Portuguese colonization and valiantly defended her realm against local

---

[1] This ("free" or "autonomous" lady) seems to have been a title. We do not know her birth name.

enemies. Their amazing stories could only reinforce this book's main claim: the period was an unprecedented—and unparalleled to this day—era of female rule.

Despite its critical significance for people in the period, this era has not received the recognition it deserves in modern historical writing. One of the reasons it was overlooked is that the sources are biased. Too often male rulers took credit for actions that their mothers or wives initiated or for diplomatic breakthroughs achieved in their name. Since men were the nominal rulers in most cases, and since court historians were hired to inflate their masters' importance and belittle the role of others around them, particularly if they were women, the image we receive is severely skewed. It is excruciatingly difficult to break free of the shackles of classic male-leaning historical narratives.[2]

In many cases, we could even show evidence for the fact that women were erased from the records. Thus, after the Mughal Emperor Shah Jahan was crowned, he instructed his court historians to efface the role of his mother-in-law Nur Jahan as the actual empress of India, and her astounding story had to be put together piecemeal by later historians. To take another example, King Henry IV of France belittled the historical importance of his mother-in-law, Queen Catherine de Medici. To correctly assess the impact of women on this era, we must therefore read the sources "against the grain."[3] In other words, we should try to uncover the actual roles that women played *despite* the efforts of men during and after their period to hijack their contributions and erase them from the pages of history.

Each of the women described in the preceding chapters deserves more than one book-length biographical study. Many, from Queen Elizabeth I of England to Nur Jahan of India, have been the subject of dozens of books and hundreds of articles. There is hardly any piece of historical evidence—letters, accounts, memoirs, chronicles—that has not been brought to light and carefully studied. Although here and there this study sheds light on previously unstudied materials or offers a different perspective on a forgotten piece of evidence, the emphasis is not on writing a new biography but on comparison and synthesis. If the main contention of this book—that women played a crucial role in government for more than a century over large parts of Eurasia—is indeed a historical phenomenon, then the stories themselves, as told by a myriad of historians from Delhi to New York are of importance only if connected into one string of narrative.

By looking at women's political achievements, their leadership qualities, their knowledge of each other, and the impact their character and rule may have had on other leading women, we may provide a basis for comparison.

---

[2] Part of this is discussed in Harvey (ed.), *Ventriloquised Voices*. See, for instance, "Matrix as Metaphor" 76–78. See also De Nicola, *Women in Mongol Iran*, 2, 4.

[3] To paraphrase Walter Benjamin's dictum, "There is no document of civilization which is not at the same time a document of barbarism. The historical materialist therefore ... regards it as his task to brush history against the grain." In Hannah Arendt (ed.), *Illuminations on the Philosophy of History* (New York: Schocken, 1969). Note Benjamin's use of "**his** task," which, ironically, proves the dictum.

Comparing their struggles to attain political power, hold on to it, and maintain it through the years against the odds, could give us insight into the making of sixteenth-century queendom. This task poses a specific dilemma: How should we go about analyzing such a widespread historical phenomenon? Each woman in this book—a crowned queen, a regent, the strong-willed wife of a monarch, or even a rich businesswoman who led her own community—operated within a unique set of circumstances, with a singular chain of events that led her to power and enabled her to hold on to it, a surfeit of rivals and misogynistic attitudes she had to overcome, and a set of specific political crises in which she managed to prevail over rivals. The method I ended up with is telling the story from each dynasty's perspective. The protagonists' rise to power, their actions, their connections with other leading women of the dynasty, and the way they handed the torch down to the next generation were thus described from within their own space and in relation to other women in their dynasty.

The main advantages of this approach are the contextualization of each life story within the history of the specific dynasty and a fuller explanation of the circumstances through which each of these women rose to power and developed her individual network. Another advantage is the multigenerational story arc that, in most of the cases examined here, is strikingly similar. While in almost every case only a handful of women reached the apex of power, their achievement was often the result of several generations of women who had painstakingly blazed the path for them. The same is true for the latest stage. Marie de Medici, Zaynab Begum, Kösem Sultan, and Nur Jahan, the most powerful women of their era, acted in similar ways, sometimes abusing the power they held and bringing about the end of the queendom period. By focusing on each dynasty separately, we were able to follow these precursors and the consequences of holding power.

What this approach is liable to obfuscate, though, is the horizontal comparison. Focusing on a single dynasty's trajectory in each chapter makes it more difficult to see the emergent network and to compare each of the phases to its parallels in other political systems so that wider conclusions and an overarching system could be deduced. This is the main subject of the current chapter.

Our protagonists in East and West alike were often connected to each other as part of a web of foreign relations. Thus, when two ruling women established a connection between them—as did, for example, the Mughal royal consort Hamida Begum and her Safavid contemporary Shahzada Sultanum, or Queen Catherine de Medici and her Ottoman counterpart Nurbanu Sultan—this relationship is described twice: once from the vantage point of one queen and then again through the eyes of her interlocutor. Taken together, the book's chapters thus aim to create a *Rashomon*, a story told from several angles at once. And through telling it from these multiple points of view, a rudimentary pattern and the outlines of a network could rise out of the haze.

The Power of Character

The context in which sixteenth-century female rule emerged was described in the introduction to this book and in the chapters themselves. Yet such external causes alone would not have sufficed. They had to be complemented by other necessary conditions, namely, the right women and the right constellations of power at court. Indeed, in each case of female sovereignty it was the remarkable personality of a single woman that accounted for her rise to power, often in the face of adversity. If structural change and serendipity are to thank for granting some of our protagonists the *opportunity* to shine, their ultimate success in *holding on to power* is owed in equal part to their courage and wisdom and to their steadfastness in the face of powerful rivals for the throne. As we have seen, the successful women leaders of the time consistently employed a mixture of iron will, political acumen, and a judicious use of "the power of weakness."

Catherine de Medici, an orphan girl shunted between monasteries and palaces, became queen of France through a series of serendipitous twists of fate but went on to govern making the most of her status as a king's widow and regent for her young sons. She maneuvered her rivals away from the throne and held on to the reins of power even after her son reached adulthood. Shahzadeh Sultanum, sister of the Safavid Shah Tahmasp, shone as an adviser to her brother even as a young girl and ended up governing the Safavid empire at his side, subduing her rivals and guiding the state to peace and prosperity. In the Mughal Empire, Nur Jahan, taken to the emperor's harem as the widow of a traitor, soon became the real locus of power in the kingdom, leading armies to battle and even minting her own coins. The Marrano Dona Gracia, persecuted for Judaizing, came into her own when her husband left her a hefty inheritance and went on to become one of the richest and most powerful women in Europe. In the Ottoman Empire, Hurrem Sultan, originally a slave girl of humble origins, defied an entire harem as she captured the heart of the sultan and became his partner in government. In England, stricken from the line of succession to the throne, and replaced by another, Mary I built an army of insurrection, and fought for the crown she believed was hers by right.

Only during this century-long interlude did the new structural elements of early modernity mesh so seamlessly with women's strength of character to allow them to play crucial governing roles in so many places at once.

Neither East nor West

One of the first conclusions to be drawn from these stories is how misleading the largely artificial boundary between East and West is. This divide is so deeply ingrained in both literature and living culture, so casually projected backward to the early modern world, that we tend to subsume all history under it. True, this sense of a divided world has a basis in early modern dynamics. On the one hand the inexorable march of the Ottomans into Europe, which first crested in the conquest of Constantinople and then continued to the gates of Vienna, and on the other the Catholic conquest of Spain and parts of North Africa, led both Christians and Muslims to fear devastation by the opposing side. Yet, conditioned as we are by the growing divide between imagined and uniform "Wests" and "Easts," it is almost impossible for us to grasp that in the sixteenth century, East and West were in many ways closer to each other than they were in recent times. The sense of a *qualitative* gap, a deep political, intellectual, and scientific abyss that separates an advanced West from a less developed East was absent. Wisdom, tolerance, righteousness, and scientific innovation were found on both sides, as were narrow-mindedness and arbitrary cruelty. Harbingers of democracy, equality, and freedom of thought, which we so readily relate to Western values, were just as visible on the eastern side of the divide, and the religious intolerance identified today mainly with Islam could more easily be attributed to early modern Christianity. Instead of a fortified wall separating the two civilizational conglomerates, it would be better to picture this imaginary line as a series of gates. Once again I return to Carlo Ginzburg's by-now-famous sixteenth-century miller, Menocchio, who, during his interrogation by the Inquisition admitted to having said that he had been *"born a Christian and so desired to live as a Christian, but if he had been born a Turk, he would have wanted to remain a Turk."*[4] These were things that a Christian in earlier centuries would not have dared think, much less say. Perhaps Menocchio was unique among people of his era, but his idea reflected a growing awareness of the relativity of faith and the sense that there is much to learn from the other side.

But before we delve into the *similarities* of East and West as regards women and sovereign power, a few sentences are in order on the *differences*. For one thing, there were clear divergences in the path to power. It is true that mistresses and concubines of Western European kings could and did attain power. Diane de Poitiers in France and Anne Boleyn or Jane Seymour in England are cases in point. But in most cases examined in this book, women in the West reached practical sovereignty more easily when they were "beyond sexuality" and, hence, became ungendered in a way. Elizabeth overcame this hurdle by being depicted as the Virgin Queen. Both Catherine and Marie de Medici began to wield real power only after they made widowhood their defining characteristic, constantly wore black clothes, and created daily rites of mourning. In a sense that was also true of Mary Queen of Scots, who returned to Scotland as widow of King Francis II of France.

In the Muslim world, by contrast, sex was the highway to power. *All* the Ottoman sultanas started out as beautiful harem odalisques who captured the sultan's heart and gained power, although most of them were shrewd enough to know when to trade sexual attraction for friendship and wise counsel. While most reached the apex of their power as royal mothers, quite a few women, including Hurrem, Nurbanu, and Safiye, held the reins of power while still young and attractive. The same was true for at least some of the Safavid queens, including Tajlu Khanum, Mahd-i Ulya, and perhaps even Shahzada Sultanum

---

[4] Ginzburg, *The Cheese and the Worms*, 49.

(although claims that her brother Shah Tahmasp was in love with her were never proven). In the Mughal world, admittedly, the idea of women holding sovereign power was so deeply ingrained from the beginning that all women— young and old, wives, aunts, and daughters—could attain governmental power. But even there, most of the queens, including Hamida Begum, Nur Jahan, and Mumtaz Mahal, initially rose to power as beloveds of an emperor.

Yet, the commonalities between East and West are much more obvious. First, despite the frequent wars and the rhetoric of *jihad* and *crusade*, all the Muslim empires were allied with Western powers, and for most of the sixteenth and seventeenth centuries, Muslim-Christian alliances were the rule, not the exception. In 1525, France's queen mother, Louise of Savoy, sent an envoy to the Ottoman sultanic couple, Hurrem and Suleiman, and requested their assistance in freeing her son, held in captivity in Spain. Following that initial contact, an alliance gradually took shape between France and the Ottomans. It was to become one of the hallmarks of both empires' diplomacy for many decades. A mirror image of this coalition was the attempt by the Habsburgs to ally themselves with the Safavid empire in order to outflank the French-Ottoman alliance. And despite occasional squabbles over sales and monopolies, the Mughals set up a trade and security collaboration with the Portuguese in the Indian Ocean. Somewhat later in the game, during Elizabeth's time, England signed treaties with the Ottomans to counter the Spanish threat, and sent envoys and merchants to the other Muslim empires, including the Safavids, the Mughals, and the ruling dynasty of Morocco. In hindsight many of these alliances were interpreted as a prelude to imperialism and domination over the non-European world, but at this early phase they were treaties between equals.

Moreover, ruling families across the Christian-Muslim divide believed they were historically related by royal blood. This was not totally imaginary. Needless to say, the royal families in England, France, Spain, the Habsburg Empire, Poland, and Russia, as well as many other kingdoms and dukedoms in Europe— whether Catholic, Protestant, or Orthodox—were related to each other through generations of intermarriage. By the turn of the fifteenth century, such marriages became endogamous rather than exogamous, that is they became, at least in the minds of the period's monarchs, marriages *inside* a vast royal family. The same is true for the Muslim dynasties. The Ottomans, Safavids, and Mughals were bound together by an origin myth of descent from adjacent Turko-Mongol tribes of Central Asia and from the great Genghisid khans, which had some basis in truth. Although they did not intermarry, all Muslim dynasties also inserted a vague lineage leading to the prophet Muhammad or to the early "righteous" caliphs into their genealogies. Such genealogies, though by and large invented traditions, enabled them to claim a shared ancestry.

Less well known are the threads that connected Muslim dynasties to Christian ones across the imaginary divide. In the first two centuries of the Ottoman state's existence, before it perceived itself as a world empire, sultans and crown princes married Christian princesses from the Byzantine Empire, the Bulgarian and Serbian kingdoms, and other Balkan monarchies to cement political alliances. These princesses' families were also related to the high aristocracies of Europe and Russia. A sultan born in the 1500s could therefore claim that he was also part of this extended royal family that spanned Europe and Asia and traced its roots to Roman antiquity. When the small Ottoman principality grew to become a world empire, sultans decided that political marriages were beneath them and had offspring only with their harem slaves. But as these harem slaves rose through the ranks, some of them also claimed descent from European nobility.

To take one example, Nurbanu Sultan was abducted at a young age from an island in the Adriatic Sea and sold to the harem. She went on to become chief consort to Sultan Selim II, mother of Sultan Murad III and a sovereign in her own right. But after becoming Selim's favorite, she asked for confirmation from the Venetian authorities that she was indeed the daughter of Venetian aristocrats. Venice confirmed. Even if, as modern research claims, there was no truth to the assertion, and the Venetian authorities lied to curry favor with the Ottoman sultanate, her son, the future sultan Murad, could still present himself as a scion of both Ottoman emperors and Venetian aristocrats.

To some extent, this was also true of the Safavids. Shah Ismail's mother was the scion of Roman-Byzantine and Georgian royalty on her mother's side. The shah, founder of the Safavid dynasty, depicted himself and, hence, his successors as representing a fusion of Christianity and Islam. Some of the Safavid shahs' wives were also of Armenian and Georgian nobility by descent.

There were no known blood relations between the Mughals and European dynasties. The Mughals prided themselves on being of pure Mongol and Timurid stock. Yet there were persistent rumors in the West that Akbar, the greatest Mughal emperor, married a Portuguese wife. While this remains doubtful, it demonstrates the will on both sides to establish such a connection. The fact that Akbar included Portuguese Jesuit missionaries in his ongoing discussion about the nature of religion and faith, gave them permission to build a church in Agra, adopted some of their theological concepts, and had several of his sons educated by them shows that he was indeed interested in such contacts. It is also significant that Akbar's mother held the title "Mariam Makani" ("occupying the place of Mary") and that he bestowed on his main wife, Harkha Bai, the title "Mariam uz-Zamani" ("Mary of her time").

One of the most dramatic catalysts for the fusion of East and West during this period was the arrival of exiled Iberian Jews in the Muslim world, culminating a few decades after their expulsion from Spain. While many of their relatives who formally converted to Christianity remained in western Europe, thousands of Spanish, Portuguese, and Italian Jews emigrated to the Ottoman Empire and to North Africa. Some even made their way to the Portuguese colonies in Asia and thence to the Mughal court. Considered outsiders on both sides of the religious divide, they brought with them new skills and a knowledge of cultures and languages. Perhaps more importantly, they shared a powerful network that connected Ottomans, Safavids, and Mughals to their Tudor, Valois, or Medici counterparts.

The Three Phases of Queendom

Women's road to the top perch was long and often arduous. Some of those who would go on to govern empires, like Hurrem, Nurbanu, Safiye, and Kösem, started out as kidnapped slave girls, ignorant and uncivilized at least in the eyes of their captors. Others who came from noble or well-to-do families, such as Hamida Begum and Nur Jahan, were reluctantly married off and sent to foreign lands without their consent. Some queens-to-be, such as Mary and Elizabeth of England, were orphans whose mothers fell from grace and were declared illegitimate. Others, such as Catherine de Medici, were sent away as young girls to strict monasteries. Even in those rare cases when they were brought up in royal palaces as queens-to-be, even when they were married in lavish ceremonies to future kings in their homelands, they often started off as neglected wives and had to acquiesce to their husbands' philandering in open view of the court and the public.

And despite the differences in provenance, in all the cases examined here a similar multigenerational narrative arc could be traced. Initially, one or two women blazed the trail, defying deeply ingrained male privilege, and others stepped into the space they created and expanded it. Thus, appointed regent for her minor brother at the end of the fifteenth century and governing wisely, Princess Anne of France broke the barrier on female sovereignty. A few years later, it was her protégé Louise of Savoy who, as queen mother, widened the breach. When Catherine de Medici found her opening three decades later, she was able to step into that space.

In the Mughal Empire, it was Babur's grandmother, Aisan Daulat Begum, and his sister Khanzada Begum who spearheaded Mughal female sovereignty by demonstrating their wisdom, determination, and strategic foresight. In later generations, court women were able to build on these foundations. In England, Katherine of Aragon performed the same function and bequeathed to her daughter Mary, through her own example and the intellectual contributions of Renaissance humanists that she commissioned, a model of queendom that Mary I could take forward and pass on to her half-sister, Elizabeth. And in the Safavid Empire it was Tajlu Khanum, the founder's intrepid wife, and her daughter Shahzada Sultanum, who set the stage for queens in subsequent decades.

The second and third generations of queens were engaged in what Max Weber termed "routinization of charisma."[5] In the Ottoman Empire, Nurbanu asserted special privileges, invented public rituals, and acquired the formal state-recognized power that later became identified with the role of the *valide*. In the Safavid Empire, Parikhan Khanum, Shahzada Sultanum's niece, was the first woman to be recognized by both courtiers and the population at large as sovereign in her own right. Catherine de Medici styled herself "Gouvernante de France" with all the trappings of a sovereign, including scepter, seal, and

---

[5] Max Weber, *The Theory of Social and Economic Organizations*, trans. A. M. Henderson and Talcott Parsons. (New York: The Free Press, 1947), 358–392.

throne. And Elizabeth of England rode into London at the head of a royal procession and proceeded to set laws, court ceremonies, and other rites in stone in order to redefine her powers as independent female sovereign. All these women have ushered in government by women as an accepted norm by creating traditions, institutionalizing ceremonies, enlarging their households, and taking upon themselves ever bigger chunks of state responsibility, sidelining their male kin who were formally in charge.

At this stage, frustrated male members of the elite often sought ways to curb the power of ruling women. In Safavid Iran and the Mughal Empire, those male monarchs who were powerful enough to challenge entrenched female rule insisted on sequestering women in the harem and limiting their freedom of movement. In France and England, attempts were made to force queens to marry and cede power to their royal husbands or in-laws. But even after such steps were taken to limit their access to government, formidable women succeeded in carving a ruling niche for themselves, even to a greater degree than before. Kösem Sultan, sidelined several times and sent to a harem outside the palace, returned to become the uncontested ruler of the Ottoman Empire. She presided over state council meetings, appointed, and dismissed ministers, signed peace treaties, and declared war. In the Mughal Empire, even after women were relegated to the harem in the previous generation, Nur Jahan was recognized as the true sovereign. In France, Marie de Medici became regent and *de facto* queen, despite the opprobrium surrounding women's rule after the fall of Catherine de Medici. These queens have stretched the notion of women's government to its limits for the time period.

But this ultimate phase—a full and defiant takeover of government—had its price. As long as women ruled from behind the scenes using their male kin as the public face of sovereignty, blame could be shared by them or even placed squarely on the shoulders of the incompetent king. But once they dropped the mask and governed directly, they also had to account for fiascos and mistakes. In many cases, women were more successful than men in the same positions, but whereas men's failures were often blamed on external circumstances or inept ministers, those of women were, as a rule, attributed to their gender.

Small wonder, then, that their success ended up reinforcing misogynistic views and put an end to the extraordinary era of queendom. All protagonists of this third phase suffered attempts to either eliminate them physically or strike them from the history books. Kösem Sultan was strangled by harem guardians at her rivals' orders. Nur Jahan was demoted by the next emperor and exiled, and her era erased from the chronicles. In France, Marie de Medici was forced into exile and died poor and neglected. Even those queens of the Jews from Istanbul, such as Esther Handali and Esperanza Malchi, were assassinated by their rivals who were threatened by their power at court.

Constructing Sovereignty

Since rule was still thought to be a male privilege, and since there were hardly any women in state officialdom and none in the military, our protagonists encountered a male-dominated aristocracy and bureaucracy and a general view of women as timid, overly emotional, lacking in reason, and ignorant about state affairs. Facing male resistance every step of the way, each woman who reached the top rung on the ladder had to build her own support base and to insure that her opinions were respected and her orders obeyed. They needed to make their subalterns understand that *they* were in charge, not the male figureheads in whose name they governed. Yet, since the circumstances in which they climbed to the top were different in every case, each one had to shore up her status by different means.

Here, too, the schematic division into "East" and "West" is misleading. The difficulties facing women in Safavid Iran, for example, were more akin to those faced by their distant French peers than to those of their Ottoman neighbors. Slave girls taken into the Ottoman harem first had to attract the sultan's attention, overcoming competition by other concubines. Once noticed by the sultan in a faceless throng of potential consorts, they had to bear him a son, steer the boy through the many challenges posed by harem rivals, and make sure their son would defeat the other concubines' sons in the contest for the throne. Once in power, with their husband or minor son secure on the throne, they also had to convince the elite and the public at large of their own wisdom, courage, far-sightedness, and commitment to the dynasty. This was notoriously difficult in a tradition that forced women to remain unseen in public and forbade the minting of their faces on coins. They had to build their reputation as sovereigns by using competent emissaries, constructing social welfare institutions, building elite alliances, and rendering assistance to those who petitioned them for help. A sultan's consort who could put her name to a mosque complex, bind an army general to her service by promotion through the ranks, or add a high-ranking minister to her network by arranging marriage to a princess would thus strengthen her powerbase. At some point they also organized public displays of power and generosity as they were driven, veiled, through the streets of the capital, doling out fistfuls of coins and accepting petitions.

For women in Safavid Iran and Mughal India the problem was very different. Those who came to hold power were always freeborn and most were part of the royal family by marriage or descent. Following Mongol traditions, sovereignty was invested not just in the male members but in the entire dynasty, and therefore women had a better springboard to positions of authority. Also, unlike Ottoman women, at least in the first century of Safavid and Mughal rule, women moved around freely. Although they were bound to cover their heads, paying lip service to Islamic tradition, Mughal and Safavid royal women owned houses outside the palace, rode horses like men, and joined their male relatives on hunting expeditions and even on the battlefield. Yet perhaps because they enjoyed so many liberties and were often in the public eye, they were also faced with suspicions of sexual misconduct, accusations of incompetence, and general misogyny. To counter all this, they also needed to create a basis of power in much the same way as the Ottoman sultanas, by proving their devotion to Islam, contributing to holy sites, erecting public buildings, donating money to charities, and orchestrating ostentatious parades.

Though not constrained by the traditions that made it difficult for Muslim women to ucover their faces in public, women in France had serious legal hurdles of their own to overcome. An ancient feudal regulation, dredged up from oblivion to prevent an English takeover of the throne, prohibited women's sovereignty even when they were first in line. Those who were in the vanguard of their rise in the early sixteenth century had to resort to special decrees and other legal means to protect their status, gradually chipping away at the law. Thus, Francis I was obliged to send letters to Parliament to explain why he had appointed his mother, Louise of Savoy, regent in his absence. Louise, in her turn, had books published extolling her virtues as the king's mother to convince the public that she was up to the task. Two generations later, to make a similar point, Catherine de Medici instructed that during her son's coronation, her throne would be placed on the same level as his.

In England, Princess Mary and her young sister Elizabeth had to contend with yet another problem. They were both declared illegitimate early on, Mary when her father's marriage to Katherine of Aragon was annulled and Elizabeth when her mother Anne Boleyn was executed for adultery and treason. Both daughters regained their father's grudging recognition in later years but still had to rebuild their reputation in the eyes of the English aristocracy and public. They also had to build a case against other contestants, such as Lady Jane Grey or their cousin Mary, Queen of Scots, who had a strong claim to the English throne not tarnished by scandal. The problem was amplified by the internal religious struggle. Mary I, a devout Catholic, acceded to the throne after the death of her brother Edward, who sided with the Reformation, and fought to restore Catholicism. Elizabeth, who took over from Mary, struggled to bring the kingdom back into reform mode.

But while the road to power was different in each dynasty, there were also significant similarities. Men most often predicated their legitimacy on war—fighting against the state's enemies, vanquishing them, and taking their land. While not shying away from war when deemed necessary, women tended to prefer diplomacy whenever possible and often engaged in negotiations with women on the other side. This was also true in the internal arena. Catherine de Medici's defining trait was the constant attempt to balance Protestants and Catholics. Nur Jahan both showed herself a devout Muslim by contributing to mosques and madrasas and followed the Hindu darshan rites of worship. Elizabeth of England bit her tongue to allow liberties for the Catholics, although her own sympathies clearly lay with the Anglican Church; and Shahzada Sultanum, a devout Shiite who had sent huge sums of money to

Imam Reza's mosque in Mashhad, sent illuminated Qurans and prayer rugs to her Sunni Ottoman counterpart for the Suleimaniye mosque in Istanbul.

A hurdle that queens faced everywhere was the fact that all state institutions were *manned* by men, and having their orders followed was a constant daily struggle. One strategy employed by women to overcome this hurdle was the habitual use of "the power of weakness" to motivate their male underlings. Women rulers often resorted to claiming that they needed male assistance and protection. The themes used by women to portray themselves to the public, such as the black-clad grieving widow (Catherine de Medici), the virgin queen (Elizabeth), or the beloved wife or mother (Nur Jahan, Nurbanu), were also subtly intended to convey that sense of frailty and the need for male assistance. Yet when a demonstration of command was necessary, they changed tack without hesitation, as described so eloquently in Queen Elizabeth's famous speech to her soldiers: "*I know I have the body of a weak and feeble woman, but I have the heart and stomach of a king.*"

Weaving a Net

The simultaneous rise of a large number of women to positions of power is an important historical phenomenon in itself. But a further question needs to be answered: What did these women know about each other? Were they influenced by the rise of other women to positions of power or by their acts of leadership? Did they maintain any sort of contact with each other? To answer these questions, we must look at several different means of early-modern communication between royal courts.

The first was meetings face to face. Although not uncommon, the long distances, large retinues, displays of fanfare, wealth and power, and complex arrangements involved in personal meetings on the monarchic level often made such meetings cumbersome and difficult to set up. Their main purposes were to parlay, to conclude a marriage agreement, or to sign a treaty. Even before the sixteenth century royal women were frequently sent to rival courts to conduct negotiations, both because they were assumed to be more patient and less threatening than their male counterparts and to make sure that failure to reach an agreement would not taint the male monarch and would allow him to maintain his posture as a warrior king.

One of the most famous examples of royal women coming together to determine the future of their realms was the meeting in 1529 in the town of Cambrai between Louise of Savoy, queen mother of France, and Margaret of Austria, aunt of Emperor Charles V. In three weeks of intense negotiations, Louise and Margaret hammered out a peace treaty between France and the Habsburg Empire, which came to be known as the Peace of the Ladies. Another example is the meeting between Shahzada Sultanum, Shah Tahmasp's sister, and Hamida Begum, Emperor Humayun's wife. Their discussions led to an agreement between the Safavids and the Mughals that enabled the Mughal couple to recapture Hindustan.

A second method, simpler and more immediate than meeting in person, was sending an envoy or emissary to carry a message or conduct negotiations on behalf of a monarch. Thus, Queen Louise of Savoy sent her emissary to Hurrem Sultan in 1525 to request Ottoman assistance in freeing her son. Hurrem also established contact through emissaries with Shahzada Sultanum after long years of devastating wars between the Ottomans and the Safavids. Together the two women orchestrated a series of negotiations that led to the signing of the Amasya Treaty and two decades of peace between their countries. Once the peace was established, the two continued to correspond, sending royal gifts to each other to seal the peace and allay fears of religious strife and renewed violence.

The exchange of letters and gifts was an age-old practice, but as new global routes opened up, the velocity and frequency of correspondence increased tenfold. Thousands of letters were sent and received by sovereigns during this period, and they seem to have played a major role in the creation of female networks. Hurrem corresponded with Louise of Savoy, queen of France, and with Bona Sforza of Poland. Nurbanu Sultan exchanged letters with Queen Catherine de Medici and with the doges of Venice; and Safiye Sultan maintained a correspondence with Queen Elizabeth of England. These communications became the core of the military and economic alliance between these countries and led to long years of stable relations.

Such means of communication were underpinned in many cases by connections between underlings. One thing to bear in mind was that networks usually began at home. Young queens understood at an early stage that in order to protect themselves and their offspring, they had to rely on powerful courtiers and on information that they painstakingly collected and assessed from their retainers. Since many of these courtiers and agents were skilled bureaucrats, physicians, and bankers, they moved easily between the royal courts of Europe and those of the Muslim world. One example of such networking across the East-West divide are the travels of Dona Gracia. Moving from Lisbon to Antwerp and amassing a huge fortune from the booming international trade, she then transferred her affairs to Lyons, Venice, and Ferrara successively and ended up as a banker and consultant to Hurrem Sultan. Throughout her travels she met kings, queens, and princesses, lending money, attending dinner parties, passing on messages from other courts, and sharing information gleaned from her network of agents.

Once the great European universities admitted converted Jews, they were literally inundated with them. Many of those who converted to Christianity were able to read Arabic and Hebrew and integrate the wealth of older Muslim and Jewish medical treatises with the new discoveries of Renaissance era medicine. After graduation, they found themselves in great demand by the monarchs of Europe and the Middle East. These physicians, some of whom returned to Judaism, remained in close contact with each other. By midcentury, almost every monarch in Europe and the Mediterranean region had a senior Jewish or Marrano physician in their service. It was not uncommon for a physician in the

Ottoman court to have relatives in the retinue of the French, English, or Polish monarchs. They soon began to double as advisors and diplomats. As Rhoads Murphey points out, in the Ottoman Empire, "a position as private body physician to a well-placed official or to the sultan himself provided a natural opportunity for the physician to act as his patron's adviser and representative in nonmedical matters. Due to their command of foreign languages, the employment of recently immigrated Jews as diplomatic envoys was both usual and expected."[6] Since both groups—royal women and Marrano/Jewish physicians—felt marginalized by the dominant religion's male establishment, they often allied with each other.

These networks were complemented and later superseded by missionary networks reinvigorated by the masses of new "heathen" populations reached by new shipping routes. The aim of the Society of Jesus, founded by Ignatius de Loyola in the 1540s, was to halt the spread of the Lutheran heresy, strengthen the Catholic Church, spread its teachings over "newly discovered" lands, and bring the errant churches of the East back into Rome's fold. Joined by a number of Jewish converts in its early days, the society took over from Marrano networks in foreign lands. During the late sixteenth and seventeenth centuries Jesuit emissaries were sent to all corners of the globe, from Mexico and Peru to Ethiopia, China, and India. Their reports became a major networking device for the emerging world order and certainly brought Eastern queendom to the attention of royal women in Western Europe, encouraging them to demand recognition.[7]

Finally, with the emergence of the printing press, prose and fiction also became important networking devices. Books recounting the stories of past queens, protofeminist writings, such as those of de Pizan, Vives, More, and Castiglione, were translated and subversively advanced the idea of women in public office, as did plays written about such figures as Hurrem/Roxelana, the Ottoman slave girl who rose to power. While some of these plays described the wiles of women who came to power in the "heathen" Muslim world, the presentation of a strong-willed and majestic queen must have had an important impact on European royal women such as Elizabeth Tudor or Catherine de Medici.

---

[6] Murphey, "Jewish Contribution to Ottoman Medicine," 64. See also Heyd, "Moses Hamon," 152. Roth, *History of the Marranos*, claims that the Marrano doctors were allowed to keep medical tracts in Hebrew, but nothing else.

[7] Maryks, "Jesuit Order as Synagogue," 61–66. Subrahmanyam, *Three Ways to be Alien*, 134–139.

CHAPTER 9

Conclusion: How and Why Did It End?

From the 1650s onward, royal women receded into the background. In the Ottoman Empire after Kösem, in the Safavid Empire after Zaynab Begum, and in the Mughal Empire after Nur Jahan and Mumtaz Mahal, we hardly even know their names. In Christian Europe, the names may still be known to historians of monarchy, but in France after Marie de Medici, in England after Elizabeth, and even in Jewish communities after Dona Gracia Mendes and the two *kiras*, women remained behind the scenes and did not play as prominent a role as they did during this short efflorescence.

Historians have offered several possible reasons for this shift. A common one, used, for instance, by Ottoman historians explaining the end of the "sultanate of women," is that eventually mismanagement by women caught up with the state and brought it to the brink of ruin. Realizing that they had no other option, the ruling women had to hand over the reins of power to capable men of state, notably the grand vizier. This is doubtful not just because it is prejudiced but also because so often in the past men brought their states to the brink of extinction, but none of them ever thought that the solution would be to hand the state over to women, or even to suggest that men more capable than them should be put in charge.

Other explanations may be more relevant. To paraphrase Paul Kennedy's description of the end of empires, one such explanation is "female overstretch."[1] As described in Chap. 8, in each of the monarchies examined in this book women, be they Ottoman concubines, Safavid princesses, or French royal consorts, gradually built their power until it reached a certain zenith. At some point this power exceeded the limits acceptable to males in the kingdom who formally kept holding on to all positions of power in the government, the army,

---

[1] Paul Kennedy, *The Rise and Fall of the Great Powers: Economic Change and Military Conflict from 1500 to 2000* (Vintage, 2010).

and the bureaucracy. While they could stomach women serving as regents for kings during their minority or pulling the strings *behind* the throne, once they appeared up front, shedding their supposed feminine incapacity and displaying the authority and self-assuredness associated with male domination, they transgressed the limits of early modern culture and were seen as too dangerous. Kings, princes, aristocrats, and royal council members came together to put an end to the streak of female rule.

Other reasons have to do with tectonic shifts in the political system and are therefore not particular to women. They just happened to occur during this specific period. Queendom fell prey to other historical shifts that took place during the seventeenth century. One dynamic we could point to is the growing complexity of government. In the sixteenth century, government could still be overseen by one very talented man or woman pulling the strings, but a century later this was no longer possible. State machineries became highly articulated bodies, with such heavy bureaucracies, that an absolutist monarchy could no longer conduct on its own. Running the government required bureaucratic skills, and monarchs found it harder and harder to rule. The same transition that created an opening for women in the early 1500s—from a peripatetic state bureaucracy to a sedentary one—shifted once again to close that opening a century later. It is no accident that both the Ottoman Turhan Sultan in 1656 and France's Queen Anne of Austria a decade earlier, asked their chief ministers, Mehmed Köprülü Pasha and Cardinal Jules Mazarin, respectively, to take charge of government. This was the age of the bureaucrat.

Which brings us to the last set of causes, which have to do with the rise of nationalism. Doubts about the need for monarchy itself began to appear in intellectual circles in the late seventeenth century. Although royalty was still revered, the idea of a dynasty ruling over a multiethnic group of subjects "by the grace of God" was gradually replaced by that of monarchy as the emblem of a nation. Its elevated status now derived not from heaven but rather from the sanctity of the eternal nation itself. At least in Europe, the nation was now depicted and imagined as a female figure, a mother or a beloved female who should be protected from being kidnapped or raped by enemies. In that kind of atmosphere, there was need for a strong, masculine figure to defend the nation. It was harder to imagine women in this role.

Such ideas of nation did not take root in the Asian world in the sixteenth century, but another phenomenon was at play there, marginalizing women. As we saw, for much of the sixteenth century royal ladies were free to come and go as they pleased. It was not uncommon to see princesses riding with men to the hunt, and women's participation in festivities, processions, and royal parties was taken for granted. There were no obstacles to prevent a woman from exercising power in court, giving orders to viziers, or participating in divan meetings. This style of government, adapted by and large from Mongol tradition, gradually gave way to an orthodox etiquette that demanded clear separation between men and women. In most Muslim monarchies, women were incarcerated inside the harem and required the consent of their male guardian to leave. While that in itself was not an insurmountable obstacle, and we saw that in the Ottoman case women were able to govern the state from *within* the confines of the harem, it did make it more difficult for women to attain power and to maintain constant contact with their underlings. It had to be done through intermediaries, and power gradually shifted from the harem women to intermediaries such as the eunuchs who served as harem security guards and could come and go as they pleased.

As a result of all these developments, female sovereignty and power were pushed back into the shadows in the mid-seventeenth century. It took a hundred years for leading women in the West to enter the realm of male politics once again. In the Orient, it took even longer.

BIBLIOGRAPHY

PRIMARY SOURCES

Archivio di Stato—Venezia

Giacomo Soranzo to Venetian Senate, Pera 4 July 1566 (A.S.V. Senato Dispacci Constantinopoli, filza 1. No. 36)
BAC   Bailo a Constantinopoli
CollRel Collegio-Relazioni
NotAtti Notarile-Atti
SDC   Senato Dispacci, Constantinopoli
SDCop   Senato Dispacci, Copie modern
SdelC   Senato Deliberazioni, Constantinopoli

Les Archives Nationales, France

Correspondence of the ambassador in Constantinople (De Morvilliers, July 1549, and onwards).

The Medici Archive Project (online)
National Archives, UK

Calendar of State Papers, Foreign, Elizabeth, 23 vols.

Başbakanlik Osmanlı Devlet Arşivi

The Akbarnāma of Abu-l-fazl, translated from the Persian by H. Beveridge, I.C.S. (retired). Calcutta: Bibliotheca Indica, 1897.

Alberi, Eugenio, *Relazioni degli ambasciatori veneti al senato durante il secolo decimosesto*. Series 3, vols. 1–3. Florence: 1840–55 X

d'Alessandri, Vincentio. "*Narrative of... V. d'Alessandri, Ambassador to the King of Persia*," tr. and ed. from Italian by Charles Grey as *A Narrative of Italian Travels in Persia, in the Fifteenth and Sixteen Centuries*, Hakluyt Society series 49, pt. 2, London, 1873.

Bajetta, Carlo M., *Elizabeth I's Italian Letters*. Palgrave, 2017.

Busbecq, Ogier Ghislen de. *Turkish Letters*. Sickle Moon Books, 2001.

De la Ferriere, Hector. (ed.), *Lettres de Catherine de Medicis*, 11 vols. Paris: Imprimerie Nationale, 1880–1963.

Ellis, Henry. Ed., *Original Letters Illustrative of English History* (London, R. Bentley), 1846.

Faierstein, Morris M., *The Book of Visions: The Diary of Rabbi Hayyim Vita*, (Sefer Ha-Hezyonot) Hebrew. Jerusalem, Yad Ben Zvi, 2005.

Green, Mary Anne Everett. *Letters of Royal and Illustrious Ladies of Great Britain: From the Commencement of the Twelfth Century to the Close of the Reign of Queen Mary*. Vol. 1. H. Colburn, 1846.

Guiffrey, G. (ed.), *Lettres inedits de Diane de Poitiers*. Paris, 1866.

Gulbadan Begum, *Humayun-Nama*, trans. Annette S. Beveridge (Lahore: Sang-e-meel Publications, 1974).

Jahangir, Alexander Rogers, and Henry Beveridge. "The Tuzuk-i-Jahangiri; or." *Memoirs of Jahangir* (1909).

von Klarwill, Victor. (ed.) *The Fugger Newsletters: Being a Selection of Unpublished Letters from the Correspondences of the House of Fugger During the Years 1568–1605*, trans. Pauline de Chary. New York and London: The Knickerbocker Press, 1926.

Knox, John. *The First Blast of the Trumpet Against the Monstrous Regiment of Women: 1558*.

Labanoff, A. *Lettres Inedites de Marie Stuart 1558–1587*. London, 1839.

Membré, Michele. *Mission to the Lord Sophy of Persia (1539–1542)*. School of Oriental and African Studies, University of London, 1993.

Olearius, Adam. *The Voyages & Travels of the Ambassadors from the Duke of Holstein, to the Great Duke of Muscovy, and the King of Persia: Begun in the Year M. DC. XXXIII and Finish'd in M. DC. XXXIX: Containing a Compleat History of Muscovy, Tartary, Persia, and Other Adjacent Countries: with Several Publick Transactions Reaching Neer the Present Times: in Seven Books: Illustrated with Diverse Accurate Mapps and Figures*. Thomas Dring, and John Starkey, and are to be sold at their shops. 2nd Edition, 1669.

Pizan, Christine de. *The Book of the City of Ladies*, translated by Rosalind Brown-Grant. Penguin, 1990.

The Remonstrance Made by the Queene-mother of France, to the King Her Sonne, for Remedy of Such Disorders and Abuses as She Pretendeth to be in the Present

Gouernement and Managing of Affaires of State, in the Realme of France...: Faithfully Translated Out of French (Newberry, 1619)

Rumlu, Hasan-i. "A Chronicle of the Early Safavids Being the Ahsanu't-Tawârîkh." Translated by C.N. Seddon. *Oriental Institute, Baroda* (1934).

Rycaut, Paul. *The History of the Turkish Empire from the Year 1623 to the Year 1677 Containing the Reigns of the Three Last Emperours, Viz., Sultan Morat or Amurat IV, Sultan Ibrahim, and Sultan Mahomet IV, His Son, the XIII Emperour Now Reigning.* Printed by J.M. for John Starkey..., 1680

Strickland, A., *Letters of Mary, Queen of Scots and Documents connected with her Personal History.* London, 1844.

Uluçay, Çatağay, *Osmanlı Sultanlarına Aşk Mektupları.* Istanbul: Ufuk Kitapları, 2001 (1950).

Uluçay, Çatağay, *Haremden Mektuplar.* Istanbul: Vakit Matbaası, 1956.

Usque, Samuel. *Consolation for the Tribulations of Israel,* (Martin A. Cohn, ed.), Philadelphia 1965 (Originally published in Ferrara, 1553).

Wood, M.A., *Letters of Royal and Illustrious Women of Great Britain.* London 1846.

Secondary Sources

Adams, Simon. "Elizabeth I, the Succession and Foreign Policy." *History Today* 53.5 (2003): 42–48.

Adelman, Howard Tzvi. "The Venetian Identities of Beatrice and Brianda de Luna." *Nashim: A Journal of Jewish Women's Studies and Gender Issues.* 2013.

Ágoston, Gabor. "Information, Ideology, and Limits of Imperial Policy: Ottoman Grand Strategy in the Context of Ottoman–Habsburg Rivalry." In *The Early Modern Ottomans: Remapping the Empire,* edited by Virginia H. Aksan and Daniel Goffman, 75–103. Cambridge: Cambridge University Press, 2007.

Al-'Afia, Abdelkader. *Amirat al-Jibal: Al-Hurra bint 'Ali Ibn Rashid.* Tetouan: Maktabat an-Nur, 1989.

Alfani, Guido, and Roberta Frigeni. "Inequality (un) perceived: The emergence of a discourse on economic inequality from the Middle Ages to the Age of Revolution." *The Journal of European Economic History* 45.1 (2016): 21–66.

Andrade. SENHORA, A. ILLVSTRISSIMA, and DONA GRACIA NASCI. "A Senhora e os destinos da Nação Portuguesa: o caminho de Amato Lusitano e de Duarte Gomes." *Cadernos de Estudos Sefarditas* 10–11 (2011): 87–130.

Andrea, Bernadette. *Women and Islam in early modern English literature.* Cambridge University Press, 2008.

Angard, Laurent. "Marguerite de Valois et 'La Querelle des femmes': des Mémoires au Discours docte et subtil." *Cahiers du GADGES* 9.1 (2011): 117–137.

Arbel, Benjamin. "Nūr Bānū (c. 1530–1583)." *Turcica* 24 (1992): 241–259.

Ashraf, Razi. "Ottoman–Mughal Political Relations circa 1500–1923." *The Eurasia Studies Society Journal* 2/2 (March 2013), 1–7.

Austen, Ralph A. "Marginalization, stagnation, and growth: the trans-Saharan caravan trade in the era of European expansion, 1500–1900." *The Rise of Merchant Empires: Long-Distance Trade in the Early Modern World, 1350–1750* (1990): 311–41.

Babayan, Katheryn, "The 'Aqa'id al-Nisa': A Glimpse at Safavid Women in Local Isfahani Culture," in Gavin R. G. Hambly (ed.), *Women in the Medieval Islamic World*, New York: Palgrave, 1998, pp. 349–82.

Balabanlilar, Lisa. "The Begims of the mystic feast: Turco-Mongol tradition in the Mughal harem." *The Journal of Asian Studies* 69.1 (2010): 123–147.

Batiffol, Louis. "Marie de Medicis." *Revue Historique* 89.Fasc. 2 (1905): 225–271.

Beck, Lois, and Guity Nashat, eds. *from 1800 to the Islamic Republic*. University of Illinois Press, 2004.

Benson, Pamela Joseph. *Invention of the Renaissance Woman: The Challenge of Female Independence in the Literature and Thought of Italy and England*. Penn State Press, 2010.

Ben-Zaken, Avner. "The Revolving planets and the revolving clocks: Circulating mechanical objects in the Mediterranean." *History of Science* 49.2 (2011): 125–148.

Berchet, Guglielmo. *La repubblica di Venezia e la Persia*, Turin: G.B. Paravia, 1865; facs. Edition, Tehran, 1976.

Bernard, George W. "The Fall of Anne Boleyn." *The English Historical Review* 106.CCCCXX (1991): 584–610.

Birjandifar, Nazak. *Royal Women and Politics in Safavid Iran*. Diss. McGill University, 2005.

Birnbaum, Marianna D. *The long journey of Gracia Mendes*. Central European University Press, 2003.

Braudel, Fernand. *The Mediterranean and the Mediterranean World in the Age of Philip II: Volume II*. Oakland, CA: University of California Press, 1995.

Braudel, Fernand. *Civilization and capitalism, 15th-18th century, vol. III: The perspective of the world*. Vol. 3. University of California Press, 1992.

Brioist, Pascal, Laure Fagnart, and Cédric Michon. *Louise de Savoie (1476–1531)*. Presses universitaires François-Rabelais, 2018.

Broomhall, Susan. "'My daughter, my dear': the correspondence of Catherine de Médicis and Elisabeth de Valois," *Women's History Review* (2015), no. 4, 548–569.

Brown, Cynthia J. "7. Family Female Networking in Early Sixteenth-Century France." *Women and Power at the French Court, 1483–1563*: 209.

Browne, Lauren Rose. "Elizabeth of York: Tudor trophy wife." *Tudor and Stuart Consorts: Power, Influence, and Dynasty*. Cham: Springer International Publishing, 2022. 19–40.

Brummett, Palmira Johnson. *Ottoman Seapower and Levantine Diplomacy in the Age of Discovery.* SUNY series in the Social and Economic History of the Middle East. Albany, NY: State University of New York Press, 1994.

Burdelez, Ivana. "The Role of Ragusan Jews in the History of the Mediterranean Countries." In *Jews, Christians and Muslims in the Mediterranean World after 1492,* edited by Alisia Meyuhas Ginio, 190–197. London: Frank Cass and Company Limited, 1992.

Burian, Orhan. "Türk–İngiliz Münasebetlerinin İlk Yılları." *Ankara Üniversitesi Dil ve Tarih-Coğra ya Fakültesi Dergisi* IX (1951): 1–17.

Burke, Peter. *The Italian Renaissance: Culture and Society in Italy.* Princeton University Press, 1986.

Burke, Peter. "Early Modern Venice as a Center of Information and Communication." In Martin, John and Dennis Romano (eds.) *Venice Reconsidered.* Baltimore 389–419.

Carpenter, Jennifer. and Sally Beth MacLean, *Power of the Weak: Studies on Medieval Women.* Urbana: 1995.

Cartwright, Julia. *Christina of Denmark, duchess of Milan and Lorraine, 1522–1590.* BoD—Books on Demand, 2018.

Carlson, Ethan. "Power, Presents, and Persuasion: Early English Diplomacy with Mughal India." *Erişim Tarihi* 19 (2019).

Casale, Giancarlo. *The Ottoman Age of Exploration.* New York: Oxford University Press, 2010.

Casale, Giancarlo. "An Ottoman Intelligence Report from the mid-Sixteenth Century Indian Ocean." *Journal of Turkish Studies* 31 (2007): 181–188.

de Castro, Filipe Vieira. *The pepper wreck: a Portuguese Indiaman at the mouth of the Tagus river.* Texas A&M University Press, 2005.

Çetiner, Yılmaz, *Haremde bir Venedikli: Nurbanu Sultan.* Istanbul: Remzi Kitabevi, 2001.

Chamberlin, Ann. *Reign of the Favoured Women.* New York: Saint Martins Press, 1998.

Chambers, Anne. *Granuaile: Grace O'Malley—Ireland's Pirate Queen, C. 1530–1603.* Gill & Macmillan, 2009.

McCartney, Elizabeth. "In the Queen's Word: Perceptions of Regency Government Gleaned from the Correspondence of Catherine de Medicis" in Couchman, Jane and Ann Crabb, *Women's Letters Across Europe, 1400–1700.* Ashgate, 2005.

Choksy, Jamsheed K., and M. Usman Hasan. "An Emissary from Akbar to 'Abbās I: Inscriptions, Texts, and the Career of Amīr Muḥammad Ma'ṣūm al-Bhakkarī." *Journal of the Royal Asiatic Society* 1.1 (1991): 19–29.

Clot, André. *Suleiman the Magnificent,* trans. M. Reisz. Saqi Books (2005).

Collins, James B. *The state in early modern France.* Cambridge University Press, 1995.

Cook, B.J. "Like Philip and Mary on a Shilling": the Literary Legacy of a Tudor Coin. *The Numismatic Chronicle (1966-)* (2017): 399–411.

Cook, Rifka. "A Pilgrimage to a Personality: Dona Gracia Mendes," in Bryan Kirschen (ed.) *Judeo-Spanish and the Making of a Community*. Vol. 1st unabridged, Cambridge Scholars Publishing, 2015, pp. 152–168.

Costa, Palmira Fontes da, and Teresa Nobre Carvalho. "Between East and West: Garcia de Orta's Colloquies and the circulation of medical knowledge in the sixteenth century." *Asclepio. Revista de Historia de la Medicina y de la Ciencia* 65.1 (2013), pp. 1–13.

Cox, Virginia. *Women's writing in Italy, 1400–1650*. JHU Press, 2008.

Crawford, Katherine. "Catherine de Médicis and the Performance of Political Motherhood," *Sixteenth Century Journal* (2000), 31(3), pp. 643–673.

Daoud, *Ta'rikh Titwān* (12 vols. Matba'at al-khalij al-Arabi, 1959)

Da Silva Tavim, Jose Alberto Rodrigues. "In the Shadow of Empire: Portuguese Jewish Communities in the Sixteenth Century." In Brockey, Liam Matthew (ed.), *Portuguese Colonial Cities in the Early Modern World*. Ashgate, 2008.

Dale, Stephen F., *The Muslim Empires of the Ottomans, Safavids and Mughals*. Cambridge University Press, 2010.

da Silva Tavim, José Alberto Rodrigues. "La" Materia Oriental en el trayecto de dos personalidades judías del Imperio Otomano: Joao Micas/D. Yosef Nasí, Álvaro Mendes/D. Shelomó Ibn Ya'ish. *Hispania judaica bulletin* 7 (2010): 211–232.

Davis, Natalie Zemon. "Decentering History: Local Stories and Cultural Crossings in a Global World. *History and Theory* 50/2 (May 2011), 188–202.

Davis, Natalie Zemon. *Society and culture in early modern France: eight essays*. Stanford University Press, 197.

Davis, Natalie Zemon. *Trickster Travels: A Sixteenth Century Muslim between Worlds*. New York: Hill and Wang, 2006.

Davis, Natalie Zemon. "'Women's history' in transition: The European case." *Feminist Studies* 3.3/4 (1976): 83–103.

Daybell, James. "Gender, Obedience, and Authority in Sixteenth-Century Women's Letters." *The Sixteenth Century Journal* (2010): 49–67.

De Nicola, Bruno. *Women in Mongol Iran: The Khatuns, 1206–1335*. Edinburgh University Press, 2017.

Doran, Susan. *Elizabeth I and her Circle*. OUP Oxford, 2015.

Doran, Susan. *Monarchy and matrimony: the courtships of Elizabeth I*. Routledge, 2002.

Doran, Susan. "Elizabeth I and Catherine de'Medici." in Glenn Richardson, *The Contending Kingdoms*. Routledge, 2016: 129–144.

Doumenjou, Marie Favereau, and Liesbeth Geevers. "The Golden Horde, the Spanish Habsburg Monarchy, and the Construction of Ruling Dynasties." *Prince, Pen, and Sword: Eurasian Perspectives*. Brill, 2018. 452–512.

Duindam, Jeroen. *Dynasties: A global history of power, 1300–1800*. Cambridge University Press, 2016.

Dumas, Juliette. "Une diplomatie par les femmes: le cas des princesses ottomanes à l'aube de l'époque moderne." dans Mehdi Jerad, *Femme et diplomatie aux époques moderne et contemporaine*, (2017).

Duncan, Sarah. *Mary I: Gender, Power, and Ceremony in the Reign of England's First Queen*. Springer, 2012.

Dursteler, Eric R. *Renegade Women: Gender, Identity, and Boundaries in the Early Modern Mediterranean*. Baltimore: The Johns Hopkins University Press, 2011.

Dursteler, Eric R., "On Bazaars and Battlefields: Recent Scholarship on Mediterranean Cultural Contacts." *Journal of Early Modern History* 15 (2011): 413–434.

Dursteler, Eric. "Describing or Distorting the 'Turk'?: The *relazioni* of the Venetian Ambassadors in Constantinople as Historical Source." *Acta Historiae* 19/1–2 (2011), 231–248.

Dursteler, Eric R., "Fatima Hatun nee Beatrice Michiel: Renegade Women in the Early Modern Mediterranean." *The Medieval History Journal* 12/2 (2009): 355–382.

Edwards, Clara Cary. "Relations of Shah Abbas the Great, of Persia, with the Mogul Emperors, Akbar and Jahangir." *Journal of the American Oriental Society* 35 (1915): 247–268.

Edwards, John. *Mary I: England's catholic queen*. Yale University Press, 2011.

Eichberger, Dagmar. "Margareta of Austria. A Princess with ambition and political insight." (2005): 48–55.

Eisenbichler, Konrad, ed. *The Cultural World of Eleonora di Toledo: Duchess of Florence and Siena*. Routledge, 2017.

Elston, Timothy G. "Transformation or Continuity? Sixteenth-Century Education and the Legacy of Catherine of Aragon, Mary I, and Juan Luis Vives." *"High and Mighty Queens" of Early Modern England: Realities and Representations*. Palgrave Macmillan, New York, 2003. 11–26.

Ergin, Nina. "Ottoman Royal Women's Spaces: The Acoustic Dimension." *Journal of Women's History* 26/1, 89–111.

Evans, Sara Margaret. *Personal politics: The roots of women's liberation in the civil rights movement and the new left*. Vintage, 1980.

Evans, Richard J. *The feminists: women's emancipation movements in Europe, America and Australasia 1840–1920*. Routledge, 2012.

Fairchilds, Cissie C., *Women in early modern Europe, 1500–1700*. Vol. 3. Pearson Education, 2007.

Febvre, L. *The Problem of Unbelief in the Sixteenth Century*. Cambridge, MA, 1942.

Federici, Federico M. "A Servant of Two Masters: The Translator Michel Angelo Corai as a Tuscan Diplomat (1599–1609)." *Translators, Interpreters, and Cultural Negotiators*. Palgrave Macmillan, London, 2014. 81–104.

Ferrier, Ronald. "Women in Safavid Iran: the evidence of European travelers." in Gavin Hambly (ed.) *Women in the Medieval Islamic World*. Palgrave Macmillan, 1999. pp. 383–406.

Fichtner, Paula S. *The Habsburg Empire: From Dynasticism to Multinationalism*. Vol. 52. Krieger Publishing Company, 1997.

Findly, Ellison Banks. *Nur Jahan, Empress of Mughal India*. Oxford University Press on Demand, 1993.

Fischel, Walter J., "Jews and Judaism at the Court of the Moghul Emperors in Medieval India." *Proceedings of the American Academy for Jewish Research*, 18 (1948–1949), 137–177.

Fram, Edward. *My Dear Daughter: Rabbi Benjamin Slonik and the Education of Jewish Women in Sixteenth-Century Poland*. Vol. 33. ISD LLC, 2007.

Friedrich, Markus. "Government and Information-Management in Early Modern Europe: The Case of the Society of Jesus." *Journal of Early Modern History* 12 (2008): 539–563.

Franceschini, Chiara. "*Los Scholares son cosa de su excelentia, como lo es toda la Compania*: Eleonora di Toledo and the Jesuits." In Konrad Eisenbachler (ed.) *The Cultural World of Eleonora di Toledo: Duchess of Florence and Siena*. Routledge, 2004.

Freedman, Estelle. *No turning back: The history of feminism and the future of women*. Ballantine Books, 2007.

Freitag, Ulrike. And Achim von Oppen, "Introduction. 'Translocality': An Approach to Connection and Transfer in Area Studies" in idem, (eds), *Translocality: The Study of Globalising Processes from a Southern Perspective*. Leiden, Brill. 2010.

Galante, Abraham. *Esther Kyra, d'apres de nouveaux documents* (Contribution à l'Histoire des Juifs de Turquie). Constantinople, 1926.

Galanté, Abraham. *Médecins Juifs au Service de la Turquie*. Istanbul: Imprimerie Babok, 1938.

Garshowitz, Libby. "Gracia Mendes: Power, Influence and Intrigue." In *Power of the Weak: Studies on Medieval Women*. edited by Jennifer Carpenter and Sally Beth MacLean, 94–125. Urbana, 1995.

Ghereghlou, Kioumars. "Zaynab Begum," *Encyclopædia Iranica*, online edition, 2016..

Gholsorkhi, Shohreh. "Pari Khan Khanum: A Masterful Princess." *Iranian Studies* 28/3–4 (Summer–Autumn 1995), 143–156.

Ginzburg, Carlo. *The cheese and the worms: the cosmos of a sixteenth-century miller*. JHU Press, 1992.

Godden, Rumer, *Gulbadan: Portrait of a Rose Princess at the Mughal Court*, New York [The Viking Press], 1981.

Goldstone, Jack A., "Trends or Cycles?: The Economic History of East–West Contact in the Early Modern World." *Journal of the Economic and Social History of the Orient* XXXVI no. 2 (1993), pp. 104–19.

Gommans, Jos. "Continuity and change in the Indian Ocean basin." in Jerry H. Bentley, Sanjay Subrahmanyam, and Merry Wiesner-Hanks: *The Cambridge World History: Volume 6, The Construction of a Global World*: 1400–1800. Cambridge University Press, 2015.

Goodwin, Godfrey. *Islamic Architecture: Ottoman Turkey*. Scorpion Publications, 1977.

Greene, Molly. *A Shared World: Christians and Muslims in the Early Modern Mediterranean*, Princeton, 2000.

Griffi, Filena Patroni. "Documenti inediti sulle attività economiche degli Abravanel in Italia meridionale (1492–1543)." *La Rassegna mensile di Israel* 63.2 (1997): 27–38.

Grimau, Rodolfo Gil. "Sayyida al-Hurra, mujer marroquí de origen andalusí." *Anaquel de estudios árabes* 11 (2000): 311–20.

Grunbaum-Ballin, P. *Joseph Naci: Duc de Naxos*. Paris and The Hague, 1968.

De Guaras, Antonio. *The Accession of Queen Mary: Being the Contemporary Narrative of Antonio de Guaras, a Spanish Merchant Resident in London*. Lawrence and Bullen, 1892.

Gökbilgin, M. Tayyib. "Venedik Devlet Arşivindeki Vesikalar Külliyatında Kanuni Sultan Süleyman Devri Belgeleri." *Belgeler: Türk Tarih Belgeleri Dergisi* I (July 1964): 119–220.

Görgün-Baran, Aylin. "A woman leader in Ottoman history: Kösem Sultan (1589–1651)." *Women Leaders in Chaotic Environments*. Springer, Cham, 2016. 71–86.

Gürkan, Emrah Safa, *Espionage in the 16th Century Mediterranean: Secret Diplomacy, Mediterranean Go-betweens and the Ottoman Habsburg Rivalry*. Dissertation, Georgetown University, 2012.

Gürkan, Emrah Safa. "Mediating boundaries: Mediterranean go-betweens and cross-confessional diplomacy in Constantinople, 1560–1600." *Journal of Early Modern History* 19.2–3 (2015): 107–128.

Guy, John. '*My Heart is My Own': The Life of Mary Queen of Scots*. London: 4th Estate, 2009.

Halaçoğlu, Yusuf. *Osmanlılarda Ulaşım ve Haberleşme: Menziller*. Ankara: PTT Genel Müdürlüğü, 2002.

Hambly, Gavin R. G. (ed.), *Women in the Medieval Islamic World*. New York: Palgrave, 1998, pp. 349–82.

Hamill, Kelsey Anne. "Her mind has no womanly weakness": The Humanist Studies of Princess Elizabeth, 1538–1558. MS thesis. Graduate Studies, 2017.

Hansen, Kathryn. "The Viragnana in North Indian History: Myth and Popular Culture." *Economic and Political Weekly* 23/18 (April 30, 1988) 25–33.

Harrison, George Bagshawe. *The Letters of Queen Elizabeth I*. London: Cassell, 1935.

Havlioğlu, Didem. *Mihrî Hatun: Performance, Gender Bending, and Subversion in Ottoman Intellectual History*. Syracuse NY: Syracuse University Press, 2017.

Hellman, Clarisse Doris. *The comet of 1577: Its Place in the History of Astronomy*. Columbia University Press, 1944.

Herber, Courtney. "Katherine of Aragon: Diligent Diplomat and Learned Queen." *Tudor and Stuart Consorts: Power, Influence, and Dynasty*. Cham: Springer International Publishing, 2022. 41–58.

Hess, Andrew C. "The Moriscos: An Ottoman Fifth Column is the Sixteenth-Century Spain." *American Historical Review* LXXIV (October 1968): 1–25.

Heyd, Uriel. "Moses Hamon, Chief Jewish Physician to Sultan Süleymān the Magnificent." *Oriens* 16.1 (1963): 152–170.

Holmberg, Eva Johanna. "Jews of All Trades: Jews and their Professions in Early Modern English Travel Writing." *Journeys* 14/2 (2013), 27-49.

Hopkins, Lisa. *Women who would be Kings: Female Rulers of the Sixteenth Century.* New York: St. Martin's Press, 1991.

Howard, Henry. *A defensatiue against the poyson of supposed Prophesies.* Printed by J. Charlewood, 1583.

Iftikhar, Rukhsana. "Behind the Veil: An Analytical Study of Political Domination of Mughal Women." *Quarterly Research Journal of Islamic and Oriental* 87 (2012): 11-29

Isom-Verhaaren, Christine. *Allies with the Infidel: The Ottoman and French Alliance in the Sixteenth Century.* London: I. B. Tauris, 2011.

Işıksel, Güneş. "A letter of chahzade Selîm to Charles IX of France on the 'Nassi Affair'." *Cuadernos de Estudos Sefarditas* 7 (2007): 247–254.

Jahandideh, Mitra and Shahab Khaefi., "Women's Status During the Safavid Period." *Recent Researches in Social Science, Digital Convergence, Manufacturing and Tourism.*

Jackson, Peter, and Lawrence Lockhart, eds. *The Cambridge History of Iran.* Vol. 6. Cambridge University Press, 1986.

Jačov, Marco. "La Tragica fine della Regina Bona Sforza e della Sultana Roxelana." *Folia Historica Cracoviensia* 26.1 (2020): 41–55.

James, Catherine. "Bogus or Bona Fide: The Legitimacy of the Tudor Dynasty at the Accession of Henry VIII." *North Alabama Historical Review* 1.1 (2011): 3.

Karo, Yoseph., *Avkat Rochel.* Edited by Yeruham Fishel (Leipzig, 1859), 69–72.

Kapoor, R. C. "Abu'l Fazl, independent discoverer of the Great Comet of 1577." *Journal of Astronomical History and Heritage* 18 (2015): 249–260.

Karami, MH. "A Study of "She-Kings" in Nezami's View." *Journal of Poetry Studies* 2:2 (2010): 133–159.

Kayaalp, Pinar. *The Empress Nurbanu and Ottoman Politics in the Sixteenth Century: Building the Atik Valide.* Routledge, 2018.

Kienholz, Mary L., *Opium Traders and their Worlds, Volume One: A Revisionist Expose of the World's Greatest Opium Traders.* iUniverse, 2008.

Klooster, Wim. "Sephardic Migration and the Growth of European Long-Distance Trade." *Studia Rosenthaliana*, 35/2 (2001), 121–132.

Koenigsberger, H.G., George L. Mosse and G.Q. Bowler, *Europe in the Sixteenth Century.* Longman, 1968.

Köse, Metin Ziyaç, *Doğu Akdeniz'de Casuslar ve Tacirler: Osmanlı Devleti ve Ragusa İişkileri 1500–1600.* İstanbul: Giza Yayınları, 2000.

Kütükoğlu, Bekir. *Osmanlı- iran Siyâsî Münâsebetleri I: 78–1590.* İstanbul: İstanbul Edebiyat Fakültesi Matbaası, 1962.

Lal, Ruby. Empress: *The Astonishing Reign of Nur Jahan.* New York, Norton, 2018

Lal, Ruby. "Rethinking Mughal India: Challenge of a Princess' Memoir." *Economic and Political Weekly* 38/1 (Jan. 4–10 2003) pp. 53–65.

Lamdān, Rût. *A separate people: Jewish women in Palestine, Syria, and Egypt in the sixteenth century.* Vol. 26. Brill, 2000.

De Lamar, Jensen. "Catherine de Medici and her Florentine Friends." *The Sixteenth Century Journal* 9/2, (July 1978), 57–74.

Langdon, Gabrielle. *Medici Women: Portraits of Power, Love and Betrayal from the Court of duke Cosimo I*. University of Toronto Press, 2006.

Lebbady, Hasna. "Women in northern Morocco: between the documentary and the imaginary." *Alif: Journal of Comparative Poetics* 32 (2012): 127–152.

Leoni, Aron di Leone. "Manoel Lopez Bichacho, a XVIth century leader of the Portuguese Nation in Antwerp and in Pesaro." *Sefarad* 59.1 (2018): 77–100.

Leoni, Aron di Leone. "La diplomazia estense e l'immigrazione dei cristiani nuovi a Ferrara al tempo di Ercole II," *Nuova Rivista Storica* 78, 2 (1994) 294–326.

Le Strange, Guy, ed. *Don Juan of Persia: A Shi'ah Catholic 1560–1604*. Vol. 6. Routledge, 2013.

Levin, Carole. *The heart and stomach of a king: Elizabeth I and the politics of sex and power*. University of Pennsylvania Press, 2013.

Levin, Carole. *The Reign and Life of Queen Elizabeth I: Politics, Culture, and Society*. Springer Nature, 2022.

Levin, Carole, and Christine Stewart-Nuñez, eds. *Scholars and Poets Talk about Queens*. Springer, 2015.

Levy, Avigdor, ed. *Jews, Turks, and Ottomans: A Shared History, Fifteenth Through the Twentieth Century*. Syracuse University Press, 2002.

Loades, David. *Elizabeth I*. Hambledon and London, 2003.

Loureiro, Rui Manuel. "Turning Japanese? The Experiences and Writings of a Portuguese Jesuit in 16th Century Japan." In Dejanirah Couto and Francois Lachaud (eds.), *Empires Éloignés: L'Europe et le Japon (XVI-XIXe Siecles)*. Paris, École Française d'Extrême-Orient, 2000, 155–168.

Lushcheno, Marina. "The Correspondence of Ottoman Women during the Early Modern Period (16th-18th Centuries): Overview of the Current State of Research, Problems and Perspectives" in Fatma Türe and Birsen Talay Keşoğlu (eds.), *Women's Memory: The Problem of the Sources*, (Cambridge Scholars Publishing, 2011).

Maclagan, Edward. *The Jesuits and the Great Mogul*. Burns, Oates and Washbourne, 1932.

Madar, Heather. "Before the Odalisque: Renaissance Representations of Elite Ottoman Women." *Early Modern Women* (2011): 1–41.

Marmen, Cynthia. "Entre mentalités et traditions à la cour de France: le pouvoir politique de Catherine de Médicis vu par ses opposants au temps des Guerres de religion." (2018).

Martins, Paulo Nuno. "Medicine in Portugal in the Medieval Ages: A contribution to the history of science." *History of Medicine On-Line* (2017): 1–7.

Maryks, Robert Aleksander. *The Jesuit Order as a Synagogue of Jews: Jesuits of Jewish Ancestry and Purity-of-Blood Laws in the Early Society of Jesus*. Brill, 2010. *JSTOR*, .

Matar, Nabil. *Turks, Moors, and Englishmen in the age of discovery*. Columbia University Press, 1999.

Mathee, Rudi. "From the Battlefield to the harem: Did women's seclusion increase from early to late Safavid times?" in Colin P. Mitchell (ed.), *New Perspectives on Safavid Iran: Empire and Society*. New York, Routledge, 2011, pp. 97–120.

Mauro, Frédéric. "Merchant Communities, 1350–1750." in James D. Tracy (ed.), *The Rise of merchant empires: long-distance trade in the early modern world* 1350-1750. Cambridge University Press, 1990, pp. 255–86.

McCartney, Elizabeth. "In the Queen's Word: Perceptions of Regency Government Gleaned from the Correspondence of Catherine de Médicis" in Jane Couchman and Ann Crabb, *Women's Letters Across Europe, 1400–1700*. Ashgate, 2005.

McMahon, Keith. "Women Rulers in Imperial China." *Nan Nü* 15.2 (2013): 179–218.

Medvei, Victor Cornelius. "The illness and death of Mary Tudor." *Journal of the Royal Society of Medicine* 80.12 (1987): 766–770.

Mernissi, Fatima. *The forgotten queens of Islam*. University of Minnesota Press, 1997.

Merserve, Margaret. "The Sophy: News of Shah Ismail Safavi in Renaissance Europe." *Journal of Early Modern History*, 18 (2014), 579–608.

Michalewicz, Nathan. "Franco-Ottoman Diplomacy during the French Wars of Religion, 1559–1610". Diss. George Mason University, 2020.

Misra, Rekha. *Women in Mughal India, 1526–1748 AD*. Munshiram Manoharlal, 1967.

Mitchell, Colin P., ed. *New perspectives on Safavid Iran: empire and society*. Taylor & Francis, 2011.

Mitchell, Colin P. "Provincial chancelleries and local lines of authority in sixteenth-century Safavid Iran." *Oriente Moderno* 88.2 (2008): 483–507

Mukherjee, Soma. *Royal Mughal Ladies and their contributions*. Gyan Books, 2001.

Nichols, John Gough, ed. *The Chronicle of Queen Jane: And of Two Years of Queen Mary, and Especially of the Rebellion of Sir Thomas Wyat*. No. 48. Camden Society, 1801.

Norrie, Aidan, and Joseph Massey. *Tudor and Stuart Consorts: Power, Influence, and Dynasty*. Springer International Publishing, 2022.

Novoa, James W. Nelson. "Documents from the Secret Vatican Archives Regarding the History of the New Christians in the Low Countries (1536–1542)." *Hispania judaica bulletin* 6 (2008): 173–186.

Ogasawara, Hiroyuki. "Enter the Mongols: A Study of the Ottoman Historiography in the 15th and 16th Centuries." *Osmanlı Araştırmaları* 51.51 (2018): 1–28.

Özgen, Elif. "Grand Vizier Koca Sinan Paşa and factional politics in the court of Murad III." Diss. İstanbul Bilgi Üniversitesi, 2010.

Paiter, Marcella. "Toscani alla Corte di Maria dei Medici regina di Francia." *Archivio Storico Italiano* 98.3/4 (375/376) (1940): 83–108.

Palandri, Eletto. *Les Négotiations Politiques et Religieuses entre La Toscane et La France a l'époque de Cosme Premier et de Catherine de Médicis 1544–1580).* Paris: Imprimerie Jules de Meester à Roulers, 1908.

Pedani, Maria Pia. "Safiye's Household and Venetian Diplomacy." *Turcica* 32 (2000): 9–31.

Pedani-Fabris, Maria Pia. *I doumenti turchi dell-archivio di stato di Venezia, inventario della miscellanea,* Rome, Ministeri per i beni culturali e ambientali, 1994.

Pedani-Fabris, Maria Pia. "Veneziani a Costantinopoli alla fine del XVI secolo." *Quaderni di studi arabi,* supplement to vol. 5, 67–84.

Peirce, Leslie. *The Imperial Harem.* Oxford University Press, 1993.

Peirce, Leslie. *Empress of the East: How a European Slave Girl Became Queen of the Ottoman Empire.* New York: Basic Books, 2017.

Perrine, Serge. "Marie de Guise Reine des Ecossais." *Memoires de l'Academie Nationale de Metz,* 2016, 209–223.

Piterberg, Gabriel. *An Ottoman Tragedy: History and Historiography at Play.* University of California Press, 2003.

Phillips, Carla Rahn. "The growth and composition of trade in the Iberian empires, 1450–1750." *The rise of merchant empires: Long-distance trade in the early modern world* 1350-1750 (1990): 34–101.

Prange, Sebastian R. "'Measuring by the bushel': reweighing the Indian Ocean pepper trade." *Historical Research* 84.224 (2011): 212–235.

Pryor, Felix. *Elizabeth I: Her Life in Letters.* University of California Press, 2003.

Pullapilly, Cyriac K., "Missionary Tropics: The Catholic Frontier in India (16th-17th Centuries)." *The Catholic Historical Review,* 93/2 (2007), 407–408.

Ravid, Benjamin. "Money, Love and Power Politics in Sixteenth Century Venice: The Perpetual Banishment and Subsequent Pardon of Joseph Nasi." In *Italia Judaica, Atti del I Convegno internazionale, Bari, 18–22 maggio 1981.* Rome, 1983, 159–181.

Reznik, Jacob. *Le Duc Joseph de Naxos, contribution à l'histoire juive du XVIe siècle: thèse pour le doctorat d'Université présentée à la Faculté des lettres de l'Université de Paris par Jacob Reznik.* Lipschutz, 1936 (Short version published in Hebrew as Jacob Harozen, *Don Yosef Nasi* [Masada, 1960]).

Ricci, Giovanni. *Ossessione turca: in una retrovia Cristiana dell'Europa moderna.* Bologna, Il Mulino, 2002.

Richards, Judith M. *Elizabeth I.* Routledge, 2013.

Richards, Judith M. "'To promote a woman to beare rule': talking of queens in mid-Tudor England." *The Sixteenth Century Journal* (1997): 101–121.

Robin, Diana Maury, Anne R. Larsen, and Carole Levin. *Encyclopedia of Women in the Renaissance: Italy, France, and England.* ABC-CLIO, 2007.

Robin, Diana. *Publishing Women: Salons, the Presses, and the Counter-Reformation in Sixteenth-Century Italy.* University of Chicago Press, 2007.

Roth, Cecil, and Herman P. Salomon. *A History of the Marranos.* Philadelphia: Jewish Publication Society of America, 1932.

Roth, Cecil. *Doña Gracia of the House of Nasi*. Philadelphia, 1948.

Roth, Cecil. "Joseph Nasi, Duke of Naxos, and the Counts of Savoy." *The Jewish Quarterly Review* 57 (1967): 460–472.

Roth, Cecil, *The House of Nasi, The Duke of Naxos*. New York: Greenwood Press, 1948.

Roth, Cecil. *Dr. Solomon Ashkenazi and the Election to the Throne of Poland, 1574–5*. University Press, 1960.

Rothbard, Wojciech Szymon. "The cultural influence and artistic patronage of Queen Bona Sforza in early 16th century Poland-Lithuania." Dissertation. Central European University, 2010.

Rothman, E. Natalie. *Brokering Empire: Trans-Imperial Subjects between Venice and Istanbul*. Ithaca: Cornell University Press, 2012.

Rothman, E. Natalie. "Afterword: Intermediaries, Mediation, and Cross-Confessional Diplomacy in the Early Modern Mediterranean." *Journal of Early Modern History* 19.2–3 (2015): 245–259.

Sadlak, Erin A., "Epistolary Negotiations: Mary the French Queen and the Politics of Letter-Writing." *Sixteenth Century Journal* 41/3 (Fall 2010), 691–711.

Salomon, Herman Prins and Aron di Leone Leoni. "Mendes, Benveniste, De Luna, Micas, Nasci: The State of the Art (1532–1558)." *Jewish Quarterly Review* 88 (1998): 135–211.

Samson, Alexander. "Mary and Philip: The Marriage of Tudor England and Habsburg Spain." *Mary and Philip*. Manchester University Press, 2020.

Sanz, Amelia, Francesca Scott, and Suzan van Dijk, eds. *Women Telling Nations*. Vol. 1. Rodopi, 2014.

Saperstein, Marc. "Martyrs, Merchants and Rabbis: Jewish Communal Conflict as Reflected in the Responsa on the Boycott of Ancona," *Jewish Social Studies* 43 (1981): 215–228.

Schrieve, Hal. "Gulbadan and Nur Jahan: The Role of Women in the Creation of the Mughal Court and Imperial Policy." Seminary paper, University of Washington, 2015.

Schwartz, Laura. "Infidel feminism: Secularism, religion and women's emancipation, England 1830–1914." (2017).

Segre, Renata. "Sephardic Refugees in Ferrara: Two Notable Families." In *Crisis and Creativity in the Sephardic World, 1391–1648*, edited by Benjamin Gampel, 164–185. New York: 1997.

Seth, Mesrovb Jacob. *Armenians in India, from the Earliest Times to the Present Day: A Work of Original Research*. Asian Educational Services, 1983.

Sharma, Sunita. "The Exponential Role of the Women Protagonists in the Formative Years of Babur—Linkages Revisited." *Proceedings of the Indian History Congress*. Vol. 73. Indian History Congress, 2012.

Sher Banu A. L. Khan, *Sovereign Women in a Muslim Kingdom: The Sultanahs of Aceh, 1641–1699*, Ithaca: Southeast Asia Program Publications, an imprint of Cornell University Press, 2017.

Sicard, Frédérique. "Continuity and Identity at the Court of France: Parties around Queen Marie de Medici and Queen Anne of Austria." *Libros de la Corte 2* (2015), 95–111.
Singer, Amy. *Constructing Ottoman beneficence: An imperial soup kitchen in Jerusalem*. SUNY Press, 2012.
Skilliter, Susan A., "The Letters of the Venetian 'Sultana' Nur Banu and her Kira to Venice," in *Studia Turculogica Memoriae Alexii Bombaci Dicata*, eds. A. Gallotta and U. Marazzi (Naples, 1892), pp. 515–36.
Skilliter, Susan A., "Three letters from the Ottoman 'Sultana' Safiye to Queen Elizabeth I," in *Documents from Islamic Chanceries*, ed. S. M. Stern. Oxford, Bruno Cassirer, 1965, pp. 119–57.
Skilliter, Susan A. *Catherine de' Médicis Turkish Ladies-in-waiting; a Dilemma in Franco-Ottoman Diplomatic Relations*. 1975.
Sluhovsky, Moshe. "History as Voyeurism: From Marguerite de Valois to La Reine Margot." *Rethinking History* 4.2 (2000): 193–210.
Sola, Emilio. *Los que van y vienen: Información y fronteras en el Mediterráneo clasico del siglo XVI*. Alcalá de Henares: Universidad de Alcalá, 2005.
Spagni, Emilio. *Una sultana veneziana*. VC Federico, 1900.
Subrahamanian, Sanjay. (ed.) *Merchant Networks in the Early Modern World, 1450–1800*. London and New York: Routledge, 1996.
Subrahamanian, Sanjay. "Connected Histories: Notes toward a Reconfiguration of Early Modern Eurasia." *Modern Asian Studies* 31/3 (Jul. 1997), 735–762.
Subrahmanyam, Sanjay. *Three ways to be alien: travails and encounters in the early modern world*. UPNE, 2011.
Szuppe, Maria. "La participation des femmes de la famille royale à l'exercice du pouvoir en Iran safavide au XVIe siècle.(Première partie). L'importance politique et sociale de la parenté matrilinéaire." *Studia iranica (Paris)* 23.2 (1994): 211–25.
Szuppe, Maria. *Status,* "Knowledge, and Politics: Women in Sixteenth-Century Safavid Iran," in Lois Beck and Guity Nashat, eds. *Women in Iran from 1800 to the Islamic Republic*. University of Illinois Press, 2004.
Taylor, Larissa Juliet. *The Virgin Warrior: The Life and Death of Joan of Arc*. Yale University Press, 2009.
Tezcan, Baki. "The Debut of Kösem Sultan's Political Career." *Turcica* 40 (2008): 347–359.
Thomas, Joy. "The Indian Pepper and the German Copper in the Indo Portuguese Trade in the Sixteenth Century." *Proceedings of the Indian History Congress*. Vol. 42. Indian History Congress, 1981.
Tracy, James D., ed., *The Rise of Merchant Empires: Long-distance Trade in the Early Modern World, 1350–1750*. New York, Cambridge University Press, 1990.
Tracy, James D., ed., *The Political Economy of Merchant Empires: State Power and World Trade, 1350–1750*. New York, Cambridge University Press, 1991.

Unat, Faik Reşit. *Osmanlı Sefirleri ve Sefaretnameleri.* Ankara: Türk Tarih Kurumu Yayınları, 1968.

Valensi, Lucette. *The Birth of the Despot: Venice and the Sublime Porte.* Ithaca: Cornell University Press, 1993.

Van Gelder, Maartje, and Tijana Krstić. "Introduction: cross-confessional diplomacy and diplomatic intermediaries in the early modern Mediterranean." *Journal of Early Modern History* 19.2–3 (2015): 93–105.

Viaud, Aude. *Lettres des souverains portugais a Charles-Quint et a l'Imperatrice (1528–1532).* Lisbon and Paris, Centre Culturel Calouste Gulbenian, 1994.

Vella, Andrew P. *An Elizabethan–Ottoman Conspiracy.* Royal University of Malta, 1972.

Vives, Juan Luis, *The Education of a Christian Woman: A Sixteenth Century Manual* (University of Chicago Press, 2000).

Walker, Greg. "Rethinking the fall of Anne Boleyn." *The Historical Journal* 45.1 (2002): 1–29

Walthall, Anne, ed. *Servants of the Dynasty: Palace Women in World History.* Vol. 7. University of California Press, 2008.

Wellman, Kathleen. *Queens and Mistresses of Renaissance France.* Yale University Press, 2013.

Wheatcroft, Andrew. *The Enemy at the Gate: Habsburgs, Ottomans, and the Battle for Europe.* Basic Books, 2009.

Wilson, Katharina M., ed. *Women Writers of the Renaissance and Reformation.* University of Georgia Press, 1987.

Woodacre, Elena, ed. *A Companion to Global Queenship.* Amsterdam University Press, 2018.

Woodacre, Elena, et al., eds. *The Routledge History of Monarchy.* Routledge, 2019.

Wriedt, Markus. "Christian Networks in the Early Modern Period." *European History Online.*

Yermolenko, Galina. "Roxolana: 'The Greatest Empress of the East'." *The Muslim World* 95.2 (2005): 231–248.

Yermolenko, Galina I., ed. *Roxolana in European Literature, History and Culture.* Routledge, 2016.

Zaman, Taymiya R. "Instructive Memory: An Analysis of Auto/Biographical Writing in Early Mughal India." *Journal of the Economic and Social History of the Orient* 54.5 (2011): 677–700.

Zarinebaf-Shahr, Fariba. "Economic activities of Safavid women in the shrine-city of Ardabil." *Iranian Studies* 31.2 (1998): 247–261.

Zum Kolk, Caroline. "The household of the Queen of France in the Sixteenth Century." *The Court Historian* 14.1

Index[1]

A

Abbas "The Great" (shah), 122
Abenaish, Solomon (Ibn Yaish, Alvaro Mendes), 44, 202, 203, 240
Abrabanel, Benvenida, 8, 11, 135, 150–153, 161–164, 170, 171
Abrabanel, Samuel, 150, 151, 153, 162, 164
Abu'l-Fazl, 2, 76, 78, 79, 80n47, 82
Account of the Miracles performed by the Holy Eucharist (book by Henry Parker), 225
Adams, Simon, 242
Adrian VI (pope), 187
Affaitati, Gian Carlo, 141, 146
Affaitati family, 141
Afghanistan, 57, 58, 69, 98
Afonso (king of Portugal), 162
Africa, 4, 137, 170
Agincourt, battle of, 174
Agra, 2, 40, 65, 69, 70, 74–76, 80, 82, 84, 85, 87, 89, 90, 93, 197, 255
Ahmed I, 14, 47, 48
Aisan Daulat Begum, 83
Akbar, Jalal al-Din (emperor), 2, 4, 39, 69, 73–80, 80n50, 82–85, 88, 106, 107, 125, 255
Alamshah Begum (Martha, Halime), 98
Aleppo, 169
Alexander I (king of Georgia), 97
Alfonso d'Este (duke of Ferrara), 198
Algiers, 13, 168
Alhambra, 134
Amasya, Amasya treaty, 28, 108n42, 109, 120, 127, 261
Amber, 80
America, Americas, 84, 138, 167, 170, 198, 238, 240
Amiens, 210
Ancona, 31, 154, 157, 159–161
Anglican Church, 237, 259
Angola, 249
Angoulême, 177, 178, 211
Anne of Austria (wife of Louis XIII), 212, 264
Anne of Cleves, 222
Anne of France (Anne of Beujeu), 8, 104, 176–178, 183, 186, 212, 220, 256
Anne (queen of England), 248, 249
Antwerp, 30, 132, 136–138, 140–147, 149, 150, 155, 156, 170, 261
Aq Qoyunlu state, 97
Arthur (English prince), 214, 215, 219
Arundel, Earl of, 224
Ascham, Roger, 232

---

[1] Note: Page numbers followed by 'n' refer to notes.

© The Author(s), under exclusive license to Springer Nature Switzerland AG 2024
D. Ze'evi, *Queens Around the World, 1520–1620*,
https://doi.org/10.1007/978-3-031-58634-7

Ashkenazi, Solomon (physician, diplomat), 35, 36, 38, 44, 155, 168, 169, 201, 202
Askari, 66, 68, 69, 73, 74
Asaf Khan, 79, 87, 89–92
Athias, Yom Tov (Jeronimo Vargas), 153
Aurangzeb (emperor), 91–93
Aylmer, John, 32
Azerbaijan, 120, 122, 125n105

B

Babayan, Kathryn, 103, 128
Babington plot, 237
Babur, Zahir al-Din (emperor), 9, 57, 59–66, 66n22, 69, 73, 87, 178, 256
Baghdad, 13, 27, 50, 51, 101
Bagrationi, 97
Bahadur Khan (Sultan of Gujarat), 69, 76
Bahram (Safavid prince), 100, 102, 106, 108, 111
Bairam Khan, 75–78
Barton, Edward, 44, 170, 241
Baş kadın (chief consort), 15, 19
Bayezid (Ottoman prince), 28, 35
Bayonne, 184, 198, 199
Bayram Pasha, 51
Beatrice de Luna, *see* Gracia Mendes (Dona)
Beatrice la Chica (Reina), 141
Beatrice Michiel (Fatma Hatun), 20, 43, 169
Beg, Ali Quli, 84
Begum, Aisan Daulat, 9, 59–63, 178, 256
Begum, Alamshah (Martha, Halima), 98
Begum, Arjumand Banu, *see* Mahal, Mumtaz
Benveniste, Abraham, 136
Benveniste, Moses, 44
Besançon, 146
Bhakkari, Farid, 88
Bharmal, Raja, 80
Bible, 8, 153, 163, 191, 219, 220, 233, 234, 236
Bingham, Richard, 247, 248
Bir Narayan, 78
Birun, 15
Black eunuch, 15, 15n4, 16, 20, 48n97

Blanche of Castile, 177
Blois, 205, 211
Blue mosque (Sultan Ahmet Camii), 37
Boadicea (queen), 224
Boleyn, Anne, 10, 18n11, 132, 141, 190, 219–238, 253, 259
Boleyn, Thomas, 220
Bomberg, Daniel, 142, 144
Bona Sforza (queen of Poland), 10, 21, 22, 25, 133, 167, 181, 249, 261
Book of the City of Ladies, 7, 174–176
Bordeaux, 184
Börte, 58, 59
Bosphorus, 37, 156
Bounin, Gabriel, 31, 196
Bourbon, 176, 180
Bourke, Risdeárd (Richard), 247
Bragadin, Pietro, 17, 19
Braudel, Frenand, 230
Brianda de Luna (Reina), 136, 137, 140–143, 141n23, 141n26, 145, 149, 153, 156, 158
Brittany, 176
Brussels, 145, 146, 212
Budapest, 13
Burghley (lord), 246
Busbeck, Ogier Ghiselin de, 161
Byzantine empire, Byzantium, 14, 95, 97, 99, 254

C

Calais, 192, 199, 220, 228, 230
Calvin, John/Calvinism, 230, 231
Cambrai, 183, 184, 260
Canfeda Hatun, 42
Capsali, Elijah, 155
Castiglione, Balthazar, 8, 262
Catherine de Medici, 10, 12, 31, 32, 36, 38, 39, 68, 109, 133, 168, 185–206, 208, 210, 212, 220, 235, 239, 242, 250–253, 256, 257, 259–262
Catherine of Austria (queen of Portugal), 139, 142
Catholics, 6, 39, 109, 135–137, 142, 153, 170, 187, 191, 194, 196, 198–201, 204, 205, 207, 219, 224, 225, 227–228, 230, 232, 233,

235–237, 240, 242–245, 253, 254, 259
Cecilia Venier-Baffo, *see* Nurbanu Sultan
Chagatai kingdom, 58, 60
Chaldiran (Battle), 26, 100
Charles IV of France, 173, 173n2
Charles IX of France, 195, 197–203
Charles V, Habsburg emperor (King Carlos of Spain), 12, 21, 36, 137, 140, 141n23, 142, 143, 146, 147, 147n50, 150, 155, 158, 160, 161, 163, 164, 167, 177, 179, 180, 183, 184, 186, 187, 190, 192n39, 215, 216, 219, 221, 226, 227, 242, 260
Charles VIII of France, 176
Charles, Duke of Luynes, 211
Charles de Bourbon, 180, 181, 183
Charles Habsburg (archduke), 220
Charles of Angoulême, 177
Chenonceau palace, 190, 199
China, 4, 58, 262
Chishti, Shaikh Salim, 80
Christina of Denmark, 142, 146
Cihangir (Ottoman prince), 20, 31
City of Ladies (The, book), 103, 176
Claude (queen, wife of Francis I), 180, 185, 220
Clement VII (pope), 139, 140, 163, 183, 186–189, 219, 221
Columbus, Christopher, 4, 12, 133, 134, 214
Comet (c/1577 v. 1), 1–12, 84, 116, 237, 249
Compiègne, Chateau de, 211
Concino Concini (Marquis d'Ancre), 210
Connacht Province, 246, 247
Consolation for the Tribulations of Israel (book), 152, 162
Constantinople, 14, 43, 59, 95, 99, 100, 132, 153n70, 166, 252
    See also Istanbul
Contarini, Cecilia (dogaressa), 148, 192
Contarini, Simon, 48
Cosimo de Medici (duke), 20, 143, 152, 164, 190, 198, 203
Cranmer, Thomas (Archbishop of Canterbury), 221, 227
Crete, 38
Crimea, 14n2, 17, 52, 120

Cromwell, Thomas, 131, 132, 141, 219, 221
Cum Nimis Absurdum (papal edict), 159
Crypto-Jews, *see* Marranos
Cyprus, 38, 161

D

Dandolo, Matteo, 148n55, 186
Dandolo, Zilia (Dogaressa), 148
Dara Shukoh (Mughal prince), 91–93
Darnley (Lord), 243, 244
Dausburg (cardinal), 147
Dayan Khan, 58
de Coligny, Gaspar, 200
De Luna, Alvaro, 136
de Paz, Duarte, 139
de Pizan, Christine, 7, 103, 174, 176, 177
de Sande, Alvaro, 195
Delhi, 65, 69–71, 74, 75, 78, 250
Della Rovere family, 187, 188
Della Valle, Pietro, 124
D'entragues, Henriette, 206
Derschwam, Hans, 157
Despina Khatun (Theodora), 96–98
Devşirme, 157
Diane de Poitiers, 146, 185–190, 192, 199, 253
Dianora Dori, *see* Leonora Galigai (Dianora Dori)
Dil Dar Begum, 72
Din-i Ilahi, 4
Dona Gracia, *see* Gracia Mendes (Dona)
Dónal O'Flaherty, 246, 247
Donato, Francesco (doge of Venice), 148, 153
Don Carlos (prince, son of Philip II), 195, 196
Don Juan of Persia, 99, 119n82, 122n91, 133
Drake, Francis, 238, 239
Dudley, John (duke of Northumberland), 223, 224
Dudley, Robert (Earl of Leicester), 235, 243
Duke of Belle Garde, 206
Dumas, Alexandre, 201
Durgavati (Rani, Queen), 78–79, 249

Dutch, *see* Netherlands
Dyalogue Defensyve for Women, against Malycyous Detractours (book), 218

E
Edict of Nantes, 209
Edirne Gate, 32, 155
Edward III of England, 173, 213
Edward VI of England, 232
Eleanor Habsburg (wife of Francis I), 184
Eleonora di Toledo, 150, 152, 162–164, 170
Elizabeth I of England, 1, 2, 10, 32, 44, 45, 75, 82, 92, 116, 124, 169, 191, 199, 201, 204, 207, 214, 220–224, 226–228, 230–248, 250, 253, 254, 256, 257, 259–261, 263
Elizabeth of Austria, 200
Elizabeth of Valois (queen of Spain, wife of Philip II), 192
Emmanuel-Philibert (duke of Savoy), 198
Enderun, 15
Enriques, Agostino, 158
Eóghan Ó Máille, 246
Ercole II d'Este (duke of Ferrara), 142, 146, 149–152, 164
Eric XIV of Sweden, 235
Exile, 6, 10, 69, 76, 84, 132, 135, 152, 163, 212, 257

F
Fakhri of Herat, 8, 84, 102, 103
Farnese, Alessandro, *see* Paul III (pope)
Fatehpur Sikri, 76–78, 80, 84
Ferdinand I, duke of Tuscany, 21, 124
Ferdinand Habsburg, 192, 192n39
Ferdinando de Medici, 206
Ferdinand of Aragon, 12, 12n25
Fergana Valley, 59, 62
Ferrara, 30, 44, 136, 136n7, 141n25, 142, 146, 149–155, 158, 162n93, 164, 170, 198, 261
Fetva, fatwa, 50, 54
Field of the Cloth of Gold (*Camp du Drap d'Or*), 180, 182, 216

Finch, William, 82
First Blast of the Trumpet (Book by John Knox), 32
Flanders, *see* Netherlands
Florence, 30, 124, 132, 143, 164, 170, 187, 188, 190, 203, 206, 212
France, 6, 6n11, 8–10, 12, 21, 32, 36, 38, 39, 44, 55, 104, 133, 135, 145, 146, 148n55, 150, 152, 156, 161, 168, 170, 173–213, 215, 216, 220, 223, 226–228, 230, 235, 237, 239, 242, 242n74, 244–247, 250, 252–254, 256, 257, 259–261, 263
Francesco de Medici, 206
Francis I of France, 10, 21, 23, 177–181, 183–190, 203, 216, 220, 226, 259
Francis II of France, 194–197, 242, 253
Francis (crown prince of France, son of Francis I), 186
Francis Hercule (French prince), 201, 201n60, 205, 235
Francisco of Aragon (don), 143, 145
Frangipani, Jean, 21n23, 181, 183
Fryer, Dr. John, 129, 129n115
Fugger family, 139, 146

G
Galata, 20, 155, 156, 168
Galigai, Leonora, 206
Gazanfer Ağa, 43
Genghis Khan, 11, 14, 14n2, 57–59, 61, 96, 102
Georgia, 97, 99, 122
Geraldini, Alessandro, 214
Ghamsar, 125
Ghetto, 148, 159
Ghiyas, *see* I'timad ud-Daula
Gholam, 124
Gibraltar, 134
Ginzburg, Carlo, 5n10, 253
Giray, Adil, 120, 122, 122n91
Gomes, Tomaso, 154
Gomez, Duarte, 158
Gondwana, 78, 79, 249
Gracia Mendes (Dona), 4, 8, 30–32, 34, 135–161, 153n70, 156n78, 164, 167, 170, 171, 194, 239, 261, 263
Granada, 6, 12, 132, 134, 214

Grey, Jane, 223, 224, 226, 235, 259
Guise family, 195, 196, 200, 204
Gulbadan Begum, 39, 64, 65, 67–80, 82–84, 93, 106, 205
Gunpowder empires, 5–6, 95

H
Habsburg empire, family, 10, 12, 133, 146, 179, 192, 226, 254, 260
Hafsa (mother of Sultan Suleiman), 17, 22, 24, 36, 40, 166
Hagia Sophia (*Aya Sofya*), 25, 40
Halima, *see* Alamshah Begum (Martha, Halime)
Halime Sultan, 48
Hamida Banu Begum, 69–80, 105–108, 255, 260
Hamon, Moshe, 149, 153, 156, 157, 160, 167
Handali, Esther, 11, 20, 43, 135, 149, 156–158, 156n78, 165–170, 257
Handan Sultan, 46
Haqiqi (pen name of Parikhan Khanum), 110
Harborne, WIlliam, 44, 240, 241
Harem, vii, 14–20, 23, 26, 27, 30, 31, 33–37, 40, 42, 46–48, 51, 52, 54, 62, 64, 70, 76–78, 80, 85, 92, 100, 110, 112, 115, 122–124, 126–129, 129n114, 157, 158, 165, 165n106, 166, 168, 169, 214, 240, 252, 253, 255, 257, 258, 265
Harkha Bai, Mariam uz-Zamani, 80–85, 92, 255
Haseki sultan, 15, 19
Hatfield House, 221, 222, 224, 231
Haydar (Safavid prince), 84, 98, 112–114, 114n67, 118
Henrietta Maria (daughter of Marie de Medici), 212
Henry II of Bourbon, Prince of Condé, 210
Henry II of France, 145, 146, 190, 239, 242
Henry III of France, (Henry of Poland, de Valois), 36, 246
Henry IV of Castile, 132

Henry IV of France (Henry of Navarre), 250
Henry VII of England, 176, 214, 215
Henry VIII of England (Tudor), 10, 133, 140, 141, 168, 180, 182, 190, 215, 217, 218, 220, 227, 232–234, 236, 242
Henry Howard, 2
Herat, 73, 84, 100, 119, 123
Hindal, 66, 68–74, 70n30, 107
Hinduism, 80
Hindustan, 4, 5, 9, 11, 12, 30, 44, 57–93, 105, 107, 108, 133, 137–139, 142, 147, 149, 158, 164, 238, 250, 260, 262
Hochstetter family, 138
Hö'elun, 58, 59
Howard, Catherine, 2, 222
Huguenots, 194–196, 194n44, 198–204, 210, 245
Humayun (emperor), 9, 65–74, 70n30, 76, 77, 105–108, 108n40, 197, 260
Humayun-nama, 64, 65, 67, 70
Hundred Years' War, 173, 173n3, 176, 214, 230
Hungary, 10, 21, 25, 33, 149, 157, 158, 166, 167, 181, 249
Huri Khan Khanum, 122
al-Hurra, Al-Sayyida, 10, 249
Hurrem Sultan (Roxelana, Anastasia Lisowska), vii, 10, 17–32, 51, 104, 109, 149, 155, 157, 158, 166, 181, 197, 252, 261, 262
Husayn, Shah Sultan (last Safavid shah), 129
Hussey, John, 141

I
Ibrahim (Sultan), 22, 23, 23n29, 27, 52–54, 104
Ibrahim Lodi, 69
Ibrahim Pasha (grand vizier), 23, 25
Ilkhanid state, 102
Imam Quli, 89
India, *see* Hindustan
Inquisition, 134, 135, 135n6, 137, 139, 140, 142, 150, 154, 214, 253

Instruction of a Christian woman (book, *De Institutione Feminae Christinae*), 217
Iran, 11, 26, 26n38, 28, 31, 37, 39, 64, 68, 69, 74, 76, 77, 83, 84, 95
Isabella d'Este, 150
Isabella Jagiellon, 25, 158, 167, 249
Isabella of Castile, 12, 132, 214, 214n2
Isfahan, 103, 106, 125–127
Ismail I (shah), 98
Ismihan Sultan (Ottoman princess), 39, 42, 201
Istanbul, 2, 2n7, 15, 18–21, 21n23, 24n31, 26, 28, 30, 32, 32n52, 36, 36n65, 39, 39n77, 42–44, 46, 47, 50–53, 108, 108n42, 112, 136, 148, 149, 153–158, 161, 166, 168, 170, 181, 183, 195, 197, 202, 203, 214, 240, 257, 260
I'timad ud-Daula, 84, 85, 87, 89

J
Jaberi, Salman, 113, 115
Jahanara (Jahan Ara), 92–93
Jahangir, Salim(emperor), 9, 80–92, 82n53
James I of England (James VI of Scotland), 208, 243
James IV of Scotland, 215
James V of Scotland, 194, 223, 242
Janissary, Janissaries, 18, 26, 49, 100
Jawahir al-'Ajāib (book by Fakhri of Herat), 84
Jeanne d'Albret, 199, 220
Jehanne Medici, 211
Jenkinson (English merchant), 238, 239
Jesuits (Society of Jesus), 134, 210, 245, 255, 262
Jewels of Wonder (*book*), 8, 102
Jews (Jewish, Judaism), 4, 11n24, 12n25, 30, 31, 131–171, 214, 231, 257, 261, 262
Jharokha (viewing balcony), 88
Jizya (poll tax), 125
Joan of Arc, 175–177, 175n6
Joanna "the Mad," 12
Joanna of Austria, 206
João III (king of Portugal), 137, 139

João MIques, *see* Joseph Nasi (Don, Joao Miques)
John IV (king of Trebizond), 96
Joseph Nasi (Don, Joao Miques), 30, 34, 35, 38, 44, 141, 153n70, 154, 158, 161, 194, 202
Judaizing, 131n1, 140, 142, 145, 149, 216, 252
Jülich succession, 207

K
Kabul, 62, 70, 73–76
Kalé Kartanou, *see* Nurbanu Sultan
Kalfa, 15
Kamran, 66, 68–70, 73, 74, 107
Kandahar, 69, 73, 74, 84, 108
Kashan, 121, 125
Katherine of Aragon (Catalina), 8, 10, 12, 18n11, 133, 141, 168, 190, 214–220, 256, 259
Kennedy, Paul, 263
Khan, Adham, 78
Khan, Afshar, 110, 119
Khan, Ali Qoli, 123, 124
Khanzada Begum, 9, 59, 63–69, 256
Khayr al-Nisa' Begum, *see* Mahd-i Ulya
Khodabanda Mohammad (shah), 84, 115n68, 117–124, 119n80, 119n82
Khorasan, 100, 122
Khurram (*Mughal prince*), *see Shah Jahan*
Khusrau (Mughal prince), 82, 85
Kira, 20, 20n19, 23, 26, 32, 38, 42–45, 149, 156, 165–170, 240, 263
Knox, John, 32, 230, 231
Köprülü Mehmed Pasha, 55, 264
Kösem Sultan, 10, 37, 47–56, 92, 127, 206, 211, 212, 251, 257
Krakow, Cracow, 21, 36, 181, 202
Kul (*kapı kulları*), 15
Külliye (Mosque complex), 24, 25, 38
Kütahya, 33
Kyiv, 58

L
Ladli (Nur Jahan's daughter), 85, 87, 90
Lahore, 73, 76, 83, 84, 87, 91
Lal, Ruby, 70, 76, 84n57

La Rochelle, 201
La Soltane (play), 31, 196
Learned and Subtle Discourse (*book*), 205
Le Havre, 199
Leo X (Pope, Giovanni de Medici), 178, 187
Leonora Galigai (Dianora Dori), 210, 211
Les Misérables, 210
Leuven, 141, 144
Lisbon, 30, 132, 136–140, 142, 143, 145, 155, 156
Lisowska, Anastasia, *see* Sultan, Hurrem
Lombardy, 10, 21, 178, 180
Lopez, Rodrigo, 44, 240
Lorenzo de Medici, 187
Louis IX "Saint Louis" of France, 177
Louis XI of France, 176
Louis XII of France, 150, 177
Louis XIII of France, 207, 210–212
Louis XIV of France, 103, 212
Louise of Savoy, vii, 10, 21, 21n23, 23, 173, 177–184, 186, 190, 197, 212, 254, 256, 259–261
Low Countries, *see* Netherlands
Loyola, Ignazio, 134, 262
Ludlow Castle, 224
Lusitanus, Amatus (Haviv Ha-Sephardi), 141, 150
Lutfallah Shirazi Mirza, 124
Lyon, 145, 146, 150, 152, 164, 198, 207, 261

M

Machiavelli, Niccolo, 23
Madeleine de la Tour d'Auvergne, 187
Madrid, 183, 184, 188, 214
Magellan, Ferdinand, 4, 238
Mahabat Khan, 91–92
Mahal, Mumtaz, 92
Maham Anaga, 91
Maham Begum, 65
Mahd-i Ulya, 118
Mahd-I Ulya Begum, 10
Mahidevran, 17, 18, 23
Mahin Banu, *see* Shahzada Sultanum
Maitland, William, 243
Makhfi (pen name of Nur Jahan), 84

Malchi, Esperanza, 11, 43–45, 135, 165–170, 240, 257
Maluku Islands, 238
Malvezzi, Giovanni, 167
Mamluks, Mamluk sultanate, 59
Mandukhai (*queen of North Yuan*), 11, 12, 58–60
Manduul Khan, 58
Manisa, 17, 24, 34–36, 38, 41
Manuel I (king of Portugal), 139
Marash, 118
Margaret (Margot, queen, wife of Henry IV), 184, 194, 205
Margaret of Austria, 10, 177, 183, 185, 220, 260
Margaret of Beaufort, 225
Margaret (Sister of Francis I), 137, 177, 181, 183, 186, 188, 196, 199, 200, 203, 220, 223, 260
Mariam Makani, *see* Hamida Banu Begum
Mariam uz-Zamani, *see* Harkha Bai, Mariam uz-Zamani
Marie de Medici, 10, 12, 205–212, 251, 253, 257, 263
Marignano, Battle of, 180
Marranos, 11, 11n24, 12, 31, 44, 131, 131n1, 134, 135, 137, 140–143, 148, 150, 156, 160, 167, 194, 202, 241, 261, 262, 262n6
Marseilles, 188, 207
Martha, *see* Alamshah Begum (Martha, Halime)
Mary (queen, wife of William III of England), 248
Mary I of England, 32, 133, 214, 222–228, 231, 256, 259
Mary of Hungary, 10, 30, 142, 147n50
Mary Queen of Scots (Mary Stewart), 204, 214, 236, 237n58, 242–246, 253, 259
Mary Wollstonecraft, 9
Matilda (Maude, Queen), 224
Matthee, Rudi, 129, 129n114
Mawsillu (tribe), 100
Maximillian II (prince, emperor), 144, 145, 158
Mazandaran, 118, 121
Mazarin (cardinal), 212, 264

Mecca, 13, 25, 39, 78, 81, 93
Mehmed IV, 54
Mehmet II "The Conqueror," 14
Mehmet III, 14
Membre, Michel, 102, 105
Mendes, Alvaro, *see* Abenaish, Solomon
Mendes, Diogo (Meir), 137–143, 147n51, 149, 150
Mendes-Benveniste, Francisco, 137
Menocchio, 5n10, 253
Mihrimah complex, 28, 32, 37, 55
Mihrimah (princess), 19, 25, 26, 28, 31–33, 32n53, 35, 37, 39, 55, 110, 156, 158, 161, 166, 168, 194, 195
Mihr un-Nisa, *see* Nur Jahan
Milan, 30, 146, 180, 183
Mildenhall, John, 82
Miques, Agostinho, 136
Miques, Bernardo, 141
Miques, Joao, 30, 136, 144, 153n70, 154, 194
Mirza Khan, 120, 121, 124
Mirza, Alqas (Safavid prince), 27, 100, 107, 108, 108n42, 110n52, 113, 116, 263
Missionaries, 134, 255, 262
Moffan, Nicholas, 239
Mohács (battle of), 21
Mohammad Khodabanda, *see* Khodabanda Mohammad (shah)
Molcho, Shlomo (Diogo Pires), 163
Moldavia/Moldavians, 26, 97, 157, 167
Mongol empire/Mongols, 11, 14, 14n2, 57–59, 61, 64, 67–69, 83, 103, 255, 258, 264
Monluc (French envoy), 36, 202
Montmorency, 191
More, Thomas, 8, 182, 218, 220, 262
Morocco, 10, 134, 170, 249, 254
Morosini (Venetian ambassador), 42
Mosso, Jacob, 160
Mughal empire (Mughals), 9, 39, 51, 57, 59, 64, 69, 90, 92, 106, 108, 252, 256, 257, 263
Muhibbi, *see* Suleiman, Suleyman "The Magnificent" (sultan)
Mumtaz Mahal, 9, 87, 90, 92–93, 254, 263

Murad III, 2, 14, 36, 37, 41, 169, 202, 240, 255
Murad IV, 14, 50, 127
Murphey, Rhoads, 262
Murshid Qoli Khan Ustajlu, 123
Mustafa Ali (Ottoman author), 41
Mustafa (Ottoman prince), 18, 30, 31, 156, 196, 239
Mustafa (Sultan), 16n5, 17, 48–50, 52, 53, 128
Mystic feast, 67–69, 197
Mytilene (Lesbos), 44, 203

N

Naples, Napoli, 30, 143, 150, 160, 162, 164, 170, 183, 192n39, 226
Navagero, Bernardo, 18, 31
Naxos, 34, 38, 141, 161
Necipoğlu, Gülrü, 103
Netherlands, 5, 8, 10, 30, 93, 134, 140–143, 145, 146, 147n50, 152, 153, 167, 183, 187, 191, 192n39, 199, 201–205, 220, 230, 235, 240, 245, 249
Normandy, 210
Nostradamus, 192, 198, 199, 204
Nurbanu Sultan, 2, 34, 112, 197, 251, 255, 260, 261
Nur Jahan, 4, 9, 62, 78, 84–92, 206, 250–252, 254, 256, 257, 259, 260, 263
Nzinga (queen of Ndongo and Matamba), 249

O

Odalisque (odalık), 15, 23, 253
Oirats, 59
Old Valide mosque (Atik valide camii), 37
Olympe de Gouges, 9
O'Malley, Grace (*Gráinne Ní Máille*), 10, 214, 246–248
Opalinski, Piotr, 22
Orghina Khatun, 58
Orléans, 175, 176
Osman Ghazi, 13
Osman (Sultan), 36, 46–50

Ottoman empire (Ottomans), 10, 12–56, 92, 99, 104, 134, 135, 138, 143, 143n36, 148, 157, 170, 181, 194, 202, 210–212, 239, 241, 252, 255–257, 262, 263

P
Palos de la Frontera, 134
Parikhan Khanum (Pari Khan), 1, 1n2, 10, 39, 84, 95, 110–119, 128, 129, 256
Paris, 36, 147n50, 158, 174, 181, 183, 184, 191, 204, 205, 208, 210, 211, 217
Parker, Henry (Lord Morley), 225
Parr, Catherine, 222, 223, 232
Passi, David, 44
Pasternak, Boris, 164
Patriarchy (Patriarchal), 7, 242
Paul III (pope), 140, 144, 221
Paul IV (pope), 31, 159–161
Pavia, Battle of, 180, 187
Peace of the Ladies, *see* Treaty of Cambrai
Pedro de Toledo (Don, viceroy of Naples), 150, 162
Peirce, Leslie, 15n3
Pelsaert, Francisco, 89
Pepper trade, 140
Percy, Henry (son of Northumberland), 131, 132, 220
Perspective of the World (book), 230
Pétremol (French ambassador), 197
Philip II (king of Spain), 44, 132n3, 191, 192, 192n39, 195, 198, 210, 232, 235, 247
Philter Montalto, 210
Pisa, 143
Pius V (pope), 236, 239, 244
Piyale Pasha, 195
Plague, 2, 50
Poland, Polish-Lithuanian Commonwealth, 201, 202
Portugal, 4, 6, 12, 44, 82, 135–140, 135n6, 142, 143, 145, 147, 150, 152, 160, 162, 164
Preveza, Battle of, 149
Priuli, Lorenzo (doge of Venice), 148

Prospero, Bartolomeo, 150, 151
Protestants, 6, 32, 44, 109, 170, 187, 191, 194, 198–205, 209, 226–228, 231, 232, 235, 240–242, 245, 254, 259

Q
Qahqaha castle, 112, 113, 115
Qazvin, 1, 111, 115–121, 123, 126–128, 238
Qizilbash, 98–100, 103, 108, 112, 114, 116, 120, 122–125, 125n102
Qom, 102
Quruq, 129, 129n114
Qutlugh Nigar Khanum, 59

R
Rabbi, 155, 160, 166
Ragusa (Dubrovnik), 44, 154
Rareş, Petru, 26
Recep Pasha, 51
Reconquista, 12, 134
Renaissance, 6, 8, 21, 150, 171, 188, 214, 216, 256, 261
Reuveni, David, 163
Richelieu (cardinal), 211, 212
Ridolfi Plot, 237, 245
Roe, Thomas, 88
Rohatyn (town in Ukraine), 17
Rome, 44, 139, 143, 148n55, 155, 159, 183, 187, 188, 219, 221, 227, 236, 262
Roth, Cecil, 138
Roxelana, Roxolana, *see* Hurrem Sultan (Roxelana, Anastasia Lisowska)
Rustem Pasha, 25, 28, 32, 108, 156, 161, 166, 167, 194, 196
Rycaut, Paul, 50–52

S
Safavid (empire), 1, 2, 6, 8, 11–13, 23, 26–28, 26n39, 39, 49–51, 55, 57, 62, 64, 69, 73–75, 84, 89, 95, 100, 104, 106, 110, 121, 155, 252, 254, 256, 263
Safed (Safad), 4

Safi (shah), 127, 128
Safiye Sultan, 2, 44, 168, 169, 241, 261
St. Bartholomew massacre, 200, 201, 204, 245
Salic Law, 173, 173n3, 176, 177, 184, 213, 214
Salim (Mughal prince), *see* Jahangir, Salim(emperor)
Salima (Jahangir's wet nurse), 82
Saljuq-Shah Begum, 102
Salon (town in France), 198, 205
Salonica (Thessaloniki), 44, 154, 155
Salviati, 152, 195
Samarkand, 59, 62, 64
Sam Mirza, *see* Safi (shah)
Saruhan, 40
Savoy, 177, 210
Scotland, 10, 12, 194, 196, 213, 215, 219, 223, 225, 228, 236, 242–244, 246, 253
Sejm (Polish Assembly), 202
Selim I "The Grim," 17, 100
Selim II, 14, 39, 40, 202, 255
Şeyhülislam, Chief mufti, 54
Seymour, Edward, 223
Seymour, Jane, 221, 222, 253
Seymour, Thomas, 232
Sforza family, 146
Shah Jahan, 83, 86, 87
Shah Jahan (emperor), 9, 51, 83, 85, 86, 90–93, 250
Shah Jahan Nama, 91
Shah Safi, *see* Safi (shah)
Shahzada Sultanum, 10n23, 100, 102–110, 125n106, 260
Shalimar Bagh, 87
Shaybani Khan, 64
Shaykh Haydar, 98
Shaykh Safi al-Din, 98
Shazada Sultan, 28, 64
Sher Shah Suri, 69, 70, 74
Shia (Shi'a), 6, 73, 74, 77, 98, 98n6, 99, 104, 110
Shiraz, 102, 113, 117–119
Shuja' (Safavid prince), 27, 100, 107, 108, 110n52, 113, 116, 117, 119, 263
Sicily, 160, 162, 192n39
Sigismund Augustus of Poland, 201
Sigismund of Poland, 10, 21, 181
Sikandra, 89
Sipahis, 166
Sokollu Mehmed Pasha, 33, 36, 38
Spain, 6, 10, 12, 12n25, 21, 39, 43, 44, 51, 99, 132n3, 133–137, 140, 143, 150, 162–164, 166–168, 179–181, 186, 191, 192, 192n39, 194, 195, 197, 198, 202, 209, 211, 213–215, 225–228, 232, 234, 237–241, 245, 247, 253–255
Spanish Armada, 42, 169, 241
Srinagar, 87
Strongilla, Stranhilla (Fatma Hanım, *kira*), 165, 166
Suleiman, Suleyman "The Magnificent" (sultan), vii, 10, 14, 16n5, 17–28, 31–37, 54, 55, 108, 109n45, 110, 143, 149, 153, 153n70, 155–158, 160, 161, 166, 167, 181–183, 194, 196, 239, 254
Sultan, Aşub, 55
Sultan, Hurrem, 17
Sultan's mother, *see* Valide/Valide sultan
Sultanum Begum (Mughal princess), 68, 119n80
Sunna, 99
Szigetvar (Fortress, siege), 33
Szuppe, Maria, 101, 119n80, 119n81, 129

T

Tabriz, 26, 27, 97, 99, 100, 122
Tahmasp, Tahmasb (Shah), 1, 10, 27, 28, 39, 64, 73, 74, 84, 100–102, 104, 104n31, 106–115, 109n45, 119, 119n80, 122–124, 128, 156, 239, 252, 254, 260
Taj Mahal, 90, 92
Tajlu Khanum, 64, 73, 99–128, 253, 256
Takiyuddin (Taqi ad-Dīn), 2
Tamerlane, *see* Timurlenk
Tatars, Tatar Khan, 17
Temüjin, *see* Genghis Khan
Theodora, *see* Despina Khatun (Theodora)
Tiberias, 161
Timar, 166

INDEX   293

Timur Lenk, 59n6
Timurid empire (Timurids), 11, 59, 61, 65, 68, 69, 102, 103, 255
Timurlenk, 59n6, 96, 96n3
Tinos (Aegean island), 47
Titian, Tizian, 18, 19
Topkapı palace, 17, 20, 32, 34, 36, 103, 156, 157, 165
Töregene, 58, 59
Torgut (corsair and Ottoman admiral), 195
Torquemada, 134
Transylvania, 10, 25, 26, 157, 167, 181, 249
Treaty of Cambrai, 184, 185, 260
Treaty of Cateau-Cambrésis, 191
Treaty of Etaples, 176
Treaty of Madrid, 183, 188
Treaty of Saint-Germain-en-laye, 199
Treaty of the More, 182
Trebizond, Trabzon, 95–97
Tunis, 195, 202
Turan, 89
Turhan Sultan, 130, 264
Turkey Company, 239
Tuscany, Toscana, 124, 143, 152, 157, 158, 162, 164, 187, 190, 206
Twyne, Thomas, 1, 2, 237

U
Ukraine/Ukrainian/Ruthenia, 17, 17n8, 27, 55
Umar Shaikh Mirza, 59, 60
Üsküdar, 37
Usque, Abraham (Duarte Pinel), 153
Usque, Samuel, 152
Uzbekistan/Uzbeks, 58, 64, 68, 69, 73, 78, 120, 122, 125n104
Uzun Hasan, 96–98, 96n3

V
Valencia, 137, 217
Valide/Valide sultan, 15, 16, 16n5, 24, 31, 35–38, 40, 42–48, 51, 55, 56, 65, 130, 166, 168, 169, 256
Vanier, Cristoforo, 48
Vasco da Gama, 4, 137
Vaughan, Robert, 218
Venice Company, 239
Venice/Venetians, 17–19, 20n20, 23, 30, 31, 34, 38, 38n72, 38n73, 42–44, 43n85, 48, 53, 55, 97, 102, 136–138, 141n24, 142, 143, 145–150, 152–162, 153n70, 165, 166, 168–170, 186, 192, 199, 239, 255, 261
Versailles, 103
Vives, Juan Louis, 8, 216–218, 220, 262

W
Wales, 215, 224, 246n89
Wallachia, 202
War of Mother and Son, 211
Weber, Max, 256
Welser family, 138
William III of England, 248
Winchester Cathedral, 226
Wolsey, Thomas (Cardinal), 173, 182, 220

Y
Yamuna River, 67, 89
Yazd, 125

Z
Zapolya, John, 21–22, 25, 26, 158, 167, 181
Zaynab Begum, 251
Zaynab Khanum, 10
Zoroastrians, 125

The manufacturer's authorised representative in the EU is Springer Nature Customer Service Centre GmbH, Europaplatz 3, 69115 Heidelberg, Germany. If you have any concerns regarding our products, please contact ProductSafety@springernature.com

Printed and bound by CPI Group (UK) Ltd, Croydon, CR0 4YY

23/03/2026

02076466-0015